THE ACTS OF
NATHAN
THE PROPHET

The Acts of Nathan the Prophet

Interior Book Design and Layout by
www.integrativeink.com

ISBN: 978-0-9826092-1-7

HAPPY EASTER
2010

My Dearest (2nd Wife),

Thank you for having an open mind and allowing me to explain myself. I have so much to tell you it is hard to know where to start, but a journey of 1000 miles begins with one step.

Sometime in the 90's I was getting life insurance and thought about the future of my children. I didn't want to give them my life long earnings only to be squandered. I wanted to give them a little piece (financially and spiritually) of me for a lifetime. I checked into my theory and discovered that I would have to hire an attorney to prepare a trust and that would be costly. So I just did like everyone else, bought a policy and designated beneficiaries.

When Hurricane Ivan was approaching the Gulf Coast I had a financial Tsunami going on in my life already. I turned to God for help. I was doing all the talking and He was talking to me, but I could not hear. My heart was just becoming ready to accept the Wonderful Counselor as my guide. I didn't know who this Counselor was and muddled through making everyone think I had lost my mind. You already know the turmoil this created in my life.

After a year of reinventing myself, I met you. I was head over heels in love with you from the first time I saw you. I was drawn to you because of your Faith in our Father and the kindness I witnessed you doing. I knew that I had a purpose for God, but I had already lost one family and decided to conform to society and not go out on a limb for God. I always find it amazing to watch the reactions of people when you mention our Creator. Wow, what have we become? I too struggled with witnessing for Him. I didn't know how to react. Am I doing what I do for His Glory or mine? I tried to join in with the church and every time I found judgment and betrayal. I would so love to go to a House of Worship and allow my vulnerabilities to be seen and accepted. My God accepts and forgives them and my transgressors prey upon them.

I guess we can classify our relationship as a rebound marriage. We immediately had to start dealing with financial issues that could be a strain on the strongest of marriages. I was still that rat in the maze searching for my next cheese station financially and spiritually. Although I did not find the financial cheese while with you, you introduced me to the spiritual cheese.

I saw myself being drawn back into the rat race with no future to look forward to. I had lost your respect and love. I just could not go back to what I had tried so hard to break free from. I had to allow myself time for the reinvention to take hold in my life. I knew that I could not finish my purpose with you in my life and I knew that I could not remain in a loveless relationship. You were my catalyst for striving to complete my purpose for God. I wanted to be able to show you that I was not insane, just possess something to arcane for you and others to accept.

After our separation, I hibernated and drank heavily. I still thought there was hope of getting back together. Several months went by and I took the advice "the best way to get over a woman is to get another one". I was with enough women to know that I had lost my soul mate. I just had no feelings for these women and I hated giving them false hope of any kind of relationship. It so went against my grain.

My drinking had began to haunt me again as it has so many times in my past. I put it down completely and picked up the project that has plagued me for five yrs. I thought all I would need to do is put the website together. I attempted to accomplish this myself and realized quickly that this was way over my head.

It was when I discovered that I didn't need just one website, I needed two that resonated in my brain and brought me back to the Two–Sided Scroll. I had spent so much time on the Vessel, I had not given the Lamb His due. I always used a blanket approach on the proceeds for God going to pay for socialized healthcare.

I was inspired by the Holy Spirit and put together Gods Legacy Trust LLC in one day. This is when I realized that I am responsible for establishing an Earthly, Everlasting Entity so that Jesus Christ may establish His Throne and dwell with His people healing them.

That is when I started my intensive research to find out who I am and if I truly do have a purpose for Him. Remember, I still have yet to have anyone refute my claims that legacywillandtrust. com will accomplish what I say it will.

I read the Bible, I searched the internet, I found what I sought. Once I started putting the pieces together, more and more fell into place that encouraged me to endeavor to persevere. I only had the Wonderful Counselor as my guide. I was instructed to write down what I had seen, heard, read and experienced. While I awaited my first book to be published and my websites to be built, I still had a burning desire to share what my observations of our world are and what our Creator would think of it. It's not a pretty picture.

I was so proud of myself for finishing the manuscript of five years of my life. I guess pride does cometh before the fall, because my manuscript was not accepted by the one that inspired me. It was the worst Christmas I have ever and pray to have had. I slipped into a very intoxicated state of mind with total devastation of my heart. I had lost you and had to gain strength from our Father to continue. I knew that I had a Gift and it would be difficult to deliver, I just didn't know it would tear my heart in two. My soul mate or my God. I will always choose our Creator, I pray He will provide a soul mate for me.

I was told by several people that the second manic episode was completely obscure to them. I knew that I had to explain it, but I didn't know I'd be writing another book to do so. It was the only way that I could encapsulate what the Holy Spirit was putting on my heart. It was way too much for me to write down, so I used my gift of Aletheia to capture the essence of the message. As I started to revisit the episode, the Holy Spirit began to plummet me with more thoughts. Many I had before that I had put on the lost tapes. I knew that I had wisdom that would help the masses and hopefully reintroduce God's people back to Him. It is the travesties that man places on man, that allows Satan to rule over God's people. I pray I can clear up a lot of confusion for people as they go through this trial and error period. It's still the same rule book, but a modern day look at it. I pray that my Father is pleased with my efforts, all I do is for Him. Yes, it is a slippery slope and I am scared. I will face Jesus and He will be my defense counselor before our God. If trying to establish Him an Everlasting, Earthly Kingdom in which He may heal and dwell among us is wrong, then I don't want to be right.

Now the acts of David the king, first and last, behold, they are written in the history of Samuel the seer, and in the Book of Nathan the prophet, and in the history of Gad the seer; - 1 Chronicles 29:29

And the rest of the acts of Solomon first and last, are they not written in the Acts of Nathan the prophet, and in the prophecy of Ahijah the Shilonite, and in the visions of Iddo the seer concerning Jeroboam the son of Nebat? - 2 Chronicles 9:29

Daniel prophesied Jesus riding in on a donkey. Jesus fulfilled prophecy. The Bible is a prophetic book and I contend that the lost books may be prophetic for the future and our present day. I am proud to be a humble servant of the Lord and blessed to deliver His Gift. The revealing of the Seven Sealed Two-Sided Scroll, His Last Will and Testament.

Notice the statement "first and last". The author is referring to lineage. I do not claim to be in that royal lineage, but I have been inspired to fulfill their individual quests for God, to fulfill prophecy and create a Kingdom on Earth for our Savior.

Gods Last Will and Testament
Book of Nathan
The Acts of Nathan the Prophet
Book of Nathan II

I Will always Love and Care for you. You are the Keeper of my Heart, please guard it well.

Your Brother in Christ,
Nate

TABLE OF CONTENTS

FOREWORD

<u>Darren S Chamlee</u> To understand the meaning of what is happening in all prophecies is to have received the Reward of the Seven Seals from the Lamb or at this time from the Chosen Vessel); and I have set thee so: thou wast upon the holy mountain of God; thou hast walked up and down in the midst of the stones of fire.

All life upon the earth since the fall of Adam and Eve, consists of what God condemned in the first creation. Now everyone is to choose their destiny. God saved every spirit that was destroyed in the first creation, placing the spirits in more glorious bodies to inhabit and enjoy through eternity; having a new heart and a new mind, knowing only the knowledge of good without the evil knowledge. Everyone in this world of sin, has experienced the good things (sunshine, food, friendship) with the evil things. Each individual makes the choice for themselves, as their conscience directs through the enlightenment of God's Word in their mind. Thereby knowing which destiny they will fulfill in the prophetic Word of God.

The righteous accept the Seven Seals Revelation into their right hand and eat the scroll as John did in Rev.10:10, thereby receive God's revealed surname (Koresh) into their forehead (mind; understanding the scroll). The wicked choose an interpretation of God's Word by their ministers and churches, which are supported by the government of man, being part of the Beast. The Beast's number is six, because on the sixth day God created the beasts and man.

Nathan Isbell Thanks for the forward my friend. If you think of anything else, give me a post.

Darren S Chamlee These are actually excerpts from a piece called the Hidden Manna, Return to the Future and Back Again.

Nathan Isbell Really, I thought you were writing about my purpose for God. No kidding, even the verbiage or did you change that up?

Darren S Chamlee That was my understanding in another's words.....I thought you might have appreciated it.

Darren S Chamlee It's kind of freaky what is revealed when we seek to understand.

Nathan Isbell You will understand what "IT" is that we all seek, when you understand that 666 can be so much more attractive. You can interpret so many things the way you want by what is on your personal agenda. It is very freaky, I went through "IT". I think that anyone that has truly had a spiritual awakening can see "IT", but they don't understand "IT". There are those that fake "IT" to make "IT" and there are those that MOCK WHAT THEY DO NOT UNDERSTAND and the vocally robust continue to rule over God's people.

Darren S Chamlee August 4 at 2:30pm
Which side of the fence?

If you ever wondered which side of the fence you sit on, this is a greattest!

If a Republican doesn't like guns, he doesn't buy one.

If a Democrat doesn't like guns, he wants all guns outlawed.

If a Republican is a vegetarian, he doesn't eat meat.

If a Democrat is a vegetarian, he wants all meat products banned for everyone.

If a Republican is homosexual, he quietly leads his life.

If a Democrat is homosexual, he demands legislated respect.

If a Republican is down-and-out, he thinks about how to better his situation.

A Democrat wonders who is going to take care of him.

If a Republican doesn't like a talk show host, he switches channels.

Democrats demand that those they don't like be shut down.

If a Republican is a non-believer, he doesn't go to church.

A Democrat non-believer wants any mention of God and religion silenced.

If a Republican decides he needs health care, he goes about shopping for it, or may choose a job that provides it.

A Democrat demands that the rest of us pay for his.

If a Republican reads this, he'll forward it so his friends know how to vote in November!

A Democrat will delete it because he's "offended".

Well, I forwarded it. A little humor to lighten the load. "D"

<u>Nathan Isbell</u> Big D,I used to believe that, but the Republicans can be too strict in some areas and loosy goosy when they want to get into the Democrats pants. I believe we need a new party, the Leper Party. A party of the rest of us folks that do most of the living, working, paying and dying around here.

<u>Darren S Chamlee</u>
You're right! They're all freaking crooked!

PREFACE

I would like to dedicate this book to Jesus Christ my Lord and Savior and my ever so Wonderful Counselor. He wasn't just with me this time, He carried me. He Will carry all Lepers that will receive Him. He is the portal to the Father.

While I awaited my first book to be revealed to the World, I was still climbing the walls with the thoughts that the Holy Spirit was putting on my heart. I was told to write my thoughts down. These thoughts are what I have seen, heard, read, experienced and what the Holy Spirit puts on my heart that resonated in my brain. That is all. I do not wish to challenge anyone on their beliefs, just as I do not wish to be challenged on mine. Let my words speak for themselves and the Father be my Judge. I throw myself at His mercy, for I feel that I am doing what I was intended to do for Christ. It is a very slippery slope and I hope and pray that I am doing His Will. I am convinced in my heart that I am doing His Will and will accept the consequences on Judgment Day.

I must ask forgiveness from all that I have offended and will offend. I only speak the Truth as I deem it based on my own frame of reference. I will have error in my judgment and my words will always need to be questioned and subject to critical analysis. Just as I would expect from our Leaders and peers. Also I ask for forgiveness for my own gift of ADHD and the tangents of stories derived thereof.

This is a Love, Love Lost and hopefully Redemption story. As you know, alcohol and cigarettes have been my demons for most of my life and they have robbed me for more than half of it. I did clean up my act when I picked the book and website project up. I wanted to prove to my (2nd Wife) that I was not crazy and was just trying to fulfill my purpose. That didn't work out to well for me, although I give her full credit for being the catalyst for me finishing this project. After my attempt fell on deaf ears, my heart was broken and I was a crushed man. I put myself into a hibernation mode and began drinking again. How many of you can relate? I wanted to click forward my future to the point of the discovery and success of Gods Last Will and Testament. I was clicking my way to death and I knew it. I also knew that I needed to come out of this hibernation state come spring or seek counsel.

A lot of this book was written while I was drinking. Let me first apologize to my God and then to all of His people. I was not being the Witness for Him that He has prepared. I knew exactly what I was doing to my body. I wanted it. I wanted my days to be short. I wanted my senses to be numb. I wanted to be alone. I wanted to talk to God. The alcoholic in me justified the drinking to be able to connect with God better. If you are an alcoholic or addict, you know how creative we are. We are all creative in our ways as to not reveal our own leprosy. What demon has a hold on you that hinders you from living a full life with Christ?

You may not like my path. It may not be the path that you would choose. Of my own free will do I choose the path that I am on. I will be alone when I meet my maker. I alone will be judged by my decisions in life and you won't be there to hold my hand. Jesus will hold my hand and plead my case before the Father. I am who I am and I am in Christ. This is My Path as I try and complete My Purpose for Our One and Only Father who art in Heaven. Aren't all paths to GOD GOOD?

Lord, please forgive me of my transgressions just as I have forgiven my transgressors. Please save this wretched sinner from an eternity of torment in the pits of Hell, an extension of what I have created here of my own free will.

Please Lord, I believe in You. I believe you died for my sins. I believe you arose to Heaven to be with our Father. I believe you sent the "Wonderful Counselor", the Holy Spirit to speak to all hearts that would listen unto You. Please Lord take the soul of this humble servant when you see the time fit, that My Purpose for you is complete.

Lord, please enable me to harness my demons and live a clean and healthy life. Please speak to Your people and ask them to pray for me, for when they pray for me, they are praying for their own family leper. He or She is there, whether they are aware of it or not.

-The Prophet Nathan
a humble servant of the Lord

PREFACE XX

06/25/2010

Hello,

My name is Nathan and I'm an alcoholic. This is my story as I embark on a life without alcohol. My public confession of Faith is both Humiliating and Redeeming. Humiliating that I confess all. Redeeming that I have nothing to hide. I'm just like you. Have you ever been Naked with Jesus before? Come and join us, it is very revealing. Naked being a metaphor for bearing your soul to Christ. But if you want to get Naked, go right ahead. LOL I wish I was with you. Hey, that's not to imply that the Father condones Naked Churches for all you perverted fruit loops. (I wish I could join, but I have restraint) Just that you will be Judged by only one God and your God sees your soul. So why hide it?

I have asked our Father to help me battle the demon that has controlled my entire adult life. He sent me the Holy Spirit aka "Wonderful Counselor". He spoke to my heart and I answered. We had a long chat. There is a place in my heart where I allowed my own Demon to enter of my own free will. My Demon became so strong and was doing everything in it's power to destroy what my Lord had put on my heart. I would have to say that we all have a Judas in our lives. Something that betrays us and we betray ourselves because it is what we want. Or what we think we want?

Even with my Faith, as powerful as it is in the Father, the Son, and the Holy Spirit, I am powerless over my Demon Alcohol. I need the help of my fellow brother. I can not do this without Him or Them. I have battled many Demons in my life. This is by far the most difficult one to slay.

I am not a writer. But I was compelled to write down my thoughts. I am not a Saint, but a walking, functioning alcoholic. I have committed many sins and have begged for forgiveness. I pray that I am doing what I was intended to to do, because I'm not sure with my mind, but I am sure with my heart. I won't defend myself because my Lord has told me to let you read what is written and make up your own minds what you believe.

This book was written with a broken heart and in a drunken state of mind. I guess I can honestly say, "Thanks Judas", thanks for being in my life so that I could find my Purpose for God. Now it is time for me to conquer my Demon and become the Witness that I was intended to be. For His Glory and Not His Shame. I believe He revealed my purpose for Him because I went searching for it. Why would He choose me? A drunk, intelligent, used car salesman. The question I asked myself was, "Why not Me"? I have nothing to lose and all to gain. I've lost it all and with His Grace I am gaining it back with Serenity. How can you kick a horse that is down? How can you spit on someone that portrays a deep part of yourself? How can you crucify someone that tells the truth as hurtful as it may be?

My Dearest Judas, "Good Night Sweetheart, well it's time to go." "Thanks for the Memories". I learned more from my mistakes than I ever did from my triumphs. Thanks again my brother, for fulfilling the role that you were intended for. It must have been a torment from Hell. I asked my brother Jesus Christ to forgive our brother Judas for His betrayal. I know in my heart what His answer would be, a resounding "Yes my Brother" you are forgiven. For all that you did was the Fathers Plan and exemplified all Man for us to measure ourselves by. Satan becomes the flesh when you allow him to come into your heart. Judas is our scapegoat to learn by. And we all have a Judas in our hearts.

I have written names and dates and I want you to know that I am not a Seer. "Not My Area". It was just wishful thinking on my part based on what I believe would be best for our Country. I'll leave the fortune telling and other crazy stuff to the false prophets. Speaking of Prophet. A Prophet is one who speaks from God. It pays nothing and cost plenty. Anyone can be a Prophet of God, all you do is accept Him into your heart and start talking to Him. You just have to train your heart to listen. Your eyes will be blind, your ears will be deaf, your lips will yearn to taste. Your Heart will Hear Him. When you praise and witness, you are a prophet of God. You don't get a wand or a funny hat and robe. I still haven't received any checks from the Board of Prophets, but now that you are here, we can file a grievance with the union. LOL

Lord,

My inept writing skills may have people confused about the Gift and message that you demand I deliver. I have opened my heart and soul to all that would listen. I have confessed my sins publicly. I have begged for forgiveness. I have faced betrayal, denial, torment, humiliation etc... What else must I face to do your will? Lord, give me the strength to convey all my craziness in an encapsulated cliff note type version. I am sooo.... ready to get this off my plate and I just don't care anymore.

I do care because I'll have to carry you.
I don't care because I love you.

TELL THEM

Hang on, you're putting me on the spot again. I need to pray. I'm going to my fourth twelve step meeting and when I get back. I WILL!!!

One more thing before I go. All I ever wanted in life was to be Loved. Maybe I can find "IT" amongst the Lepers. I thought that all I needed was my Lord Jesus Christ to love me and I would be content. I must confess Lord, I love you with all my heart, but I need the love of my brothers and sisters as well. Deliver us all from the Demons that distract us from the Masters Plan and let us erect His Everlasting Earthly Kingdom built with the bricks of Mankind for the Glory of God and allow Him to dwell among us and Heal us.

Gotta go I'm late. Typical LOL.

I think I have found the Island of Misfit Toys. And I finally fit in. There are dentists, doctors, lawyers, teachers, city workers etc... Rudolph the Red nose Drunk. But you can call me Nathan. LOL I see Hope that these misfits can help this misfit slay the Dragon that has been dragging me down my entire adult life. I can see right now that I must add another chapter to the continuing saga we call Life. But I have orders to bring you up to date in a concise manner, all of this that has come to pass.

He saw some of the misfit toys had a disregard for Santa, but believed in a higher power. He didn't blame the man for his belief, after all, he was stuck on an Island with a weak Lion in control. He wondered why that Lion would not go over to Santa and get in his face and say "HEY, what about us. Don't we get any Love". The Lion was wise to not give them their love. For he knew Santa would just say something like, "IT" is here. "IT" has been here the whole time. Come on over here and get your Gift. We didn't forget you. You chose to isolate yourself because you had been hurt. Santa has a Gift for you. He gives you a purpose in life. He asks that your purpose be to help others to find their own purpose and that will enable you to find your own purpose in the process.

He thought about that for a moment and his revelation was, what is it that I want? (A typical Me Me thought) I want to be loved. So if you give, you receive. Hmmm....if I love someone else that is in need of love, maybe I will receive it as well. But who is in need? He pondered. They wear such beautiful masks during the day.

Once upon a Time,

There lived a good boy with great parents that did all he could do to please everyone. He studied real hard and got good grades. Traveled the World as a Navy brat. He participated in most sports and scouting activities. He had a great childhood, learning many valuable things that began to establish his frame of reference and allowed him to make right and wrong decisions. He was told that mistakes were bad and we don't want to make mistakes. He was never told that mistakes can be good if we learn from them.

He wasn't the smartest kid, he wasn't the most handsome, he wasn't the most athletic...He was pretty much the tall skinny kid with glasses. No self-confidence, but with an inner glow that he was more, just waiting for his opportunity. And always willing to put it all on the line.

Searching for a mentor to emulate, he was educated and exposed to the work place. Not fully realizing that many things had been omitted in his studies. But due to his laziness to learn and ego of having "IT" figured out, he began to chase his dream to be rich.

He engaged as most do, into the "Rat Race" game. Being convinced of his superior intellect, he blazed his own trail in most endeavors he pursued. So when he finally found something that he perceived as his opportunity, he bet the family farm. I think you can fill in your own blanks as to the result of that.

Faced with failure, the options began to run through his mind. All life lines had been exhausted and there was no Hope of recovering from this blow. He chose to ask God for help and made the mistake of telling his loved ones about it. Holy Crap did that open a can of worms for him. Shortly there after he found himself broke, isolated and yearning for his family back. Once he made this commitment to God, there was no going back to save this relationship. He moved on and put the encounter on the back burner and shortly after that, found the love of his life. Imagine, finding the love of his life in just two dates into the singles world. That's a lucky somebody huh?

He was actually lucky to have this person come into his life, because she was ultimately the catalyst for him completing his purpose for God that he hadn't quite figured out just yet. He built his frame of reference more and more. Not only was he re-inventing himself spiritually, but he searched for any source of wisdom that could quench a thirst that seemed unquenchable.

He recalls a seed that had been planted when he attempted to prepare his own Last Will and Testament, but the seed fell on undernourished soil and went into hibernation in his subconscious. When faced with a financial tsunami, he reached for the seed and no one believed him, nor would even take the time to listen. You see, he had fallen on a path of alcohol and as any alcoholic and their friends will tell you. "Blame it on the a-a-a-a-a-alcohol." His words meant nothing because he was no longer even considered worthy to be heard. He tried to reach people he did not know, people that were in an influential position to no avail. They had become to important to hear anything past their own agendasHe set out to take on the project all alone. Yet still didn't realize what this project was until he started to search for his purpose for God. It was at this point that all the pieces began to come together. That his purpose was to ….. still didn't have all the pieces. He continued the search and the obstacles kept getting larger and the praise kept being challenged. What am I doing? Everyone thinks I'm crazy, think I'll have another drink. I must not listen to them. I must endeavor to persevere. He would say to himself.

After five yrs of aimlessly searching for contentment in a drunken state of mind, he started asking pointed questions for the purpose of his own existence. At first he would answer his own questions with his own drunk witted remarks. When his own remarks began to reveal his own existence, that is when he realized that he was now listening to the Holy Spirit and had been for a very long time. He just hadn't been taught to listen with his heart. His remarks didn't seem to be his own, but from a state of mind, even as inebriated as his mind had become. His answers were now coming faster than his own quandaries. He had given control over to the Holy Spirit and he became the interviewee. He had no reason to not be honest with the Spirit. No one would laugh, but himself laughing at himself to avoid crying and change the outlook of the situation. He chose Hope over Despair and he did this by realizing that tomorrow is a new day and he couldn't really do anything about his performance yesterday, but ask for forgiveness wholeheartedly as he had done so many times in the past. Make any type of retribution for those actions and then forgive himself.

He took on challenges that he never thought he would have to face. He built websites even as intimidated by the computer as he was. He published books, the concept that seemed to be an impossible dream at the time. He overcame any comfort zone issue that kept him from completing his purpose for God. He sobered up while he compiled his notes and created a manuscript. This book would fulfill his purpose, get his children back, wipe out all of his Demons and be the "IT" that could finally solve "IT" so he could rest knowing "IT" is all under control. This manuscript would get his lost love back and he would live happily ever after, so he thought. She was his catalyst that gave him strength to continue. He wanted her to see what "IT" was, he was doing for Christ to prove he was a Godly man wearing the suit of a sinner for all to see. So would that like make me a sheep in wolves clothing? Yes, I think it would, he proclaimed.

That kick in the teeth was all it took to send him where he had frequented twice before. Back to God to fix him. He would pray, Lord, I'm broken again. Please fix me. But this time he would not be fixed until he had completed what he had started and release the cause for his unrest and the unrest of his forefathers. He knew what his purpose for God was and that was to deliver God's Gift at all costs. Wow, what a ride, he reflected.

He had already been on this path twice and had learned from his past mistakes of mania. He had learned how to control this state of mind and enjoy the euphoria. He had learned how to control his alcoholism and finish his purpose by not controlling it and letting the alcohol completely take control in a controlled environment. He did as little drinking and driving as possible and most of it was on the short drive to the liquor store to refuel for the experience. He challenged his demon alcohol to a duel. Our Lord was up for the challenge and seemed like he had been waiting a long time on the sidelines, waiting to play. Kind of like, "Put Me in Coach, I'm Ready to Play". Okay kid, show 'em what you got. He couldn't definitively answer for the future outcome because it will take a lifetime, but he had very high hopes for Jesus. Now that he had found some like-kind disciples that he anxiously wanted to call his friends.

He was convinced that he was connecting better with God while intoxicated. He had even justified his Demon to the Almighty. Like, "You Talking to Me". If you want me, you got to take me like I am. So God allowed him all the rope he requested. He was so very smart after all. You know, solving the two largest riddles of Mankind and all. He just got so damn smart, no one wanted to be around him and he couldn't figure it out. He had so much to share with everyone. He realized that he was alone on the plane that he was on. A plane with no captain or cocktail waitress. That's a bitch. He had popped his head outside the box to look in and find out what the hell is happening to his world. In his circle of influence, no one could see past themselves. This is a quest that I must make alone, he thought.

All I need is this bottle and that's all I need. And this lamp, I need that. All I need is this bottle, this lamp and that's all I need and this chair. I need this. That's it, that's all I need. This bottle, this lamp and this chair and that other bottle in case I run out. - The Jerk

God blessed him financially to pursue his Passions and Demons. He procrastinated about his purpose for God and escalated his thirst for justified mental pain relief. He was blessed not to have hurt himself or anyone else except the loved ones that he left in his wake of self-destruction. He wondered, how many knots can I tie myself up in before I run out of rope? The Lord replied to his heart...

YOUR TIME HAS COME
YOUR TIME HAS GONE
IT IS YOUR TIME
TO INSPIRE THY
BROTHER
I WILL
GIVE YOU
TIME
TAKE IT
DAMN THY HAND

He reaches his hand out to his Leper brothers and sisters and finds they are reaching even more passionately than himself. He prays and is thankful for the opportunity to find love, happiness and contentment again. He is thankful for that one last chance that God gives to us all before we meet Him. He is convinced that he has a gift from God and will remain in unrest until it is delivered. He knows that if it is to be delivered on the wings of a Dragon, it will most certainly fail. With his new circle of Leper friends, he is certain he can imprison "IT" for a thousand years and fulfill his purpose. He humbles himself to ask of his brothers and sister in Christ. He cries out: I thought you were all I need? I don't need anyone else but you Lord. My brothers hurt me, my sisters hate me. Why do you forsake him? Why do you bless him? My brothers and sister in Christ, he needs your help with this cross that he bears for us all. Who will succeed him if he fails to deliver God's Gift? Who will help carry him?

My Leper Brothers and Sisters in Christ, I need your help. I do not possess the talents to complete my purpose for God. I have hired a web designer and have not gotten satisfaction. I beg of you to search your heart and help me with this project. By helping me, you may find your own purpose. What a gift I am offering you. What a "Gift" I AM... has offered me.

Thank you Lord, thank you for sending the Wonderful Counselor to direct my thoughts. Thank you for blocking my path and showing me yours. I was never meant to accomplish this purpose without the help from my brothers and sisters was I? It was my arrogance and frustration with my brothers that made me think I could do it alone. But I know that I am never alone because I will always have You. I know that I will join You soon enough. I know I will be judged for my actions or the lack thereof. I know You put on my heart, the Salvation of Mankind. Who'd have thunk it.

You always have worked in mysterious ways. I guess your coming has got to come with a little crazy doesn't it? I never thought you'd come on a surfboard shooting fire balls from your ass or anything. I just could have never imagined me being one of the two witnesses. If that is even who I am. All I know is that I was compelled to do what I have done and then get the hell out of the way. Let God's people finish this Gift. My talents can only go so far before I have to enlist the assistance from my very talented brother. If my brother hasn't discovered his talents, it is my talent to help him to discover them.

Lord, you know my soft spot is with the handicapped. Physically and mentally. I could never be around them and I did not know how to judge my own heart in this arena. I have a new facebook friend in Kenya Africa. His name is Jumaa Mtuku and lives in the Nairobi Homes. He is handicapped and was asking me for a laptop computer so that he may better connect with the world. I told him that I had something better than a laptop, I have a concept that will grow charity and provide them with so much more. He thanked me and is praying for me now. I guess the reason the handicapped have always made me sick at my stomach is because my heart was hurting so much. I recognize the challenges they face as they attempt to find or give purpose to themselves or to another individual searching for their own.

You know every time I thought it couldn't get worse, it either got worse or God showed me how bad things could be and to stop whining about a very blessed life that I have lived.

If I can please get my Leper Brothers and Sisters to pray with me now.

GOD,
Grant me the SERENITY to
accept the things I cannot change.
The COURAGE to change
the things that I can
and the WISDOM to
know the difference.

He could not have beaten Himself to the point of death. He could not carry the cross alone. He could not dig the hole to hoist the cross. He could not put on a crown of thorns. He could not climb up the cross. He could not drive nails into His hands and feet securing Himself to the cross. He could not feed Himself sour wine on the cross. He could not pierce His side for the blood and water to rush from on the cross. He could not free himself from the cross. He could not have rolled back the stone of His earthly tomb. He required the help from His brothers. Our Father sat back and watched it happen with tears as any true Father would. Because that is our Covenant. It's of our own free will what to believe. And we suffer the consequences of those decisions. Christs' death was planned. Yeah, it was an inside job. Christ was here to deliver a message of hope and love. He knew exactly what His purpose for the Father was. His purpose was to save us from our sins and let us know that there would be a time that He would come back. He promised to send the "Wonderful Counselor". He asks for us not to be sad for His leaving. He knew the program folks. I'm not so sure that any of us would want to endure that type of torment for their brother. It's not mankind that beats me down my brother. It is the lure of mankinds creations. The sad part is, I give myself every lash. Lash after lash after lash. I can either keep lashing and die, or I can realize that I am doing it to myself of my own free will. I can recognize it once and for all, so I can make attempts to correct and control "IT". "IT" is my Demon.

MY BROTHERS
I AM
HERE
I WILL
HEAL

He was risen to be at the right hand of the Father. He kept His promise by sending back the "Wonderful Counselor" aka The Holy Spirit. You will witness a battle as prophesied. Just not a battle like you were expecting. It is a battle that is in each and everyone of us. We just all have different Demons that tear us away from our true purpose here on Earth.

I pray with our Fathers Grace that I will be able to touch your heart in a way that you know how to find your purpose in life and that is to help someone else find there's. I ask you to pray for me as I embark on my journey of sobriety, for when you pray for me, you pray for the Lepers in your own family. Whether you know who they are or not.

The drunk in me wanted to apologize for anyone I offend and it started off something like you sons of B....'s LOL The sober me asks for your forgiveness and love as I share the Truth from the perspective of a brother that has lived through many of the same circumstances as you have. What I have not experienced for myself, I gained by your articulations. The Holy Spirit demanded that I share.

You know, I was in one of my more clever drunken modes when I asked Carol this question. If you were to describe yourself as a spice, what spice would it be?

ginger .... once you peel the outer cover off
you get something firm and fragrant ...

Isn't that a great answer. Hey, she has a lot of great answers and I'm sure her story can touch some folks. We laughed if God's books take off, if she would write the "Book of Carolpaetra". LOL LO L... I guess you had to be there. Her story is one that I have heard before. I have not experienced it except through her articulation. Therefore, she would tell the story much better than I could ever.

Anthropomorphism - an animal or non-human object portraying human characteristics

If our Father had asked me the same question. Like what kind of a spice would you be for Me? I would normally be able to pull something out of my ass right away and everyone would laugh. But now that I am reprogramming, I would have to have some time to think it through. You see, I will strive to have the best answer for our God, so that I can have the lime light. Do you see the correlation between this behavior and the behavior of "Scurry" and "Him"? "Scurry" is so weak with his Demon, he couldn't pull a greasy string out of a rats ass. "Him" has said, screw it, there has to be something better and went seeking. These are characters from the book "Who Moved My Cheese".

I understand perfectly what Jesus was referring to when He said He could only give us so much information and was dying to give more. His message was a message of Hope and Love. We could not grasp all that He wanted to share. That is why He sent back a "Wonderful Counselor" and a Wonderful Counselor He is, if you will listen to your heart instead of your mind occasionally. Or pull your head out of your ass. Whichever works for you. LOL You can allow your heart to be involved in your decision making process. I promise you, it makes life a hell of a lot easier. "Jesus take the wheel".

Anything that is Free, the Hogs are first in line at the trough. The pigs that need to be fattened are left out. Remember God's Gift is for the pigs, the truly needy. Look past yourselves my brothers and sisters and let the truly needy have what they need. Remember, Hogs are slaughtered and Pigs are fed. You will be judged harshly on this account.

Sounds like we need to break out the old highlighter on that one. Or do you need another version.

I'd like to hear Gov. Romney's version on how the healthcare plan worked out for his state. Something tells me that every Hog in the state ran to get the Doctor to look at the corn on their big toe. I could be wrong, quite often I am. We can always agree to disagree, but that solves nothing. Let's examine the facts shall we. Let God be the test pilot for free healthcare and with our charity, slop the Hogs because the pigs need to be fed, watered, sheltered, clothed and cared for. God and you know who's in need and who's in greed.

PREFACE XXX

8/15/2010

Good Evening Lord, thanks for a great sober day with You. I will be 8 wks sober tomorrow and I will be out of town for my 60 day mark. I find it necessary to see if I can encapsulate the journey that I have been on in a short and understandable letter to my brothers and sisters in Christ. I pray that You can confine my thoughts and make a point that they can understand. Thanks. I just remembered what you put on my heart last night. I almost forgot because I didn't want to get out of bed and write it down. LOL

Lord, what happened to Rudolph and the Dentist after that Glorious Night?

Rudolph the red nose reindeer. What an epic tale. One that continues to this very day. It all began with the birth of a deer that was different. Rudolph was very wise because he had been on many trips with Santa and didn't mind sharing the experience with his fellow deer that would listen. None of the deer had seen Santa, but they knew that Santa was in Rudolph's heart and that he spoke authoritatively for Santa. He even plotted a course of sharing gifts with every household. At least to all that would believe that Santa would come if they wished hard enough, hung stockings and sent a letter. Many would even leave carrots for the reindeer and cookies for Santa himself. The Merry 'ole Soul.

Rudolph began to tell all of the deer about the charted course of Santa. Some believed him and some did not. Some

of the Elves of Authority began to question the validity of this supposed charted course of spreading good will. They even saw it as a threat to their own authority over the deers as well as the other elves.

The head elves began to plot against Rudolph and soon found a trusted friend willing to betray Rudolph for mere silver. The elves and deer gathered and condemned Rudolph for having a charted course from Santa, when they themselves have never seen, much less ridden with Santa. And of course with their arrogance, if Santa would speak to anyone, it would be them. They are the head elves after all.

They rallied the other clueless elves until the decision to crucify Rudolph was final. Because Rudolph had already been speaking to Santa, he knew what the elves were plotting to do all along. He even made the necessary steps to prepare his fellow deer believers. He told them the things they witness must happen, so that Santa could send the spirit of Rudolph to touch the hearts of other believers. Rudolph knew it would be difficult for his deer friends to understand, so that is why he always spoke in ways that could touch everyone at different times of their life. Santa had already told Rudolph that his words would have to be timeless to reach the believer that would finally finish the charted course that has been all but burned, so others could follow.

Rudolph was stripped of his hide and hung to dry out and die. His stripped lifeless corpse was placed in a cave, sealed by stone and guarded by elves. Santa then took Rudolph for himself. Heart, mind, body and soul. Rudolph now is at the right hand of the Santa praying for Santa to penetrate the hearts of his fellow deer creating a portal for communication.

Rudolph didn't have a red nose, it was a metaphor for being able to shed light needed to blaze a trail of goodness and chart a course. No, the red nose came much later. Many generations of deer have come and gone since Rudolph ascended to the North Pole and Santa has continued his search for the deer that seeks his purpose for both Santa and Rudolph. This deer must be willing to follow blind faith in Santa and Rudolph, because he himself can only hear the Spirit of Rudolph if Santa opens the portal to his heart allowing "IT" to be filled.

Santa knew that the deer to deliver the Gift, would have a red nose of defeat and drunkenness. A dreamer among deer that have lost their dream and the dream of Rudolph.

Lord, can I stop You there. I'm tired. I want to hear all about the dreaming deer tomorrow. He sounds like a "Wild and Crazy" deer. LOL I also want to know about the dentist. You haven't mentioned him yet in your story. Good Night my Lord. Thanks for the sober day.

8/16/2010

Good afternoon Lord, please grant me another sober day. I've been running errands to get this new project started. Still have a little to do and then we will finish this story. I am in contact with the book editor to process before sending to distributor. I hope to have this done before going out of town.

Okay Lord, tell me about this dreaming deer. Wait, hold that thought. I need to make this meeting at seven. I'll be right back.

Do what you need to do to stay sober my brother. I'll be with you.

K...I'm back.

K...As I was saying, generation after generation went by as Santa waited for that special red nosed deer that would be worthy in Santa's eyes. Maybe not in the eyes of the elves or even the other deer, but Santa waited for that deer to get tired of making mistakes and living with the consequences. He waited for a deer that wanted to pick up where Rudolph had left off. A deer that wanted to emulate Rudolph and speak to Santa. By order of Santa, Rudolph left a charted course for this red nose deer to follow as well as for anyone that seeks their own path to Santa.

This red nose deer had discovered the rest of the course and began to tell the elves of authority. He had no idea the resistance he would encounter trying to shed some light on the course that Rudolph had left. Many attempts were made to be heard by the elves to no avail. The elves were more concerned with making sure that the elves that did not build toys, were taken care of by the elves and deer that do build toys. They had not seen Santa's Plan, the Plan that would complete the circle of eternal Salvation for all elves and deer that wanted to play the reindeer game of life and eternal life.

Oh this red nose deer just didn't up and hear Rudolph. He had to first allow the time portal to be opened by Santa and then the Spirit of Rudolph began to fill his heart with thoughts from Santa. This deer was given a Gift from Santa to deliver to all the elves and deer. To rejoice that Rudolph would finally be able to come back and love his deer brothers and sisters, not in a physical living sense, but a spiritual one created by the elves and deer themselves. When the red nose deer came out of his mind altered state, he realized that the chart that he himself had been tracking while seeking Santa, was now a pathway for others to find Rudolph in their own hearts, minds, bodies and souls also. This red nose deer had so many Gifts to share with everyone, but he knew that he could gain serenity if he could only help others to see that there is a real North Pole and Rudolph is the guiding light to Santa Himself. The phones lines are open to Rudolph, but might I suggest that you listen to the Spirit of Rudolph with your heart and write a letter to Santa about anything that is on your mind. Rudolph is your Deer Brother that appreciates all the carrot sticks you left him, but now it is time to pet Rudolph and make him your best friend. Watch how you approach him, but he won't bite. He wants to come home with you. Oh Herbie, can I, can I, can I, Pleeeeeeaaaaaasssssse...I'll take real good care of him. I'll feed him, talk to him and take him out for walks everyday.

We'll see, he does seem to like you. Let me check with the head elf and make sure that it doesn't interfere with any of his toy making agendas. You may have to wait a time longer, the head elves are busy trying to come up with ideas to deliver new toys with less deer and more elves. The sleigh continues to get heavier as the elves greedily pile in, not sure how much longer it will be before the deer won't be able to get it off the ground. It might be faster if you had some of that dust. Things have been a little tough working on all of these rotten teeth that the elves hide. The Fairy dust greases the elves personal toy building machines. They have climate machines, energy machines, communication machines, propaganda machines etc...all designed to further their own personal toy empire. Which machine do you wish to grease to deliver this Gift from Santa?

I have no dust to grease the machine, but I do believe in the Dream Machine of Santa. Rudolph finished the plan as best he could, it is up to his Deer Brothers and Sisters to fulfill the Dream of Rudolph and Santa alike.

I'm not sure why many of the elves and deer began to question the charted course of Santa, but I guess Rudolph has been gone for so long now and many deer have gotten off course as they forged their own course. I guess this made it a little easier for the elves to prove there was no Santa Claus at all and Rudolph got what he had coming to him. Besides, many of those same elves survive on the longevity of the head elves machines. With no Fairy dust for them, their personal machines breaks down and Santa will just have to wait yet another year before delivering his gift to all the good little boys and girls.

But don't count the red nose deer out to fast. He no longer has a red nose, but the vision of the most famous reindeer of all and Santa's last Gift, his Will and Testament.

Great story. Does Santa's Will ever get read to the elves and deer alike? Just to even see if the game is worth playing?

"IT" may crash burn, but "IT" is looking pretty good so far. Thanks to the Top Guns of Santa.

Awesome tale Lord. I'm ready to call it a night. I may get beat up over using some pagan stuff, but I don't give a rats ass. I want to question who determines what is pagan and what is not. I like Santa and if the myth resonates with people as a positive pathway to God, then I say great and screw you. I'm not worshiping Santa, I'm gaining a better understanding of the Father, Son and Holy Spirit and I pray you are too. Thanks for another sober day Lord. I really just don't think about "IT" much any more. But I know "IT" patiently waits for the rest of my days.

Just thought of something else. I wonder if Cornelius ever found that Silver lining he tirelessly sought. I sure spent the worst part of my life trying to find that Silver and Gold for myself.

REFLECTIONS

6/27/2010

I am reflecting back to all that I have been through. The Joy, sorrow, memories good and bad. How I had been trained. How I had been deceived. How I dealt with "IT". How I sought after "IT". It's a pretty shaky set of rules if you ask me. Rules that can be easily taken out of context as I am soooo..... discovering with these damn texting and emails. I can't hear your heart nor can your brother. We already have enough wars going on abroad because we do not speak the same tongue as our adversaries. Now we are wanting to destroy our own little worlds to each other, because texting is cool. Texting is easily taken out of context and the next text may be your last to a great friend that took your text out of context. "Like wake up girlfriend, I didn't mean it like that".

Damn, even sober I still got it. Keep 'em coming Lord, I missed out on my daughter's life. Show me what it would have been like. I would have liked to have been there. I would have liked to see her first date pick her up at the door. I would like to have consoled her on her first break up. I would have liked matching her funds and buying a first clunker. I would have explained the benefits of working for something are far greater than being given something. I would have waxed it for her and followed her to college to make sure the piece made it. I would have hugged and kissed her on the cheek to let her know that I will always be here for her. I would have rejoiced in her accomplishments and grieved in her sorrows. I did what I could do. I prayed for her and I endeavored to persevere. Sometimes you just have to choose God.

I do question myself if I am doing all of this while being possessed by my demon alcohol. Hell Yes, who are you trying to kid. Because even though I'm..., what was Monday morning since I was drunk. He still lingers around every corner. He waits for me to say, screw 'em pour me a big one.

If this book doesn't convince you that I am fulfilling prophecy, then I guess I'm not the salesman God thought I was. But I know in my heart I'm His number three salesman. Second to Jesus Christ our Lord and Savior and third to the "Wonderful Counselor". I'm searching for the other witness. I need some competition witnessing for our Father. I know who you are. Come and claim your prize. My new name in Christ is Ophiuchus. Brother, tell me your new name in Christ. I want to know your name and what it means for the Glory of God. Now live it and live with the consequences of your decisions made of your own free will.

When you are ready to reach the point of honesty with yourself, your heart might be in the right place, but your mind is not. Unfortunately we all have a Judas tucked away in our hearts. Even Peter had a Judas tucked away for his denial. When you learn to hear with your heart, you will have alter egos to chat with. It reminds me of Kazoo in the Flintstones. Understand just as Fred did, you make choices and live with the consequences thereof. Do you remember Kazoo telling Fred, "I told you so Dum Dum".

I share these stories from movies of my past, so it can become your frame of reference for generations to come. As generations pass, new generations emerge. Because we are all about ourselves and our immediate surroundings, it is very easy to forget the lessons of the past. We just have to much going on in our own lives to bother with Andy Griffith. Hey, I still kick myself to this day that I didn't get this t-shirt. It was a picture of Floyd the Barber laced in Pink and the caption was Pink Floyd. I'm a huge fan of both, but I'm Otis the town drunk, so what do I know. LOL Or Reverend Jim on Taxi. I loved it when he started playing the piano after embarrassing the red head chick. He says after playing eloquently, "I must have learned how to do that sometime". So hey, if you're a drunk, I know at least you are laughing with me. Not so sure about everyone else. Screw 'em let me get you another round and

3

we'll talk about how we won the war. LOL You're my good friend. What did you say your name was?

This is worth mentioning again. Why are you coming home half drunk? I ran out of money, get off my ass. I'm not sure how much difference alcohol made in my life. I know it controlled it. I know it robbed me of memories. But you know, I'm the type person that likes to look at the bright side. How can I learn from it and control it? I don't have a freaking clue and that is why I am seeking help from others that have been where I am now or worse. I guess one could say that I paid a healthy sum for therapy. I paid it with opportunity costs of life. If alcohol was my medicine for my mental therapy to deal with life, then I paid a lot for therapy.

So what happens after I fulfill my purpose. Will there be a ticker tape parade in my honor? Will there be a monument of me carved in a mountain? Will there be songs written about me? I wouldn't know because I've been warned about my vanity. So any thanks and praise you may have, make your checks and money orders payable to...LOL too funny, but true. Gods Legacy Trust LLC. He is so ready to have His Kingdom here on Earth, to invest into His children and Heal the Sick with the Praise from thy brother. Just thought of something. If I'm this great salesman, I could be a great scam artist as well. Maybe that is why the website was blocked from my control. So the control could be of the people. That's how I wanted it, I just didn't know how to have an entity without a member. Don't worry, we'll get the lawyers to draw it up. I hope you will know me well enough when this is all over, that a scam is the furthest thing from my mind. Isn't it a shame that we even have to discuss that. I can't say as I blame you. I have been bent over enough myself and if we don't change our direction, the Government is going to give us a screwing like we have never seen or could ever get out of. There will be no option but to screw the working class to pay for all of the entitlements that the non-working class get to enjoy at our expense.

"Share the Wealth" I like it. Try this on for size, "Share the Labor" and you will share in the wealth that you create for yourself and gain a sense of pride from your accomplishments.

But hell, I always thought the clean air tax was fair. I just never got my bottle of it or shown the stations where I can refill it. What the hell, let's have a sunshine tax. All days that are cloudless days, there will be no tax. But it must remain that way for the full 24 hrs and it doesn't fall on Sunday. Otherwise there will be a sunshine tax. So let it be written, so let it be done. If my memory serves me correctly and believe me when I tell you, you better question me. LOL Jesus was seeing the same tax crap going on in his time. Over taxation to the point of upheaval. That is one of the things that He fought for and ruffled some feathers to say the least. He was exposing the truth and it didn't sit well with the people that He was going to get into their pocket. Is it just me or do you see a cycle here?

Hey, here's a thought. We could text our dialogue to our Global adversaries, get taken out of context and go ahead and get it on. Which is exactly what is happening right now because we do not speak their tongue. A tongue that was forged from birth. They will follow their frame of reference and we will follow ours. And the corrupt that use our Father as a divisive God will fuel their own egos or are they just confused. Right..."Oh, you mean the secret Nuclear research facility". Let there be no doubt that we all serve the same God. A God of Peace. I'm so over this war thing, aren't you? Did you see me flip my hair back. LOL "Like" aren't you? I think we all are over it. I think as a planet we are ready to step up to the plate and except our place and do all that we can for the Glory of God. Hate when I do that, I sound like a preacher.

Maybe we can derive the answer from that story of Saladin and Nathan the Wise. Yes, I think there is great wisdom in that story. Let's see Saladin was the powerful Muslim that exhausted his resources funding wars. Hmm...sounds like U.S. The Jew had gained wealth and could easily be pursued. And the Christian, well he hadn't showed up yet. How was it that Nathan the Wise managed to escape an ugly situation when he was being set up for treason to be thrown in jail or worse, have his funds confiscated? He found out what Saladin's needs were and satisfied them to accomplish a win win for both parties.

So if we were truly able to know the needs of the Muslim people, we could create a win win situation? What if the power of Caesar is in charge and he does not represent the sentiments of the people? Yet is in control of their destiny. Hey, don't blame me. I chose Rambo and 007. You're the one that went in head first. It's cool though, we learn not to make the same mistake and live with the consequences of our actions. Not to get ghetto with it, but somebody ought to pop a cap in that little sawed off Iranian ass. Or convince me that his intentions are not to wipe Israel off the globe for his own self fame. Sounds like some serious short man syndrome to me. Hey Ghadafi, hows it hanging? Brilliant plan of Reagan and can be yours "if the price is right". Awwww.... Mercenaries...oh damn, what movie did I see that in? Robin Hood with Kevin Costner. Whew...that would have irritated me all day.

So let's recap here for a moment and say we're the big dog on the block. We went to obedience class and learned to interact well with the other dogs. But there are a few in the bunch that just keep pissing us off. A little nip here and a little nip there. There is one in particular that has rallied friends and they bit the shit out of us. Because the big dog had not gained complete control over anger, he bit back. Not knowing exactly where to bite, but knew it would set a precedence that this big dog will bite back if provoked enough. As we lick our wounds this same smaller dog just will not quit. He justifies his motivations with his other dog friends. You've seen them, the oil painting with dogs playing cards. Classic, I have it right next to my velvet Elvis picture and below my Ankh of Tau picture. I do have good taste. LOL But these dogs aren't playing for their pack, they play for themselves and use God as their playing cards. With as much controversy as Religion has had for the centuries, wouldn't that be where you would find the corrupt working the system to their advantage? The Living Word can be easily maneuvered to fit ones objective. Thus, Christ like or Anti-Christ like.

Speaking of working the system to their advantage. Don't we have that going on right here in our country? Honestly ask yourselves this question. Do I spend more time on how to beat the system out of money or contribute to it? You ignorant human being, it really is not your fault. You are ignorant, helpless, lazy, bitter, self righteous and pretty much a blight on the face of the earth. The system was built by loving human beings to have charity and reach out to help their neighbor. You have turned it into your opportunity to retire. Are you the money changers of today? You take my money and the money of your working brother and kick back and waller in the meager contentment that your brother has provided. If I were a politician that didn't care about you. I would keep you in your sty and promise you more slop. My agenda and fame would continue your imprisonment while I profited from your ignorance.

Did you get your bowl of free slop? It's right over there. No my brother, I will plant a garden and harvest for a bountiful feast. My slop will be there tomorrow for you to enjoy as long as I have your vote. If you earnestly need my charity, then please, come in and break bread with me. You are who the charity was meant to fulfill. Do not feel shame by accepting my charity. I have more shame giving it. The shame that I can not do more for those that truly are in need. And the shame that our greedy brothers can not see past themselves. But the world needs shit shovelers too. Speaking of shoveling shit.

Hey if anyone wants to blame me for the oil spill they can. We are going to be shoveling shit here for a long time. I should have never made that crack about Global Warming sending sharks to ruin my summer. Reminds me of Dan Akroyd thinking of the Marsh Mellow Man in Ghost Busters. I guess if that is my first prophecy to come through, it would be a quickie. And I don't like quickies, I prefer longies. LOL So let's stop placing blame and get this shit cleaned up. BTW...a longie is a Legacy.

Oh so you are prophesying now are you? I'll do anything I can to sell you on God's Gift. He hired a salesman, so ? ? ? me. Nah, not going there. Let it be a game of hang man for yourselves. I can't wait to get in front of my Judge.

DID YOU DO ALL IN YOUR
POWER
TO DELIVER
MY GIFT

After I finish this second book, do the ten radio interviews and pray that someone helps me finish your website, I'm going to have to say yes. "That's my final answer". I must have peace of mind Lord.

Okay, so freaking talk to me. Did I win? LOL Or did I just make a complete ass out of myself again? It's cool, I have a lot of training in that area. But Lord, I'd rather make a complete ass out of myself proclaiming your Holy Name with my favorite lamp shade on, rather than have to go through life without you in my heart and knowing that I didn't do all in my power to fulfill my purpose for You. The "at all costs" clause was a little tough. But was one Hell of a great excuse to drink.

I don't have to know that you are right there anymore. I'm up your butt, I'm like velcro. At least that is what I have been told by my friends when it comes to women. LOL Don't come to any sudden halts on me, my head will be so far up your ass. Hey, c'mon. Come back please. A little humor and some burnt offerings pleases our God. At least that is what I believe. What do you believe? NO!!! After an intensive inventory of your life. I mean an honest to goodness come to Jesus meeting. What do you believe? Are you following the beliefs of someone that you are emulating? Or are you following what you have researched and willing to make a decision as to what you believe and live with the consequences?

Sign my ass up for the I believe my Savior Jesus Christ died for my sins and was risen from the grave. Ho Hum, now give me my pass. Really, no Really??? Did you really think that that was all there was to it? Well I'm generally a nice person. That's nice, I'm glad to hear that. We need more nice people like you in this world. I must pay you a compliment, if the world were filled with people like you we would be living in a world that looks a whole lot like what we got. Oh, thank you. You're so kind. Besides baby, with that dress, it's all about you now isn't it? Ooooooh....Nathan

I still got my Mo Jo Baby, I can insult your intelligence, get your vote and still shag you. Yeah Baby. Oh don't take offense Baby, Dr. Evil has deliberately omitted things from the development of your mind and you were so easy Baby, because you didn't come looking for "IT". And when you did, your brothers capitalized on your naivety. MuuuHua How does Dr. Evil make that laugh in script?

Damn, this is funny stuff. I think I'm funnier sober than I was drunk. But I'll reserve judgment for you. You all are so damn good at it. Alcohol has served its last purpose in my life. God Willing.

Okay, so maybe I'm a little over the top. I haven't heard anything from the Father for a few moments. I better do a sound check. Marco!!!

POLO!!!

9

That's the great thing about God. He never leaves you. He just gives you enough rope to get away. Get away from what, is your decision and there will always be enough rope for you... Sorry, I can't go there. I have heard your stories. I have wept with you. I can give you my thanks and hand in friendship. My thanks for allowing me to understand where you are at and what you have been through, before I found myself in a similar circumstance. I guess you could say I watched how you putted your ball, saw the curves and could avoid them if I'm very careful. My hand in friendship is a hand up, not a hand out. With enough practice, we can both birdie this hole. My friend, my brother.

I think I need to take smoking out of my life as well. YA THINK!!! You Moron. I can feel it hurting me. Not drinking has even pushed me to it more. Why are these stupid things so difficult to remove from our lives? I hear that they're putting carpet glue into them so you don't get drunk and burn your house down. Yuck, now I'm inhaling carpet glue. How can I be so smart and so stupid at the same time? I'm quitting right after I finish this pack. Right, heard that one before. At least your not going to kill anyone but yourself with that one. So let me buy you a pack. And remember me on election day. More freebies coming your way. Hey, I know what you're doing. You think because I smoke cigarettes that I am not that smart and you can get over on me. If you deliberately destroy the body, I would say that would definitively characterize you. It may not exemplify you, but the odds are increased that you would have a lower level of intellect due to harmful decisions that you make for yourself. All right, just wanted to clear that up. I thought you were insulting me. You weren't were you? It is a pretty stupid habit. Pray for me and I'll pray for you.

Lord, please allow me to control the Demons that control me and rob me of my life. More importantly, give me the strength and wisdom to help someone else through their pain so that I may discover how easy mine is to get through. What am I bitching about?

I will end this day telling you about the twelve step meeting I just went to. An out of town visitor shared an analogy about Santa. I was dying to tell everyone that I had just been writing about that. But I refrained and thanked her, but I couldn't resist telling everyone my misfit toy analogy. I am just such a "all about me kind of guy". I have got to fix that. I just want to tell everyone that has been sober for years, hey, good news. I've allowed the Lord into my heart and I'm never going to forget Him again. I know what I would get for a response. Yeah, good for you. Keep coming back. LOL They are right, I can stumble at any time and I have already heard the tale and can tell it so well myself.

6/28/2010

Productive day editing book. Had some issues that I had to deal with today that would have ordinarily been all the excuse I needed to get a bottle and pass out. I'm not feeling as comfortable as I was. But I do know I haven't had a drink for seven days. If I had not heard their compassionate stories about that first drink, I would have had one tonight. Thank you Lord for giving me another day without Alcohol. I want to use my Demon as a beacon for You. I bring you the Head of Alcohol on a silver platter. He just has always kept growing new heads. I won't start making promises to you Lord, but I will start making real promises to myself. When I can commit a promise to You. I want to make damn sure I can keep "IT".

6/29/2010

I'm wondering what I will do with all of my time when I finish this book. It has helped to have this project to focus on and redirect my energy. I am in a manic state of mind now and have been for the last couple of days. Every time I pick up my purpose for God, I just get way out there. I like to put on a little Enigma

11

and pray as I write. Hey, I guess this is like a personal facebook diary. This book is full of "What's on your mind?" You talking to me, cause if your talking to me, I'll tell you what's on my mind.

Hey I discovered that a characteristic of the disease alcoholism is to have a "Save the World" mindset. This concerns me greatly. If they have admitted their crazy ideas came from the bottle, why can't I? You know I kind of think that it is Gods Plan like everything else is, once you take the time to put two and two together. Us crazy bastards are the ones that create shit for everyone to enjoy. But just like the semen strive and struggle to fertilize the egg, it only takes one for conception. So maybe I am a member of the lucky sperm club after all.

Do you mean to tell me that my concept that will re-instate birthrights, create a propagating, everlasting, taxable income stream is all just alcohol talking to me? Are you telling me that if I donate to a charity and they only get half of the profits and the other half is to be re-invested that I won't be donating for an eternity? Don't tell me that all of my future heirs will not get a check from me with my inspirational words on it. Couldn't we use this newly created, from thin air, taxable income stream to rebuild social security? If lots and lots of money were invested into the market place, wouldn't that create jobs? I just thought maybe I was the one that had been given a Gift and now I see that it is just this disease that I have. Damn, it has embarrassed me my whole life. It would have been nice to witness God having an Everlasting, Earthly Entity where He would fund His Health Care Centers and heal the sick. Just kind of sounds like Jesus, doesn't it? Well, at least I know now that I have a disease that inspired me to witness for our Father and to put down all of this craziness and go back to work with all of the other elves. I thought about being a dentist, but yuck, your breath. So I ended up with the red nose and I'm ready to guide His sleigh for one night. We'll have to see about tomorrow, tomorrow. I'm taking it one day at a time and praising Him every minute of the day.

I am seeing co-dependence in me more and more. I have always had this insecurity. Maybe that is why I always want to be at the center of attention. I have been using a big lure to catch the fish that I want and I think I'm fooling the real fish telling them I'm going for big fish. Truth be told, I don't know what I'd do if I had a Marlin on the line. LOL Cut and Release maybe? No, not my clingy ass. We're going to mount that Baby and I can tell all my friends how I caught her. Whoo Hoo, look at my trophy wife that I will worship and she will make my life a living Hell trying to please her for another shot of booty. I can see how this can repel anyone, but when you are in excitement, you just want to be excited. I just have to learn how to be excited being with someone without being up their ass. But if you're not up their ass, they think your avoiding them. Hey, like I said before, I failed in the relationship category. Good luck, I think they all have snakes in their head and I'm a learned snake charmer and get bit repeatedly. LOL

Well, that didn't take long. I got a Marlin on the line. Let's see how long it takes for me to screw it up. I think I'll try a new strategy since I'm sober. I think I will just be me. She seemed to like my wit. Wait til she meets Mr. Crazy. I'm not a bad catch myself. Now that I am beginning to understand who I am and who I do not want to be. I'm worthy of a Marlin, I take care of myself physically for the most part. Except when I destroy my body with my Demons. I'm fairly attractive, financially sound and have a spiritual belief that guides me. Yeah, without my Demons, I'm even more attractive. To a point of controlled vanity. You have to watch those boundaries of ego and depression with negative self-talk.

Speaking of Mr. Crazy, the other night I was talking to a new Leper friend. He says he became the best witness for Sobriety while he was hammered. It reminded me of my whole God thing. "Repent and thou shalt be Saved" and Hic Cup doesn't quite go together does it? I pray that my Father will use my wasted life for the benefit of others that are struggling and prevent others that may. It really is not of your control if you are one of "those" type people. I like to refer to us not as Lepers, although it's perfect, but undiscovered creative minds. If you have this mind like I do, you will medicate it to fruition. It is a disease that you were born with. Your mind must always be turning. You must be focused on something, otherwise your mind pleads to rest. You have to discover what releases your mind for yourselves. Some do yoga, biking, gardening etc...I have found that I like to write and express my thoughts. I've never written a goal down in my life and I'm not starting now. I want to live day by day and enjoy the days I have left. It sounds like a pipe dream for me because of all the hell I've been through. But now, life is good and I will only create my own hell for myself by allowing my Demons to destroy me.

I have changed some things in my life. I strive to change some things in my life. I fail at changing things in my life. I guess that is why so many marriages fail and grow apart. As we grow, we don't always grow at the same rate spiritually. Just like in the maze that we are in, some will cautiously sniff out new cheese and others will scurry into bad decisions. Some will be reluctant, but will begin to seek and others will never know what the purpose for their lives ever meant. Okay, I can finally answer the quandary put on my heart after reading "Who Moved My Cheese". Just got it, no shit. I'm Scurry and Him. I have scurried around my whole life like a chicken with it's head cut off, I don't think I was wobbling because my head was cut off literally, but cut off from reality. I am Him because I began to seek Him. And He guided my heart to places that I have never been. He showed me where I had been and where I do not want to go. No stairway to Heaven, it's my purpose to build it with the Bricks of Mankind. Not only for us to go up, but for Him to come down and Heal us.

Man, this is some pretty good stuff wouldn't you agree? I think I'll put it in a book and give God 90% of the proceeds so His Earthly Entity can start healing the sick.

Oh, you're a salesman. I must admit my heart was filled for a moment then came you. The Salesman. The lowly, drunk, used car salesman.

Look Lady, I don't give a rats …

Stop, pause, think and decide.

Thanks Kazoo, I was fixing to rip her a new one.

Oh forgive me, I didn't mean to say that out loud and it wasn't in reference to you. The term "Salesman" just brought back memories of my late husband. He drank himself to death thinking that he had a solution to all the Worlds problems. Now what is it that you are selling young man.

Uhhhhh.....Right. I am fulfilling my purpose for God and I am seeking someone that has the technological talent that can build our Master the tool needed, so that we may pass along birthrights that will ultimately be our Worlds Salvation.

Uhhhhh....Do you have a card? You sound just like my late husband. His name was Nathan and he used to say he was given a gift from God. What a loon.

Yes mamn, I can certainly understand where you are coming from. We don't want any one running around here trying to deliver a gift from God. He's in a better place now, I can assure you.

What were you saying about technology?

Yes mamn, I am trying to find someone that can build a computer website. They need to be pure at heart and passionate about what they believe in.

Oh well is that all, hand me my purse. My sisters, cousins, nephew is a complete geek. He's always playing those video games when he should be out exercising them lungs. Here's his number, call him.

I sure will and thanks. He sounds just like the man for the job. He has to be someone special to create something that will live in infamy. Something so special that it blossoms into World Peace.

That's him alright.

I'll give him a call. Yeah, right. Get me the hell out of here.

Look Dum Dum, what does it hurt to call him?

Kazoo, I just don't want to call him. He's a geek for crying out loud.

Yeah, that's telling him. Hit the road Kazoo.

It's your decision Dum Dum.

You know, maybe Kazoo is right and I should call. I shouldn't judge someone by using someone else as the barometer. I'm going to call him right now. Hang on.

Hello

Hello Poindexter

Yes, hang on. Let me turn my video game down.

Hey, I'm on hold, but I just busted a gut. Thought I'd share. LMAO

Hello this is Poindexter, can I help you?

Hi Poindexter, I was referred to you by your...uh..Aunt's... uh.. a relative of yours. She says you may be able to help me.

How can I help?

I am trying to design a website that will enable everyone to create their own Living Will, Will and Living Trust free of charge and right from their own home PC. There's a lot more to the story, but for now, let me say that I am looking for a spiritual man than has the talents and passion to build this site.

I am that man. I too have been searching to fulfill my purpose for our Father and I am honored that you would ask me. I will build a glorious website. One like no other. I have the skills and I have the technology. The Vessel deserves great care and planning, one that is not scurried into. One that is everlasting. One with Passion.

Son of a bitch, who'd have thunk it Poindexter. You're a Lion in sheep's clothing too huh? I would have never found you had I not tried to seek you.

Do you think I could drive to K-Mart and pick up some underwear? I'm a very good driver.

Sure Poindexter, whatever you need brother. I got you covered and so will the Hanes.

Hey, I sure hope we can get some endorsements here. It's for a good cause after all. And as a reminder to everyone that thinks I'm in it for the money. I only get 10% from the concession stand for eternity. Everything else goes to Gods Legacy Trust LLC to heal the sick for an Eternity. I like the sound of that. Say it again Mufasa. "ETERNITY".

You know, I bet if we took a poll of people asking them if they have ever heard of the Seven Sealed, Two-Sided Scroll, the largest riddle of Mankind, the riddle that would be our Salvation; I would guess that only .666% would have ever heard of it. I know that I hadn't.

Your purpose in Life is to help someone else find theirs. You purpose is to help Mankind and so is mine. Mine may be a little Grandiose for you to comprehend, but I have the Courage to change the things that I can. The Wisdom to know when I need help from my brother and the Serenity that comes with fulfillment for our Father.

And hey, if you're going to go down, you might as well go down in a blaze of Glory for our Creator. So step back non-believers, I'm shooting the whole load. LOL

You still got it Baby, even sober and it's so much more fun this way. You still got your Mo Jo Baby.

Do you know what it is like to not be able to use your legs, Gump?

Ya..Yuh...You're still Lt. Dan, Lt. Dan. - Forrest Gump

I AM
HIM

I find Him, when I seek Him
I become Him, when I am Him
I WILL pray for HIM, to know Him.

Him is Thy Brother
Thy Brother is
HIM

Hey, I got invited to go to a half way house for a meeting tomorrow. I'm excited to see where I could have ended up had it not been for wonderful parents. I want to learn what it is like to not have alcohol in my life. I need an negative incentive to help me strive to be more.

Tonight's meeting was about gaining trust after you become sober. It was pretty heartbreaking to hear the stories about the separation from the family and it was rejoicing to hear about being given the trust to care for a child. It was probably a good thing I was traveling all those years as my children were growing up. I couldn't take care of myself after hours.

As I pace the floor with jealousy that is not warranted, I think about a good tumbler full of Vodka on the rocks. That's my chosen poison. Then I wonder what drunken text and email I'll fire off and have to ask for forgiveness tomorrow. I want to be in a relationship, but I fear I may run off a good one if I find her in my present state of mind. I think I may be being succumbed to loneliness. It is not my desire, but I think it is part of my recovery and I don't think I have the power just yet to deal with my co-dependence issues. I have enough on my plate already. I want to tackle my Demons one at the time. I think if I can take the Shepard out, the flock will disburse. So, Mr. Vodka I rebuke you in the name of the Holy Spirit. He has spoken to my heart and will hold my hand during this battle, you and me. I have my Savior on my side and you have my disease on yours.

Lord, I submit to your Will for my Life. If I have not done your Will, please have mercy on this sinner that he take a stand and witness for You and what was promised. I have chosen to piss my life away and I don't believe in waste. So Lord, let my life not be a waste. Let your children digest your Living Word and save them from the Demons that they will find. I especially pray for our future prophets to not poison your minds with the poisons they give you for your gift. Explore your talent and express it sanely. Believe me, the crazy shit don't work. So stop, pause, think and then decide. I know what's going on in your mind. Somehow saving the World will somehow make us feel better about ourselves, so we can stop beating ourselves up over the drunken fiasco last night.

The problem that he is having is, He really believes that he was given a Gift from the "Wonderful Counselor" aka Holy Spirit. And he can not be heard. He knows not to stop. He knows how to be sane. He knows that he will be met with...well, everything. He knows that he has been told to disappear and remain anonymous. He knows his hands have been tied to mercenaries building a website without the passion one needs for a project of this magnitude. He knows he is tired, so I'll thank my God now for another day of Sobriety and say good night.

Good Night Jesus my brother, Mr. Miagi, Kazoo, Hank, etc... and you my Demon. I say good night to you and thank you. If it weren't for you, I'd have never stumbled over my purpose for God.

One more thing before You let me go. I hope it is your guidance to free me from the obligation to build these websites and not laziness on my part. I already have $3000 invested Lord and our mercenary has not performed. I ask of You to place "IT" in the hands of your children and take me out of the loop. If I have to do "IT", "IT" might drive me to drinking again. LOL That is one talent that I am thankful to have a brother to count on.

"IT"
IS IN
GOOD HANDS
"IT"
IS IN
GODS HANDS
NOW

Thank you my brother, I so want to emulate You and please the Father. I gotta tell you. I feel a sign of relief coming over me knowing that I am almost done. I will get to see His Mighty reach in my lifetime. I can feel it. "Imagine Turning To God For Change". Doesn't that slogan just talk to you? It would if you had a trained heart to listen. Start listening to your heart for a change and see where that gets you. I'll speak for myself when I tell you that my mind was not doing a very good job. I've benched him and seeking what is really important to me and those I can touch. Our Lord cries out to touch your heart and he has used me to be his Vessel to reach you. Are you in my story? Which one of my alter egos are you? Or are you my Judge? What story made you cry? What joke made you laugh? What offended you and why? What hit closest to home for you? What do you believe? What is your dream? Don't tell me, tell Him. I don't have time to listen to you. I'm way to busy. I'm way to busy missing my life. You and I will be heard, if it is only heard by our Lord. So you might as well line up for His freebies. He's passing them out to anyone that wants to help his brother strive for more. Honestly, I don't think it's a freebie at all. I think you got to want it like you have never wanted before. How much does it cost to be a friend? How much does empathy costs? The opportunity costs are measured by your decisions of your own free will. My demon costs me 30 yrs of my life. I think I have had enough of that therapy, thank you very much.

6/30/2010

Good Morning God. Please grant me another day of sobriety. Just got off the phone with my good friend Darren. He loved the preface and is going to see if he can help me with publicity. You never know what someone will get tinkled over as they read what I have written. He loved the line about no pilot or cocktail waitress, what a bitch. LOL I love to make people laugh. I gain a fulfillment in my heart by adding something to your day. Your purpose doesn't have to be as grandiose as mine. Your purpose could be to brighten others day with a smile. It's truly amazing what a smile and a few kind words can do. You just never know when it will trigger someone to make a change in their life. Your smile is touching people in ways that you can not comprehend, because we all get touched in different ways. So Smile You're on God's Camera.

You know I'm kind of embarrassed to say this, but you know I have no shame before our Father. I started to think how funny this is. In our present day time of technology, you should be able to be heard. What I discovered at the twelve step meetings is that everyone wants to be heard. It makes it difficult for true prophets to deliver their message from God. So before you continue to blog up the airways with non-sense because you're hammered, and hey I'm guilty too, ask yourself, is what I am saying and doing for His Glory or for my own.

"If you 'aint got no money, take your broke ass home." Tell the Lord your love for Him in private unless at a setting where it is appropriate. Many conversations have been monopolized because the speaker likes to hear themselves speak. I am a great bloviator and always attempting to be the star of the show. It's all about me. Wow, that's going to be a tough one to take out of my life. I'm thinking hibernation until after I launch the books. I can always get a booty call when I need it. Yeah, if that Marlin I had on the line doesn't sniff back at the bait, I'll take a break.

It's been a great Spring, what I remember of it. I did go to Vegas and yes, what happens in Vegas, stays in Vegas. In my case it will stay because I don't remember much of it. I do remember getting kicked out of a club. LOL Cause that is when I went and made money at Black Jack, drunker than Cooter Brown. Hell I was giving the fist with everyone at the table. Half of them didn't speak English, so I had to screw with them. I mean, cmon. That's a given people. Don't we mock what we don't understand. If I went to their country, would I want to be screwed with? Abso-freakin-lutely Baby, I can recognize when I'm being screwed with and will join in on the fun and if you didn't screw with me, I'd become a wall flower with shyness. Give me your best shot is all I have to say. I may not speak their verbal tongues, but I speak their heart tongue. And it's not some yibbity yabbity bullshit no one understands but yourself. Because if you are honest with yourself, you would recognize that it is a performance. But who the Hell am I to Judge you, I'm a Leper. Please continue, I enjoy a good performance and so does the Father. If that is on your heart, give it to Him freely. Maybe it's something only you and He can understand. Damn, I'm learning Father. I'm learning not to be so quick to judge.

The sexual tension is incredible in this manic state. My mind tells me I don't need a relationship right now. My Mini Me Mind tells me something different. Believe me when I tell you this, for some men, it can drive them insane. It is a enormously huge demon that I am blessed to have control over. I would love to listen to someone else's story of how they conquered it. I just flirt with that Demon and I have a Doctors script to take him out and exercise him at least daily or as needed for pain. The other pain that I have in my life somehow is released when sexual tension is released for me anyway. But I'm sure that no one else thinks this way. Right......MuuuaHuuuuaaa Dr. Evil loves your little dirty secrets. Oh, he can sure use shame to hold you hostage. Shame has taken many a life. I have so much shame for what I have made out of my life. I want a redeemed life by fulfilling my purpose. At least it won't all be for NOT.

I'm guilty. I'm guilty of condemning you of your sin, while I secretly fantasize about it. It is my restraint that allows me not to chase those Demons. And knowing me, I'd be addicted after the first time. I know what displeases the Father and I do all in my power to be a witness for Him. It's just damn, that girls got a fine ass. Those are my horns growing and I have many of them.

Do you remember the cartoon, when the character would push one lump on his head down and another would arise in a different place? Keep pushing them down and "keep coming back". I'm excited about today's meeting. It gives me a reason to shower and get out of the house.

Lord, thank you for blessing me financially to afford me the time to spend with you. This has become a full time gig working for you. But it is a piece of work that in your hands will blossom to a better world. A World where You dwell among us with your Everlasting, Healing, Loving, Earthly, Entity. And that is when my forefathers and myself can rest knowing the World is truly in God's Hands. He has a place in everyone's heart and can fix the broken ones here on earth as it is in Heaven. If you have ever been given your life back, stand up and tell me your tale. If you have not, shut the hell up, you can not articulate what you have not experienced for yourself. I try to articulate the horrors that others have been exposed to. An articulation will fall extremely short of the experience. If you don't think alcohol is a powerful Demon, brother, tell me your Demon and we'll get drunk and one up each other all night. "You think you got it bad, let me tell you about ME" cause I really didn't hear shit you said and could really give a shit. I just want to be heard. I want you to listen. No don't go, get him another round on me. So what are your problems? Well, I ...; that's great, now let me tell you about my problems. LOL What a drunken buffoon I have been.

So Doc, what do you think?

Tell me why you think alcoholism destroyed your life?

Well Doc, as a young man out of college I had a vision of a Yaught and a Trophy wife and I lost that vision. So I settled with a Bass Boat and a Road Whore and I lost that vision. Now I have a vision of a Hard On and an inner tube and there both going down. LOL Laugh you schmucks.

Hey I just thought of this, imagine that. LOL Us Lepers are the easiest bunch to get riled up because we have all been searching for our purpose. I knew there was a reason for me to join with my Leper brothers and sisters. You can't wait to heard either and nor can I. As a conglomerate group of reformed assholes, we have a pretty good voice. But we also know that that is not in the rules for the twelve step program. So sorry for getting you riled up. But I do need your prayers and support and if you could just help me with this website. Thank you, you're so kind. My that's a nice shade of blue your wearing, it matches your eyes. Look pal, do you want some booty or not? Is this the sexual revolution that I am hearing about? I am sooooooo.......down. But give me some time to pray about it, I may decide differently later. Especially if I give birth to a consequence or have to disclose an "oh shit" for the rest of my life to any future partners.

I have got to get out of this house. I'm going to take a shower and go to the gym. I'll start my work out by lifting that heavy ass phone and call my sponsor to let him know that I'll be at the meeting tonight. Man, I hate that shit. I haven't reported in for years, except to my folks and children. But I'm nine days sober, so I'm going to keep doing it.

I'm sitting here writing and having a great time in my manic state and it has started to rain a bit. I can use my creative avoidance and say to conserve time and because of the light rain, I'll go to the gym right before the meeting and kill two birds with one stone. Dude, why are you trying to conserve time? It is still just me planning, me planning to get drunk. I can leave the house anytime I want now. But I really don't want to go far unless I am pushed. I am feeling this program giving me the push that I need to re-emerge into society. I just don't know if I can fit in anymore. I am crazy after all.

What's with this Tweety Bird. I don't need to know when you are taking a crap or when you get a piece of ass. It's not my business and no one should care. That would be the old me. Alas, the new me has learned to listen with my heart. (can you tell it's dripping with sarcasm) My heart tells me that you are battling insecurity issues and vanity is screaming to be noticed. I will pray for you. Those Demons will eat your ass up.

I can't emphasis this one enough. If I have a vote, a black ball if you will. That will determine the fate of predators. I vote black. Your brother Jesus and our Father may forgive you, but I can not and will not forgive you. It causes a life time of pain for your prey. It WILL cause you pain eternally. Restraint guys, it is the measure of a man. Not the measurement of his member that matches his I.Q. If there is anyone in the room that has not heard me on how powerful the Demon between our legs is, listen up. There are ways to control this Demon and if man would stop suppressing men long enough, we could get a tax, keep it clean and safe and call it for what it is. Prostitution, a very needed industry that has been filled for centuries and the corrupt have corrupted it by suppressing it.

Oh shit, brain fart. If I am one of the witnesses, the other witness is you. My brother. I'm listening to my heart Father. Now my brother, be a Man and take your place in the household as a Real Godly Man. So that you can show our Father you are seeking your purpose by helping those that seek for their own.

Hey I was just thinking about masturbating. You know that movie out now with the vampires that are in control of themselves and feast on the blood of animals. They say the comparison for us is like eating tofu everyday. I would say that's a pretty good analogy of masturbation. It satisfies, but there is nothing like the warmth that comes from another human being, especially one that you love and would go to the ends of the earth for. I haven't seen how all of this ends just yet and I hope it takes a while longer now that I'm sober. But I think that perfect scenario is a fantasy. If you have it in your marriage, God blessed you. For the rest of us, we're still wearing our masks and making poor decisions. BTW...I masturbated hours ago, we'll go again later if prescribed by the Doc.

You know, you always have to thank God first so you can thank Him for sending "Them" to you in your time of need. Thank God for my parents. I love "Them".

If their were these Vampires that lived among us and had learned restraint, would you love them even knowing at any time their thirst for human blood could become an insane manic moment? Could you see yourselves setting up a blood bank so that they may quench their thirst from time to time to keep themselves in check about restraint? What would you think of the donors of such a bank? That's an interesting quandary? Pause here for a moment and think before you decide.

If their were these Insane Males that lived among us and had learned restraint, would you love them even knowing at any time their thirst for the warmth of another human being could become Vampirish at any moment? Could you see yourselves setting up a flesh bank so that they may quench their thirst from time to time to keep themselves in check about restraint? What would you think of the donors for such a bank? Is there more empathy in our hearts for Vampires than there is empathy in our hearts for Mankind? This is a Demon that is uncontrollable for many Vampires. How can we make these Vampires a non-threat to the well being of our society, get a tax, clean up the corruption and make it safe for human beings to do what they are going to do anyway of their own free will? I say that if you can not find in yourselves to aspire for more, then I want you safe and I want you to give your Mom and Dad a call and let them know that you are alright. They worry about you. If not them, your Father and Brother in Christ worry about you, we love you. Give Christ a call.

If one has empathy for Vampires, maybe one should re-evaluate fundamentalist Christian values and determine if there is another alternative that would still be pleasing to our Father. As a dad, I vote for the safety and the call. These are the values of the Leper Party made up with just one member with multiple personalities and we will throw ourselves at our Fathers feet for mercy. For we were all made broken, begged to be forgiven and the fortunate Demon slayers will rejoice in our Fathers Love. The corrupt will no longer have anything to corrupt and those predators will move to new suppressed ground to prey upon the laws of the land.

I wonder what society would dictate as the appropriate appearance and conduct in handling the Vampire environment that dispenses Human Blood. Red Lights, filth, beatings and disease or Bright Lights, sanitary, safe and optional group meetings on restraining your Demons.

The chair of our meeting tonight has expressed some expertise in the area of Bi-Polar and Schizophrenia. I was diagnosed Bi-Polar and I think after reading this, I qualify for the Schizophrenia part as well. I wonder if I could get some great drugs? I'm an alcoholic. That is my personal diagnosis and I don't need any damn pills to pull me through this Demon that I am battling. I just have to take alcohol out of my life. I'll conquer the other Demons later. This one is going to kill me. I asked this expert in my opinion because he has experienced trying to save the world syndrome as well, to give me his prognosis on my behavior based on this preface and chapter I am writing now. I am very concerned that I exemplify the characteristics, but I am convinced that I am right. And unless someone can definitively rebuke Gods Last Will and Testament, them I must endeavor to persevere.

"Why couldn't people just understand that I just felt like running" - Forrest Gump

I just felt like drinking, why couldn't people just understand that I wanted to numb my pain and fast forward my life? Hell, I understood it. I wanted to either Kill myself or control my Demon. So being the coward that I am, I stepped back and let Christ fight my battle. I am with Christ, so what Demon can stand against me? My naked soul is displayed for your public scrutiny. Step up like your brothers before you and choose your weapon to lash me with. When you choose your weapon of choice to lash me, make sure it is the same weapon that you lash yourself with.

This has duel meanings to me. When Forrest lost his girl after just making love to her the night before. The girl that was the keeper of his heart. He had to cleanse. He had to run her out of his system so that he could reach a point of acceptance and contentment. He was also running to find out what type of chocolate he would get. His destiny and purpose in life. His heart has been scarred and he can not do anything about that. So he gains serenity by accepting something he has no control over. He has the courage to pick his life up and make something of himself. And he has the wisdom to seek God for guidance. My peers wisdom says "STOP FORREST". My Lords wisdom says "ENDEAVOR TO PERSEVERE". Forrest's wisdom says "I've already gone this far, I might as well go all the way". So if my peers vote stop and my Lord, Forrest and the Wonderful Counselor say go. That's three to one, I like the odds. Hey, don't worry about me being on a slippery slope. I have a get out of hell free card. I had to earn it though. I had to totally humiliate myself before all of God's children and confess my sins. Most are allowed to confess in private as they search for their purpose. My purpose is for all mankind, so all mankind must be allowed to see my naked soul and learn from my mistakes and triumphs. I will be your Judas, so you can gauge your own lives using the consequences of my decisions. I pray you have control over your Judas as I battle mine. I lost it all and have been redeemed. How much will you lose before you have Christ challenge the Demons in your life? You do know that you have Demons in your life, don't you? If you don't, I want

29

to read your book. Sinless words haven't been spoken since uh-hhh....since Jesus.

Forrest was given his purpose by God. He was given a life that he could pour all of his wisdom into and fulfill his own purpose by giving back to another human being.

I am not tempting you Lord, but surely you wouldn't allow me to hang myself out here for You and You leave me hanging.

KEEP HANGING
YOU'RE ALMOST THERE
YOUR BROTHER WILL HELP
I PROMISE

I have always been my brothers keeper, am I now my brother and in need of being kept?

BINGO

I can't live with that. Thank you Father, I will need a booster shot of God everyday. I will need a booster shot of Spiritual Medication. Hear my Prayers and Speak to my heart Lord, I'm listening now.

Thank you Lord for another sober day. Good Night.

7/1/2010

Good Morning God. Lord please grant me another sober day.

I started running just like Jenny had told me to do and when I looked back, there was no one there.
- Forrest Gump

Are you a Prophet of God? Do you witness for God? Do you pray to God for your brother? Do you pray to God for yourselves? (That's a no brainer) Are you a prepared Prophet or do you just want to tell the Lepers that Jesus loves them and get the Hell out of there? What would you do if a Leper that you were witnessing to said, I need your help? Can you help me? If you can not be prepared for that scenario, then sit your monkey ass at home. You are creating more harm than good. This may have been the last time this Leper would reach for a hand up and yours wasn't really there for Him. Your hand is to busy stroking yourself to make yourself feel better about you. I'm not saying to stop spooning out the slop at Thanksgiving and Christmas, I'm just saying that if you want to reach out and touch one of the undesirables, you best be prepared. Are you?

He will be with you in just a moment, would you like a cigarette, booze, drugs, sex or Rock and Roll while you wait. It's free. This may be your last time to party like a Rock Star. This book has a plethora of excuses if you haven't prepared one for yourself already. Our God aims to please, He gives you so many chances. Did you reach out for yours? Hey, that's none of your damn business. You're right, it is not my business. But if you were a Leper, I didn't want to miss you and possibly discover my purpose along the way. Good Luck, He shouldn't be much longer. The one in there now has been awhile, it must be one Hell of a pleading tale.

Had my first meeting with my twelve step sponsor. He is a Pharmacist by trade, so you know he had some good shit during his Demonic battle. As I try and tell my story to him, he is trying to stick to the curriculum. He had told me before to refrain from interjecting my comments, but just to listen and learn from others that have succeeded in controlling their Demon. By the end of our meeting I had a revelation. I can not try and rally my Leper brothers and sisters. They are holding on by a thread themselves. I remember a Leper friend telling me after he had been asked to look after something, his response was; I have a hard enough time keeping up with Woody. Woody don't have time for you. I understand my Leper brother, pray for me and let me learn from you. I do not want to upset your apple cart and that is not my intention. I am seeking another Lion, not another Lamb. A Lioness wouldn't be to bad either. Rrrrroooooaaaaarrrhh....

Okay, back to the twelve step program. My sponsor had already given me one assignment and I finished that the first night. He gave me a twelve step daily to do list to follow:

1. Pray in the morning for a sober day.
2. Have Daily Reflection
3. Do something nice for someone and don't tell them.
4. Go to a twelve step meeting
5. Call your sponsor
6. Read at least two pages in the twelve step Big Book
7. Pray at night and give thanks for another sober day.

Homework:
1. Read Bill's Story
2. Listen to Disease of Perception

Cool, that doesn't sound to hard. If I can gain control over my Demon, I would do just about anything. Well not anything, I will always exercise my own judgment based on my frame of reference. For I know the decisions I make will reap consequences that I and I alone must live with.

Pants on the ground, pants on the ground. Looking like a fool with your pants on the ground. I have had my pants on the ground serving my Demon for years. I looked like a fool with my pants on the ground. I am not ashamed to pull my pants down for Christ and for all to see and hear my confession of Faith and Love for our Savior.

I had just started my drive to Orange Bch, Al for the 7 o'clock meeting and ran into traffic. It was great. I turned around because I knew that I would never make it and I had so much happiness in my heart that I would have not been able to remember all of the thoughts that raced through my mind. It's the fourth of July 2010 weekend, the weather sucks and we got oil on the beach. Our summer is ruined, just as I had asked for it not to be. The GREAT part about seeing all the traffic was seeing all the unity. Not only to celebrate the Independence of our Great Nation, but to do what we can to help our struggling brother on the beach. It's amazing what we can do as a people when we become of the people, by the people and for the people. In God We Trust. It is Faith, Hope, Charity and Love that will sustain this Great Empire.

The Faith that there is a God greater than ourselves.

The Hope for a better tomorrow.

The Eternal Charity of God's Gift. "LEGACY"

The Love of our brothers and sisters in Christ.

How am I doing Father?

POLO!

Smart ass brother of mine. I love you Jesus. I still owe you that wedgie for all you put me through. Thank you. Thank you for saving my life. You're all I have had to lean on for years now. How can anyone understand what I am doing?

TWEETY?

Oh, hell no. I don't want anyone up my ass like that. I'll stick my vanity and my balls in my lunch box before that happens.

ANONYMITY?

Perfect!!!

TOLD YOU SO

"LIKE" I know you did, but you don't have to rub my nose in it.

SURE?

Yes Father, all I do is for Your Glory not mine. I am your humble servant to deliver Your Great Gift and I will get out of the way to witness Your Mighty Hand. I haven't forgotten.

WHAT?
THIS IS GOD
REMINDING NATHAN
TO SHUT UP

Yeah, I like that one. I have seen the greatest of salespeople keep selling a product that is already sold, to the point that he talked himself right out of a sale. I pray that I am the salesman you thought I was. No wonder John wept if you allowed him to see my drunk ass. I would have bet against me and I never do that. I play to win baby. If your kitchen is to Hot, get out of your Hell. If I can't sell you on God's Gift, could I interest you in some cool God Slogan T-shirts? LOL LOL LOL God, with you as a partner, we will make a fortune. 90% for you and 10% for me just from the concession stand, right? That's the deal. Let's Shake on "IT".

ETERNALLY

I do like the sound of that. Eternally. It is a message that we, God's children, are either still oblivious to God's Last Will and Testament or you've lost your Faith and really just don't give a shit about much of nothing anymore. You went out full and came back bitter. Life has beat you down. There is no Hope. Brother, I tell you that there is Hope. The Master's Plan is our Salvation.

When the prostitute was to be stoned to death. Jesus said, he among you without sin, cast the first stone. He then told the prostitute, go and sin no more. Now knowing my brother Jesus Christ like I do, I would have to say that He was inspiring her to make more out of her life. I really don't think He was condemning her for doing what she has to do to eat and feed a family. This person may exemplify the lowest of the food chain in your eyes, but I say this person provides a noble service to keep the insane Vampires that dwell among us in Restraint. Ask Melvin P. Thorpe from "The Best Lil Whorehouse in Texas" how he wants to view this issue and see if it coincides with your own. "Texas, has a whorehouse in it", thank God. Those Vampires prey upon their own. Our Father in my humble opinion, will close that loop hole excuse for being a predator. Incest, Rape, Bizarre shit will no longer be forgivable. If it ever was.

It is difficult to continue on my purpose for God. I am a laughing stock. Lord, they do not understand. Their blinders will not allow them to see. Or is it me that has blinders on Lord? Am I allowing my Demons to completely embarrass me once and for all. Thank God. Let's do it. Let's exercise the Demon without releasing him. Let's learn how to control him. I need help and you may also.

Tough night Lord. I see now that I can not have any influence of a woman right now. It can easily tilt my balance and cause me to drink. Now I will just have to contend with the loneliness while I attempt to gain control of my life. A life without alcohol would be a life without a bully that kicks your ass all over the playground everyday and causes you great humiliation. Guess I may just need to make more meetings if I get lonely. I can not falter this time Lord. I want to prove it to You and myself. I will not be beaten down. I will rise up and be the witness for You that You so desire for me to be. All you bitches go home. The snakes in your heads are getting in mine. Let me get my head straight and then come back. Especially you, my brunette cutie. Such a fine ass. Ummm Ummm Ummm. Such an insane ass OnYaMama. What the Hell, a little political humor is good for the soul.

That wasn't racist was it? I don't want to start any shit over racism. One has to wonder at what point does one rely on ones own abilities and put ones crutch down and join the struggle of a one Mankind under One God. Are you the "ONE" that models, destroys or exemplifies what your race should be? It's a struggle for all of us brother and we are all in this together. Let's get past the bullshit of the color of someone's skin. Show God who you are on the inside. Your discriminating brother is a moron and his generation will grow out and a new generation of God's Children will grow in.

I've been hearing some of the Lepers question the Big Book when it comes to praying for yourselves. Thank you my brother. That's what I'm talking about. Always Respectfully Question Authority. Even when it is a great authority. The twelve step program has saved many lives and I pray that I will be one of them. But I'm praying for me a lot. I need help. I will pray for and nurture my brother, but sometimes I just want a little alone time with the Father so He can nurture me. Like a child that curls up to his mother on the couch, watches TV and falls asleep knowing he is safe and loved. We never stop yearning for that closeness and the fortunate find it in a mate, but is available to us all with the Father's undying Love for you. You will feel His presence if you stop looking for it with your mind and feel Him on your heart.

Alright you got to stop hitting chili peppers up everyone's ass. Now listen to me. Drop your ball over your left shoulder. What? Do it. Now put a golf tee behind your right ear. What does all of this mean? It means shit, but if you need some Hocus Pocus for

36

you to Focus. I give you humility. Now kick some ass and let's go home. - Tin Cup and a little bit of me. LOL Loved the nickname, "Clank".

We are drawn to prey upon the misfortunes of others. I don't know exactly why that is other than greed. You can witness it at someones death and the heirs fight amongst themselves to get what they got coming to them. Even if it costs them their sibling. I'll give you an example how it works in sales. Have you ever had one of those meat delivery trucks come rolling into your driveway and the distraught driver/salesman explains that the cooling element just went out on his truck and if you want a steal on some steaks, now's the time because all of this will go in the dumpster tomorrow. Cha Ching, sucker born everyday. How about the asphalt Gypsies. They run around looking for pot holes and tell the owners of businesses that they just finished a job and this load on the truck will harden if they don't use it. They will make you a great deal. Is this dishonest to prey upon your greed? You are getting what you want at a perceived value. No this is selling and what can cause salespeople to catch a bad wrap. A good salesman will give you what you want, because he knows if he can fill your need, his needs will be filled as well. All this shit says the same thing don't it? You will find your purpose by helping others to find theirs. I'm selling my ass off to get you to buy into God's Gift. Create yourselves a personal trust and Legacy. No charge. Watch the change in our World when God is the Shepard and has the Gold and Silver to heal the sick. Gods Legacy Trust LLC. His Everlasting Earthly Entity. His Kingdom, here on Earth as it is in Heaven.

I asked for your help with my Demon alcohol because it was killing me. I now humbly ask for your help with my Demon Cigarettes, they are killing me.

Rough day today Lord. There is no way I could have made it today had it not been for your guidance and those damn meetings.

37

I love them. They're addictive. Good night my Lord and Savior. Thanks for the sober day.

Hey, I'm still up. I sat down to watch a little TV to relax and I flipped through the religious channels and found this preacher making up stories and promising folks to have their prayer answered if they would just send him $1000.00.

Why don't you just give me a thousand dollars and we can go out back where I will kick you in the nuts and we can call it a day? - Vegas Vacation

The religious predators sicken me. Using God's name for their own self-gain. I'm not sure where the Father, Son and the Holy Spirit stand on this one, but I got a black ball for your ass.

7/2/2010

Good Morning God. Please help me make it through this weekend. It's going to be a rough ride. I'm going to force myself to get out alone. Not my thing, but what is my thing? Right.... Drinking. I haven't discovered a new thing for myself. Guess I'll do a little fishing and see if I can catch a Marlin and by the end of the night, decide if I want to take a croaker home. Not my thing either, but I do have needs.

I can't remember the last time I spent a 4th of July weekend sober if I ever did. I know that I can not cower to my Demon, but I must face him head on. If I continue to hibernate my Demon may not be being consumed by me, but has defeated me by consuming me. I will not settle for an island of misfit toys as my only outlet. I will re-emerge a sober witness for Christ. A drunken witness destroys our Father's Plan. I know that this is something that I must do for Him and me, but I will need help. I will need new direction and focus. Thank God I am still working on this book. My mind will not stop turning, it keeps me in total unrest. What does God want me to do? Over and over and over again. If you don't understand this by now, it has been like Whoopi getting serenaded by Patrick Swayze (RIP my beloved brother) "King Henry the Eighth I Am". Even with this in my head, God is speaking to my heart and demanding I do this. Make a complete idiot out of myself. Why is it when you proclaim your Love for your Lord and Savior people look at you like you have lost your mind? I would have to say that Loving our Creator has somehow been perverted by all of the weirdos out there wearing panty hose on their heads, beating tambourines and passing out flowers at the airport. Or they see a Pastor so worried about getting into your pocket book, they just manage to squeeze in some of God's Word between commercials. Or they have seen supposed men of God go down in a blaze as they anoint themselves as Judge and Jury over your lives and even delve into their own perversions using their position of power serving themselves, not our Father. They're just name dropping to see what is in it for them. Bastards. You are the ones that have made it very difficult for God's children to come to believe again. The last time they wanted to Come, so did you. But you were thinking of a different kind of Cum. Sorry guys, but a few bad apples does spoil the barrel in this case.

Brothers and Sisters in Christ. There are many men of God, but remember that they are still men. All men have horns, it is how we are made. Period, end of discussion. It is their restraint that measures them with the yardstick of God. Never let your guard down, but love one another. I know, what a crock of shit we have made of this world that we would have to become this shielded. Lord, I can brush off pretty much all of the sticks and stones will break your bones shit, but those predators really hit close to home and can change my World if I am not careful and aware of my surroundings. Has man really become evil or has it always been this way? This could really give you a complex about people wanting to bend you over at every street corner and you know what? They have that concern in other countries of the

World. We are just blessed to live in God's new promised land. The brothers we left behind to hold down God's fort are still being persecuted.

Time can be our blessing or enemy. Depending on what we do with time. I think sometimes. Do you think? But most of the time I can't finish my thought before something triggers me to go off on a tangent and lose the great thought that I was working on because I'm off to another great thought before I could finish my first or even my second thought. Crazy isn't it. I think it is a gift and I love it. I don't want your man made drugs to control this and lose control because your elixirs erase the line of reality for me. Why do you think folks are killing folks. I can go to the Doc right now and get a multitude of shit and sell it as party favors to my friends. Hell, I don't even have to go to the street corner. Hey, that's really not a bad idea. Hmmmmm.....economy has been pretty tough, so I could have justification. Do you see how our minds work my brother. You have the same thoughts, you just may have more control of yours. People like me can get themselves in trouble if are not very careful. We were born with a much more powerful Demon. I tell you the truth, what it is that we are trying to medicate is, we were supposed to be so much more in this life and life beat us down. So we relinquished command. This medication takes TIME and eventually will put our dreams to rest or our bodies whichever one comes first. Your Demons don't give a shit. Dead or Alive even better for them to witness for me. Their Lord Satan. I am so loved by the diseased.

Holy Shit Lord, are you fixing to bring me through some exorcist shit or something. Cool, don't scare me to much and I don't have any pea soup in the pantry. Lord, we've done this already haven't we? Right....I have been my own Demon for a long time now haven't I? Right....Maybe it was me that was the problem. Ya think maybe a little? I have been witnessing for my Demon alcohol. I have become one of those predators that want to tell you how you should live your life and get hammered and live mine the way the hell I want. At least I'm not asking for a Love offering for my books with the complete 3 CD collection of these inspirational words, but wait. If you order now, we will throw in the cross and nails. I'm selling my books. Yes the Prophet wants a Profit. 90% for God and 10% for me. Screw you brother, I got to eat to. My God wants to feed me well, for when He is fed, so am I eternally. I'm pretty smart for a drunk huh? A Leper of society. One of "those". Pssst....do you see him right there, stay away from him, let me whisper....I don't want my God to hear me sin. He's praising God like for real. What's up with that girlfriend? So weird, just keeping it real girl. You know what I'm saying, what's up with dat? Keep this on the down low, gossiping can have repercussions for me and you know that I can really only dish it out. I aint taking shit unless I can get high off of it. But that's just you and me girlfriend. You know what I'm saying?

No girlfriend, I really don't. I have seen him and I am actually quite envious that he has managed to figure out a way of really connecting with the Holy Spirit. He is feeling the Love that I yearn for in my own life, but you and I medicate ourselves to ease our pain. His pain has been removed. So, no girlfriend. I do not understand tearing down the image that we so desperately seek. Love, to be Loved and to Hope for a better tomorrow. I'm actually pretty miserable girlfriend. I see my life slipping by me and I have already wasted most of it chasing Demons.

Like I told you, I was flipping through the religious channels I saw a woman giving great advice to other women. She was saying not to put up with pricks. Hell, we're being taught to be pricks because that is what most of you are drawn to. Hard to figure out except to say that whatever we can have at any time is not as desirable as the challenge to have what we can not. It is just like accepting our Christ as our Lord and Savior. You can have Him at any time, but you seek a different God to serve. You seek Dr. Feel Good and it does feel soooooo..... good until the ride is over, which they all come to an end and you live with the consequences of your decisions and unfortunately these short sided decisions can last a lifetime. First came drinks, then came sex, then came Jr. in a baby carriage. Animal instinct is difficult to control. If you can not control "IT"

I will tell you the truth. I want a partner that is an extension of me except when I need time to spend "time" with our Father. I guess that makes me clingy. I am so clinging on to my Lord and Savior right now. He is all I have left to cling to. No one understands and listens to me more than Him. He reads every word that I write. He guides my words so that they Honor Him. If I am a poor witness for you Father, I am sorry. I am a wretched sinner and I want to redeem myself in your presence. I want to be pure of heart, mind, body and soul when that Glorious day comes for me to meet you face to face.

I wish "IT" didn't have to be so dramatic, but I am delivering a Gift from God to all Mankind. Dude, that has got to come with some crazy drama and it does. Keep reading and keep coming back.

Just as we have seen in our text. How are text can be taken out of context. Wayyyyyyy..... to easy. The words of our Lord and Savior can be taken out of context to fit the text of a Leader that has his own text and his text is to be your Judge and Jury to fuel his own personal perverted Demons. So shall we pause for a moment of texting? LOL

You are your best witness for your worst Demon. Damn, did that just come out of my mouth. I want to hear it in your words Father.

I AM...
I WILL...
YOU ARE...
YOU WILL...

42

He's good isn't He. You could pray a month on that one and still not scratch the surface. Or I could just sell you a t-shirt and pray the Holy Spirit will touch your heart soon. How about a hat and coffee mug with that Salvation you're buying. I'm kidding about the t-shirt thing because I think it is wonderful for you to wear a badge of Honor for our Lord. He just wants you to get past your check writing mentality and get a little dirty. Check writing mentality that tells you that you have written checks to the church for years so your Salvation should be paid in full. Whooptie Shit. Have you ever touched another human beings heart? Have you ever had your heart touched by another human being? It's called Love people, not an open orgy. Although I would have loved to have been their Baby. We could do a little remixing Baby. Do a shag to the left to the left to the left, do a shag to the right to the right to the right. Now walk it on down, walk it on down, walk it on down. Yeah Baby, let's "Shag". As much as I want to join in and play, you know I have many horns, I must consider if my Father would approve. I think I would be happier if I could find one that didn't bitch and whine and mope and not give up the booty. No, I've already done that. I think I will be a little pickier the next time and keep my Demon between my legs well exercised so that I can make better decisions for a lifetime partner. Young Love is beautiful. Young decisions usually equal disaster unless you have the tenacity and commitment to support one another in every Love Language in the order that your partner understands. Reference "The Five Love Languages" by Dr. Gary Chapman.

I've got to get out from behind this computer, so I'm going to shower and masturbate, then head to the gym and try to read a little at the beach. No, on second thought. I think I'd just like to sit there and enjoy the peace regardless of the oil. Might be a little tough finding peace this weekend with all of the ass that will be running around there. See you later, I'm going to see if I can spear one. LOL I let the Marlin off the hook and didn't recast. She was special in her own mind. And I'm sure she is. I just didn't want to blow something that might be perfect until I gain a grip

43

on my alcoholism. Or does that just sound like creative avoidance because I'm terrified of the pain they can inflict on the male heart.

I'm thinking I might just go down and look at the Marlins and spear a Croaker to quench my human warmth thirst.

Those Goofy Bastards are about the best thing I got going is this miserable World.

Isn't that a little politically incorrect?

Screw that, I don't care what anyone believes. I know what I believe and no one is going to tell me different.

Cool – There's Something About Mary

My words are politically incorrect for a reason brother. I am very sane. I am leading where you want to go. I am leading where you need to go. I am leading a horse to water, but I can not make him drink. Make mine a Vodka on the rocks, but that's another story. What I am trying to tell you brother, I am a Salesman sent by God to get you to buy in to His Gift. And I Will get your attention anyway I can. I love the politically correct one. So much corruption, it just makes it to easy to be right.

Oh, I forgot I took a shit earlier. Just in case anyone wanted to know. Isn't that just a little too much information TMI girlfriend. Are you suffering from a superiority complex or do you just want "your pants on the ground" and bent over being humiliated and labeled.

You goes around doing that kind of stuff, you get a Rep. You don't want no Rep.

Hey, Screw You Rocky.

Screw me, yeah screw me. Who am I to tell nobody nothing
– Rocky

My name is Nobody. My Father's Name is God. My Brother
and Savior's Name is Jesus Christ. My Wonderful Counselor's
name is The Holy Spirit. I'd like to introduce you to my Family.
That's Moses over there with the hot brunette and you remember
Abraham don't you. The one behind the bar pouring the drinks
is Judas. Yeah, my brother couldn't stay mad at him for long. He
loves Him and He is His Brother. He just made Him a Slave and
He doesn't mind the deal. He just couldn't bear the thought of
roasting His ass for something He had really no control over. Oh
did He beg? More than is conscionable. Yeah, I always thought
He got kind of a raw deal too. Y'all got any Red Bull, I'm driving
tonight. I wish I could drink, it looks like so much fun.

Does the Wealth pay off in Heaven or does the Wealth pay off
the God "WE" serve here?

Good night God. Thanks for another sober day.

7/3/2010

Good Morning God. I faced my Demon alcohol head on last
night, even after repeated temptations from a sister that I had
known from an earlier time. I managed to hang on and not drink,
but of course the Demon between my legs began demanding to
be exercised and my blood bank donor wanted a contract in order
to quench my Vampirish needs. Had I not had control over that
Demon, I may make decisions based on my Demons needs and
not my own. I am just getting started with battling my Greatest
Demon alcohol, so I just don't need anything that can give my
Demon an advantage to the detriment of my own self will. So I
have controlled my Vampire and exercised good judgment and
restraint by not allowing my Demon alcohol to influence my de-

cisions. My blood donor has left this morning and I still thirst for Blood. If the Vampire Blood Bank were open, I would quench my thirst in a clean, safe, healthy environment, just like going to the Doc. Dr. Feel Good. Alas, they are not open, so I will settle for Tofu this morning, exercise the Demon myself per Doctors prescribed orders and exercise RESRAINT!!! I will not become a predator and prey upon the innocent, but I can understand why some Vampires have difficulty with their own restraint. Did you see how my Vampire brother reacted with a single paper cut and a single drop of blood. (Twilight) I don't damn my brother for the way he is made, I damn the system that corruptly suppresses what Man craves with the perverted interpretation of God's Word to fit with their own corrupt agenda. Or is it just plain ignorance? I don't think it is ignorance. I think it is a classic example of Young Lady/Old Lady. Your interpretation is either based on your own frame of reference or you give all of your control over to those that you want to emulate, thus relieving yourselves of discovering your purpose for God and signing up for; Yeah, I believe Jesus was crucified on the cross and rose in three days. Honey, would you pick up my pass for Salvation while your downtown cheating on me with your boss, because he pays more attention to you than I do? I'm in the middle of this ballgame and the season is just getting started. I do like my Angels in the Outfield. Oh Honey? Would you grab me a beer and make me a sandwich before you go? Don't worry about cleaning up the mess, you can do that when you get home. Check out this new video game I picked up today. Do you want to have Sex? Huh, you've having these headaches a lot here lately. Have you been to the Doc.

You damn right you worthless sack of shit. I went to Dr. Feel Good and even picked up a paycheck to take care of your sorry ass. I just don't know why I put up with "IT". I just don't know why I can not overcome my comfort zones to leave. I just don't know why I don't report you when you hurt me. I just don't know why I did nothing, when you hurt our child. You are a predator and you frighten me. I can not fight this Demon of the flesh alone and I don't think God will physically intervene. I think God will mentally intervene and allow you to search your heart for the answers and yes, doing nothing is an answer and you must live with the consequences of your decisions. If you are anything like me, He spoke to my heart and told me to seek help from my brothers and sisters in Christ to battle a Demon that was to Large for me to handle alone. So my smoking Demon has gained strength as I battle my alcohol Demon and self medicate my Vampirish thirst. Don't worry about all of your Demons right now. Battle your one true Satan and his Demons will follow with your renewed strength with Faith in a power greater than yourself. The Power of God. Submit your weaknesses over to Him and ask Him for help. Then turn to your brother and say; I need your help too.

Do you remember that movie Brewsters Millions. He had to spend 30 millions dollars in 30 days to inherit his real inheritance of 300 million. The catch was, he couldn't tell anyone why he was blowing the money like a drunker sailor. His friends kept trying to stop him because they were unaware of the deal. My friends know not what I am attempting to do for our Lord.

God has been chipped away from U.S. Generation after Generation. I can't imagine what our forefathers are thinking right now. Yes I can, What the Freak are you doing? We busted our asses to get to the promised land and gave thanks to God for allowing safe passage and still thanked him for the struggles that come with establishing a Free Nation. This Freedom that you enjoy today comes from the sweat, blood and tears of your forefathers that just wanted something a little better for their children than they had for themselves.

Mr Owl,
How many generations does it take for God's children to forget where they came from, forget You are the Father and Savior, forget to enlighten the commoners financial intelligence, forget

Faith, forget Hopes and Dreams and most of all, forget to help our fellow man?

Let's find out. Your parents generation struggled with depression and fought for a better life for you. Your generation is somehow entitled to everything you have and now your kids generation must have everything or they have nothing. So my answer to the quandary is 3. Can I have one of those red tootsie pops? Make that three in different colors and beliefs. Islamic, Jews and Christians. They all have a different flavor and they all taste good when they haven't been tainted by the corrupt that want more than their fair share. They want God's share and God can not fulfill His Promise to us without the help of His Children. We got to want it people. We have got to want God's Gift to the World. LEGACY. What Legacy will this Generation leave to this World? What Legacy will God take in our History? If I were a betting man, which I am, I'd have to be all in on Satan right now. If you truly examine the state of our Global affairs, we need to be all in for God right now. But I'm just one man and can only do what "I am" compelled to do. "I will" watch how God's Gift is received and place my bets accordingly.

I'd love to talk to you about what is going on if you can have an open mind. My thoughts and interpretation are way out there, I know. But look at where the current religious and political leaders have gotten us. "Imagine Turning to God for Change".

You asked me via a facebook friend if I had figured out the 144,000 that are chosen yet. No man, I've been drinking and trying to figure out which one of the 24 elders leg I will have to hump to get a dry martini when I get there, if my only talent that I have to offer is humping. I've been told that Judas is tending bar because our brother Jesus couldn't stand to punish Him any longer, because it was all in the Father's script. And after all, Judas is our brother that took the dive for us to characterize all of our own Demons and learn from our mistakes. Judas has been one great teacher. I don't know about you, but I have learned a lot more from my failures than I ever did from my triumphs. I want to get shit faced on the blood of Jesus Christ.

I am reminded of the man I know that let his demon alcohol influence his Vampire and it cost $247,000.00 That's an expensive pint of blood in that it creates an opportunity for Satan to live when a new soul is brought into this World, a soul that was not wanted. This is not a good start to the struggle of Life and I can only pray that these souls will endeavor to persevere and place the blame on the Demons of our ancestors and their creation thereof.

As I sit here not doing any of the things that I told myself I was going to do, I think about my Demon. There really is but one thing that is holding me back from tying one on and that is that damn meeting at 8. I have exercised my Vampire, wrote in my journal and now feeling alone. I love being alone, but I don't like feeling alone. When I feel alone is when I want to betray myself, because I am only sneaking around on myself.

WHY HAVE YOU COME TO ME NOW? WHY DIDN'T YOU COME BEFORE NOW?

I didn't understand Lord, my frame of reference did not include you. How can I accept something I don't understand? I was serving another God, my Lord. I was serving Satan and his band of Demons and there was no room in my heart for you. There was only room in my heart for the seed of your Gift to mankind to be hibernated in my subconscious until my back was against the wall and forced me to seek your guidance.

WHAT GRADE WOULD YOU GIVE YOURSELF AT-TEMPTING TO DO MY WILL?

If I asked you Father, while I am still in the process of completing my purpose for you, what grade would you give me? I would have to give myself an F. Failure.

"A" – ADMIRABLE "B" – BRAVE "C" – CHARITABLE "D" – DEFEATOR OF THYSELF "E" – EXCELLENT EFFORT "F" – FAITH VS. FAILURE "G" – THAT BELONGS TO FRED SANFORD "H" – HUMILITY and HUMOR "I" – IS-A-BELL NECESSARY TO CALL YOU HOME?

No Lord, Nathan J. Isbell is Home. Thanks for giving the reader another illustration of 666. You find what you seek and can interpret to fit your own agenda and so can World Leaders. Hey, what's the J stand for in my name? Or the next letter of your grading system?

ASK
HEART

Dig it, I can do that now. Now that I have trained my mind to listen to it. And the only thing that matters is what I believe in my heart. I have accepted the Lord Jesus Christ to come into my heart and be my "Wonderful Counselor". I have to go to my heart to seek my guidance and wisdom from our Lord. That seed, that Gift carved out just enough in my subconscious to "Wake me up, before I GO GO". I was a Goner and I wanted to be, BTW G is for Goner. But I have Faith in that magic seed, I envision, drum roll please. I envision a stairway built to Heaven using the bricks of Mankind and our Lord and Savior may come from Heaven and dwell among us and empathetically Heal us on the inside and out. His Promised Everlasting Kingdom here on Earth as prophesied. Gods Legacy Trust LLC.

Can you feel "IT" Capt. Compost – Pet Detective - When Nature Calls

Lord, your flesh was ripped from your body to prepare your soul for the Father. You have patiently waited with the Father hoping someone would hear the Holy Spirit and Witness for you like a true prophet. Let them rip into me oh, Lord. Just as they ripped into you. I can understand where your head was those last days. You have prepared yourself to do the thing that you must for the Father and are willing to suffer the consequences of that decision. Let them rip Lord, I'm ready to be with you. You may have liked them, I'm sick of them and would humbly walk in your steps to give myself to the Father for my brothers and my sins. But I will not be the coward that Judas was and I will learn from His mistake. I will punish myself by being the Brother I have always wanted to be and lost that dream. The opportunity costs of being a brother to help a brother are endless and so are the opportunities.

I suppose "S" would stand for satisfactory Salesman?

YOU NEVER ASKED ME FOR A GRADE ON "GODS LAST WILL AND TESTAMENT", I GIVE "IT" AS YOU PROCLAIM "IT". "S"

ASK ME

As I have told you Lord, "S" is not good enough for me and I pray this book will do you more Glory. I ask of you now Lord, what grade do you give my acts of drunkenness as I make a complete ass out of myself for all to see?

FOR THE ACTS OF NATHAN THE PROPHET, I GIVE YOU AN "S". IT IS A HANG MAN RIDDLE THAT ALLOWS ALL MY CHILDREN TO PROCLAIM THEIR OWN MEANING OF THEIR GRADE "S". JUST AS MANY HAVE LIVED THROUGH JUDAS, SO SHALL THEY LIVE THROUGH NATHAN THE PROPHET AND LEARN FROM HIS MISTAKES.

Too easy, I love it when you speak directly to me. SAVED, that's my finally answer.

WRONG SHOW BROTHER. THIS IS THE FAMILY FEUD. SURVEY SAYS # 1 ANSWER. THIS SHOW IS A LITTLE DIFFERENT THOUGH. THE TOP FIVE ANSWERS ARE DIFFERENT FOR EVERYONE AT DIFFERENT TIMES IN THEIR LIFE. "S" IS A PERSONAL GRADING SYSTEM. MOST CHOOSE "SELF" AS THEIR # 1 ANSWER.

All Men, brother Jesus. Myself included. Praise the Lord.

I wanna be a prophet for God, soooo.... freakin bad. Smiling next to Jesus and the King.

I wanna be on the cover of, God's magazine. Healing all my children like it's no big thing.

Cause every time I close my eyes. I pray that I have given you pride. It's You that I wish to please, oh please Lord tell me why, please tell me why, cause I'm already a billionaire. Whoa ooh Whoa oo, I'm already a billionaire.

All for your Glory my Lord and Savior. All for your Glory. I'm out of here like an anonymous alcoholic. Your humble servant will humbly request his prize when he meets you Lord.

ASK NOW

Damn, I hate when you do that. I need to go to a meeting and I will pray about it. I pray that my Leper brothers and sister will fill my heart with the Holy Spirit. My own quandary is like the Genie giving three wishes and you don't want to waste any and in my case, you grant me but one. This is a very deep quandary Lord. Thanks, you know how I love a riddle.

Just got back. Great meeting. We discussed taking that first drink. Oh, the number of times that I have said I will just get a half pint only to get into the store and be frugal and get the fifth. I will ration it as I rationalize everything. I heard many stories of no self control and my stories had only just begun.

Lord, can we pick this up in the morning. I just really want to speak to You with my heart tonight and I'm getting tired and losing focus. I'm sober and I want to thank You for a great day. Good Night Father and my brother Jesus, it's heart to heart time with the Wonderful Counselor. And don't let me forget to tell you about my sponsor getting on my ass tonight.

Before I forget Lord, about my prize. Let me witness your Gift take root and begin to flourish with my own sober eyes. For I would have helped Mankind and fulfilled my purpose for You, with the Guidance of the Wonderful Counselor. Night now.

7/4/2010

Happy Birthday America and Good Morning God. God pleeeeeeeeeeeeeeeeaaaassse grant me a sober day today. 7/4/1776 – 07/4/2010 So it's our 234th birthday as a Free Nation. Well I'd have to say we had a pretty good run at being a Worldwide Global Empire. I just have to wonder how many more years do we have before the History books will forever mark a date, a date at which time the Greatest Empire the World has ever known will fall. An Empire founded on Judea Christian principles. The radical Islamic terrorist will have been successful in destroying God's Promised land that our Forefathers had fought and struggled so hard to attain.

Have you notice that even the greatest of sitcoms always have an end? We love them at first and wouldn't think of missing a show. But after a while we begin to miss a few and figure we'll catch it later on TVO. But things get busy and we never get around to it. So we watch the show a few weeks later and enjoy it, but it is losing it's luster as time goes on. It kind of gets predictable. As human beings, we are always on the look out for something a little different. Something a little flashier and exciting. Our God has been the same throughout time. But just speaking from America's time, after 234 yrs of God being chipped away from our society by the Political and Religious Pharisees of the day, as they all begin to push their own agendas and not Gods, we will fall. Just as sitcoms fizzle out, so will our God if something different doesn't happen soon. This parable can be used in many facets of your life. Have a heart to heart with the Wonderful Counselor, He really is wonderful. You just have to see for yourselves.

The birthing pains of Christ are building in intensity my brother just as prophesied. The time is now for God's Gift to be opened and given to the World. You say you don't want our Empire to fall, but what are you willing to do to make a change? Are you willing to give your World over to Leaders that their motivations are questionable to say the least? When will God's people stand up and fight for God. When God has been involved, a battle never lost. We have depended on God when our Face is to the ground. God depends on us to build His Everlasting, Earthly Kingdom. Why is it so hard to believe in Him?

Pfffffttttt.... God, what's He ever done for me? Look at my life and "I just prayed to a God I don't believe in".

Brother, if you don't believe in Him, why would you bother to pray for Him. You are praying for yourself to fix yourself. You need to pray for Him to fix you. He will listen and it will be your Faith in your brother that fixes you. As Jesus walked through the crowds, He felt a tug at His robe. A sense of power that transferred from His body to the body that was tugging at Him. All this person needed after putting her Faith in God was to just touch the bottom of His garment and she would be Saved. Jesus stopped immediately after sensing the Faith that this woman has. He says to her; your Faith has healed you.

Pharisees of today have been perverting that Act for a very long time anointing themselves as Spiritual Healers of Mankind. They prey upon what you believe in, they prey upon your Faith and vulnerabilities in a state of mind that is trying to make decisions with the heart. Our Father has allowed this to happen due to our Covenant. "Of our own free will". All Predators will be judged, but for now, it's no wonder people grab their pocket book or turn on the crazy alert whenever our Savior is mentioned. That Sucks a Big One. Our Father is sickened to see the Greedy gobble up the Charitable. You can chime in anytime my Lord.

HELLO, MY NAME IS I AM... AND I AM... AND I THINK I'LL JUST LISTEN TONIGHT. THANKS EVERYONE, IT'S GOOD TO BE HERE. AND A SPECIAL THANKS TO YOU NATHAN FOR CHAIRING THIS MEETING. WITH THAT, I WILL... PASS TO YOU.

You're such a smart ass, I love you brother. For those of you that don't know, that is how we introduce ourselves in twelve step meetings and you can share your story or pass. I have chosen of my own free will to share my story anonymously with you. Not for my Glory, but for the Glory of God before "I PASS".

Wow, it's hard to get another thought right now. All I can think about is when "I PASS". What have I made of my Life? What will I leave? Will anyone even remember that I was here? Will anyone care?

I WILL...

Well I know you Will, "You had me at Hello". I just wonder if I can take this wretched Life of mine and benefit mankind with it.

YOU WILL...

Will my brothers and sisters join me to erect You my Lord and Savior, an Earthly, Everlasting Entity so You may dwell among us and Heal us?

THEY WILL...

Will you grant my wish to witness your Gift rise to fruition through sober eyes?

WE'LL SEE...

You're a hard sale Lord. Everytime I try and pin You down and close my deal with You, somehow it is always put back on me.

**IF "IT" IS
TO BE
"IT"
IS UP TO
ME**

You're using my words against me aren't you? It's always been about me when I'm in my own presence. It's time we all make it about You, not me. Or did I steal your words and make them my own? I'm ready to surrender Lord, it has been about me long enough. I'm tired and I wanna go Home.

You know I was just sitting here reflecting on the things you have shared with my heart and I was thinking about the whole Him thing. Our brother being Him. The difficulty to accept Him as our brother. We haven't been able to accept him because he is imperfect unlike ourselves. Brother, just a reminder, there hasn't been a perfect brother since our brother Jesus Christ and we missed that boat. We are all imperfect brothers of a perfect brother. I'm not saying let's get together for a circle jerk over it, but I am trying to get you to open your eyes about your imperfect brother and inspire him for more. Before you start a rigorous re-invention of your brother, be selfish and start with yourself. Also understand that your brother may not want what you want. But if he wants a check, he better get off his ass and get one. That is where you may help to inspire him to discover his talents and enjoy Life and Worship our Father in anyway he sees fit. That's a very personal relationship and no one needs any butt in skiis telling them they are lighting the incense wrong or they are doing "IT" all wrong. All paths to God are good as long as God is the guiding light and His words are not manipulated for your own agenda.

"Cash for Clunkers". Now let me get this straight. You can trade in your piece of shit and get a trade allowance of "X" and you purchase a new car to stimulate the economy and remove the pieces from the streets. Novel idea, but part of the deal was to crush all automobiles that are entered into the program. Are you kidding me? Did you really crush automobiles that still had life left in them? Automobiles that could have stimulated a brother to apply for one and get a job. If it were a Cash for Food campaign, would you destroy my trade and deny the hungry? If "IT" were a Cash for God campaign, would you embrace "IT" and heal the hurting? Or deny God and your hungry, hurting brothers.

I was just thinking while creatively avoiding the gym, about that brain fart about the Two Witnesses. So just suppose for a moment that I am one of the two witnesses in Revelations. I will want my brother for the other. My brother and sister in Christ. Damn, did I just solve another riddle. I love riddles. Isn't it just like our Father to leave the door open to anyone that wants to Praise and Witness for Him. I guess in this case anyone that wants to participate can just pick up their trophy over their. Your brother has it and He can't wait to give it to you. It is the Trophy of Love and Appreciation. You came back for me my brother. Why?

YOU ARE MY
BROTHER
I AM
MY BROTHERS
KEEPER

Headed to the gym my Father and Brother. I need for the Counselor to give me a break. It's beginning to not be so Wonderful. LOL Just Kidding, but I really do need to relax my mind for a moment and I dare not lose any more thoughts than I have already while intoxicated. If this is truly for the benefit of Mankind. I'm still not sure, I'm a drunk that has been sober forrrrrr...... tomorrow will be two weeks. Yay, for me.

Good Ship, Good Crew
Hooray for "ME" and Screw You. - Dad

That ship is going down, it is just a matter of time. Sometimes you can not tell your brother that he is on the wrong path. They must figure it out on there own. Unfortunately, the more we pull at them, the more they pull away and hurt us. I pray that you can connect with your lost brother, I'm sorry, I'm lacking in expertise or even articulation in this area. So I guess "that's not my area". But you know me, I'll always pull a monkey out of my ass and add my two cents whether it belongs or not. So give me a moment to pray on it.

Lord, I'm still not hearing you. Tell me, I don't want to make a mistake here. Tell me.

PLANT
SEEDS

Man, this is some good shit. Lord, I need a break. Throw me a freakin bone here, I need to do something else. BRB

K

If you are a smart drunk like me, you learn an exit strategy just as they told us in the D.U.I. Class we attended. The problem with an exit strategy and being a smart drunk is, you can't go anywhere. You plan your day around when you plan to get hammered, which is all the time. You create a prison for yourselves without the bars.

I drove out to Leper Land today while I listened to my assignment. For what ever reason, God decided to bless me and allow my CD player to work. No shit, there were no Angels or flashes of light, the damn thing just didn't skip through both CD's. Great message, great speaker. While I was at Leper Land, I notice the purple martins were buzzing around like flies. No bird Sanctuary there yet, but maybe one day. They must have been preparing for their long migration home. Our Life time is a long migration home. How we fly along the way, is how the Father will Judge us of our worthiness.

We talked about being the lone wolf tonight. I am the lone wolf now and I am lonely. Right now the only thing that helps me keep my sanity is knowing that my Father expects more from me. I am so much more than I have become. He gives me strength, because I want to be sober for Him and myself. Great topic tonight, I didn't share. These men and women were on the same path that I have been on. Some were much further down the path, I am blessed to have them in my life now. They are yelling back saying "Go Back, It's a Dead End". I have flirted with the edge enough to know that at anytime for the rest of my life, I could find myself in a half way house. I am no better than anyone there, so how can I pass judgment on the way that they have lived their lives. I've got a Vodka Log in my eye, turn around and let me critique you.

This message may or may not resonate with the drunks, this message is for those who the drunks offend. Do not argue with a drunk. Do not encourage a drunk. Do not facilitate a drunk. Do not put up with a drunk. Let what a drunk says to you, roll off your back. Your apology will be coming from them in the morning as they are perspiring through the phone. Do not let the words of a drunk knock you off your balance. Do not preach to a drunk. Plant seeds as our Father has said. It may take many years for the seed to take root, but the drunk is the only one that can decide if he is ready to plant "IT" yet or not. As Albert Wine-stein would say; have a few glasses and become a Genius. Do you really want to have an argument with a Genius in their own mind? They haven't listened to a freakin word you have said. They are planning what they will say next when their mouth is not moving.

I believe I have found my purpose after my project ends. I want to witness for our Lord at twelve step meetings unexpectedly around the World. That way I can do what I so deeply desire to do. I desire to publicly praise Him and keep my Vanity in restraint. I'll be no different than any other visitor from out of town. I just love the brotherhood that twelve step program has. If you are from out of town, there is a booster shot of God waiting for you close by. Go and get it and share your story. Finally, somebody to listen to me besides the Hotel TV. Finally, somebody that will share their embarrassments and more importantly, how they climbed out of that insanity.

I was told back in college by a guy that looked like one of the Three Musketeers, that maybe I ought to think about not drinking. That was after I had taken out my frustrations on a washing machine in the dorm that had ruined a borrowed shirt. I ripped the top off it and took a piss in it. That ought to fix it right up. So then, I proceeded to crawl up on top of it for a long winters nap. I can't remember how I dodged that bullet, but I wish now that I had listened to the Musketeer.

Wow, when you really start to take inventory of your Life, it can be pretty depressing. But that's just me the drunk. I'm sure your world is perfect. So I'm not speaking to your lying ass, I'm speaking to the people who are hurting on the inside and wear a mask of courage. Keep your mask on, there are those that are looking to bend you over. Be careful who you allow to be your close friends. You know, the gossip girl. I will tell you this, if you would be okay to see your verbal words in print on the front page of the paper, then by all means speak your mind. When your peer is in Judgment of your brother or sister in Christ, take a non-confrontational stance. Remember, when your fair weathered friend is not with you, she says the same things about you. Don't stick your nose up their ass because they are pretty and popular, they are just as clueless as the rest of us. Do not give your control over to someone that has no business with control. A pretty smile, athlete or wealthy parents, a path of God, does not make. Always examine someone's heart, they may have a heart like your own. Those are the relationships that I would think exists, but I wouldn't know. I just trained my heart to tell my mind to shut the hell up and let the heart pray on the decision-making process for now on.

Thank you Lord for a sober 4th of July weekend. You are my Lord, Savior and Brother. Thank you for coming back for me. You didn't forget me, I forgot You Lord. I will never forget you again.

7/5/2010

Good Morning God. Please grant me a sober day.

To think about all of the times that I did not have You in my Life is pretty frightening. I guess I am very lucky to be alive, strike that, there's no guessing about it. I'm alive and sober because of you my Lord and the twelve step program will help me to stay that way. I am excited about witnessing for you to the

Lepers. I am one and I need their help to control my Demon that You have defeated for me.

I've been praying about what my twelve step sponsor said. He said that one of the steps is to do something nice for someone and not let them know it was you that did it. I don't know many people, but I do know that my (2nd Wife) is in financial trouble with no one to turn to. I haven't sent her any gift cards since May 24th. The last time we emailed, she did ask for a gift card and I sent her a check immediately. I know that was very difficult for her to ask for help. I will not preface my gift to her, I'll just send it weekly. I hope that will qualify for that step in the program.

Do not tempt the Lord, Thy God. I was just thinking about the sharks and the oil spill correlation. Lord, I don't really claim responsibility for this disaster, but what the hell, I'll ask. If the oil spill is of your doing and it comes from my proclamation then by all means show us what it means. Let it blacken the Gulf of Mexico. Let it destroy all of you wonderful creatures. Let it destroy the lives of those children that depend on it. Lord, if this is your will, show me. Pssstt....I'm trying a little reverse psychology on my brother. He'll never go for it, He knows my heart. Let this be an example of me not being a Seer, I am a Prophet of God. I tell you what I have seen, heard, read, experience and what the Holy Spirit puts on my heart. That's it, no predictions only wishful thinking. But hey, if He turns if off in the next three days, I guess I'm going to have to get me a wand, robe, funny hat and a white owl. But you can forget that tattoo on the forehead. Ouch. Do not ask your Lord to prove Himself to you by proclaiming a challenge. Unless it is a challenge for you to conquer your Demons and witness for Him while helping your brother to strive for more.

I will insert a simple note into every envelope with the gift card to (2nd Wife). The note will read;

I AM
PRAYING FOR YOU
I WILL
ALWAYS LOVE YOU

Thanks Lord, that is inspirational and I would forget it if I didn't write it down. I am kind of digging the correlation between my love for my (2nd Wife) and your Love for us all. We all are your (2nd Wives) just as You have proclaimed to my heart. The more I want her back, the more she pushes back. The more You want us back, the more Your children push back. At what age do we decide that our parents embarrass us? When are we as parents suppose to allow them to spread their own wings, knowing that they will face many turbulent storms? Do we close the door behind them? If your door is closed, then seek God's door. It is always open and a fatted calf awaits you. You will always have a Home with the Heavenly Father. When you discover your purpose in Life, then you will have Life. You must seek for your purpose through your brother.

Lord, our conversations continue to amaze me. When I think that I have shared everything that I know, You put another thought on my heart.

It's like you were inside my head and we were having GREAT SEX – Broadcast News

Today's topic was divine intervention. "Hello, hello, hello, is there anybody in there? Just nod if you can hear me. Is there anyone at home?"

I hear You Lord, I hear You.

"I have a special purpose" - The Jerk

I have a complete visual of exactly how my Lord wants for His Gift to be delivered. It is to be delivered anonymously by the Lepers of our society. I don't know why I didn't see it before, guess I was studying the young lady to much and could not see the old lady. You yearn for what I know. How to pray and hear the Wonderful Counselor. When you know how to do "IT", it's too easy. When a decision is to be made that could alter your Life. Stop, pause, pray and decide. This decision will be easy to answer with your mind, but you need to have a heart to heart with the Wonderful Counselor. He is always there for you to call on at anytime of day or night. Once you evaluate all of the possible outcomes that your decision could produce, it is your choice to choose what you feel Your Father would approve of or not. Your decision and will always be yours. I choose to witness for our Lord anonymously to my Leper brothers and sisters in Christ. That is my long term purpose for God, His children and myself to achieve sobriety.

Lord, I just don't know what to say. You've chosen to speak to my heart and I've chosen to listen. I have a perfect vision of my purpose for You. That gives me so much relief to have a sense of direction. I will be of pure heart when I meet you Lord. I'm having a little difficulty hearing you tonight, maybe it's just me and I'm a little tired or I just can't think of anything to ask You. Lord, is there anything you would like to talk to me about?

ENDEAVOR TO PERSEVERE

Yeah, I know Father. You've said that before.

I
LOVE
YOU
SON

You've never said that before. Thank you Father. I Love You with all my Heart, mind, body and soul. Sometimes I just like to hear my Father praise me with His Everlasting, Forgiving Love. Don't we all crave that sense of being Loved? My Father loves me and you, I want to make my Father proud. Don't you? He promises a better Life than the one that I am pissing away.

Thanks Lord, just needed a smoke and prayer. We'll deal with the smokes next. Let's battle this Demon together tonight. I say to you my Leper brothers and sisters in Christ. The next time you are feeling squirrelly, I implore you to write a letter to God. I want you to tell Him what is going on in your Life and convince Him that you need your Demon to make it another day. He will listen and I want you to listen as you write to Him. Listen for your helpers, listen for you betrayers. Pause for a long moment and weigh out the decision with all of the possible outcomes before you decide. Then choose for yourselves and live with the consequences of those decisions. Take responsibility for your actions, they are your actions. When there is no one else around to blame, you may be to blame. I am alone brother and I hate it. Maybe I'm to blame for where I am at now. Ya think? No I haven't, but now I Will if I can control my Demon. Ironic: Flirting with time by Tom Petty is playing on my computer.

These are the signs to look for. They are everywhere, when you are seeking your purpose you will see them. Your signs will depend on what you are seeking. If you are seeking a reason to destroy yourselves, your mind and Demon will accommodate. If you are seeking to make a difference in someone elses life, your Lord Thy God will accommodate with allowing you to find what it is you so desperately need and seek. A purpose to keep living.

This was a pretty cool study I picked up from Lou Tice. I'm especially interested in this tactic now that I am faced with the reality that my parents are getting old and won't be around much longer. This will work well if both parents are alive, but if you have a loved one suffering from a broken heart because they have lost their soul mate, try this. Give them a calendar at Christmas that maps out activities throughout the year that will include your widowed parent. I promise you, it will increase their life span because they will have something to look forward to. They will have a reason and purpose to live another day. WARNING: If you elect to do this, do not make alterations unless it's life or death and quickly reschedule. What you are screwing with could be life or death for your loved one.

Well Lord, I guess it's about time for this Crazy Manic Freak to call it a night.

Nathan, My Brother. What would you have Me say to your sarcasm?

I don't know Lord, I'm just so tired of being thought of as Crazy. I know that it is your Will that I do what I am compelled to do, but shit, I'm sick of it. I want to buy the fast pass and get my Life back.

BUY IT!!! Your Demon awaits you. Remember my Brother, I told you that "I DON'T CARE, BECAUSE I LOVE YOU". HELL, I'll give you a ride. Ever road a pink elephant or would you prefer the magic carpet ride to the liquor store?

I'd like to take this opportunity to thank all the Angels in my life that managed to successfully take the wheel from my hand and make it safely home without killing myself or worse, someone else.

I want an umpa loompa now Daddy or I'll...I'll...I'll die. - Willy Wonka modified a little LOL

Don't you just hate that threat. Good night Father, you're on a roll. I need another smoke BRB.

K

If you leave me, I will kill myself. First let me say, why would you ever give your power over to another human being? Second, understand that I have no expertise in this area. I have no frame of reference at all. I really am scared to even pray on this one, because I know I am not the one to ask. "Not my area".

How can you know what to say? Every case is different. They must search their own hearts. They must plant seeds. They must allow those seeds to take root. The soil is out of their control and can only be cultivated when it's owner is ready to plow. I AM only the seed, my children are the soil. If my seeds do not find fertile ground and the soil becomes my Master, would it not be better for Me to find a new field and give someone else a chance with this one that you have been farming. The one that you have been farming at the expense of your own life. So I say, who is killing who?

Folks, I think that monkey didn't come out of my ass at all. That really is not my area. But Damn, that's sounds right.

My Father has taught me many things. - The Godfather

So has mine, but mine are for the betterment of Mankind. Not Greed and Corruption. But the movie series was just Killer. I'm a huge fan. Al Pacino, dude, you are a bad ass. I'm glad to have an example of what I do not want to be. It displeases the Father and we will carry the chains we forge in Life eternally after Death. Your Game may be over brother, but mine will just have begun. I invite you to join us, let me get you a Bloody Mary with a twist of Jesus. Maybe that will help to clear your head. Man, if you don't have anything to hold on to, why don't you just try Jesus one time.

If they're going to drink themselves to death, then by all means do it and decrease the surplus population. - Scrooge

Be careful who you let in your head brother. The only way Jesus will ever have any room in there is if you allow Him into your heart. Your reticular activating system may draw from your subconscious, but decisions of the heart are made by the heart and the whole gang is invited to debate the issue at hand. It is your decision brother, make it a God one.

Give me some knuckles brother and let's call it a night. Thanks for another sober day.

7/6/2010

Good Morning God. What a great day to be alive!!! My parents and aunt are coming by for a visit, so I'll have to get going in a minute. I just wanted to quickly put on paper what was on my heart this morning.

As we continue our conversations Lord, I realize that I have a lifetime of stories to tell. How can one man tell everything you want me to tell them? How will they conduct their lives for your Glory?

**EYES SEE
EARS HEAR
BRAIN THINKS**

**HEART
FEELS**

**HEART
KNOWS**

ASK
HEART

Cool, I get "IT". I almost forgot Lord, please grant me another sober day. I think the reason that I almost forgot it is because I'm getting a little cocky that I haven't really been doing much thinking about a drink. Ooooooh....that's scary. That's when I start thinking I can join in on the fun and just have one beer. Well two never hurt anybody....you're my good friend, tell me I'm right and I'll buy you a drink. What did you say your name was again friend? Where are we anyway friend? What day is it? Am I bleeding?

Say something in this ear. That's the damnedest thing, I haven't heard anything in that ear since I was a kid.

Your lip stopped bleeding to George. They're not there either.

What?

Zuzu's petals. You have been granted your wish George. You've never been born. That is what you wished for isn't it George? - It's a Wonderful Life

Are you alright Danielson?

Yeah, I just wanted to face my fear before training. I guess it was pretty stupid.

Miagi say same thing to Father. Father agree, WAS stupid.
- Karate Kid

I almost forgot to tell you what my sponsor got on my ass about. It was the 4th of July weekend after all and I hadn't had a drink in a week and a half. I can handle this. So I took my blood donor to the club and had to refuse my Demon from my blood

69

donor repeatedly. I had a miserable time and couldn't wait to get out of there. As my sponsored told me, you're less than two weeks into this and your clubbing. That's pretty stupid. I had been invited to go to an outing with my friend Bill for the 4th. Whiskey and half naked women. I don't think so. I Will Pass. Those are my two largest Demons of all and they play quite well together actually. Then all of my other Demons are invited to play as well.

You have to rest your mind and allow your heart to make your decisions. What would my Father approve of? When you serve another God, you are in no position to make those decisions. Your Demon is in control of your destiny. You wake up in beds not knowing how you got there. Not exactly the role model for your Father or His children that you thought you would be. Go back to your dreams, what was I going to make out of my life when I was a Dreamer? I want to know because I'm in the middle of a freakin Nightmare. What will I make of my life? Is there still time? Am I a Goner? Can I be saved from the Hell that I have created for myself here on earth?

I don't know if this is selfish on my part. But my Vampire thirsts for Human Blood and I can't seem to find a replacement donor that fills my heart. My confusion comes in when I think about what I had. My (2nd Wife) quenches my thirst for both my Vampirish desires as well as potentially fulfill what I crave spiritually, she's so close and I can not touch her.

Nathan, I understand. All of Mankind is my (2nd Wife) and I have been trying to win back her heart since I left her to do my Father's Will. Just as you have chosen to do. You have chosen to fulfill your purpose for the Father "at all costs". I had the same assignment my brother. Did you think you were special or something?

Yes, I am special. I must be, You came back for me. I don't want to just be grateful for You raising me from the Dead. I want to witness to all of the Lepers that are truly in that desperate state of mind and let them know that there are options. I want to touch them in a way that encourages them to touch others and spread like a disease to kill a disease. I want them to know that there is Hope when there is Faith and Charity.

Hey, I need to rest my heart for a moment and get a work out in. Damn, I'm looking good. LOL
BRB K...

K...You look great brother.

Hell's Bell's by AC/DC just came on, so I'll rock out with You before I go. Love Ya Bro.

Hey if you want to Rock out with Us, go to grooveshark.com and pull it up. Yeah, that's a plug for them, maybe they can chip in for God if God has helped them.

I'm drawing a blank now Lord. Am I coming to the end of my purpose for You or just the beginning? I am already feeling that sense of fulfillment only derived from mission accomplished. God was my pilot when I was the obnoxious drunk in coach and God will be my pilot as the Witness that He wants me to become in First Class.

Do you want to talk about embarrassment. As a teen I didn't want to participate in some sports because I didn't want to shower with the other guys. My pubic hair was lacking to say the least because I was a blondie. I allowed my manhood to prevent me from reaching manhood. The funny thing is, I shave it now because I want to look younger. LOL Don't allow your judgmental peers to rob you of anything in your life. Just think, later in life they won't have any hair on their head because it has migrated to their back. The point is, don't let anything prevent you from accomplishing what you believe in, especially black mail. Let those that would use black mail as a tool against their brother, have a special place in the Masters Plan. I haven't been shown this place, "not my area". I did see a room that people were sitting around in shit and drinking coffee though. I thought, that's not so bad until I heard someone say, ok, coffee break is over, back on your heads. I don't know, maybe it had something to do with never taking your head out of your ass while you were alive.

Tonight's twelve step meeting topic was about peoples experience being their best teacher and finding their Higher Power. I didn't speak tonight. I like to pray about what I say. These are the type questions that you must reflect on and ask your heart for all the possible solutions. Then make up your mind knowing the consequences of your actions. As I have said, my brother Judas taught me a lot by learning by mistakes. But being bone headed and being bit, is the lessons that stick with you the best. Unfortunately, the Demon alcohol is very powerful and will entice you to keep coming back for more, even when you know in good conscious it's poison. I can't tell you why I chose to serve my Demon knowing damn good in well where it leads. I just did it. As the Late Great Elvis Presley would sing; "I Did "IT" My Way". I sure did and it got me no where. I want to try His Way for awhile and see how that works out for me. What the Hell do I have to lose?

As far as finding ones Higher Power. That is a part of my purpose for my Lord. I am sharing the whole process of how I found mine. I pray that you can take something from my experiences and apply it to your own life to help you to find your purpose for God. Most of us don't even try to seek "IT" until we are at the bottom pits of hell, living a lie that we have created for ourselves. The Demons that alter your judgment are the Demons to fear most. We give our power over to human beings all the time and need to be aware of that and stop. But when you give your power over to your Demon, you are no longer in control of your life and destiny derived of decisions made thereof. When you wake up one morning and find yourself here, you need to take a personal inventory of your life real quick. Where was I? Where am I? Where do I want to go? Where do I need to go? Where can I find people that understand and will listen to my crazy ass?

Well Lord, I think I'm going to have a little Tofu and call it a night. Don't laugh, our Father made me this way and I have learned to exercise restraint. Many of my brothers have not and will inflict avoidable pain on the helpless.

I would never laugh at you brother while you are trying to explain to my children how we all think regardless of the outer shields we put up. Our Father made us all in different ways, but there are distinguishable traits that can be detected early to determine proper treatment for these children and their different Demons.

Well Good Night Lord, thanks for another sober day.

7/7/2010

Good Morning my God and Lord. Your humble servant humbly request another sober day. Please don't allow anything to rattle me and tempt me to pick up my Demon alcohol.

I was just looking at the Crazy Chi Phi '81 pic that my fraternity brother Keith Petroni posted to facebook. Wow, was I a duck out of water. Still didn't have anything figured out, but I was going to be rich doing whatever it was I was to do. My dreams were bigger than life. My dreams were introduced to my Demon alcohol and it was on. I started doing things that I had never done. It was almost instantaneous for me. I was a shy person and alcohol seemed to make me the life of the party in my own mind. I was a lot of fun for the first part of the evening, but the night would fall and so would I. My Demon became my best friend and Master. I took him everywhere I went and hid him from anyone that would tell me I'm on the wrong path. I became a master at serving my Master alcohol.

I have served my Master alcohol by witnessing to my peers with passion and zeal. My Lord and Savior helps me to battle my Demon, does He deserve less passion and zeal as I gave my Master alcohol? I think NOT!!!

I used to really get fulfillment helping others. I took a sense of pride being a mentor. It's a frustrating position to worry about everyone. As time went by, I discovered that not everyone thinks like me and my Demon was gaining strength. There came a time after betrayal and awakening on my part that pushed me into my prison of isolation searching for a new Master and continuing to serve my greatest Master alcohol. I had lost my desire to help my brother. Screw him is what I thought, all I need is this bottle and God. That hasn't been playing out to well for me brother. My brother Jesus Christ came back for me and saved me. I know that He would want me to do the same for my brother, so here brother, take my hand and join us.

I was just chuckling about that bogus Minister in Australia saying that he is one of the witnesses and spokesman for both. LOL What an arrogant, betraying predator Demon of the vulnerable. Who anointed you?

If I were King of the Forest, not Prince, Duke or Earle. I would have the courage to tell you the truth.
  – The Wizard of Oz

If I am one of the witnesses, I would want all my brothers and sisters for the other. I would want the Good News to spread with Laser Light Speed. Witness to all of your friends about the Love that awaits you if you will just accept Him into your life and live with a moral code that you believe your Father would approve of. You will fall, that is a given. Ask for forgiveness, make restitution, sin no more and forgive yourself. Today is a new day, a new day that can be blessed or cursed by your own free will while re-acting to your surroundings. Take an inventory of your surroundings. Where was I? Where am I? Where do I want to be? Where do I need to be? Who are all these people that keep me where I don't want to be? Who are all of these people in my head? It is your frame of reference brother. You can only search your mind for answers when you have supplied your brain with mistakes and triumphs. What you learn from them will shape your frame of reference for your entire life.

If I were Jesus Christ and ALL were my (2nd Wives), I would be brokenhearted. I'm not my brother, but I have a broken heart. A broken heart over my (2nd Wife). She has so much potential, but she can not get past what others think of her. Shame keeps many of us in bondage not realizing all that the Father calls us to do for His Glory. Who am I to witness for the Glory of God anyway. I'm a Leper and proud of it. Take your best shot you arrogant ass. It's not like I haven't heard or lived it before.

As I stalk my (2nd Wife)'s pictures on facebook, I reflect on how much I love her. How much pain I inflicted on her with my instability. I don't know why I want to bring that pain in my heart by looking at these pics except to gain closure. "It is better to have loved and lost, than to have never loved at all". Yeah, whatever. The pain is immense and the cure I chose was poison. I'm sorry (2nd Wife). I made it very hard for you to love me.

I'm sorry (2nd Wives), our Father's Plan made it difficult for Me to explain and for you to understand. I am alive and well in all of you that would listen to the Wonderful Counselor I promised to send back.

Lord, how can one explain to another human being, that they really have found their purpose for you?

If your purpose is truly for Me, who's approval do you seek?

Damn, you're good.

Do you ask your employer, what else can I do to make your business thrive? I need for you to be successful so I can keep this job while I seek my purpose for God. Or do you just fit in collecting a check and do as little as you can get away with? Get laid off and sit around collecting unemployment as long as your empathetic employer can afford to pay it and is forced to pay it due to government regulations. What does your heart tell you to that quandary? Can you not even be honest with yourselves? Ask your heart what the Father would approve of in your life.

Hey I have to pick a publishing date of this book. I didn't really pray about that for the first one and made a decision with out guidance. Lord, I ask you. What date should this book claim as it's official publishing date?

You're here for Mary? Mary left with Woogie to go to the Prom an hour ago. LOL I'm just screwing with you. - There's something about Mary

**FULFILL YOUR
DESTINY
TAKE YOUR PLACE
WITNESS
FOR THY
GOD**

Cool, then 12/21/2012 it is. What the Hell this all means, I don't have a clue. Maybe it's Worldwide Leper Day, where we all confess our sins to our Father and to our brother and rejuvenate our Love for one another. Maybe we take this day as a day of reflection and consider how blessed we truly are, but we will only be complete if we can find our purpose by helping others to find theirs. After all, "WE ARE FAMILY, I GOT ALL MY BROTHERS AND SISTERS WITH ME". Don't judge me brothers and sisters in Christ. I have but one Judge and that is the Father. Please brother, plant seeds discreetly. I don't want to avoid you any longer, I love you. Your seeds will take root when I want to begin harvesting. Pray that I don't have to go to the pits of Hell before I wake and plant your seeds. My field was flooded with Vodka and not worthy of our Father's seed. I am cleaning up brother and so can you.

Climb that wall Siegar, you can do it. One step at a time - An Officer and a Gentleman

Don't be the sugar britches that has to slip behind the wall for a booster shot of your Demon. Get your boost by helping Siegar get over that wall. One day at a time.

To all Predators, I have been pretty hard on you and you deserve it. It is not my place to Judge you. Your Judgment Day will have a jury of your victims and only you may ask our Lord to be your defense counselor. Be wise with your pleas of forgiveness, for the Father knows your heart. He has seen it your whole life and can hit replay anytime you lie. Good Luck Brother.

"I Love You, I'll Kill You. But I'll Love You Forever" - Enigma

Oooooh, don't you just love riddles. Let's dissect this statement, shall we? First let's assume we can get past ourselves for a moment and assume "I" is our Higher Power. Let's say that we know "Love", but many of us do not. Who is "You"? Is it our Fathers children or is it Jesus Christ? "I'll" Hmmm... one could say "I'll" sounds slang for it'll. One could make the correlation between "I'll" and Ill. An illness would kill us. "Kill", our inevitable death? Christ's Death? Rob yourselves or someone else out

77

of life? "You" same answer. "But", I would say this means there are options. "I'll", I see this as the Master you wish to serve. "Love", Let's try praise and worship here. "You" same answer. "Forever", you will eternally live the life that you have chosen for yourselves here on earth.

I can only speak for myself what this speaks to my heart. My frame of reference is different from yours and I can insert any type of interpretation that fits with my agenda, but I need a smoke. BRB

K

Most songs deliver a message and we get to decide how we want to receive it. The best are the ones that allow you to explore your heart. There is no right or wrong answer to feelings, just consequences.

I took time to pray about my answer Father and before I give my answer, I have a quandary of all my Masters so I can conscionably choose who I wish to serve. Please start you answer with; "If I were your...".

If I were your **PEERS**, I would pity you, I would kill your dreams. But if you did discover something, I'd be first in line with my hand out. Until that time comes, you will be the butt of my joke because of my ignorance. And I will forever say "I told you so".

If I were your **GOVERNMENT**, I would note your outburst and quickly conceal it. I would see if it conflicted with my own agenda and publicly humiliate and intimidate you if it does. I would see that you are thoroughly investigated. One might even call it a shake down for dirt.

If I were your **DEMON**, I would put a spell on you. I would suppress God's Gifts and demand you open Man's. I would omit intelligence to the ones I wish to rule. I would dictate your thoughts, behaviors and decisions. I would lead you where you are dying to go. I will promise you the same after life as the life you have lived to the 666th degree.

If I were your **JUDAS**, I would attempt to teach you to learn by your mistakes and the mistakes of others. I would tell you about the torment serving the wrong God.

If I were your **FATHER**, I would love you like only a true Father can to His son. I'll allow you to kill yourself of your own free will. I AM your only Judge and I AM Eternal...

If I were your Savior **CHRIST**, I'd shake my head in disgust and I'd do it all over again for mankind. I'll reach out to you and cry when you don't hear me. I AM my brother's keeper and I Will come back to take my Kingdom as I was promised.

If I were your **WONDERFUL COUNSELOR**, I'd patiently wait until you could hear Me. I would challenge you to free your-self from this Demon that calls you slave. I can not kill "IT", "IT" dwells within your heart. I can help you restrain "IT". I can show you a better World if you'll allow Me into your heart where your Demon lives.

If I were your humble **SERVANT**, I would want You to train me the exact way that You did. I would want you to use me Lord, for the benefit of another. I would never forget You saved me and I would deliver your Gift "at all costs". Then I would be thankful for the punishment that You give me. A lifetime of servitude to my Leper brothers and sisters in Christ. I will anonymously wit-ness to them and allow them to help me restrain my own Demons.

Semi, you have disgraced yourself and you must be punished. You will confine yourself to our Royal Suite at the Waldorf Astoria. I want you to bathe him thoroughly and see that he gets some decent attire.

Oh, Thank You Your Majesty – Coming to America

Hey, I'm headed for a work out and a meeting. BRB You don't have to keep saying "K" unless you want to "K"

K
LOL

Why don't we have that kind of relationship with our Savior – Jerry McGuire

I really couldn't understand the topic tonight to well. A lot of discussion about the third and forth step and I was clueless to what they were. I asked my sponsor if I should be reading through them and he said that I am right where I need to be. But I'm impatient and I want to see now. So have a look with me in the morning. Good Night God. Thanks for another sober day.

7/8/2010

Good Morning God, I'm sleeping better. Grant me another sober day.

THE TWELVE STEP PROGRAM

1. We admitted we were powerless over our Demon and that our lives had become unmanageable.

I publicly confess my weakness over my Demon.

2. Came to believe that a Power greater than ourselves could restore us to sanity.

I'm alive today because of my Lord and Savior.

3. Made a decision to turn our will and our lives over to the care of God *as we understood Him.*

Ab-so-freakin-lutely

4. Made a searching and fearless moral inventory of ourselves.

Yep, done that.

5. Admitted to God, to ourselves, and to another human being the exact nature of our wrongs.

K...done that.

6. Were entirely ready to have God remove all these defects of character.

Sooooo......ready!!!

7.   Humbly asked Him to remove our shortcomings.

Many times in prayer.

8. Made a list of all persons we had harmed, and became willing to make amends to them all.

K...I'll do it.

9. Made direct amends to such people wherever possible, except when to do so would injure them or others.

K...I'll do it.

10. Continued to take personal inventory and when we were wrong promptly admitted it.

Daily

11. Sought through prayer and meditation to improve our conscious contact with God, *as we understood Him,* praying only for knowledge of His will for us and the power to carry that out.

Got an overload here, I pray I can do His Will.

12. Having had a spiritual awakening as the result of these Steps, we tried to carry this message to the Demon possessed, and to practice these principles in all our affairs.

And I will try and continue where You left off. Now, got a question for You. Once I complete all the twelve steps, can we have a drink to celebrate? LOL

OF YOUR OWN
FREE WILL

Have you ever made a proclamation to a loved one that you are only hurting yourself? I ask you this; if you hurt yourself, who is to take care of you? You know I love you, so why do you continue to hurt me by hurting yourself?

I was just reading a little of the Song of Songs by my brother Solomon. His "Game" is a lot like mine, express what is on His heart to the woman He Loves. Good thing He was King, cause that method doesn't seem to work worth a shit now. I don't think I will ever understand how a woman can be drawn to something that is bad and not appreciate the good that is looking her straight in the face. I guess it is the; I can have you at any time I want, so you're not a challenge syndrome. It's a lot like our Christ. You can have Him anytime you want, but you prefer to chase the "Bad Boys" and deny who can truly fulfill your life.

BAD BOYS, BAD BOYS
WHATCHA GONNA DO

WHATCHA GONNA DO
WHEN I COME FOR YOU

What is it with this Frankincense and Myrrh that would warrant being mentioned repeatedly while romancing His love? So much so for her to mention Him tending to His spice garden. You know, I like spices, but I don't bring to many to the bedroom unless they can bring something to the bedroom.

No longer will anything be cursed. For the throne of God and of the Lamb will be there, and His servants will worship Him. - Revelations 22 : 3

Oh, I dig it now. It is just like the woman analogy. We want what we can't have. So we have suppressed man from what comes from God and allow him to freely partake of what man has created as many peoples poison to a life of self destruction. That's makes sense, can you throw in a couple of appetizers? Oh, you did. Tobacco and Gambling. I just wanted to make sure I understood the menu that you have prepared, as you have unleashed a very Powerful Demon unto God's children with no real tools to equip themselves with. We are like lost sheep feeding on what man has created for us to dull the senses of no purpose in life. God's tools have been suppressed and corruption has emerged. I wonder if everything that man suppresses from man were readily available, would man have restraint and if he can not, can another man restrain him with love. The Love of a Brother in Christ.

If "The Acts of Nathan the Prophet" are truly the last acts of King David and King Solomon, I pray that I have done my Lord proud. I pray Your book Father, will touch the lives of Lepers and the loved ones that surround them. Please forgive me of my inequities my Lord, I am a Leper just as my brothers and sisters are. Please forgive us all of our sins and touch our hearts so that we may attempt to be conscious of our decisions. The decisions that can last an eternity. I pray my Faith in my Brother and in You will be Eternal and we can all finally rest knowing our Father has His Kingdom on Earth. Lord, we are sick and we need You to fix us. As I attempt to do your Will to fix others, You are fixing me Lord. Thanks for showing me how it is done.

You know, the more I think about it, I think I deserve two wishes. I mean Damn, I didn't know I was signing up for all of this. I thought my purpose was to just deliver the Gift. I didn't know I had to take them on to raise. But I guess if there was no one there to ever raise them, I would pray that you give me the wisdom that my parents and God have blessed me with. A fellow Leper brother mentioned being raised by alcoholics. A frame of reference instilled at birth and reared by alcoholic parents can be a difficult web to escape. Love your parents, but always respect-fully question authority and seek your purpose for God. He will give you strength if you ask your heart to tell your brain to live a Christ Like Life.

ASK

Alright, give me a sec......I pray that You grant Your children a new direction for this planet. Our direction hasn't worked out to well. Let's try God's Direction. "Imagine Turning To God for Change", "Hollywood, doesn't it just sing?" - Mannequin

DONE

Your Wish has been Granted - Big

Miagi proud of you. When do God technique right, no can defense - Karate Kid

Finally, told you so Dum Dum – Kazoo

I was just thinking what a great role the body of Christ could play in this whole Master's Plan. If they became God's Health Centers and had twelve step meetings for controlling all different kinds of Demons, wouldn't that be witnessing for You like You so desire. To witness to the Lepers so you can control your own leprosy. If only the body of Christ could heal God's children, the World would be a better place.

"IF ONLY" - You've Got Mail

What is the fate of Nathan the Prophet Lord?
What is the fate of Ophiuchus my Lord?

FAITH
HOPE
CHARITY
LOVE

FREE WILL

Yeah, I got "IT", but will they? I know my purpose for You. What is my fate Lord? What is my destiny?

ASK HEART

Damn, I just can't seem to pin You down. You're a tough customer and I got You against the ropes. I just can't seem to get You to pull the trigger and commit.

WELCOME
TO MY
KINGDOM

You know, I have got about as much chance of getting my (2nd Wife) back as Christ has to get His. What's up with that? You know what I'm saying? If I concede and accept that I will never have my (2nd Wife) back, then I must move on. Who does Christ move on to when we won't accept Him? Wait, step back non-believer. I'm getting a vision. I can see it, a little smokey but clearing. LOL I see a World destroyed by the Hand of Man that could never understand that we are all brothers and sisters in Christ and serve the same God. The God of Abraham. Will this be the Kingdom that we will leave for our God? Our children? Our neighbor? Our Country? Our Global brothers? Will this be our Legacy? The Legacy of Mankind?

Maybe we should start over with the apes, nah, that didn't seem to work either. LOL Maybe the pests, can't seem to ever get rid of those bastards, but I don't think they will give our Father the enjoyment He gains watching us run around in the maze of Life. I sure am praying we can continue, I'd like to try this World again with a better understanding of the rules. Maybe a thousand years like the original option on the contract . Since I know that this is impossible for my lifetime, I better make the most of the Life that I have left. Thank God, I get to live another day. Another day of sobriety and one day closer to fulfilling my purpose. I'm so tired Lord. I can't leave Your World like this, not knowing what I know. Please give me the Wisdom of King Solomon and Strength of King David to deliver your Gracious Gift to Mankind. I already have the heart of Tinman and You have mine.

You know, you may not like Glenn Beck. But I like his passion of exposing the truth and willing to substantiate his claims to anyone that would challenge them. I'm right there with you brother. I can find no one that can rebuke my interpretation of the

Seven Sealed, Two-Sided Scroll in the right hand of Him who sits on the Throne.

I'm not feeling it tonight Lord. Think I'll watch a little news and get riled up again. Good Night if we don't talk anymore tonight. I love you Lord and I thank you for another sober day.

7/9/2010

Good Morning God. Please grant me another sober day. I'm growing impatient as I always do. This would be about the time that I would screw anything that I am involved with up. I don't know exactly what it is that I'm looking for and I don't know if I can be content when I get there. My mind moves from one thing to the next, will I ever get to rest? It's a bitch carrying around a Gift from God. A Gift that is arcane and being delivered by a Leper. Let me ask you something Lord, are you making deals with the Devil? Or is that just Pat? LOL Because it sure sounds like the stakes for a bet. Kind of like you did with Job, the patience of Job. There's my answer folks. I may not like it, but it is an answer. I can always go and shovel shit at my once beautiful beach and I am not above doing what I have to do to support my family. It's just right now, I have educated myself to be able to use my brain instead of my back for financial support and my Lord has blessed me. He has afforded me the time to fulfill my purpose for Him and I pray that I do just that.

I used to ride around and look at houses and wonder, how the hell do people afford all that? I just didn't realize that many people are living way beyond their financial means. Now that I know, I don't envy them anymore. I know that financial nightmare all to well.

Good Night Father, I'm a little tired. Thanks for another sober day.

7/10/2010

Good Afternoon God, grant me a sober day. I had to run and meet with my twelve step sponsor and have a meeting with the group this morning. So here I am procrastinating about writing because I'm tired. As I lie in my bed trying to take a nap, the Holy Spirit keeps putting thoughts on my heart. These thoughts are things that are a part of my frame of reference and many people have not been privy to a higher state of actualization. I must share this thought before I store it back into my subconscious.

Affirmations and 30 day chip.

I will be on my cruise with my son and his friend when I hit my 30 day point of sobriety. So I will prepare my speech now.
Anyone have 30 days of Sobriety?

I do.

Clap, Clap, Clap...

I'd like to thank my Father and Creator, my Lord and Savior and my Wonderful Counselor and Guide. I'd also like to thank my Leper brothers and sisters in Christ, for if it were not for you sharing your own stories that relate to mine, I am not sure I would know my purpose for God. I didn't know the rules of the game called Life. I've spent my lifetime establishing the boundaries and suffering from the consequences. I mean really, how many times do I need to be shocked before I realize my Demons are robbing me of my life? My brother, I went searching for my purpose and I didn't have a clue how to do it. I was like a rat in a maze always packing my Demon for the trip. Man did I slam into some dead ends, but I never broke my bottle. Maybe if I had broken the bottle and gotten cut, I could have recognized it earlier? Probably not, that was a good Demon that enabled me to clear my conscious and rest my mind. It was my medicine. I justified my Demon to God. My Lord, I would say, I just seem to connect better with You when I'm drunk. And He would say, c'mon, I'll take you anyway I can get you. So I went with what was on my heart and not really giving a rats ass what anyone thought. I let Him bring me through my past. I let Him show me the present. He revealed to me what needs to be done to change the future. Gods Last Will and Testament. I kept thinking that I was done and my purpose was fulfilled. He kept guiding me with thoughts and gave me the time to think them through. He blocked my path and showed me another. A path of anonymity that would allow me to do what I so desperately want and have to do, if I want to praise and witness for Him and keep my sobriety at the same time. He put quite a bit on my plate and I want it off.

"TO DO"

1. **Fix Global Financial problems by re-instating Birth-rights.**
2. **Bring World Peace to the Three Brothers.**
3. **Give a modern day sociological perspective of God, that will enable the children of God to better equip themselves for the challenges of their own Demons as they allow them to enter into their hearts via any orifice.**
4. **Teach them how to pray.**
5. **Teach them how to listen with their heart.**
6. **Teach them how to develop a Godly frame of reference.**
7. **Teach them how to recognize 666.**
8. **Teach them how to Love one another and discover their purpose for God.**
9. **Teach them how to discover one anothers needs and level of importance.**
10. **Teach them Empathy.**
11. **Teach them about their omitted studies.**
12. **Teach them to Love your Brothers and Sisters as you Love Me.**

13. **Seek your new name in Christ and become what you so desperately want to emulate for our Father's Glory. I AM...**

Etcetera...Etcetera...Etcetera...

Pffffttttt......is that all? You hired a salesman brother, I can do "IT". Psssssst....Holy Shit brother, how am I going to do "IT". I'm not Superman, I'm a Leper.

I ask you my Brother and Sister in Christ, if you truly, truly, truly felt that the Holy Spirit had given you a Gift that would save Mankind from self destruction and no one could rebuke your theory, how would you get that message out? You can armchair quarterback me all you want. Hell, I just got drunk and started writing. I vented all my frustrations and I may have even pissed you off. The drunk in me would have said something like, the truth hurts you worthless piece of shit bastard. The new and improved Godly me would say:

**BECAUSE I LOVE YOU
I DO CARE
BECAUSE I'LL HAVE TO CARRY YOU
I MUST CARE**

I pray that you are not given a similar "to do" list to buy your way into heaven. This is just mine, and Christ and I seem to have a very similar agenda. I'm not real sure who was first, I wanted my (2nd Wife) back so I expressed everything on my heart before I am to "Pass". Our Christ was not given that luxury and His brothers robbed Him of continuing His ministry. The Living Word has been interpreted many ways over the centuries to coincide with mans agenda and frame of reference. Our Lord and Savior wants us all back, we are all His (2nd Wives) and He is our Bridegroom. What will it take to settle our monkey asses down and live a peaceful existence? I will not answer that one, because

90

I might just get what I ask for taken out of context. I think I will just send Him a text.

Lord,
I'm doing all in my power to deliver your Gift. I would have to say the Demons have got a clear cut advantage over your children. Just as my Demons have kept me in the darkness, the darkness masks the Light of the Son. I Will plant your seed Lord, "at all costs" and "IT" will be on your children whether "IT" falls on fertile soil. Let Your Last Will and Testament Be Done.
  – your humble servant Nathan

Hey, I know it don't really make a shit to anyone else but You and me, but should I start referring to myself as Ophiuchus or is that just reserved for heart to hearts?

I think I'll answer for myself this time Lord, interject anytime though. You have already caught me in this quandary. You said, if my purpose was truly for You, who's approval do I seek? I was immediately drawn to the obvious answer and that would be You, of course. Upon further evaluation, I would say that once I have done a thorough inventory of my life, I could choose a name worthy of my purpose for Christ and do everything to emulate my hero for the Glory of God. So man, if you want to tell me what your new name in Christ is, tell me with your actions first and I'll tell you if your name suits you. That is if you are allowing me to be your judge, I will gladly do so. I say your name is 666. If you say different, don't tell me, tell Him. Some things are just better left private with your God, you never know when you may want to change the direction your life is headed and a new name in Christ is more fitting for your heart. Hell, I've had lots of names given to me. Let's see there's Nathan, worthless sperm donor, crazy manic fuck, etc...but I got to choose my own name in Christ and now I get to choose to allow Christ to help me to emulate who I want to become for His Glory.

Oh man, I got so far away from affirmations, I almost forgot to tell you about them. As you write about things, write about them in a manner as if they had already happened. I guess my acceptance speech ran a little long. LOL I'm just so happy to have made it 30 days without a drink. Do you get it? Write out what you want to become and emulate "IT" to become "IT".

DEEP

LOL, I thought you'd like that. Just some tools I picked up along the way as I sought to find my purpose for God.

HEAVY

He 'aint Heavy, He's my brother. Take Your Place Lord. Guide our hearts to build Your Kingdom here on earth as it is in Heaven before We Pass.

I wanted this first chapter to be my reflections of my first 30 days of sobriety. I have to draw a line to stop sharing what I know. I am looking for peace in my life and I am hanging on by a thread myself. I'm picking up my son tomorrow and will have to make adjustments to my lifestyle. I will share when I can and when I get back from the cruise, I will share more. When my son goes home to his mother, I want to finish this. I will turn up the heat on my determination to get God's Gift heard. Then I will vanish into anonymity to witness for God until He wishes to take me Home.

I just thought of a whole lot more that should be on that "To Do" list. Like establish Your Kingdom by laying the first brick to building Gods Legacy Trust LLC. You put too much on me Lord. I Will do the best I can to make You proud to call me Son.

7/11/2010

Good Morning God. I'm headed to pick up Austin this morning, I'm very excited to see him. We'll talk later.

I don't know what I'm thinking tonight Lord. I can not seem to get that sense of balance of how things in my life should be. You've blessed me with so much and I still am in unrest. I know you have reminded me repeatedly about the fact that I am not done with my purpose and I never will be, so enjoy the ride while you live. I am going to try to do that Lord, but I am very uneasy and cautious now. I don't want to slip into paranoia, but I am so sick of seeing the self-centeredness of my brothers and sisters. I'm sick with myself as I personally give myself an inventory of my actions in my life. How self-centered I have been with my own thoughts. Sometimes you just can't see it in yourselves and someone has to point it out to you and this will normally piss you off.

Not feeling it tonight Lord, check you in the morning. Thanks for another sober day. You're the Greatest God that has ever been and ever will be.

7/12/2010

Good Morning God. Please grant me another sober day. Today is three weeks since my last drink. Hooray for me and thanks to You and my Leper friends. As I sit here pondering what to do today, I am reminded how I haven't really passed anything along to my son. Every time I want to talk to him about the ways of the World, he shuts me down. Our children have their own mentors and they come from the Media and friends. It's no wonder the wisdom of past generations is slowly dying off as it has done throughout history. What is the new frame of reference that is being instilled into our future generations subconscious? I do not see it as a Godly frame of reference. I see it as a "ALL ABOUT

ME" generation, the only thing that has changed from generation to generation is God being chipped from our lives and frame of reference. Imagine, the Greatest counselor to have ever lived and His words have been manipulated and we are suffering the consequences right now as we speak. Good news, there is still time. But time is getting very short and we must act quickly.

Lord, I will finish this soon and I will continue to spread the "Good News". I pray that your children will accept your Gift. It will be very difficult to maintain composure if I am not heard. I have answered your inquiry about when I am done. I know that I am never done, but I must get what I have to say off my heart. I understand the unrest that King David and King Solomon must feel if they are able to look down upon us. I have heard their cheers and felt their heads shaking with disgust over my performance and the performance of all of God's children. I hear my Leper brothers scream back, turn around it's a dead end. I hear my ancestors screaming to me, Endeavor to Persevere. How would I answer your question Lord? Did you do everything in your power to deliver My Gift? I am trying to do all in my power Lord, but I'm fearful of how I will be able to live with myself if this Message is not heard. I've thought about mailing the books with a note. "This is Not a Bomb", but they will blow your ass away.

How do we get people to listen? How do we get noticed? Is what we are offering, Glorify God or ourselves? Maybe Austin will go on a Hot Air Balloon ride and I could call the authorities and tell them we have another run away balloon with a child in it. I have to wonder how many times the authorities would give their all after being duped by a hoax. Peter cried wolf, it's a great story of why you should not hit the panic button unless it truly is an emergency. If you didn't get cheese on your burger, it's not a big deal. Don't call 911 you dumb ass.

Hebrews 10:38 (NKJV) Now the just shall live by faith; But if anyone draws back, My soul has no pleasure in him."

Hebrews 11:1 (NKJV) Now faith is the substance of things hoped for, the evidence of things not seen.

Romans 8:24 (NKJV) For we were saved in this hope, but hope that is seen is not hope; for why does one still hope for what he sees?

Hebrews 3:14 (NKJV) For we have become partakers of Christ if we hold the beginning of our confidence steadfast to the end.

Hebrews 11:3 (NKJV) By faith we understand that the worlds were framed by the word of God, so that the things which are seen were not made of things which are visible.

Colossians 1:16 (NKJV) For by Him all things were created that are in heaven and that are on earth, visible and invisible, whether thrones or dominions or principalities or powers. All things were created through Him and for Him.

Hebrews 9:26 (NKJV) He then would have had to suffer often since the foundation of the world; (*kosmos*) but now, once at the end of the ages (*aion*), He has appeared to put away sin by the sacrifice of Himself.

Matthew 12:32 (NKJV) Anyone who speaks a word against the Son of Man, it will be forgiven him; but whoever speaks against the Holy Spirit, it will not be forgiven him, either <u>in this age or in the age to come.</u>

Ephesians 1:21 (NKJV) far above all principality and power and might and dominion, and every name that is named, <u>not only in this age but also in that which is to come.</u>

Hebrews 11:4 (NKJV) By faith Abel offered to God a more excellent sacrifice than Cain, through which he obtained witness that he was righteous, God testifying of his gifts; and through it he being dead still speaks.

Genesis 4:1-7 (NKJV) Now Adam knew Eve his wife, and she conceived and bore Cain, and said, "I have acquired a man from the LORD." 2 Then she bore again, this time his brother Abel. Now Abel was a keeper of sheep, but Cain was a tiller of the ground. 3 And in the process of time it came to pass that Cain brought an offering of the fruit of the ground to the LORD. 4 Abel also brought of the firstborn of his flock and of their fat. And the LORD respected Abel and his offering, 5 but He did not respect Cain and his offering. And Cain was very angry, and his countenance fell. 6 So the LORD said to Cain, "Why are you angry? And why has your countenance fallen? 7 "If you do well, will you not be accepted? And if you do not do well, sin lies at the door. And its desire is for you, but you should rule over it."

Genesis 4:3 (NKJV) And in the process of time it came to pass that Cain brought an offering of the fruit of the ground to the LORD.

John 14:6 (NKJV) Jesus said to him, "I am the way, the truth, and the life. No one comes to the Father except through Me.

Acts 4:12 (NKJV) "Nor is there salvation in any other, for there is no other name under heaven given among men by which we must be saved."

Hebrews 11:5 (NKJV) By faith Enoch was taken away so that he did not see death, "and was not found, because God had taken him"; for before he was taken he had this testimony, that he pleased God.

John 3:13 (NKJV) "No one has ascended to heaven but He who came down from heaven, that is, the Son of Man who is in heaven.

Hebrews 11:6 (NKJV) But without faith it is impossible to please Him, for he who comes to God must believe that He is, and that He is a rewarder of those who diligently seek Him.

2 Chronicles 20: 20 So they rose early in the morning and went out into the Wilderness of Tekoa; and as they went out, Jehoshaphat stood and said, "Hear me, O Judah and you inhabitants of Jerusalem: Believe in the LORD your God, and you shall be established; believe His prophets, and you shall prosper."

Psalms 9:10 (NKJV) And those who know Your name will put their trust in You; For You, LORD, have not forsaken those who seek You.

I'm counting on You Lord, because I look like a damn fool to my peers. But it is Your approval that I seek. I pray that you allow the Holy Spirit to guide my path and that it is a path that all my brothers and sisters in Christ may "PASS" through to You. It is through You that we reach the Father and the Heaven He promised.

If I were a speculator, which I am. I would say that based on John 3 : 13 I have a cheering squad in Christ. He's the only one in Heaven with the Father and He beckons to me and all that can hear with their hearts. I WILL...have my promised Kingdom. Your ancestors are not in Heaven. They await for you to fulfill your purpose for God, so that you all may join Him.

Good Night God. Thanks for another sober day.

7/13/2010

Good Morning God. Please grant me a sober day. I took my son and two of his friends to the river today. I had plenty of words of wisdom racing through my mind, but I know that unless I approach it right, it will fall on deaf ears. It seems that it is very difficult for a parent to reach a child when there are other mentors in their life. Sometimes it is just better received from another authority figure. Dorothy could have told the scarecrow that he had brains, but it took the Wizard of Oz to instill into the scarecrow that he had brains if he would just use them. An authority figure encouraged a needy person to aspire for more. An authority figure can be anyone that has been there and done that and can honestly tell another human being what their own experience has been like. I don't need for you to tell me how screwed up my life is, I already know that. Tell me about how screwed up your life was and how you were able to achieve recovery.

Tonight's meeting was kind of cool. A newcomer was there and she got most of the focus, even though she was there because of a court order. I witnessed my Leper brothers and even one that never shares, elaborate their stories that hopefully will resonate in an questionably open mind. I know my first week, I really didn't hear shit. I was more interested in being heard and continuing with my purpose for God. Once I started really listening to my Lepers friends, I started to realize that they all had some kind of awakening. One man had confessed that he had been in and out of twelve step program for years and was on his last chance. I could hear his heart and it was in a complete state of confusion. I decided to share tonight. I spoke of how I am able to hear with my heart. I told them I put out a question in my mind for all of my alter egos to make a decision on. After carefully listening to all of the egos, I make a decision knowing what the consequences could be. Listening to your heart is just that easy. Understand, your frame of reference will only shed light on the decision at hand. If you have not exposed yourself to all possible consequences because they may not be in your frame of reference, you'll probably make a mistake. If you make a mistake, learn from it and put that lesson in your subconscious frame of reference for the next time a similar decision is to be made.

My friend Darren from Auburn University called me today. He asked if I had seen the Glenn Beck show. It was about the Black Panthers, you know, the ones that Forrest interrupted their Party fighting. I can honestly say that I have been a racist, ignorant bastard for much of my life. I searched for the personality that I wanted to emulate. Unfortunately, I was surrounded by racist growing up. It really doesn't matter what the color of your skin is, you will either aspire to make the system better or try and tear it down. If you take on the persona of another that is racist, you continue to be the catalyst that keeps this country divided over race. I'm sick of it, I'm so over it. We have shown as a Nation that we are over it. Sure, there will continue to be racism as long as our profiteer brother continue stirring shit over it and get paid to do it. You may have to deal with racism for a while longer. I have been told it will take three more generations to fully wipe it out of our frame of reference. If it is so easy to grow God out of our lives, why can't we out grow racism?

BROTHER OF COLOR
BROTHER OF ANOTHER MOTHER
BROTHER OF ONE FATHER
KEEPER OF THY BROTHER
ASSASIN OF THY BROTHER
FREE WILL

I'd rather you just talk to me straight up, but I will try and decipher. These enigmas are cool though, I think they can take on a personal meaning to everyone depending on the battles that wage in their minds. Let's see....we are all of "Color". We were all brought into this World by different "Mother's". We are all brothers and sisters in Christ to one "Father". Of our "own free will", we get to decide if we will "inspire" our brothers and sisters or "decimate" them.

If you are feeling a void in your life, it is the void of not really accomplishing anything that will make a difference before you "Pass". I promise you, if you will attempt to inspire God's children, you will find your purpose in Life and receive the blessing of fulfillment from the Father. You just will not know how many lives that are actually being touched by you when you live a Christ filled life. It can not be contained, it will radiate off of you through your smile and kind words. Your words can "inspire" or "decimate" the dreams of inspirational minds. It will be difficult to be cognoscente of your own words if they are not true in your heart. It is good to speak your beliefs, but understand that your beliefs have been built by what you have been exposed to. Once religious beliefs are locked into our heads, it can be very hard to see another interpretation of the "TRUTH".

Everyone seems to have their own version of "IT". I ask you this, by who's authority, gives you authority, to be my authority, when my authority, tells me to seek my authority and my authority is not a man, but a Man God that spoke with authority, an authority given unto Him by the Father until His life was taken by the authority, this is documented by good authority and the authority continues to pervert the authority, for the authority is yet to be the authority as the authority of our World. Say that three times real fast. LOL

SO WHO'S
"YO DADDY"

"Behold, the only thing greater than yourself" - Roots

And the struggle of Life begins. This statement elevates Man to be greater than God. Unfortunately, man is about himself until he is humbled by God.

100

Let's call it a night Bro. Thanks for another sober day.

NIGHT
WELL COME

7/14/2010

Good Morning God. Please grant me a sober day. I went to a great small twelve step meeting today. The topic was insanity. Everyone's stories emulated things that I had done myself. The question one has to ask oneself is, how long do I allow the insanity to rule my life? I'm not going to bore you with all of my stories of my drunkenness, you will see that in the rest of the book. You do need to hear these stories if you want to hear "turn around, go back it's a dead end". What I'm telling you is, my stories are the same as my Leper friends stories with one exception. I was given a Gift and it has kept me from sobriety and now I use "IT" to gain sobriety. I have a special purpose for my Creator. How can I possibly imagine being drunk with the weight of the World on my shoulders? I want it the Hell off as soon as possible.

I see everyone is piling on Mel Gibson these days. What a shame to watch alcoholism claim yet another big prize for Satan. As a prophet of God, we saw his passion for Christ. As a man tempted by his Demons, we see him as a poor witness for the Lord. I see him as a man that struggles with Demons just as we all do. I will pray for him. Lord, please give Mr. Gibson the strength to challenge his Demons with your help. He has been such a trumpet for you Lord, please pick him up from the mire and mold him into the witness that you had intended for his life. He is a great Godly man that has fallen victim to the Demons implanted in our society by mankind. I say; Ye without Sin, Cast the first Stone.

101

I can not believe how you have come into my life just at the right time to fulfill my purpose for You. We are begging for a new direction in Christ. I'm feeling more and more confident about being able to deliver Your Gift Lord. Your children are sooooo..... ripe with sin. I sure hope the sword You pulled out of my mouth was sharp enough for the harvest. The Truth Hurts and we can justify any belief we want to determine our truth. We will argue you down to convince you that our truth is the Divine Truth. So if you want to go to Heaven, you better do "IT" our way. I tell you the truth, it is a personal relationship that you must have with Christ and you take personal accountability for your actions for our Fathers approval. Many are so quick to take their frame of reference and tell me how I am suppose to believe in my creator. It is not a big challenge to manipulate God's Word to fit ones agenda. The only real truth to me is my interpretation of God's Truth. I have done my own research and I will be the only one to be Judged when my time comes. I don't want to say to my Lord, I didn't want to take the time to understand you Lord. I took a short cut by listening to Your supposed messengers and didn't educate myself to seek what it is that I am here for. I filled that void in my heart quite well with my Demons. I was on earth to get mine and I didn't really give a damn who I had to crush to get "IT". But, I went to church on Sunday occasionally and I always put a little in the kitty. I told people that I believe that You died for my sins on the cross and arose in three days. So since I have made this proclamation, shouldn't I be allowed in Heaven? There is no "I" in team or brotherhood. When is the last time you truly did something nice for someone else anonymously? Do you truly feel blessed to give and humbled to receive? Who's approval do you seek when you make your daily decisions? Are your decisions Christ Like or Anti-Christ Like?

Good Night Lord. Thanks for another Sober day.

102

7/15/2010

Good Morning God. Please grant me another sober day.

It still bothers me that my (2ⁿᵈ Wife) thinks I'm crazy. This is what I sent her this morning after a few pleasant emails.

(2ⁿᵈ Wife), I am fulfilling prophecy. I have done a tremendous amount of research. You will witness a battle of good and evil, but it will not come as expected. It is allowing Christ into your heart and asking for His guidance as you battle your own demons in your life. This book shows the whole process for me battling my demon alcohol and how I allowed Christ to save me with recovery. It is a battle plan that others can follow as they equip themselves to conquer their own demon. LOL Christ and I had many drunken chats about everything that was bothering me in this world. I'm not drunk or crazy, I am doing what I am compelled to do. If I were not convinced about my purpose for God, I would never subject myself to this much humiliation. So I guess that pretty much sums up what has be going on in my mind. I'll send you a copy of the new book if you would like one. Did you read the first one?

I show how I came to have a personal relationship with Jesus Christ, our Lord and Savior.

Guess I am fixing to go to the folks house this afternoon with Austin. We will play the board game Risk for hours. Austin loves World Domination. But who doesn't, there are a lot of kooks out there ruling Nations. I may even take this opportunity to reintroduce Austin to "Cashflow 101" so I can continue his financial education. I'm going to spend the night there Lord, so I'll check in when I get back. Please don't plummet my heart with more thoughts, I won't be able to remember them and share them with your children. I so want to please you Lord, I don't want to miss a thing you want me to tell them.

CHILD TIME
IS
GOD TIME

Before I leave I was just thinking this in the shower. Glenn Beck has been stereotyping dope smoking hippies as Radicals. When did the alcoholic become the pot smoker's judge? I think I will send him another email that I know he won't get.

Subject: Alcoholic Stereotypes Hippie as Radical?

Dear Glenn,

I'm a huge fan. Are you saying that all "Dope Smoking Hippies" are Radicals? When did the alcoholic become the judge for the pot smoker? I pray for your success and hope your Demon doesn't cause you to stumble, but you know it is always there. Please refrain from making a correlation between "Dope Smoking Hippies" and Radicals, you just don't have a clue how much of an audience you will lose. Keep up the great work.

Ophiuchus
Gulf Shores, Al
http://godslegacytrust.blogspot.com

7/17/2010

Good Morning God. Please grant me another sober day. Lord, you are putting more on my heart than I can remember to write down. Slow down please. "Nanny, Nanny, Poo, Poo" I have a personal relationship with Christ and you don't. Good News Brother, you can have this also if you will allow the Holy Spirit to enter your hearts and use Him as your Counselor to make your decisions Christ Like.

Lord, today is the big day. We are leaving out of Mobile, Al. on a Fun Ship. There will be half naked women and blue frozen drinks with fruit and umbrellas in them. A proverbial smorgasbord of temptations. How will I be able to restrain my Demon when my Demon is so appealing? How did King David as a lad, muster the courage of faith to face His Goliath? His Demon that would call Him Slave, His Demon that He would call Master. The Demon that would control all of His days if He allows himself to be consumed. My sponsor is right, this is crazy to face my Demons ill prepared. My sponsor doesn't understand that I am prepared and I want the fast track of recovery, for my time to deliver His Gift is running out with the sands of time and these are the "days of our lives".

I will put my faith in you Lord. When my Demon screams noises of Ecstasy that await me, I will weigh out the consequences and make my decision of my own free will. If my Demon raises so much Hell with me I can not stand it any longer, I will turn my Demon over to You. I will write out a permission slip from my Demon and I will get my Father to sign it on my heart. If I can convince You Lord that I can handle "IT" by myself, my Demon has already won and I might as well shoot myself and decrease the surplus population. But that would be the route of Judas, an after life torment that only He can articulate.Lord, I'm not sure I know how to have a good time anymore. All my perceived good times always revolved around my Demon. How will I slow my mind without self medication? How will I re-emerge into society? How will I overcome my insecurities? How can I not be so judgmental? How can I relieve myself of being in charge?

**GIVE "IT"
TO ME
"IT" IS
PAID FOR
PRAY**

I can do this. Let's bring the whole gang on this trip by not bringing the gang. Call me crazy (many do), but I want to get rid of the smokes too. Fix me Lord. Let me think through all my Demons and the losses that they have caused in my life. I will be thinking about (2nd Wife) a lot on this trip, we had cruised three times in the past. So this not so "Fun Ship" will include: 1. No Alcohol 2. No Smokes 3. Lost Love 4. No Gambling 5. A Son that is embarrassed to be seen with me 6. Books to read and a God to serve

Or of my own free will, this "Fun Ship" will include: 1. Great Food 2. New Friends 3. Ambiance of God's Beautiful Creation 4. Peace of Mind 5. Memories of a new bond with my Son 6. Books to read and a Great God to serve

I can have any type vacation I want. It is up to me to determine whether it will be a shitty time or a great time. Think about that for a moment. When I was drinking, I turned the time shitty. When I wasn't drinking, I turned the time shitty because I wasn't drinking. Please forgive me Lord, I was an ass when I wasn't an ass, I was an ass because I wanted to be an ass. I was an ass when I became an ass. I am an ass when I become an ass.

Speaking of ass, I kicked some ass yesterday playing "Risk". I allowed Dad and Austin to battle it out as I stayed quietly on the sidelines, not being confrontational and I watched them deplete and thin out their troops. I built my armies and waited for the opportune time to attack. They were so completely absorbed into their own agendas that they didn't notice me carrying out my mission. When they were at there weakest, I attacked quick and calculated. They weren't expecting what conquered them. I AM... World Domination. LOL

I believe my Nation, the Beacon for other Nations to emulate, is at it's all time weakest that I have seen in my lifetime. I already feel as if I had ascended to the Heavens and sit with the Father and the Son, we watch to see who you will serve. A Master of men will arise before the fall, and you will serve him passionately. Your Master is your Demon and the Demon in your brother. My Master is our Loving Father, Christ is my brother and the Holy Spirit is my "Wonderful Counselor". These are my Master's that I report to now. I am their humble servant and not a slave to my Demons. You can believe whatever you want, this is what I believe. I believe Christ came back for me and Saved me from the path of self destruction. Just as the guard that had his ear sliced off from the blade of Peter was reattached by Christ, Christ reattached me with reality and saved me. I will not just sit here in amazement. I will witness for Christ for what He has done for me. I will have a purpose for God to help my brother and sister in Christ battle their own Demons.

Lord, I have no idea how I got here, but I've got to pack for the cruise. Whoo Hoo, I think I'll make it a good one. I'll be back and forth K...

TIME
THINK
PRAY
FEEL
QUESTION
SEEK
DECIDE

I get to decide how this trip will turn out. I get to decide if I allow something to knock me off my game and be seduced by my Demon. Lord, can I get my Mo Jo back without my Demon?

Brother, did you ever have Mo Jo? How can you get back what you have never had?

I never had you in my heart Lord. I didn't understand how to invite you really. Yeah, I heard all that shit from people that I didn't know for real. As it has been for me in everything in my life, I have had to have my nose rubbed in it for me to accept it. I know You and I know my Demon. It is my own free will that I choose my destiny.

Just ironing my golf shirt and it reminded me of playing a round with an acquaintance. He would get real pissed off when he didn't hit well. Club throwing pissed. I suck and know I suck, cause I'm sucking on a brew. I watched a better sober golfer come to him and say; Why are you getting all pissed off, have you invested into yourself to improve your game? If you have not invested in yourself, who do you have to get pissed at? Your Brother? Here brother, let me help you by not giving you a damn thing but guidance to improving your game. Will you accept my hand in friendship and let me help you? By me helping you improve your game, I may improve mine as well.

Well, I guess I better get focused on the boys and make sure we have everything we need for the trip. Please be with me Lord. I will need Your guidance and the help from my Leper Brothers and Sisters. I'm suppose to look for friends of Bill W's. LOL Cool.

BON VOYAGE

Be Back Thursday, but You will always be on my mind. You are my Best Friend.

7/22/2010

Good Afternoon God, I'm still sober. I have so much to tell You, but first let me tell You what was on my facebook page when I got home.

I had an agnostic question the relevance of my photo to God. This is how I answered:

It is one of the many signs that I found as I searched for my purpose for God. It is my zodiac sign and the 13th sign that is real, but not in traditional zodiac literature. Ophiuchus is the God of Medicine and by establishing our Father His Everlasting, Earthly Entity "Gods Legacy Trust LLC", He may dwell among us and heal the sick for free. His Earthly Kingdom will have to built with the bricks of Mankind. Ophiuchus is also my new name in Christ. I am almost finished with my second book, "The Acts of Nathan the Prophet" (A Documented Lost Book of a Prophetic Bible) due out Oct. 2010 and "Gods Last Will and Testament" is already available on amazon.com. Which is my interpretation of the Seven Sealed, Two-Sided Scroll. (Rev 5 : 1 - 5). I am however at a standstill in creating the Websites. I have already extended $3000.00 to a designer and "my will" has been blocked by hiring a mercenary without the Passion for the job. My purpose is to deliver His Gift, not to build it. I do not possess the talents required to do so and besides, I don't want to rob someone of their own opportunity to fulfill their purpose for God. Did you ever wonder why so much emphasis was put on "Birthrights"? Esau sold his for a bowl of soup to his brother Jacob. Legacywillandtrust.com will enable everyone to establish themselves their own personal Legacy and thus re-instate birthrights and will be the Salvation of Mankind. You can check out my concept website at http://legacy-willandtrust.com/ and check out my blog which is the preface and first chapter of my second book. http://godslegacytrust.blogspot.com/ The last six years of my life have been filled with loss and triumph and I have documented the journey the whole way. So if you are interested in the solutions to the World's Largest Riddles, you might want to check it out. Riddles like of course the biggest one, what is written on the Scroll that John has pleaded for someone to decipher, but no one could even look inside. Would you like to know what exactly 666 means? It is not what you might think. Or how about the answer to who the Two Witnesses of

Revelations are? Sir Isaac Newton and Michel Nostradamus had scientific perspectives of God, "The Acts of Nathan the Prophet" is a sociological perspective. I warn you, be prepared to read a lot. Through my personal relationship with Jesus Christ our Lord and Savior, He touched my heart and taught me to listen to the "Wonderful Counselor" aka The Holy Spirit that He promised to send back. I am a sinner brother and didn't come to know the Lord until 2004. You will witness a battle as prophesied, just not what Hypocritical Christian Fundamentalist are expecting. It is a battle with my Demon Alcohol and how my Lord helped me to recovery. We all have our Demons, I just show you how the Lord came into my life and saved me. I pray people can emulate my experience to their own demonic battles and allow Christ into their hearts to take over the fight. What type of a Witness for our Lord would I be if I didn't share my experience and God's Gift. Do you remember the soldier that Peter cut off his ear and Jesus reattached it to the man's head? A Silent Saved Witness, I Am Not. I Will Deliver His Gift "at all costs".

The Prophet Nathan/Ophiuchus - a humble servant of the Lord

Anyway, I thought it was pretty cool the way You inspired me to Witness for You to an agnostic and hopefully bring him to You. I'll keep you posted.

I got a little side tracked tonight defending myself about You Lord. Can we call it a night, I promise to put on paper what You have put on my heart. This is going to be a great topic for tomorrow. How does an alcoholic discipline/educate a 14 soon to be 15 yr old about alcoholism without alienating himself and watching his son pursue the same path that cost me 30 years of my life and a continual teetering balance of sobriety?

Thanks for giving me purpose Lord, it kept me sober knowing that I would not be an acceptable witness for You if I allowed

110

myself to be controlled and be a slave to my Demons. Wow, were the temptations grand. Half naked women and frozen drinks with umbrellas being shoved in my faced repeatedly. My two biggest Demons, Booze and Booty.

Good Night Lord, it is good to be home. Sometimes the best part of a trip is just getting home. I think everyone can agree with that one and we don't have to raise taxes or launch any grenades. We can just agree or agree to disagree.

7/23/2010

Good Morning God. Please bless me with another sober day. This quandary I have for You this morning is pretty difficult to navigate my through, so that it will plant the proper seeds that I would like to see come to fruition for my son. The last night of the cruise he was brought to my cabin and I was awaken by the knocks of one of the ships officers and a security guard. They had observed Austin drinking the remains of other passengers alcoholic drinks. He also had a fifth of Smirnoff Vodka in his possession that he claims he found. I had to fill out an acknowledgment statement and he was released to my supervision. I didn't know what was the proper thing to do at that moment, it was two in the morning and I wasn't thinking clearly to make those decisions. So I had Austin brush his teeth and get into the bed with me. I patted his chest and told him not to sweat it. What I needed was time to pray for the right guidance that our Father would approve of and hopefully save my son from the same 30 year torment that I myself, had forged for myself of my own free will.

I am going to talk to my sponsor today and see if he has any suggestions. I am leaning towards confessing what alcohol has done to me and let my leper brothers and sisters explain what it has done to their lives. I can only pray that at least one of the stories will resonate in his subconscious and allow him to make better decisions when tempted with the dilemma of facing a very powerful man made Demon.

I did not have any luck with getting him to play a financial game last week that will help him throughout his life, so why should he listen to me about alcohol. I have played the game with him on several occasions and the seed has found nourished soil, but I believe I may have over watered it. A seed must be allowed time to take root and like I have done so many times in my life, I over do it. When the seed is drowned in love, it repels it and never is allowed for its roots to penetrate the soil. The soil has been washed away and the seed searches for other soil. Soil that appears to have more authority due to media credibility that is questionable to say the least. My son has a new mentor because of my shortcomings. I'll keep you posted on how the conversation goes with my sponsor. I pray to make the right decisions and I hope it can help all of you with your own parental responsibilities. It is our Demons that create secrets and shame for ourselves that rob us from the ability to mentor our own children to face the difficulties of a Godless world. A world filled with illusions that can prey upon childrens dreams.

I like to dance alone for my Father. I dance with joy that He has filled my heart with the Wisdom of King Solomon and the Strength of King David. I dance for the opportunity to serve Him as a saved witness. There is a tingling sensation that runs through my head as I feel His presence. Many times it can break me into tears, His Love is so Strong. We truly are His (2nd Wives) and He is so close, but can't quite have us completely due to our frame of reference and the Demons we have filling our hearts. You will know when you have cleansed with our Father. You will feel it, there is nothing to hide from Him. He knows you better that you know yourselves. I implore you to give your Demons to Christ, He Saves.

I reread my mentors book "Rich Dad's Conspiracy of the Rich" by Robert Kiyosaki while I was sober and on the cruise. We agree on most things except level of contentment. After reading the book and getting re-energized about getting into good debt, I came home to hear another counsel in my friend Brian. He reminded me of the torment that I had and that he presently has trying to pay this debt. The whole idea is for the asset to pay for itself and in an ideal situation it does. The problems arise when you give your contentment over to another individual. My cash position tells me that I am ready to take on this debt and be able to absorb any mishaps, but my contentment tells me to build my portfolio of passive income slower and with cash. Maybe my balls will never be as big as Mr. Kiyosaki's and I admire him for having nuts so big they have to ride shotgun, but I think I will make the most out of a humble lifestyle and worship God without having to worry about how to pay for food, water, shelter, healthcare and Freedom. My small balls will grow to big balls generation after generation eternally. It will be the Legacy that I leave on earth for the praise of our Father.

He also mentioned not liking mutual funds because of the excessive fees and not being truly diversified in the four categories. The Heirs will have a vote to control the financial predators. Businesses, Real Estate, Paper Assets and Commodities. I presently have my assets in Silver, Real Estate and cash that is doing nothing to hedge against inflation. I just don't understand the stock market and I don't want to take the time to learn it. He also mentions that people would have been better off to just place their bets aligning with the S & P 500. I pray Mr. Kiyosaki will take on the Challenge to be a member on the Two Talent Team of God's Treasury. I would place my bet on those Legacies. I believe that if I had inheritance involved, I would monitor it as much if not more than I do Fantasy Football. Because if I win, I get a better check and my world flourishes as my Savior heals the sick and gains His Earthly presence with the Kingdom of God. BTW...I never had time for fantasy football, I'm to busy chatting with my God to help my brother and save mankind from a terrible Demonic fate that it's course presently charts. I am so damn ready to give my mind a break, I guess that is why I was always sedating it with alcohol. Ask and Ye shall receive, we get to decide who we will serve. What are your seven deadly sins? What robs you of a Christ filled Life? Are you ready to ask for Christ to battle this Demon of yours?

Financial Ark: Robert used this analogy so people could understand that they need to build their own Ark's for turbulent financial and retirement times. I pray that you can see how our God was passing the same message with the story of Noah. God allowed Noah to save mankind and rebuild with faith, somehow the message was lost again over time. Gods Last Will and Testament still had not been revealed to illustrate eternal praising and birthrights. Shall we destroy our world this time with fire for a new generation to start again still clueless to our Father's Will. Our Father wants us all to build our own personal Eternal Financial Arks so that His Future Children can live in a world free from corruption and experience His Healing Powers and Merciful, Forgiving Love.

"Cattle Rancher" versus "Dairy Farmer": Robert uses this analogy to demonstrate the difference between the mindset of one that slaughters assets versus milking them. You can accumulate assets with any type of job you may have. My chosen profession is real estate, therefore I must slaughter them to feed myself and I will keep some in my portfolio to milk. I prefer to accumulate my milking assets at a slower pace and not create debt even when it is "Good Debt". I do not have a defeatist attitude, I just know the level of contentment that I need and I'm not willing to take the fast track with worry about finances. I am happy for my brothers and sisters that do and wish them all the success in the world. I'll reserve my talents with contentment and fulfilling my purpose for God mentoring others to strive for more. The Gift that I will receive for helping my brothers and sisters in Christ is "Priceless". I get to enter the Kingdom of Heaven, you can too and live a Christ filled life while we are here on Mother Earth.

Okay, talked with sponsor and Austin. I'm tired tonight, so I'll fill you in tomorrow morning. Thanks for another sober day Lord, it was a hell of a lot easier today without Pedro shoving frozen drinks in my face all day. LOL

7/24/2010

Good Morning Lord. Please grant me another sober day. I'm headed to the gym and a meeting this morning before Austin wakes up. We'll chat when I get back.

K

Hey, I'm back. The meeting was real good this morning. I think I picked up a level of respect from my Leper brothers and sisters because I passed the 30 day mark. More of them are starting to approach me now and carry on conversations. It reminds me of the movie "The Dirty Dozen" when one of the new guys was trying to befriend the veterans of war. They didn't want to get close to the new comer because most fail and die. Just like many that come to the twelve step program wanting to achieve sobriety, but they haven't given their life over to You, Christ our Lord and Savior.

So I talked to my sponsor about bringing Austin to a meeting and he didn't seem to think it was a good idea. So I had to take the mentoring lesson to my son on by myself. I took him to a Mexican restaurant and told him that his Great Grandfather died in prison because he was running moonshine. His Grandfather is a recovering alcoholic and his dad is an alcoholic that has to go to meetings to remain sober. I told him that alcoholism is a disease that is hereditary and there a very good chance that he has

115

these traits. I told him that what he had done on the cruise was things that he would have to face alone for the rest of his life and if he didn't gain an awareness of this disease it could cost him a fulfilled life. I also told him that if he ever found himself in a situation that he had been drinking or was with someone that was drinking, to call me anytime of the day or night and I would be there to pick him up and bring him home safely. I did tell him he would have to wash my car for dragging my ass out of bed. LOL This is the type relationship that I want to have with my son, one that is supportive, not one that would cause him to hide what I already know he is doing. My main concern is that he is safe and when he is not, he exercises good judgment when his judgment abilities have been mentally altered by alcohol or drugs. I am so glad that I didn't make a rash decision while we were on the ship and my emotions were running so high with irritability because of my own alcoholic shortcomings. I have planted a seed, just as my Savior has told me to do. I will not over water this seed and allow Austin an open door to come to me when he has questions, knowing that he will not face retribution for doing so. I mean really, "Go Get Me A Switch" to beat your ass with never really worked for me. Understanding and empathy is what will resonate with anyone trying to conquer their Demons and most will never consider allowing Christ to help until they are face down to the ground in tears and turmoil before they do. Then as soon as things seem to get better they allow their Demons back in where the Demons find that the new environment has be swept clean and the Demons proceeds to make up for lost time. This is when you can really see your life slip away from you, FAST.

I believe our Lord has the same open door to us. Anyone willing to ask for His help and Guidance, "IT" is always there for us to indulge in. Christ Love is Merciful and Forgiving, He is always ready for you to allow Him into your heart for a heart to heart. I wanted to either Die or get my Life back. My feet were going numb and I know that I have diabetic issues, but the lure of alcohol was stronger than my fear of death. I could not conquer this Demon on my own. I could not conquer this Demon with just Christ. I could only conquer this Demon if I had a purpose to do so. My purpose in life is to serve Christ and being a drunken Witness for our Lord and Savior is not where He wants me to be and certainly not where I want to be any longer. I pray that I am able to salvage my life and be of some benefit to others trying to accomplish the same. I was sharing some financial knowledge with a new Leper friend after the meeting. I could tell he was lapping it up and searching for answers himself. I have discovered so much and I am passionate about giving again. Today's topic was about giving to others without a sense of what do I get out of it. I reflected on that and when it was my turn to speak, I told everyone about the story of Naomi and Ruth. How they had gone out so full and life beat them down. I told them how I loved mentoring to people the things that I thought I knew and gained fulfillment from helping others. I told them how life had beat me down and sent me into a drunken life of isolation and paranoia. I can only witness for our Savior about what I have experienced and can articulate. I find that I have purpose in Life if I can help others, so I guess I'll keep going back, listening and helping.

Hey Good Night Lord, thanks for another sober day. The seeds that I planted are starting to take root. Austin and I played Cashflow 101 twice today at his request. I think he may have finally gotten what it is all about. I pray the talk about alcoholism sticks as well.

Sunday 7/25/2010

"DO OVER"

Good Morning Lord, I like today's topic. It is like we will have our own twelve step meeting this morning. Or as I like to refer to "IT", a Personal Praise and Worship Service. You have been plummeting my mind with thoughts this morning and I have prayed about them. So let's have a service shall we.

Your words make me reflect on the movie "Big". We all watched as a child named Josh became an adult instantly and faced a different atmosphere than he was used to. His frame of reference had not included the tyranny that man wages against man. It was his blind child like faith that actually made him unique in a corrupt world. He was despised by his adversaries and desired by his female co-worker as she attempts to climb the corporate pole with different talents.

When Josh presented his girlfriend the idea of coming back to childhood with him, she honestly reflected how much difficulty she had had navigating her way through adolescence. If it were me reflecting the same scenario, I would be thinking about all the mistakes I made and the pain that comes from "IT". Searching for the "TRUTH" as I go through life trying to emulate the ones that I admire presents many decisions.

As I think about Your words "Do Over", I just have to wonder how things would have been for me if somehow I could have been blessed with all the knowledge that I have now, then? I have been through so much training, read so many books and experienced life for myself. I have been on man's path for my entire life and it wasn't working out to well. Since I can not got back to being a child via a Zoltar Machine, I would like to share with my son what I know, so that he may be able to avoid many of the largest pitfalls that I endured.

I just can't tell You how excited I am to see some of my seeds take root. I want him to be able to have the knowledge to create himself a life free from Demons that will rob him of his life. I want him to have the financial success that affords him comfort, but also the time to reflect on You, how blessed he truly is and how he can make an impact in others lives.

Okay, I'll be selfish and dream the impossible dream. If I were given a chance to do life over. What would I want?

You know, I was never one of those salesman that got their quota and laid down for the rest of the month. I was always striving for more and I wanted that plaque with my name on it, so everyone could see "I am the Champion, my friend". My vanity was rewarded as well as my finances. I worked very hard and put in many hours, even working alone on the Sabbath. I earned those plaques, but because my father in law was the General Manager, everyone thought I had been given a leg up. So the reward was a bitter sweet one for me. I had no idea what was really important to me, so I chased toys to fill the void.

I would have like to have been able to recognize that my Materialistic Idols were robbing me of my life. I would have like to have been educated in all four quadrants of employment. Employee, Self Employed, Business Owner and Investor. I would like for someone to have told me how to build my financial ark, so that I could achieve a level of finances that would allow me to give back to my brothers and sisters in Christ and live a Christ filled life of contentment.

"Happiness and Contentment have been achieved" - The Coneheads

I remember when the financial planners were presenting the 401k plan. It made sense to me at the time. You just have a portion of your earnings retracted from your paycheck and give all of you financial control over to someone that you perceive as having more intelligence than yourselves. No one really talked about the scenario of not having new money come into the plan to buy the shares of the existing members as they begin to retire. We were just made to have the assumption that the Market would continue to go up and thrive. Why would anyone want to trust the market now with all of the corruption we are witnessing? The Market is in dire need of the "Circle of Life" theory. Until the Circle is Eternal, empires will continue to fall over and over again until the destruction of our World.

I would have liked to have lived in a World like our forefathers, except with the comforts of today. They had a very clear understanding that we are "ONE NATION UNDER GOD" and "IN GOD WE TRUST". I'm not sure exactly why God was chipped away from our lives over time, but generation after generation kept having sentiments of "what has God ever done for me". And the Bible, Jeez, what a playground for the corrupt. If the same passage was read by people around the world with completely different frames of reference, how many different truths would you hear? I would have liked for someone to tell me that I should always respectfully question authority. Do my own research and decide if I want my decisions to be Christ like or Anti-Christ like based on what I feel on my heart what our Father would approve. Okay, I got it. They have their own version of the truth and I have mine. I just don't want them to enforce their version on me. They will not be with me when I meet You. I know when I am sinning and I know when I am witnessing. I know I will strive for more for Your Glory and I know I serve a forgiving God when my decisions are not from You, but from man and my selfishness.

So let me see if I can recap all this for You. I want to live in a World of the Truth and have a level playing field for everyone that is willing to seek their purpose for You, thus finding their own purpose in life. I want mankind to have it better than I. I certainly don't want to see my son go through 30 yrs of his life in a drunken stupor trying to figure out the rules and utilizing mentors that will quickly prey upon his naivety.

Lord, tell me why You have allowed me to be raised in a World where you are considered uncool. A world where if you proclaim our love for You, ours peers think we have lost our minds. I want to know why we have taken You out of our lives so much over the generations that we can't even proclaim our love for a Creator, Savior and a Wonderful Counselor that speaks to us all. Has Satan won? Satan being man himself based on the decision he makes deciding who to serve.

Lord, I thank You for all of Your Gifts. I thank you for giving me the courage to endeavor to persevere for You. I thank You for giving me the wisdom to share with Your Children and mine, but Your humble servant very humbly requests the Serenity of knowing that I have completed Your Will so that I may have Peace of Mind, Heart, Body and Soul. I just can not think of leaving a World knowing what I know about You and having all the Gifts that you have shared with me and not be heard. I don't want to leave a world where God does not have a say in the outcome. It is time Lord, we are ripe. Please send Your Angels to touch their hearts and build Your Earthly Kingdom. We so cry out to be Your Harvest.

Please forgive those that know not what they do and punish those that know exactly what they do as they serve man. I am not their Judge, only the Father can Judge. He Judges with consequences, some are fair and some are not. If you always got the good deal, how would you know the bad? Learn from your mistakes and make your life revolve around a relationship with Christ first, then your peers. As you have said many times, the poor of heart will always be among us. Okay, forgive me Father. I am adding a few words to Yours and we have been warned about that. If my words have not been for thy Glory, Your humble servant begs for forgiveness of my shortcomings. I know You are using me as an instrument, let my drum be heard worldwide. "I play my drum for You. Pa Rum Pa Pum Pum."

You know what the really cool thing about having a personal relationship with You is? It's free to everyone. No membership dues or selling donuts at five in the morning on a Saturday. To be in an elite group that has trained their hearts to hear you Lord, is a membership that I want to be a part of. I get to witness to my peers of Your Love for us. And they get to be one of the Two Witnesses also. My brothers and sisters in Christ, a very elite group that serve a Loving God and are willing to be thy brothers keeper and motivator. Oops...there I go again adding words to Yours.

Tell me the Truth Lord. I have always made the case that King David's son was Nathan the Prophet. Who else would have the nuts to scold the King for plotting to get a little booty with Bathsheba. She sounds freaking HOT!!! So if Nathan the Prophet was the son of the King, he would feel a little more comfortable about challenging Him. So if all of God's children are sons and daughter's of One Father and Creator, then that would make me a son of God, just as we all are. As a Son of a Great God, I have my beliefs and my own interpretation of My Father's Word and I speak for my Father.

I WILL...
MY EARTHLY
KINGDOM

Wow, I went out for a smoke on that one and You gave me a sign. Thunder coming from the Heavens that shook the house. I'll take that as a sign of approval, I hope. If not, I'm screwed. I am so nervous being on this slippery slope Lord. I truly pray that what I am doing for You is for Your Glory and not mine. I can yield to my judgmental brothers, but I say screw them. I've been serving Y'all long enough and I want to serve my Father now. This is what I believe and you can believe anything you want. Screw it, I'm taking a shower now and going to meet with my sponsor to help me fight my Demons. I'll give You a shout when I get back Lord. Can I get a Witness??? Don't scare me like that by turning off my power Lord. I could never write this book again. I will never go back to that life of torment without You and serving my Demons. But we did have some great drunken chats though. Whoo Hoo. LOL

I pray that You give me strength to heal from my Demons wounds. I pray that I scar over so my Demon can not penetrate again. I pray You use my scars made of my own free will that left a wake of wounds for my family and for Your Family. My brothers and sisters in Christ.

Austin finally beat me at Cashflow 101. He is real proud of himself for having an understanding of a game that he was intimidated by. We are fixing to watch a movie and call it a night. Good Night Lord, thanks for another sober day.

7/26/2010

Good Morning my Savior. Please grant me another sober day. Not much on the agenda today, I'd like to work out and go to a meeting before Austin wakes up. I need to call Bill today and see what the plan for Atlanta is. I know Austin is looking forward to flying on his plane. I look forward to it every time I go. I haven't seen Bill for awhile now and I look forward to spending some time with him also. Our personalities are very different, so I enjoy his stories and he enjoys the advice I give him. We are brothers from a different mother and I love my brother. I have some great fear about the path my brother is on and who am I to preach about Demons? I will take my Father's advice and "Plant Seeds" and I will learn from my mistakes of the past, so I do not over water "IT". I can only pray that the seeds will take root, but they must first be placed into the subconscious. We have all heard that we shouldn't do something and we do it anyway. Show me how you were able to bring yourselves up from the pits of Hell here on Earth and strive to live a life without Demons. We all stumble, but which Demons are robbing you of the most? Let's start with those first. The mind altering Demons. I have to be able to make good decisions in order to perform my purpose in life. Even as painful as life can be. Do you remember when Wallace (Braveheart) refused the mind altering drug before he was tortured? He

123

said he needed to have his wits about him. There is a time to focus and there is a time to play. If you want to endanger your own life fine, I will pray for you, but don't endanger the lives of your brothers and sisters in Christ. Haven't you ever heard that there is a "TIME and PLACE" for everything? How many fingers must you lose before you catch on?

Hey I'm back and Austin is still asleep. My mind is still running in so many directions Lord. I am wondering if I have told them everything You want me to tell them. I pray that you allow me to hear the words on my heart, so that I might be the witness I was intended to be for You. Am I done Lord? Next week I will start the final edit hopefully and then off to the presses. I am so ready to be done Lord and slip into an anonymous Witness for You. I want to Witness Your Mighty Hand Heal Your Children and harness our Demons for a thousand years. A World of Peace and Love is pretty mind boggling. I pray we have not moved so past You, that we can not come home to You. What is Your Will for me Lord? Have I done all in my power to be a humble servant for You Lord? Will this testimony of a poor wretched sinner, change the direction of Your World? I believe "IT" can, but what do I know. I'm just a drunk that was saved by You and I will not remain silent about "IT".

Played Cashflow with Brian and Kim tonight. Austin won and did a great job as an auditor and coach. You learn a lot more when you can coach someone else. They make you accountable to know what you are teaching unless you silence them about your own ignorance.

Going to call it a night. Good Night Lord, thank you for another sober day.

7/27/2010

Good Morning Lord, please grant me another sober day. Our plans have changed due to a death of a friend. The funeral is on Friday, so we will not be going to Atlanta this time. These are the most difficult to understand Lord, the deaths that cut an inspiring life short. He was a young, vibrant, well spoken and a driven man. He found himself very comfortable in an environment of his peers that were all of a different race than himself. He conducted himself in a manner that was accepted by his peers, regardless of his race. I am so happy to be seeing this. Not just the acceptance, but the desire of a minority to strive for more and his fellow majority brother is there with his hand extended in acceptance and friendship. God must have a special purpose for this special young man, He literally opened His mouth and swallowed him. Our friend was taken from us in an undertow of the seas, I pray that the memories of overcoming racial boundaries will continue. I believe that our lost friend, if given the opportunity, would witness for the Lord telling everyone that Racism can be overcome. I believe he would tell you that it requires work from both sides. I believe that if this message can get out, he will have served his purpose for God and mankind. He will have planted his seed before meeting his Savior. Til we meet again my friend, thanks for fighting the good fight. Rest in Peace my brother of a different color.

Oh BTW, this is ironic. He was a Bailey and we all know about those Bailey's don't we?

"You just can't keep those Bailey's down, can you Mr. Potter?" - It's a Wonderful Life

I was just reflecting on my appearance last Christmas. I was in a full blown manic state of mind and I was going to do what I wanted to do, regardless of what others thought. There was no way I could have gotten a job and been accepted by my peers with my appearance. It did not effect them, I did not need their approval. It was when I discovered that I was embarrassing my son I realized that my appearance was not acceptable as a witness for our Father. I don't believe He would approve of my appearance, the first thing my peers see and judge me by.

I was watching an episode of "Curb Your Enthusiasm" the other night. The message was about "Casual Friday" and how the people that engage in a professional relationship don't appreciate the lack of seriousness taken by someone that will be handling their personal affairs based on their appearance. You do have to dress the part to be accepted as someone that takes life serious, when life needs to be taken seriously. Your peers do not have time to examine your heart at first glance, they judge your appearance and label whatever your demeanor personifies by that first impression. Look at yourselves, would you take yourselves seriously if you were wanting the Lords trust, let alone the trust of a potential client or friend? Do you believe your appearance exemplifies what our Father would approve of? Your Father approves of "Clean" and your brother approves of clean cut. Your brother will discover if you are pure of heart only after further examination of the decisions you make daily and so will your Father. Will your appearance allow you the opportunity for your brother to see your heart like only your Father can? If my financial planner were to conduct his business in the hot sun, I would anticipate him to dress comfortably, yet appropriately. If his business is to be conducted in an controlled environment, then I would still expect comfort ability and professionalism. We are not bartering at the fruit stands, we are building life long trust.

I'm going to take Austin to my folks today, we'll have some lunch and play Cashflow. Austin didn't want to play Cashflow last time, so I kicked his ass at Risk. LOL Since he has won the last two times at Cashflow even met with more challenges of different players, he is on fire to prevail more. I am so proud to have a son that has begun to understand financial intelligence. How many 14 yr olds do you know that know what a financial statement is? All it took was some seeds and a path, now I will sit back and watch it flourish with loving guidance. I can live vicariously through my son and bring him to know the Lord next (seeds have already been planted) and I won't over water. He's on his own with the chicks, I still don't have them figured out. He's a cutie, it will be interesting to watch. I'm afraid those are lessons that can only be experienced, not articulated. How does one explain clearly the pain derived from a broken heart? Our Christ, Our Savior has a broken heart right now for His (2nd Wives). He has a broken heart for all of us, His children.

I understand why You my Savior could not tell us everything while You were here gracing us with Your presence. You had too many seeds to plant and the only option was for You to go away and send the Wonderful Counselor. Thank you Lord for opening my eyes so that He may counsel me. I experience the same as I try to plant seeds in James Austin. He rebels when I try too hard to mentor. I could have said screw it, let him figure it out for himself. Instead I chose to plant seeds as You said to do and allow them to take root when he was ready to begin farming for a bountiful harvest. I am here for him, just as You are here for me, him and all of Your believing Children. Children of Faith for a loving forgiving God.

Lord, I am selling my ass off to Your children to believe in You. I pray I do not over sell and lose them. I just believe that these things you put on my heart are things you want me to share with them. My everyday occurrences emulates everyone's life at some point in time in their own lives. I pray I can witness for You Lord as they make their own free will decisions of who to serve. I pray to emulate You my Lord and Savior. I pray for Your Forgiveness when I fall short and make amends swiftly and accordingly. I pray to learn from my sins and to share with others when appropriate.

127

If you struggle with a heart that is too big or the nuts to face confrontation, reread my letter to my friend and brother in Christ Bill Holmes of Holmes Motors Inc. I was watching Hell's Kitchen last night with James. Just as Bill was Billy when I first met him, Austin has grown to be James, not Jim, James and I will make it a point to call him a name worthy of his knowledge that I have instilled into him and he has accepted. Anyway, the owner of this restaurant was a pathetic worm of a man. He broke down in tears and explained that his own inadequacies were derived from a driven, not loving dad. Once the mirror had been placed in front of his face, he knew he had to grow some balls and do what needed to be done for the well being of all that counted on the Legacy that his dad had left to him. The Legacy needed his leadership so that he could continue to provide well being to all that depended on the success of the business. If you are a business owner, I implore you to surround yourselves with employees that understand your success is directly related to the enthusiasm of it's people that strive to be the best at what they do and compensate them with praise and a just wage. The ones that you pamper will never fulfill their purpose until they understand the purpose of a team. So get rid of them and allow them to find themselves somewhere else. God is working here and "IT" shows.

I just got off the phone with Carli. She says she will be done with the edit this wkend. I am so ready to get started on the final edit. I don't know what the hell I am in store for, because I don't remember what I wrote. I have scanned through and I know I'm not crazy, just very drunk and raw. You know the old saying, you tell the truth when you're drunk. I'm getting very excited about watching Christ battle my Demon myself. I can't wait to eat popcorn and watch "IT" at the theaters. I'll be having a non-alcoholic beverage of course. LOL You can not tell me any of your sneaky shit that I have not already done or thought of. We can be geniuses when it comes to concealing our medicine/Demon.

Lord, I am not sure how we will end this conversation. Have I told them everything that You want me to share? Talk to me straight tonight brother. I want to be the Witness that You were expecting to show up.

Why do you ask me if you are done? Are you done? Is this not your cleansing? How far must you run to out run your Demons? You place your power in Me, I give you the power in you through Me. Your Faith in Me has cured you of your Demon. But beware, your Demon waits patiently for you to serve him once again. He is always there for you, just as I AM. Trust in Me as I have put My trust in you. My brothers and sisters of one true Father our Creator, our one true God.

I still don't think I got a clear answer, so I guess I will be done when I am done.

I WILL...
BE DONE
I AM...
DONE

God, I dig it when Your Words Live, but they are up for interpretation again. We can all fill in our own dot dot dot's, so I guess that is the point of the dots. We get to fill in the dots of our own lives to determine if we are done or not. Let Your Words speak to their heart Lord, they know their dots and spots. It is difficult to change the spots of a Leper, but it can be done with the help of a perfect brother and imperfect brothers and sisters in Christ as we all are or can be of our own free will. You have to ask yourselves will you witness for our Savior, fulfill your purpose for Him and be done. I am fulfilling my purpose for God and I will never be done witnessing for You Lord. Until that great day comes that I get to meet You face to face.

Speaking of being done Lord, I'm tired. Thanks for another sober day. You are a great God. I am so thankful to have a personal relationship with You. It's just too easy to talk to You, You are such a great listener. I'm still digging the idea that my acts will enable King David and King Solomon to be done. I pray this will finally enable them to enter the Kingdom of Heaven where they may find rest and comfort with the Father who art in Heaven. Good Night my Lord and Savior. Good Night my Father in Heaven. Good Night my Wonderful Counselor. I pray the Three Heads will look over me and guide my thoughts to be as Christ like as a sinner can confess and witness for the Glory of thy God. I look forward to talking with You tomorrow, don't keep me up all night Lord. I'd love another drunken chat with You, but I know that a drunken witness is not a witness for You at all. A drunken witness is a witness for our Demon. I pray that I have witnessed for my Demon enough. I pray that You use me as a witness for my Demon to help Your children learn from my Demonic witnessing. I can hear the gnashing of teeth coming from my Demon. He promises me so much. He lies about what he will give me. I know what the outcome will be if I surrender to his temptations. Somehow, I just don't feel alone to fight this Demon any longer. I do not have the uncontrollable urges any longer. You have Your foot upon my Demon and I have Your shield around me. I am in Your Rocking Chair, like Smokey and the Bandit. I Am safe in Your Loving Arms. I Will allow No Demon to hurt me tonight. Tomorrow is another day and the SON of God will come out tomorrow, you can bet your bottom dollar tomorrow. Dollar Hell, I have my whole life on the line. I have placed my bets on my Savior. Go ahead and "SPIN IT", I don't even have to look. My face is upon my Savior's feet, I am His humble servant and no longer a slave to my Demon alcohol. Cigarettes, "YOU"RE NEXT"!!!

My mind is racing tonight Lord. My impatience is getting the better of me. I know that Your Will will be done when You Will it to be done. It is my Will that I grow impatient with. Please accept my humble apologies for being an inadequate servant. I know I must wait upon You, hand and foot.

7/28/2010

Good Morning God. Please grant me another sober day. I'm headed to pick up James and bring him home. Six hour round trip. Ugh It's all good though, I'll have a lot of driving time to really pray without any distractions. Just don't put too much wisdom on my heart, I am not going to write it down, so don't waste it. I'll be right back.

K...Drive Careful.

I'm a little tired tonight, but I have a lot to discuss with You in the morning. Thanks for the Revelation on the ride back home. We'll talk about that and the seed that I planted in my new Leper friend. Good Night Lord, thanks for another sober day.

7/29/2010

Good Afternoon Lord, Please grant me another sober day. I just got off the phone with a great friend Carolpaetra. We had a lengthy discussion about a lot of things going on in each of our lives. My passion controlled the direction of the conversation, but that is nothing new. It has always been about me and I am working on that. It is just that I am passionate about witnessing for You and looking for any kind of sign that will help for You to touch their hearts. She has suggested that I see the movie "Julie and Julia", she says I may get something out of it. I will let You know, I'm going to watch it today. I pray that it inspires me to deliver Your wisdom.

I pray that Your children will believe, that I believe in what I am doing for You my Lord. Your humble servant can only pray for that awareness. It is up to each and everyone of them to determine what their own belief in a Higher Power is to them and be willing to accept You as their Judge and Jury, not their peers. Have You been chipped away from our lives so much, that we fear of being ostracized from our peers if we witness for You? Have You been chipped away from our culture so much, we can't see that our own survival will only come if "IT" includes You. Our one God and Creator. One Son that gave His life for ours and One Hell of a Wonderful Counselor that speaks to our hearts? Three Heads in One.

I struggled with the Holy Spirit Lord. I didn't know how to listen with my heart. I can see it in my own writing, it tracks the progression of when I allowed the scales to be removed from my eyes and see and hear with my heart. I was trying to communicate with you Lord, but I was to involved in what was in it for me at first. I had a motivation and honestly, I still do. But You have allowed me to see past me and the benefit Your Gift will be to all mankind eternally. I feel on my heart that I must put my life on hold and become the witness I was intended to be. I pray that I can accomplish this task soon Lord. Your humble servant is just about fed up with being in Limbo. I want to achieve balance in every arena of my life. I have financial intelligence. I have spiritual awareness. I want a relationship with a partner that desires to please me, as much as I desire to please her. I pray that You will grant me the latter once I allow You to defeat and remove my Demons. Until then, I am not sure where You will take my life. I'd like to witness for You worldwide at anonymous meetings. I pray that is Your Will, not mine.

Satan has won, I am defeated. This is how I felt Lord, this is how I felt when I begged of Your assistance. I was powerless over my Demon. You took me as I was, with a "AS – IS" disclaimer and allowed me to bring my Demons. Only You could have conquered this Demon and You must remain with me, for I Am to weak to be alone. I Will store You in my heart and bring You out anytime I need to make a decision. My decisions will be Christ Like as much as a wretched sinner can pray for. When I fail, I will immediately ask for forgiveness and make any retribution required for the well being of my brother in Christ. I pray that I will learn from my shortcomings and the shortcomings of others.

This is my last thought before I go get that movie, but I had to put on down on paper before I forgot "IT". On the way home with James Austin, I tried to tell him where his own family fit in to the Cashflow game. His Pop Pop had gotten lucky with some real estate deals at the end of his life, but his life was his work and at 70 yrs old with cancer, he still had to report into to work to get a check to survive on. My parents did not live the materialistic facade, yet retired in their 50's. I had been on the materialistic path and failed. I had been restored with a new Faith.

"Julie and Julia" Movie notes:

A blessed life

A life of struggle

Her passion became her release of anxiety

Acceptance of the gift of ADD

Worldly friends and confidence

Plastic friends and self-esteem

A deranged challenge 365 days

Time is always a challenge

A mentor looking to fulfill a void and a mindless search to find it

Reality check from family to kill your dreams

She is challenged to fulfill her passion

In her mind, she has a personal relationship with her icon

She desperately wanted some encouragement and when she thought she would have her first fan, it ended up being a crab.

I love how Julia's dreams were challenged by a pompass ass and she rose to the challenge, put in extra time and her heart.

Julia seems to have a supportive spouse and she fulfill his erotic desires. She also affirms his importance to her and to his work. Then he turns around and reciprocates with a compliment of love. Appreciation can be so heart breaking and fuel you to do more.

"These things are as hot as a stiff cock", Julie is shocked to see a different side of Julia.

Julie gained encouragement from followers.

Julie began to study the life of her icon and began emulating her.

Julie's friends figured out a way she could financially facilitate her passion through pay pal and the help of her fans.

Julie acknowledged her spouse and icon as her means of getting through life with contentment.

Rut Roe, "too much food and not enough sex".

Vanity has begun to set in. I have a following.

Julia listened to advisors and circumvented her opposition, the one that prevented her from fulfilling the recognition of her achievement she so desired.

The fights begin when Julie's passion becomes the focus.

The frustration sets in as the hurdles mount, but Julie receives a phone call from a reporter, she bounces back to 100%.

It was cool to watch Julia's husband defuse a confrontation by excusing himself to dance with his wife. Sometimes you just have to walk away from people that refuse to see a different side.

Julie's passion for her icon continues as she feels a spiritual connection with Julia.

Julie and her husband find light hearted humor at her icon's expense.

It was interesting to see another cook book author that was swindled out of her dream. Her dream didn't seem authentic though, because she had not tested all of the recipes. She was in it for the quick bucks for herself.

The enthusiasm that Julia had for someone loving her book was inspirational.

Just when Julie thought she might be getting her big break, then life dealt her a curve ball. When her support team came to the rescue, she bit his head off. She chased her passion until she chased off her husband.

Many distractions kept Julia from completing her passion.

Watching the partners splitting up perceived future profits and demanding a fair share for a fair share of the work is something we all deal with. Then the slacker of the group plays on the others empathy. Julia caved in and the other partner picked up the slack and did what was fair and needed to be done.

Julia's husband gets grilled by his employers and begins to question what his career was all about. Then finds comfort in knowing that Julia is pursuing her passion and she graciously included him in the efforts. He felt contentment by helping to fulfill the passion of his partner in life.

Julie begins to take a personal inventory and realizes that her world was way out of balance without her supportive husband. She respects his wishes not to share their dirty laundry with the world.

Julie is warned by her employer to not let her passion interfere with her companies objectives. She is also warned that not everyone wants to have their own anonymity broadcasted for public scrutiny.

Julie is so wrapped up in her own world, she forgets to be empathetic to her friends world. The moment she tries to be empathetic, the conversation is quickly reverted back to Julie. She is drawn to a vision of her icon as always one that would be empathetic.

Julie so wants to emulate Julia, but falls short and is learning from mistakes.

The loneliness sets in and the struggle to rekindle a relationship begins.

Once Julie had overcome her obstacles, her dream killer wants to encourage her to continue without a lot of empathy of others left in the wake.

Julie accepts the situational loss and begins to pursue her passion, just when her better half shows up to reunite their lost love.

Julia is asked to revise her work, she is asked to revise her passion. She is asked to shorten her passion due to the shear length. She begins to question her publisher's authority on her passion.

Questions arise as to the purpose of their passion. "We wanted to write a french cook book for American woman who do not have cooks". Julia is re-energized with a challenge to complete her passion. She wanted her passions to come in volumes, so as not to take anything away from her passionate followers.

Julie regains her focus, now that she has regained her balance in life.

Both Julie and Julia begin to find love again as their passions draw near to reality and finality.

Julie tells an authority that she dreams to meet Julia one day. She explains she feels Julia's precense

The reporter that crushed Julie's heart, but not her spirit.

7/29/2010

Good Morning God. Please grant me a sober day. I am sooooo.....pissed. As you might notice, I didn't thank you for a sober day for 7/27/2010. That's because I lost a day and a half worth of work. I will take that as a sign; "This is God reminding Nathan to shut up". I was wondering how I was to finish this. With help from my new friend Carol suggesting a applicable movie for me to watch, You have shown me exactly how I should end this. I will take this weekend off Lord to pray. Next week I will start the final edit of Your prophetic book and fulfill my purpose for You.

You are a great God. I am dealing with making amends to people that I have harmed in my lifetime. On the financial aspect of my transgressions, there lies a $4000 debt to a man that actually introduced me to my very good friend and brother Bill. I repaid him by stiffing him when my business went down.

I am also presently faced with another financial quandary. My new friend Carol has found herself with no transportation. I owe her nothing, she owes me nothing. We have just become close friends and I can count those on one hand. I don't want her to feel obligated to me, so how can I help her without her feeling that I am doing this for self serving reasons? She is pretty hot after all.

I have heard from some pretty reliable sources that when they made financial amends, their victims don't seem to react anything like they were expecting. Their apologies came from their hearts and pocket book, only to hear, are you crazy or just plain stupid? Or does this make you feel better now?

It sounds to me that that money had been written off years ago. I'd rather put it to good use for someone that I care about. You are a brilliant God. I'll buy a $4000 car for Carol and send the title to my victim and let him collect my debt over time that is comfortable for Carol.

Is that bad of me Lord? To use someone else to pay my debts? I call it financial intelligence and being a better Witness for You. The way I see it is, my victim is being reimbursed, my friend is getting transportation and I am receiving the forgiveness I desperately need to achieve balance. Without balance, I will never achieve Self-Actualization. I will also guarantee the note to my victim. If Carol doesn't pay it, I will. I want to trust in people again.

The Wisdom of my brother King Solomon is awesome, but my personal favorite is WWJD. What Would Jesus Do?

Lord, I just told Carol what I was doing and told her I'd draw up a contract. I know contracts forwards and backwards, but I want her to have a contract from God.

I, Carolpaetra, hereby understand that I am entering into a state of indebtedness for the amount of ($4000.00) four thousand dollars.

For that debt I will have possession and use of undetermined automotive collateral valued in excess of $4000.00.

I will make payments of $100.00 month to an undetermined victim of Nathan's and receive title once collateral is paid in full.

Times that I can pay more, I will.

If I can not meet this obligation, I will write a humble apology to my debtor and make an earnest attempt to catch up.

I understand that there will be no interest on this debt.

I understand that I will maintain state law by carrying at least minimum insurance and accept my debt regardless of the condition of said collateral after possession.

I understand that no one will repossess this collateral for debt.

I understand this debt will bug the hell out of me, because it is a debt to God and He has answered my transportation prayers.

I will humbly give thanks to Him daily and twice on Sunday. LOL That is actually the fun part when you develop a personal relationship with Him.

I understand a signature is not needed, a handshake and prayer is still a bond in Heaven and in my heart.

I pray that my victim will find forgiveness in his heart towards me and empathy towards his new sister in Christ, so that they may become life long friends.

X_____

"Sign your name across my heart, I want You to be my Savior".

Good night Lord. Thanks for another sober day.

7/31/2010

Good Morning Lord. Please grant me another sober day. Another financial quandary is headed my way. I pray that I will take the time to pray about my decision. You know I will be giving "IT" to You for Your approval for my heart. I watched Julie and Julia again yesterday and saw a different movie the second time. I will do the review on Sunday, I'd like to absorb the characters a little more. I think it is a great illustration on how we can emulate our icons. My icon just happens to be Christ. TTYL on that one k.

There really is just so much to say Lord. I pray You will reveal to my heart any shortcomings Your humble servant may have omitted.

I WILL SEE
I AM HEART
YOUR BROTHER I AM
I WILL FOREVER BE

Cool, You are a poet and I didn't know "IT". LOL You can be just so damn deep though. Carol bitches at me about being deep so much. I want to have a lighter essence. When this is complete, will You lighten my load on my heart Lord? Financially, we're good. More would be great, but not necessary for my contentment. My contentment can only be fulfilled when Your children accept You as their Lord and Savior. I must succeed in delivering Your Gift Lord. If their Salvation comes with a check, maybe they will listen. Lord, I think the only way that I will find rest in my mind is to witness "IT" for myself. Father, please let my brothers David and Solomon rest, just as I have humbly requested for myself. My mind is like a pinball machine Lord, promise me You will turn it off when You're done. We do want to save on energy and be ecologically minded. LOL True.

I pray this wonderful prayer of contentment:

God, please grant me
the **Serenity** to accept the things I can not change.
The **Courage** to change the things I can and
the **Wisdom** to know the difference.

You've given me the Wisdom of King Solomon and the Courage of King David, now Your humble servant humbly requests the Serenity that only You my Lord know at the right hand of the Father in Heaven. Please take Your Kingdom now before "IT" is too late. Steal their hearts Lord, steal them with the "Truth". There are many witnesses before me, like stars in the sky. They cry out to me for their own rest and "IT" tears me apart. They turn in their graves over regret. They regret they could not do more for their God and their Brothers and Sisters in Christ.

141

Just heard from Carli, she says that her edit is done. I'm so excited to get started. I asked her if the book impacted her and she said yes, but was struggling with it spiritually. Not exactly the comment that would inflate my ego, but after praying about it, it is the impression I want to leave. If "IT" has an impact, then people will talk about "IT". We all struggle spiritually, deciding who to serve as our God takes a lifetime of personal decisions. Then she expressed concerns over my well being, You know, a crazy check. I told her "Thanks, No Worries".

This is a tough world to be a Jesus Freak. If I were lugging a real cross down the road, I probably would be questioning my sanity more. I carry a "Gift" and I store it in my heart as I proceed through my own Life. I would have never attended the party, had it not been for my Lord giving me a Gift to give to you. I told Him how ungracious you are, I told Him who you are when I told Him about myself. I don't remember the cats name (maybe Ezekiel), but stubborn is the right word, but just does not convey justly. I hate to add words, but let's add assholes. We all got one right, you stubborn assholes. LOL Especially my stubborn saved ass. Oh yes my brother, I said Saved. Do you want what I have? I abso-freaking-lutely want to give it to you. I have it right here in the bag I stole from the Wizard of Oz. I promise to give it back to him when I get there.

What is "IT"??? I Am Dying here.

K...here you go.

What's a freaking mirror have to do with the Tea in China? Let alone my Salvation?

Christ, I'm going for a smoke. I know, don't give me shit about it. Why don't You tell them about the mirror? No parable shit though. Of course unless you think it is appropriate. I must watch my arrogance.

MIRROR, MIRROR
ON THE WALL
WHO'S THE FAIREST
OF US ALL

LOL Holy Shit, I forgot about that one. That's funny. We already know when we see You my brother, that we see perfection. What do we see, when we see me? Please Don't say cringe.

ASK HEART

You know, I think we may have already discussed this topic. I was pioneering ground that did not need to be pioneered. The path was there, I could not see "IT" for the weed. A honest, personal self evaluation is crucial to find out who we are, so that we might witness for who You are. Our Savior.

Lord, I mentioned another financial quandary earlier and it is noon and I have not received a call. (2nd Wife) sent me a text yesterday with a plea for financial help. I was busy with You and didn't hear the beep. I sent her three text back, a phone call and then an email via Facebook. She replied late in the evening saying she had not seen a missed call on her phone and that she would call in the morning. I know all to well that feeling of pride that does not allow anyone any degree of self-esteem. Humble Pie sucks, but I have acquired a taste for "IT" and wish to cut you off a big slice for yourselves. Hold your nose, lick the salt off your hand and bite into this lemon, then just shoot it down real fast. You like the effects afterwords, but despise the after taste. If you are the one hosting this humble pie party, make sure you bring something refreshing to wash it down with. Not a constant reminder of the shit you just made somebody eat. I am so blessed to have had a slice from my parents that included whipped cream and milk. I know that this is the right recipe for anyone's appetite. Only you get to decide whether you will be serving humble pie or shit on a shingle. If you are the recipient of one of these, be

143

humble and gracious. Shit on a shingle is better than no shit when you're desperate. You get to decide if you would like to ask for "more please". You may ask of the Father endlessly and eternally. You may ask of your brother when you are truly in your time of need and not there for him to be your facilitator. There lies your answer of which kind of pie you will be eating today. I do love me some humble pie, but I am very careful not to ask of my Lord until it is truly my time of need to have some.

I made my decision Lord and will live with the consequences. Bill will think I'm a pathetic chump, but it really doesn't matter what anyone thinks. It matters what I think. It matters to me what I think You will approve of. I can't see the Lord refusing me or serving me shit on a shingle. I see it as a metaphor for accepting something from someone and allowing your heart to taste "IT" or to serve "IT". Whichever side of the kitchen you find yourselves on. None of you can tell me honestly you have not tasted "IT" or served "IT" in your adult lives. Do unto others as you would have them do unto you. Open your humble pie house and serve only the best, even if you did not get the best, serve what you prayed for when you placed your own order or future orders.

Lord, you have blessed me financially, but these pies can get a little expensive.

LOOK FOR THOSE
BARE NECESSITIES
THOSE SIMPLE BARE NECESSITIES

FORGET ABOUT YOUR WORRIES
AND YOUR STRIFE

You're such a silly brother of mine, I love you Christ. LOL This is the pie I will be serving today Lord. I pray "IT" is Your recipe.

Hey (2nd Wife),

I had to get this out in today's mail. I haven't heard from you, so I will just tell you I know how hard this is for you. Please tell me by accepting this from me, that you will ask again if you are in need. I am building something for us, if there will ever be an us again. I am living with a scar, but I am learning to live without you. I pray you know how deeply I care for you. Enclosed, please find $500.00 worth of Gift cards. I hope this will take care of Back to School and groceries for awhile. Let me know.

Your Brother in Christ,
Nate

P.S.
I AM PRAYING FOR YOU.
I WILL ALWAYS LOVE YOU.

Bill just called me and reminded me that next week is his birthday and he has plans to go to the Bahamas. As badly as he needs cars, some things just take precedence over business. LOL That was always a tough lesson for me, so I drank. I would takes trips and not even leave the farm. I feel bad that I am so self-absorbed that I didn't even remember my brothers birthday. But he shouldn't feel bad, I just started being able to see past myself enough to remember my parents birthdays, just a few years ago.

I informed Carol that it would be another week before I could get up there. Sometimes I just have to accept that my schedule doesn't always coincide with others and the universe just does not revolve around ME. I do not like giving my power over to others, but many times it makes more sense to let others lead and become part of the support team for a common goal. I can witness for Christ at the back of the line, just as well as the front. It might be a little harder to be heard, but I'll get there. Or my name in Christ is not Ophiuchus, just another drunk Nathan at the back of the line. The bottom of the food chain as perceived by my hypocritical peers.

I'm going to watch Julie and Julia again tonight when I get home from my twelve step meeting. It's raining like a bitch and I could easily make that an excuse not to go, but damn it, I'm still sober after 40 days. I told You that somehow technology swallowed my notes from the first day I watched it and I told you that I saw a different movie the second time I watched it. I asked Carol to watch it under the premise that Julia was Jesus and Julie was me, Nathan. She said she wouldn't do it, she liked to watch a version of the movie that had an appeal to her own personality and she is passionate about cooking. I think that is cool how we can all extract what we want to extract, pretty much on "Any Given Sunday". Okay, let's just let everyone play shall we. Watch the movie with the premise that Julia is Christ and the two of you have the same passion that fulfilled your life. It is a bond between you that does not require words. Now insert your passion. Mine was drinking and helping people.

You know, I'm not going to write that review because there were so many things that I could have expanded on, I would have had to write another book. Aint happening, I pray. I will just leave you this one thought. Did you allow yourselves to go with the flow of the movie and assume that Julia had said those dreadful things about Julie's blog? Or did you immediately think this reporter (man) was baiting a naïve dreamer to further advance his own career with smack spoken from Julie in a confused state of mind? Learn to pray before you speak, especially when someone speaks for someone.

I am a beaten man and I speak for Christ. It is written, I think, you can bash me all you would like. I really don't give a shit what you think of me, it is not your approval I seek. But you best not be bashing on the Wonderful Counselor, because your ignorance does not allow you to know Him in a personal way.

My 365 day challenge was to publish two books for our Father, the Son and my Wonderful Counselor. I will accept no hurtful opinion of man, I want to hear it from my brothers lips that I have not done all in my power for His Glory, not mine. I chuckle at myself now reflecting on the time that I questioned myself who this Wonderful Counselor was. He is Christ when I allow Him to speak to my heart. It is wayyyyyyy....cool.

What a great day I have had Lord. Thank you for keeping me sober. I just feel like dancing tonight Lord. I want to feel Your warmth, I want to feel Your Love. Make my ass tingle Lord, You know what You do to me. Start from the left side of my brain and run through my body to my toes. Cleanse me of my sins Lord, I beg of You.

I pray to You my Father, please grant Your humble servant the opportunity to see what "IT" is that You have built in me. Jesus can't take back the lashes that I gave to myself God. I beg of you to give me the abundant life I want to live for Your pleasure. Take me now God, if that is Your Will. My soul is prepared for Judgment. But Your humble servant feels he may be able to be of more service to You for awhile longer. All I am is for You.

Good prayer Nathan. Our Father will let you know, just as He let me know. When that glorious time comes when we meet face to face, I will be here to comfort you and show You an even larger perspective of what we, together as brothers for one Father, have created and passed to mankind. Live everyday to the fullest. Love Life. I miss you all so very much. I want to heal you, but there is so much more I wish to give you from the Father. Even you Nathan, you have not seen anything yet. The hand of our Father is Earth Shaking.

What are You telling me Lord? Don't put that earthquake shit on me, I already took responsibility for the damn oil spill. I being man that is.

It's in our Father's hands, not mine. I Am a servant for the Father just as you.

Well, at least put in a good word for us to the Father.

I left you many, seek me, seek your purpose for me, seek your purpose for our Father and you will live an abundant Life. I promise. I sent you the Wonderful Counselor didn't I? I keep my promises and so does the Father. I await for my Everlasting, Earthly Kingdom as I was promised. It is the responsibility of my brothers and sisters to build this for Me in praise of the Father. I so want to hold your hands again. I so burn to minister to you. I so want to save your soul. So many have been lost to Satan and "IT" breaks my heart. Come back to Me, I Am your bridegroom. Don't leave me hanging.

You're cool. After all of this time and all of the things we have done, You still love us don't You? I do too my brother, but I really got sick of them. HA, so who's crazy now?

You are certifiably crazy brother, didn't you get a certificate and a script? LOL The Father orchestrated the whole thing. I just had to watch as you stumbled. I was always there to catch you before you went to far.

Well, I wouldn't change a thing now that I am seeing my purpose. But Damn, it's been painful.

Brother, let me ask you. How do you see me claiming my Earthly Kingdom and who will deliver our Father's Gift that even I was not privy too?

Hey, Jesus Christ. That's not fair, I've already given them the answer. You're going to put me out of a job. LOL Just heard Tom Petty sing that on Breakdown. "Go ahead and give it to me". You can do it anyway you wanna do it babe. I think we all need to

148

breakdown the barriers that keep us from our primary purpose. To live a Christ filled life.

Nathan, I believe our Father hired the right man for the job. You are a hell of a salesman and since you have been in hell with them, you can sell them on our Father's Divine Plan. "The Gift". Remember, I Will be with you every step of the way. You have nothing to fear when you stand with Me. I Am your protector and shield. So let's cop a squat and watch "IT" play out. Got any Jew Jew beans? LOL

Nah man, I'm fresh out. I don't think I even know what those are. They're not in my frame of reference. Try one of the tootsie pops, I have a question to ask You. LOL

The owl thing right? LOL Three!!!

You didn't give me a chance to ask.

All God's creations entered the Ark two by two. Three represents a a promise of a new generation.

Well that was what I was going to ask. How many generations will it take for Your Kingdom to be a Kingdom?

That is not my area, nor is "IT" the Fathers. "IT" is your area and the area of our brothers and sisters.

Hey brother, I'm a little tired. I think I will have a little more tofu and call it a night. Thanks for another sober day.

Think about "IT".

God Cha. Night Lord.

149

8/1/2010

Good Morning Lord, Please grant me a sober Sabbath. I have a confession to make this morning. Not only do I have the accountability to go to a twelve step meeting, but I was given a task from a brother. I know excuses are like assholes, we all got one, but my mind was wrapped up in You yesterday. I could have lied and told my brother I did feed the dogs last night, but my Father would know I lied. I could have let this shortcoming of mine rob me of a great day with You if I worried that my brother would find out if I am a liar. Because of what I learned from the steps, I promptly admitted my wrong doings and asked for forgiveness from my brother. I was forgiven and thanked for what I did do. Whewwww.....I feel better.

Some of the Lepers have spoken of going back to Church and having a different experience now that they are sober. I might give it a try today, I haven't been to a Church in quite some time. But I have been to a Worship Service daily while I try to become sober. We have a worship service that is a little different than the main service. I see it as Christ utilizing His body to heal many on the inside. All that seek help. I'm going to go, I pray that I will be able to hear Your message. I pray that I don't just sit there and make plans how this body of Christ will heal us on the outside as well as the in. God's Health Care Centers, the body of Christ. Don't just tell me how the body of Christ heals, "SHOW ME".

I was watching the news a few months ago and they were discussing the financial feasibility of saving someone with illnesses that did not have health coverage. I understand the financial aspect of this heartlessness, just not the empathy of man towards their fellow man. Who among you would offer up your own son as sacrifice to the concept of financial feasibility? Don't worry about picking up stones, here's a scalpel, slit His throat and decrease the surplus population.

Hey, I just got up from a nap after the service. I have been praying what to say, because this is Holy Ground that I am treading on here. I pray to You Father, Brother and especially You, my Wonderful Counselor. Don't let me screw this up. Today's topic is Facing the Future.

I enjoy the music during praise and worship time. I knew that I was in complete control on what I wanted to take out of the service. I could already sense the tenseness welling up in me as I entered into a den of hypocrites. I was looking sharp and had all of my defense shields up. I watched the hands go up to You Father and I so wanted to believe and join in with them. I so want to believe they raise their hands to You and not to their peers. One guy was dancing up a storm and doing many hand gestures. It reminded me of what I like to do when I am in the privacy of my home, for only You my Father to see my heart and for me to feel Your Loving Presence. Lord, I beg you to remove the cynical Judge in my heart that likes to play God. I do not know their hearts, I don't even know their names. When the hell did I get anointed to be their King? Rock On Brother, you worship anyway you see fit. I hope to join you one day.

The service started off with a baby recognition. The pastor explained that many Churches have a baby dedication with baptism, but the beliefs of his Church is that each individual must accept the Lord Jesus Christ as their Personal Savior to be baptized. He didn't go as far as to say, if you don't do "IT" this way, you're going to burn in Hell, but he did make it clear that there are different beliefs of the same God.

The pastor took a cheap shot at Astrology with no fear of retribution or substantiation needed for the claim. Just a blanket approach over Astrology, palm readers and Hocus Pocus. I believe the stars have been instrumental in guiding many cultures for many centuries. Do you think the compass we have today, would have worked back then? Probably so, but they didn't have one and used the stars to pinpoint many things, even the birth place of Christ Himself. No one bitched when the Three Wise Men showed up with Gifts of Gold, Frankincense and Myrrh. The latter two being considered more valuable than Gold due to their unique medicinal qualities. I mean really, when you are in pain, do you want medicine or money? Bring on God's Med's for my Leper ass, I've had enough of mans.

There once was a young Indian brave that began to question his existence. He went to his dad and asked him if there was any significance to his and his siblings names. His dad replied: I always look to the stars for guidance, then I look for the first thing that I see. When your sister was born, the first thing I saw was a beam of light coming from the moon. So I named her Moonbeam. When your brother was born, the first thing I saw was a deer running through the forest, so I named him Running Deer. Why do you ask Two Dogs Humping? LOL I thought it was funny.

BEWARE
FALSE PROPHETS
TRUST IN ME
IN GOD WE TRUST

Thanks for the sign Lord. Today's sermon is on James 4:13-17. And remember I just graduated my son to James. Ha, there's another 666 sign or is "IT" a sign from my Lord. I guess "IT" will depend on how I personally want to decipher the sign.

The scripture speaks of the confusion involved in interpreting God's Will. So they live day by day seeking His Divine Plan for their lives. The problem is, no one has revealed my Father's Divine Plan, the Seven Sealed Two-Sided Scroll, His Last Will and Testament. @my brother James. Please don't condemn me for boasting about revealing the Father's Divine Plan. I deliver His Gift under a humble veal of anonymity. I will remind you of

152

Your own words: "Remember, it is sin to know what you ought to do and then not do it." - James 4:17 I'm doing the best that I can with the talents I have been given by the Father.

The Parable of the Rich Fool – Luke 12 : 13 - 20

13Someone in the crowd said to him, "Teacher, tell my brother to divide the inheritance with me."

14Jesus replied, "Man, who appointed me a judge or an arbiter between you?" 15Then he said to them, "Watch out! Be on your guard against all kinds of greed; a man's life does not consist in the abundance of his possessions."

16And he told them this parable: "The ground of a certain rich man produced a good crop. 17He thought to himself, 'What shall I do? I have no place to store my crops.'

18"Then he said, 'This is what I'll do. I will tear down my barns and build bigger ones, and there I will store all my grain and my goods. 19And I'll say to myself, "You have plenty of good things laid up for many years. Take life easy; eat, drink and be merry." '

20"But God said to him, 'You fool! This very night your life will be demanded from you. Then who will get what you have prepared for yourself?'

21"This is how it will be with anyone who stores up things for himself but is not rich toward God."

This was the ending scripture of today's service. The pastor emphasized the three things you can do with your life and they were by his interpretation 1. Waste "IT" 2, Spend "IT" or 3. Invest "IT". I understand the first two, but Invest "IT" in what? God? Or the Church? Is the Body of Christ aka the Church, healing God's children so my offering is helping my brother and myself when needed? Or are you building new bowling alley's for outreach to those that fit in? Who's Legacy are you building as you make additions to your Churches? God's or your own? But who the Hell am I to Judge? Only the Father has that authority. Not even Christ, who will do His best to defend you before the Father, can Judge you.

Well Father, I should be getting started with the final edit tomorrow. I will end this book now, but I feel the need to continue the blog. My purpose for You has consumed me for the last six years and I could be consumed into a blog, but that is not what I was promised. That would not be an abundant life, would "IT"? I'm not sure, so I'll leave "IT" open. "IT" may be the best source for me to Witness for You Worldwide.

Good Night my Lord and Savior, thanks for another sober day.

8/2/2010

Good Morning God. Please grant me another sober day. I begin the final edit today, so I will be ending this chapter of my Saved Life with a prayer.

My Lord, the only begotten Son of God, my Savior and Brother. I pray to You to speak to our Father, for I know, no one reaches the Father if not through You. I am a Son of Man and a Child of God. I believe You gave Your Life for us, so the Father would forgive us of our sins. I believe You arose from the dead and now sit at the right hand of the Father. I believe You watch over me and sent the Wonderful Counselor to be my guide. I believe You speak to my heart, even when my heart could not hear. I believe I found my purpose for You when I went seeking "IT" and not my Demon. I believe You came back for me and saved me from my Demon. I believe when You told us You would be coming back, You meant You would be coming back through us as Witnesses for God our Father. My brothers and sisters in Christ may or may not believe in me, it is their choice. I believe if I were in Your Holy sandals, I would do the same as You for my brothers and sisters in Christ. I ask You now brother, Do You Believe in Me, Your Brother in need of keeping?

- Your humble servant Ophiuchus

I died believing in You. You ALL are my brothers and sisters of One True Father, our Creator, our GOD. I LOVE YOU WITH ALL MY HEART AND SOUL.

C U SOON

Are you speaking in tongues again brother? LOL At least I can understand You now. Let's not make it too soon, I AM...just beginning to learn how to enjoy this World our Father has graciously provided for us. If our Father has a say in the future, it will be bright from the light of the Son. If man continues to dictate where to steer this World, 666 has won and the destruction of our Father's Creation will come from the mind of man. Unless God Will's differently.

PRESS HARD
THREE COPIES
SALVATION

SOOOOOOLLLLLLDDDDDDD!!! All Three Heads get ONE.

Hey look, if you leave out the S on sold, you get 6 "O"'s, 6 "L"'s and 6 "D"'s. Whatever do you think "IT" means? Mom, Can you check my closet before you turn out the light? I checked yours. I hide my Demons there to play with later. What's your excuse?

"We All Got One"
ETCETERA...ETCETERA...ETCETERA...
NOW GO FORTH
AS SHEEP AMONG MEN
AND SHARE THE
GOOD NEWS
I WILL
MY KINGDOM
LIFE DEPENDS UPON
"IT"

Good Night Lord, thanks for another sober day.

8/3/2010

Good afternoon Lord. I've doing a lot of praying this morning about taking on the editing myself. I'm concerned about things that may have become lost and my context being altered to someone else's frame of reference.

I closed on the new house project yesterday and I am ready to hire a subcontractor to do the work. I got a call from a subcontractor that I've used in the past and I really like him and his work. It's a little slow, but who am I to judge, so am I. As long as I am paying for the job, I don't mind taking the extra time to help him out. The problem is, I suggested that he increase the tools of his trade and he chose not to. This job will require more tools than his he has in his box. I called another subcontractor that possesses all the tools needed for the job and I am willing to delay the project and pay extra for the convenience of not having to hire several subcontractors. By not inspiring to be more in life, cost my friend and brother in Christ the job. As much as it hurts me not to help him, I must consider the time taken away from my purpose by being to hands on to the job. My occupation is how I get paid and eat. My Lord is my Life and my Savior. I prefer to spend more time with Him, so I aspired to be more.

I had a great day of editing and ready to call it a night. Thanks for another sober day Lord. I am looking forward and dreading this task. I will have to revisit all of the emotions that tore me apart, I'm looking forward to the ones that make me laugh. I'm so excited, I'm almost done with my purpose for You. Then I can witness for You while I maintain my control over my own Demon alcohol.

8/4/2010

Good Morning Lord. Please grant me another sober day. I had a good morning with three friends. One is still a little apprehensive to believe, but believes that I believe. One believes to a point and is using what I have shared to develop his own passive income and the other is in total belief and giving me the encouragement I so desperately need to hear.

I won't be attending my brother's birthday trip to the Bahamas because my lifestyle does not fit in right now. I'm not drinking and I'm not chasing women. I have to clear my head and finish my purpose for God, so I can have peace and serenity. I could allow my feeling to be hurt by not getting an invite, but after the Super Bowl, Las Vegas and Billy Bow Legs, I best sit my crazy monkey ass at the house until I am completely in control of my Demons and focus on my sobriety, one day at a time.

Okay, back to editing the book. I know that I will have to expand upon the thoughts and I can do that on the audio version. I'm so excited to share my wealth of knowledge that the Lord blessed me with, by sticking a cattle prod up my ass to go and get "IT".

I was just thinking here while editing and wanted to remember to share this with you. After I spoke with Darren, he asked if (2ⁿᵈ Wife) had read what I had written her? I didn't know for sure, but I could only hope that she hadn't and I was mistaken about the warmth of her heart. If I were Christ, I would have to wonder where He stands with all of us, His (2ⁿᵈ Wives)? I guess that is why I stand with such a forgiving heart for (2ⁿᵈ Wife), how could she possibly understand my purpose for God, when my mannerisms exemplified a "crazy manic fuck" trying to deliver the Father's Divine Plan. But I do grow weary and I will move on with my life if man doesn't destroy "IT" first. Maybe whatever is left after a nuclear holocaust, our Savior can finally have His Kingdom. Because God will be all that is left for us to hold on to. As my Leper friends yell back to me; "Turn around, Go Back it's a DEAD END" I find strength that if they can do "IT", so can I. My ancestors scream to my heart the same thing, but they are referring to their revelation at their deaths; Coulda, Shoulda and Woulda. "If Only" I had known the truth and a personal relationship with a God as I know Him. Great emphasis on the "I" in this case. How personal are you with our God? I ask you this, if you were to keep a personal journal, would it be alright to share your thoughts with everyone? Question yourselves about the ones that you would not want to share with the class and determine in your heart if our Father would approve.

Calling it a night Lord. Thanks for another sober day.

8/5/2010

Good Morning Lord, I'm feeling good. I'm still battling these cigarettes on my own, but please grant me another sober day. I'm going to try eating some of that nicotine gum today. I'm hurting in my chest and I'm scared, but then again, I'm not. But I don't want to be stupid about "IT". "IT" is killing me and I can feel "IT". What is "IT" that I gain from "IT". If I were watching myself as a rat in a maze, I would be thinking: "Look at that one, he got one of his Demons removed by the Lord and then he jumps harder on another one. Put that on his record. I give him an "S" for STUPID. Make sure that he is taken care of, but don't give him any responsibilities. Anyone that stupid can not be trusted to care for others in the Kingdom of Heaven. He can certainly still come, the Father loves all of His children. "IT" just shows that he is not capable of making self-will decisions without Christ just yet and that's kind of stupid." But, that's the story with Man.

I found some problems in the book. I had double cut and paste a couple of things and that is why I thought I lost my Julie and Julia notes. So good, we will just have a movie review after all. After I finish this edit, I'm on a mission to be done.

Hey, went and looked at some houses with Brian and had lunch. Brian was telling me about one of our deals falling was through and I began to tell Brian how to do his job. I wasn't being hard on him for the deal falling apart, I was being hard on him for not following up with the customer. My training was they either buy or die. He already had this much time invested, he might as well try and overcome the objections and sell them something for his daily bread. It was just a few short weeks ago he was telling me he was desperate and the credit card business was his only option and it was what he "Had" to do. Now that a few things have changed in an ever changing career financially, he has forgotten what he almost "Had" to do and trimming out what he needs to do. This almost stemmed to a fight until I stepped in and apologized for trying to motivate him for more. The reason I owed him the apology is, I would have to ask myself what my own motivation level is at the time of encouragement, to make a honest assessment of how I would have reacted in his shoes. I think I will stick to planting quick seeds, some will find fertile soil and some will not and that goes for everyone, especially me. I'm a hard head. I knew there was an Old Lady there somewhere, but I could just not see her for many years.

8/6/2010

Good Morning God. I got so wrapped in You last night, I forgot to say good night in this journal. So thanks for the sober day and can I have another. My plans have been confirmed to see Carolpaetra this weekend and go to Atlanta. We are planning to see some body exhibit that she has mentioned an interest in and then probably do Six Flags on the way home Sunday. I really started digging the rides at the end of the day, the last time we went. I am also looking forward to the warmth of another human being that understands me a little. LOL It really is eye opening to realize that our society views people with outspoken positive views as a nuts and applaud the nuts that publicly denounce our Creator.

What do you have a think of that Mr. Spock.

If I have told you one time, I have told you a thousand times. Humans are not logical, you dumb ass. This is the last time I Will remind you.

We're at the end of our rope and if we don't let God into our World, our World will cease to be a World. I don't normally do this, please forgive me God for taking Your Holy name in Vain. I just think that this point needs to be emphasized with Your Holy Name. It would be a GOD DAMN SHAME to destroy such a beautiful Creation.

I'm sure feeling that old Indian crying feelings from my youth. I see His visions and I see mans, by envisioning the destruction already illustrated at the movie theaters. I just have to wonder how many signs do are dumb asses need before we realize that we are writing our own prophecy at the theaters. So the computers are what finally evolve for our God's entertainment. That makes a lot of sense, it has worked for our children and robbed them of quality family time. Spend some time with a child that is trained by a machine and then spend some time with a child that is trained by a loving parent. It will astound you. We have to accept that the home environment will not always be suitable to properly raise a child that has a gift and a desire to be more for the Glory of God. Our schools must take on this task. There is so much to talk about here, I just can't even begin to start. I will just say one thing in print and let you let your mind wander. Second thought, I'm not that clever. You give it to them brother it is You that I wish to serve.

TIME

That's "IT", Time? I feel You. We have had some great quality time You and I, haven't we?

YES
GOOD TIMES

I'm glad You're back.

I only left you for a time and now it is my time to comeback. Nathan, You have freed the genie of the bottle. You have rubbed that lamp hard enough that your brothers and sisters will witness the Holy Spirit through You. Isn't He just the most Wonderful Counselor You have ever listened to?

Whhooooooooaaaaaaa Lord. Let me catch up. Do you mean to tell me, that when I told you that all I needed was this lamp, this chair and these bottles and that's all I need, You were preparing me for when I ran out of the desire for more bottles. Let me sit down in this here chair and think about that for a moment. I have been rubbing the shit out of this lamp. I just didn't know how to have a personal relationship with You and neither do they. But they do now. LOL HooRay

161

Lord, if there would be one final wish in that lamp. I know I have used two and I hope they were not frivolous in thine eyes. Your humble servant has decided. If You were to grant me a third wish, I wish that my brothers and sisters in Christ, come to understand how to have that personal relationship with Jesus Christ our Lord and Savior and understand that we all are children of the same God. Lord, show us Mother Nature and stop all of this bickering between the Heat Miser and Mr. Freeze aka Dr. Jekyll and Mr. Hyde. I'm sick of "IT" and I'm sure You are too. You know, I never saw that movie, but I always referred to it when I was referring to my two personalities. I think I will need to go rent that this weekend. I'll try to remember on my way to Atlanta. I better write "IT" down.

VERY
COOL
I Thought
I Had

I thought so, but I'm trying not to get to cocky now that I'm Sober. LOL Hey, let me get back to editing before I pack. Love Ya.

K...Love You Too

Facilitating and Cash Flow

"You've Got To Give To God" - (2nd Wife)

I was just reflecting playing cashflow with (2nd Wife), her children and Austin. I always remember her making it a point to give to God when she landed on the spot. But when she drew the card for helping a relative, she opted not to help, the same as we all did.

I found myself playing with Austin this last time with the same mission that I had been on when I was chasing materialism. I just realized what I have done. I have put my son on the path of materialism equipped with financial knowledge, but with no spiritual awareness or empathy for his brothers and sisters in Christ. There is still time Lord, now that I have his interest with the Gold, I can now expose him to the God and teach him how to pray and hear You with his heart. Like a Snow Dad from Jack Frost.

The message that I take away from that card that is a desperate plea for help from a relative, really hits home this morning. My aunt is widowed, working and broke like the rest of us. She seeks advice from her sister, my mom. My mom is now seeking advice from me for her sister, my aunt. I guess I have rebuilt the trust that I once had. It would have been much easier to just not get involved, but this is my family and I am so alone and not alone.

We'll talk some more on this, I have a lot more to share. I have to get ready for the trip. Please pray for me, my brothers and sisters in Christ. You don't know me, but I know You. I pray for You everyday, You are my brothers and sisters in Christ and I gotta love You all. Yeah, Even You.

NATHAN'S
AUTO SALES
251-666-2345
WE FINANCE ANYONE
EVEN YOU

My brothers and sisters screwed me on that one didn't they Lord. Let me see if I can pull a little Voo Doo, Hocus Pocus out of my ass, so you can focus how man can manipulate man. Do you see the 666 in my business phone number. If man is the one, would that complete the sequence? If God were the 1, would He?

You could say, hey, you did that on purpose to manipulate us. Brother, when I made that sign, I was drunk and chasing the wrong dream. What does it mean to you? It means shit to me, but an understanding how manipulating predators can pervert the word of God when they present their own context of the context as long as "IT" fits with the "TRUTH" that has been instilled into their frame of reference since birth. Or they could just be screwing with you to get what they want. Pants on the ground, pants on the ground. We've been looking like fools with our Pants on the Ground. I haven't screwed with the interpretation of the 251, remember, it means shit. Be careful as you put your own dots together as you search for your own purpose for God. Many false prophets will help you to connect them for pay or status. Have a heart to heart with our Father, like you have now been trained to do and you will find the peace and serenity that only the Father, the Son and the Wonder Counselor can give. I am really digging the Wonderful Counselor who is in fact the Holy Spirit of Jesus Christ Himself. If it weren't for Him, I'd have no one to talk to, or even cared to talk to. He makes me see things differently and pushes me to re-engage. Talk to me Goose. Talk to me. Talk to me God. Talk to me. Let me listen for a change, after all it is "OUR TIME". Mr. Hand and mine. So who is sitting on the Throne with the Scroll in their right hand. Is it the Father or the Son?

You know Lord, I was just thinking. (A frightening thing, I know. - The Beauty and the Beast) The Father has always been portrayed as an entity, so the bodily vision that John had, must have been You, my Savior. You had been given the Will of the Father, but it wasn't the right time to reveal "IT". Lord, how could You have possibly explained "IT" any better than You did. I get "IT" and I'll explain "IT" to your children and mine

FAITH
HOPE
CHARITY
LOVE

FRUITFUL
BIRTHRIGHTS
LEGACY
KINGDOM
PEACE
HEAVEN

I'm not exactly sure how you want to title these ten proclamations, the Commandments has already been taken. LOL I see that we have made it to step 5. Be Fruitful and Multiply.

Sorry, I got hung up. - Rambo XX

Let's see here now. I have explained the birthrights as best I can. It will create everyone a personal Legacy and a Legacy for God. His Kingdom will emerge, grow our economy and heal the sick for free. We will live in peace as "IT" is in Heaven.

TEN STEPS TO
SALVATION?

I Love "IT" my brother. "Ten Steps to Salvation" "IT" Will be. Man, I better get in the shower, I'm going to be late again. I hate to leave You, but I really must go.

Well Good Bye my Brother
Good Bye

Silly, LMAO I'm going to spend some "Time" with someone that proclaims to be "LOVING LIFE" on her facebook page, but I know she struggles as we all do. TTYL

Thanks Lord for answering my silent prayer. I will let them build the consequence cards on Your New Game of Life.

8/9/2010

Good Afternoon Lord, thanks for keeping me sober, "IT" was an awesome weekend. I have lots of notes. I'm so glad Carolpaetra insisted I bring a notepad, although "IT" does become a way for me to get out of balance. I even suggested an egg timer for the amount of time I was allotted to Witness for You. They can stand only so much at a time Lord.

Well, let's go over my notes shall we. I know I left some blanks to fill in and I Will do my best to do Your Will.

I'm too tired. TTYL Thanks for a great sober day Lord. Good Night my Brother. I really can't wait to see You, but please give me some more time to do the Fathers Will if that is His Will. Ask Him for me please. Ask Him to grant me "Time".

Time has been granted by the Father. Rest tonight, chat tomorrow. The Father has been taken for granted long enough, "IT" is TIME.

"You Say You Want a Revolution"? How about a Reflection of my Revelation? Good Night my brothers and sisters in Christ. I Am really sick of you, but you are my family under One Father. My Blood – His Blood. I Will always care for all of you. It is His Will that I do so. My Will checked out years ago, I made a contract with Satan. I drank his blood and he drained my Life from me. My Ex-Master called me Slave, I gladly gave him my life progressively over Time. I allowed Life to beat me down and Satan/666/Mankind/The Beast had won. My Lord and Savior came back for me. He Saved me and can save you as well. I picked up my mat brother, I can finally see the fourth dimension. I left you a road map to a personal relationship with Christ. It is your decision which path to choose. This path is now written on the trees and will never be gobbled up by the Demonic birds again. Our Lord Lives. I really can't blame you for not hearing Him, I was pretty much a dumb ass too. There is a young lady and old, if you will look harder and with your heart. The signs are all around when you evaluate every decision by WWJD. When He truly is in your heart, He is all you think about and everything else works around His Will, not mine. I can't wait to see what the future prophets will think of to better their brothers lives when their creativity is not suppressed. This path only scratches the surface of the fourth dimension.

I want to talk to you about the Body Exhibit, but I've got to lie down now. BRB brother.

K

Real Quick. Carolpaetra said "THEY" couldn't determine if the Exhibit was art or science. Can't you see that it is both. "IT" is God's Greatest Creation, Mankind. "We've only just begun... to live". A World with You as my Shepard and I shall not WANT. I lie down now, in greener pastures. Speak to me Lord, I haven't had a dream in a long time. Put a thought on my heart Lord as I lie down to rest my body. How can your servant touch their hearts, so they may dream again. My dream is just a dream. My brothers and sisters in Christ can make MY DREAM a reality, by building Your Everlasting, Earthly Kingdom my Lord. My Savior.

When you trust Me, I want to know your dreams and nightmares. I want to know you intimately. I want to know your essence and soul. I want to know you eternally. I can only know you by your heart and the Father will be your Judge. Tell me what is on your hearts and give "IT" to Me. I AM... your biggest fan. I WILL...encourage you. Now pick up your Damn mat, leave your crutch and let's go Home. Your Loved Ones Await You.

I thought you said Good Night brother?

Yeah, well...it's a never ending party when you show up. But sometimes I do like "IT" when the Wonderful Counselor takes a nap.

DREAM TIME

8/10/2010

I am finding new clues, connecting more dots and confirming my purpose for God. When I analyzed the symbol of Ophiuchus, my assessment was from my heart. The little cross with the loop at the top, I proclaimed as being You and I. The Helpers. I have done further research on the little cross and it's called the Ankh of Tau, the Key of Life. I'd like for you see what I have found as I penetrate the fourth dimension and bring back information like an Avatar. I have got to watch that movie now. Tried to watch it all weekend with Carolpaetra, but it's three hours long. Damn that's long. There are so many other things to do when you have found the phallus of Osiris and have the eye of Horus the Falcon. A school will emerge and it will train children to understand the fourth dimension. Not everyone will be able to attend. Come, pull the sword from the stone for your personal admittance.

Good Morning Lord, please grant me another sober day. Sorry, forgot. I was just so excited this morning. No dream last night, but I did have a vision after I researched the Ankh of Tau. Please make them understand that "IT" is not a symbol that I wish to serve, but I do use them as signs from past generations to communicate a timeless message.

Quick note: Broken Contracts: They didn't even want to know why I wanted out after 6 yrs of loyal patronage. If they do not want to learn from their customers the mistakes that may have cost them the business and be of better service in the future, Let them fail. Does Christ have that same option?

168

I just looked at the next bill and they are charging me $45.00 for some charge that I am not familiar with. Now I have a cable bill that is $117.00 and I don't even have any paid channels like HBO and the clan. So of course I pick up that heavy ass phone myself and go through the whole hold process, wondering if I will speak to someone from Bangladesh. No offense, I just can't understand your ass. I was very fortunate this time, I could either go through the computer operated system that never works for me or I could incur an additional $5.00 charge to talk to the sucker over seas. The phone rings and it's Bill. I begin to tell him my dilemma and he empathizes with the businesses, saying, man, I'm sick of the whiney ass babies, it's only a few extra dollars to absorb business costs. I told him that he had missed the entire point of the confrontation. Businesses are being squeezed by our government and making cutbacks and raising fees or adding fees to what was once considered a free service for doing business with them. I am now to pay a bill for services once provided for free and the hidden tax is hidden from the ignorant that think they are being helped. THIS IS A SILENT TAX!!! You really didn't think Obama was pulling this money out of his ass did you? When you give shit away, somebodies got to pay for that shit. By the time that shit gets through all the hands that are greased, it's a smaller turd than one that would have been gladly given from the sweat from your brothers brow, rather than what your government made him shit for you to have.

I think "IT" goes something like; "You Make Your Bed, Now Lie In "IT"". I just had to make that point clear with the rod to my (1st Wife) that has requested more money for a daughter that I have no contact with for the last six years by her choice, not mine. (1st Wife) says Lauren was crying. (1st Wife) didn't inform Lauren that she was the one that created that bed and I told her to lie in it. The phone must have been awfully heavy for Lauren, I hope she can live with the shame I have caused her. My parents hearts have ached for six years over the loss of their granddaughter. Lauren got a check written to her today and I wrote what it was "for". "Court Awarded College Support". It broke my heart and I didn't put any cash nor a note in the envelope, as I had always done in the past. This was a cold hearted ruthless court awarded contract that could have been so much more for Lauren. She was robbed by the ignorance and greed of my (1ˢᵗ Wife) and I am just as much at fault for not being the man in the relationship and having a truly Godly Home when I was there. I am living with the repercussions of my own actions and decisions made, when I was young, dumb and full of cum. The altered mind just has to go without saying, if you were to know me. When will Dr. Jekyll be available? The appointment book became filled with Mr. Hide.

Sent: Mon, August 9, 2010 10:48:13 PM
Subject: Update

Nathan,
I have not heard from you concerning child support. Lauren is short $1000. this semester. The pell grant money she was getting through my taxes was cut this year. I feel really bad for her. My parents and yours paid for our education. We have let her down. She works very hard and was crying on the phone tonight because she has to pay her rent. She depends on your $350.00. If there is any way you can contribute more this semester it would be greatly appreciated.

Austin is starting back to school on Thursday and I need school supplies and clothes.

On Aug 10, 2010, at 8:00 AM, nathan isbell wrote:

(1ˢᵗ Wife),

I guess I let this month slip away. I really thought I had sent checks out. They will go out today.

Sorry,
Nathan

P.S.
I haven't heard from Lauren in Six long years, her choice, not mine. I will always love her, but we all make a bed.

(1st Wife) wrote:

Thanks for sending the child support check.

I understand but it takes two. It is not just her fault. She starts to maybe forgive you and you show up on you tube for all her friends to laugh at. Not good. You have to think about your children when you do things like that on my space and you tube. The internet can get you in trouble, you have to be careful.

You have been made to support her by attorney's. You have never given her anything from your heart. Just because you want to.

You have made your bed too. According to your websites, you are a Christian. You need to take a look at what you have done as a Christian for your daughter. Not helping others is not Christian.

The time has finally come Lord. It is time for Lauren to know the truth. I love how You arranged everything. What are the chances of a lost friend finding me after 30 years? What are the chances that he is in an authority position and has access to all Auburn University students? My friend offered to speak with Lauren before and I put him on hold. The time was not right because I have not finished my purpose, but the time is drawing near. I hated to hear that my daughter was suffering from humiliation created by me and her peers gained a laugh at my expense and hers. My heart breaks, but I will always choose God over anything or anyone. How can I turn my back on my Savior, especially at this point. Do

I have anything to lose with my relationship with my daughter at this point? I think not. I asked my friend to call her in and count out the remaining $650 she was short in cash . I asked my friend to tell her about me and her grieving grandparents, he knows us all intimately. I am very blessed to have a friend and brother in Christ to help me with correcting my Life Long decisions. If I had to choose who I would want to confront my daughter, it would be this brother. He has a passion in things that I have witnessed and when he gets on a roll it reminds me of me. LOL He has an inner strength that I am confident he will convey to my daughter. I pray that he can plant seeds, so she may begin to seek. She can start with where she comes from and work her way up to me being an Avatar teaching the World about the fourth dimension and blazing a trail for others to follow as they search for spiritual actualization.

How's this sound? Did you know that your dad is a recovering alcoholic that had a spiritual awakening and discovered his purpose for God in the process. Yeah, he has shown us by him going through the portal to God, how we can all have a personal relationship with our Savior. Some will be plagued with disease and others search to fulfill a void in their lives. Regardless, there is a path for others to track their own tears to achieve spiritual oneness with our Father, the Son and the Holy Spirit.

I don't know what to tell you my brother. I know you will do your best and your words will make much more of an impact than mine. In her mind and the mind of others, I'm Crazy. I pray for the Wonderful Counselor to make your words to my daughter, music to her ears.

IT IS TIME

Lord, the closer I become to the end, You keep putting more on my plate. I pray to You to allow your humble servant to finish his purpose for You and deliver the Father's Gift to all Mankind.

I'm tired Lord. Let's call it a night. Good Night my Savior, thanks for another sober day. How do Avatars sleep? I'm going to take a very large sleeping pill and go to bed. LOL No, I'm past that Hellish time in my life. I'll just lie down and dream of a world with You as our Everlasting King.

8/11/2010

Good Morning Lord, please grant me another sober day. Great Tofu this morning thinking of Carolpaetra. I needed to release that energy so that I can better focus on You my Lord. Let's finish this brother, I'm so tired. I am mentally drained, like a vampire that humans have sucked the life out of. I started to cut and paste all the shit about the Ankh of Tau, but let me read it all and give You my interpretation Lord. Oh Joy, another slippery slope. I will challenge them all to have a better understanding of You my Lord. I am a Nethinim and I do interpret signs from God. I do go through the portal of Life and bring back messages from the past to fix the future. I am closing in to finding my complete purpose for You my Lord. I know "IT", You are showing me how to explain "IT" to a generation that can't survive without "IT". "IT" is You, my Lord and Savior, my Brother in Christ, the Son of God. "IT" is proof positive to the Father, how much you love each and everyone of us.

Jesus loves me, this I know. For the Bible tells me so.

Nah, think I'll cut and paste. This is the opinion of someone else and like always, subject to critical analysis.

Really Lord, why are you blocking me from using someone elses words for credibility to point out the signs that I am following? Cut and Paste would be a Hell of a lot easier.

I ASKED YOU
YOUR THOUGHTS

K...I'll do "IT" under protest. Plagiarizing is so much easier. To explain "IT", I must understand "IT".

WAX ON
WAX OFF
LOL

Funny, just not too funny for me. I've painted Your fence, washed your cars, sanded your floors, "IT" has been a bitch to deliver this Gift.

Nathan, when you drunkenly installed your first garage door opener, you were reluctant to follow directions as you have always been. It took you all day and there were times when all seemed lost. You screwed up, but you successfully completed your assignment. How long would it take you to instruct someone else to accomplish the same task when you are in a sober state of mind?

"IT" really wouldn't take long at all Lord. I learned from my mistakes and had a guide the whole time. Maybe "IT" was my altered mind that created so much difficulty in the project.

NOW SHOW YOUR BROTHERS AND SISTERS HOW TO GO THROUGH THE PORTAL AND SPEAK DIRECTLY TO ME WITH THEIR HEARTS.

That could take a life time my Lord.

I KNOW

Damn, I was blocked again. I hoped there would be something on youtube. Guess I'm just gonna have to read. "IT" sucks, but vital. I'll talk to you in a couple of hours.

"IT" didn't take long after all, once I stopped going off in tangents and there were many to chase. Anyway, let me tell You my interpretation of the Ankh of Tau.

Help me Brother, I want to get this right.

CROSS

The cross represents protection to many cultures.

CIRCLE

The Circle of Eternal Life. Rebirth, Reincarnation, one lifetime is not enough to understand evolution.

DOT

The impregnation of a gifted reincarnated generation. Some will be born with Gifts beyond our understanding and need to be encouraged, not sedated. Their minds run wild trying to understand the void. Their Gifts will bring comfort to us all and they will have fulfilled their own purpose for God and profited from their developed wisdom.

AVATAR

One that has achieved Self-actualization and chooses to help mankind strive "at all costs", so the World may survive eternally. His purpose for God is an act of humility and selflessness. His Acts of Perseverance and Benevolence will be judged by the Father, not his peers.

ANKH OF TAU

The Key to our Father's Kingdom, a Key to Christs' heart and our own. A Red Phone to Christ to speak to the Father on our behalf, we are all so screwed up. A Portal in our hearts that allows Christ to penetrate our soul with the Wonderful Counselor.

Hey, that wasn't too bad. Let's get to the wkend notes now. I can't get my dragon to work, so I guess I will do "IT" manually again. Besides, I don't want to get to spoiled. I might perceive that I am entitled and get cut off all together. We will get cut off over and over again until we complete God's Will. The Eternal Circle of Life.

Daily Bread versus owning a bakery. Brian is coming over again to talk. We have been discussing many things that plague his finances. He spent an enormous amount of man hours learning a trade that would provide him with a passive income, but the rabbits have appeared again. "IT" is rabbit season and he craves their Lucky feet. I reminded him that rabbit season will be over again soon, just as "IT" always comes and goes. I insisted he hone his duck calls during rabbit season, so he will be prepared to hunt duck when the season arises. The importance of hunting ducks is not to slaughter them, but to raise them and live off their eggs. Rabbit season will be here again soon enough my brother, but the eggs will feed you your daily bread and you are the owner of the bakery.

If you missed the Lucky feet analogy within an analogy, you are not alone. You have not trained your mind to see more than just one frame of reference. The Lucky feet will provide the daily bread, but raising the rabbits will multiply rapidly. Let's raise both and slaughter what is needed for our daily bread and nurture what we need to survive without worry of starvation. If the marketability of the lucky feet goes down, we survive on the eggs. If the ducks stop laying, we eat them.

Let's begin to grow our Dream now that our daily bread is taken care of shall we. If you don't, I may be selling a Hummer for your relatives because you took your own life. You must have purpose to be alive or you will die and decrease the surplus population. What is your dream, have you been working on "IT" since your youth. Does "IT" glorify God or does "IT" glorify yourself? Pick up your Dream, or your shovel, your choice.

If you offer assistance to your brother or sister in Christ, you must search your heart for who you are assisting. Them or yourselves. Your intentions may be in the right place, but your vanity may prevail and an opportunity to witness for the Lord becomes your platform. That is why "IT" is so much easier to witness for the Lord without our peers knowing who to thank for this great gift, no matter the size or thought. If you must witness for the Lord in this situation, allow your peer to be a part of the whole process and let them make the final decision when you have made them abreast of all known options. Do not make the decision for them to acquire control for yourselves.

Who are you? Who am I? Who are they? My demons have no face, they wear a mask. My demon is The Beast in myself, The Beast in you, The Beast you create and The Beast you become suppressing man. Who can I completely take my mask off around and not feel shame? If you can find this in a partner, you both will be very happy you took yours off and made decisions based on the facts. Not a temporary facade of who you would like to be to close your deal and cause a lifetime of pain. Be yourselves and be free.

ADD is like deviating off your original window and opening new tabs, but forgetting the tabs you have open. It's like chasing rabbits. Try distracting a person with ADD with new topics without them knowing what you are doing. They will never finish the first thought. Loads of fun at parties. LOL Or is "IT".

The Spice Game is a game of senses. Carolpaetra has her children trained by their sense of smell to recognize spices. You can exercise your senses if you work them out, achieve Self-actualization and find your purpose for God. Look at the people born with deficiencies, they compensate for the impairment to fulfill their own importance of existing. Smell good sensations are living vicariously through your children by reflecting on your own youth.

"You can't make me have your frame of reference, you can only tell me about your frame of reference. I decide what I put in my frame of reference." - Carolpaetra

If your partner does something that bothers you, be honest with them. Don't let it be one of the pet peeves you bring out of your arsenal when you have "The Fight". It is courtesy to your partner to let them know what bothers you and it should also be courtesy to accept your partners feelings and make changes appropriately. If you can not, discus how you both can agree to disagree and attempt to pray about your decisions. If your partner is an 8 cylinder motor and running on 4, before running them to the shop, check and see how many cylinders you are running on. You might find happiness and contentment with your partner if you both challenge each other to run on 6. Some things about an individual's persona can not be altered. "IT" is hard to change your spots, but "IT" can be done if you can see them.

MY DREAM

Lord, tell them my dream to their hearts. Please.

LIFE,
BUT A DREAM
BEGIN TO DREAM
DREAM TO BEGIN
BUILD A DREAM

DREAM TO DESTROY
LIVE A DREAM
DREAM TO DIE

Row, Row, Row your boat, gently down the stream. Merrily, Merrily, Merrily, Merrily Life is but a Dream. That's freaking awesome Lord. I'll come back to that. I want to tell them about my specific recurring dream. Not one that just made a one time impact, but one that haunted my whole life.

When I was a kid, I would write down my dreams when I would wake in the night. I would write them down in a slumber so when I woke up, I could remember the thoughts. I didn't do that all of the time, that would have required commitment. LOL They were all craziness and I quickly discarded them the next day. But one dream remained with me. I was being chased by monsters. Monsters with no face. I could not see who or what they were. All I could do was try to run to escape them. I was terrified and as soon as I began to run, a Hurricane type wind would blow me at a stand still and my demons drew closer.

That's as far as I ever made it in that dream before waking in a cold sweat. I used to blame the sweats on alcohol because that's easy and a catch all for any problem I had. I haven't had the dream for quite some time now, but I do still have the sweats and I can't remember any dreams. The Tooth Fairy or the Molena-tor one, finally got my last baby tooth. I sedated my dreams and became an Elf.

Lord, I don't think you understand my humble request. We can all be taken out of context, even you. I was talking about my dream, not my dream for you.

INTERPRET YOUR DREAM
WITH MY DREAM

That's too much writing right now brother. I got your message, I'll decipher "IT" later. I am having an awesome weekend with Carolpaetra. I saw her heart through drunken eyes and stepped on my dick again. I saw her heart again this time with sober eyes and she and I are different, but the same. BTW...my dick is fine, thank you very much. LOL

Lord, before I forget to tell them, I don't need a shrink or a fortune teller to interpret my dreams. After a real honest self evaluation, I believe your dream will become my dream. My dream was consumed by my faceless demon, Your dream for me, Saved me.

The Predator Family Effect. Is there a man among us or do we cower to 666. Does man understand what 666 does to man, when the man has an altered state of mind and allows 666 (The Beast), to justify the pleasure to man and man doesn't pray to examine the consequences that 666 will inflict? 666 is the Beast in:

"ALL MEN"
EVEN YOU!!!

What could possibly be on the mind of a predator when they rip the heart and soul out of an innocent victim?

JACK THE RIPPER
666 WILL BURN WITH LUST
666 WILL STALK HIS PREY
666 WILL BELIEVE IN YOUNG BLOOD
666 WILL MAKE HIS DECISION
666 WILL RIP THE HEART
666 WILL TAKE THE SOULS
666 WILL HAVE PAIN ETERNALLY
666 WILL BURN IN HELL
666 MAY HAVE A CHANCE
666 WILL HAVE A JURY OF LAMBS
666 WILL DIE AND LIVE IN HELL

666 WILL HAVE NO FACE
666 WILL HAVE NO HEART
666 WILL HAVE NO SOUL
666 WILL BE RESTRAINED WITH LOVE
666 WILL BE UNDERSTOOD
666 WILL BE MAN
MAN WILL BE 666
GOD WILLS MANKIND
666 WILLS MAN

I can only pray my Lord. I Pray I don't have to kill a predator they preys upon mine. I haven't faced those decisions and I don't want to.

IF YOU ARE IN NEED
HAVE ONE
IF YOU ARE IN GREED
CHOKE ON ONE

How long must "IT" take for us to learn our way out of this maze? We are the Rats and we are slaves to big Fat ones. Alcohol, Cigarettes, restrained LUST, Gambling, Substitutes of man to replace God's Gifts. Pinocchio is still a boy on strings and 666 finds what 666 seeks.

I AM
TAKEN FOR GRANTED
I WILL
HAVE MY PROMISED
KINGDOM

Yes You are my Lord, with my last breath I will attempt to do Your Will and lay the first brick to your Everlasting, Earthly Kingdom.

Swearing is for the ignorant. Words are like a shell game. Do you educate yourself or pick up a shell and get screwed?

Clean text would write *&^%$#@^& because it adds nothing but shit, fills the void of ignorance and emphasizes points that would be more appropriate with a mastery of the Kings English.

I AM A SLAVE TO ONE MASTER
A SERVANT TO ONE BROTHER
WHO AM I?
WHO ARE YOU TO ME?

Too easy, I'm a slave to one Father and a servant to the brotherhood of mankind.

THAT IS THE YOUNG, DO YOU SEE THE OLD?

You are a slave to the Father and a servant of mankind. I am Your brother in Christ and You are my Savior.

WOULD THE MASTER HAVE YOU AS A SLAVE, WHEN I YOUR SAVIOR WOULD HAVE YOU FOR A SERVANT?

I am a slave for many Demons. Why should my Father warrant less?

THE KINGS NEW WARDROBE
THE NAKED TRUTH
WHAT IS 666 SELLING?
WHEN YOU LAUGH AT THE KING
LAUGH AT YOURSELVES
FOR YOU OWN ATTIRE

Lord, I bare my soul to You and my brothers and sisters in You, so that they may find You. Hansel and Gretel left a breadcrumb trail and it was gobbled up by the birds. Your words are marked on the trees. The power of the printed Word.

Sexual immorality is in my heart, but "IT" is a sin. So I live vicariously through your experiences and my own as I exercise Restraint over My Demon Willie. For "IT" is not His Will, "IT" is mine. If all is forgiven, can I ever trust you to restrain your Demon, if I can't restrain my own? Don't tempt thy God and don't tempt thy Demon.

Decisions points of a relationship. Do we make "IT" work or cut and run gambling to find the love you once had in each other. Sometimes relationships run there course. Too bad for you, too bad for me, too bad for my kids and your kids. How intimate did we know each others hearts before we did the deal? Beware 666 is the salesman to satisfy the thirst of his own personal demons that call him slave and he calls MASTERS.

If your childrens boat is sinking, do you throw them a rope or do they throw you two anchors? When your boat begins to sink from the excess weight, do you jump in the boat with your children, a boat with your true partner or keep bailing? Life is but a Dream.

Do not live in shame or guilt. A parent can only plant seeds and pray they find fertile soil. It's the same for our God.

Okay Lord, I'm caught up now. Tomorrow I begin editing the 2nd Manic Episode Revisited, this ought to be fun. LOL Little tired tonight so, Good Night my brother. Thanks for another sober day. I pray a silent prayer...I just don't know, I just don't know. Let "IT" be Your Will, not mine. Give me the strength to Endeavor to Persevere. I'm so beat down. My blood is drained just as Yours was my Lord. Your Blood has been sold my Savior. I am selling mine for You. My life is out of balance and my Demon awaits to promise "IT". "IT" will never be completely out of my life and can end "IT" at any time. I pray to You Father, crush the head of the serpent that wishes to be my Master, the other serpents will follow. Tough night Lord, thanks for being here for me.

NO WORRIES

No Worries, I'm good and You are Great. You are the thread that I cling to.

8/12/2010

Good Morning Lord, please grant me another sober day. Happy Ramadan. I don't know what that is because "IT" is not in my frame of reference. But if "IT" is a pathway to God, then I say Happy Ramadan. Doing a lot of processing this morning Lord. I am so close, I feel the sense of relief coming over my exhausted sober body. I have to finish the edit and I have mapped out my strategy. Lots of irons in the fire right now. TTYL.

Had a good day of editing today. As I go through the 2nd manic episode, I realize that many things that I was trying to encapsulate will be lost due to not giving myself the trigger that I need to expand on or I was drunk and tripping. LOL Hey, I did the best I could. You try going into the fourth dimension and bringing something back for the betterment of your brother and we'll judge your performance. I got a big fat "S" from my Savior. I'm working on turning "IT" from SELF to SAVED.

I am also experiencing for myself as I read my own words, how much time it will take for people to ponder each thought. It has been mentally exhausting retracing my drunken steps. It almost seems like an enigma within an enigma. I knew there was a lot of wisdom that I was extracting from the movies of my past, that ultimately formed my frame of reference.

Good Night my Lord and personal Savior. Thanks for coming back for me. I'm feeling alive again, but very tired. Thanks for another sober day.

8/13/2010 Friday the 13th

Good Morning Brother, please grant me another sober day. I'm getting close to completing the first final edit. This is the part that I dislike the most and probably why I never complete other things in my life. I do not like to go over material that I have already been through. I'm an idea man, not a follow through man. Well back to editing, ugh. The emotional roller coaster is ready to go again.

Humiliation is the gateway to Humility. I heard that last night at a meeting, I didn't catch who the guy was quoting. It made me think of my thermos. I have my Lamp, Chair and many empty bottles. I just forgot to tell you about my thermos that I was holding behind my back so I wouldn't be embarrassed about my Vampirish needs. Until we begin to address the things we have in the closet, we will never be free. God's children will continue to bump around forging the same ground that you covered, because you keep secrets.

IF I ONLY KNEW THEN
WHAT I KNOW NOW

Okay, back to editing. I have to get this done soon. "IT" is coming to a HEAD. Pardon the pun, where's my thermos. I need some Tofu to clear my mind and be productive. If not, the Vampire may haunt my thoughts all day. I see you blushing, I Am You. Are you capable of humility? "IT" is the pathway to the Portal. How bad do you want to speak to God? Go back in your minds to the playground of your youth. If you never had an imaginary friend, I didn't, find Him now and bring Him back through the

Portal with you. Now begin to ask Him questions in your mind and keep a personal journal of your daily conversations. I never did this, but "IT" is such a relief to get "IT" off my mind and on paper. I feel like I have given my problems over to Christ when I do that. I try to live a Christ filled life and the Karma has been phenomenal. Build your frame of reference and begin to seek your purpose.

Gotta go see what my crazy ass is saying now. It's kind of funny now, the drunk is interpreting what the manic has written down while in the fourth dimension. This ought to be interesting. I don't want to massage what is written, because "IT" was a completely different state of mind on both occasions. You might say that I don't want to disturb the evidence room and distort the facts, even as arcane as they appear.

I'm glad that Darren reminded me about blood and brainwashing. I just don't want to get my hopes up to high and be let down again. My heart has hardened and the feelings suppressed. "IT" hurts too much to play with. My purpose is for all mankind and I must Endeavor to Persevere. "At ALL Costs".

I was just questioning my own benevolence and I erupted in laughter. The only thing I'm getting financially off this project is 10% from the concession stand. Throw me a fricking bone here, doing all of this shit is killing me. Now I'd like for you to imagine Jesus Christ, our Lord and Savior saying the same for our Father. I sure would like to see the Body of Christ heal the sick, so much so, He will have the other 90% for His Everlasting, Earthly Entity. I pray Your Kingdom will be built quickly Lord, the "TIME" draws near.

Hey, real quick. I just slipped through that portal and brought back a thought. Do you remember when in Star Trek IV, they released the whales? The humans had to figure out first who the message was for and did, but did anyone else interpret the message of hope. "IT" was the reincarnation of an extinct species. The hope comes from rebirth of a new future with old species Mankind. Can we suppress 666 this time, now that we know who he is?

My movie came today. Dr. Jekyll and Mr. Hyde. I can't wait to watch "IT". I know there is a message, I pray to catch "IT" in the fourth dimension.

I can not believe this movie has not been re-made to illustrate narcotics abuse. We will talk about that in the morning. Good Night Lord, thanks for another sober day. I'm exhausted.

I've been thinking about my publishing date. 12/21/2012 doesn't really mean anything to me directly, but 6/21/10 does. That is my Sobriety date. It represents a new beginning for me, a rebirth. Also, "IT" is cool how the numbers add up. 6+2+1+10=18 or 6+21-10=18. 18/3=6 6+6+6=18 3x6=18. Oh my, this is a Devil Date. One more illustration of how silly we are as we try to interpret 666 with ignorance.

8/14/2010

Good Morning Lord. Please grant me another sober day. BTW...I wonder how many of them realize that 6+21-10=17 not 18. "IT" is just like the shell game. If I am fast enough, I can manipulate you without you knowing "IT".

Less than 100 pages to edit and I will be done. Yaaaaaa HOOOOOO!!!!!! I'm coming down the home stretch and I feel I have a grasp of what my entire purpose is, but I will let that be His Will for my life for Him. I'm dreading the audio version and I'm excited. I pray that I can bring as much passion to my words this time, as I did when I initially wrote them. I will do my best, but most of my emotions have been drained. Just as you are beat into your little Elf world, I have been beaten trying to prove that just because I have a Red Nose, doesn't mean that I can't guide the sleigh in the most turbulent times. Brother, I don't have the strength to guide shit, but maybe I can shed a little light on "IT" for some else to lead.

I have learned so much in my lifetime. I was compelled to share. I ask you, if you were a crab that managed to make it out of the bucket and could easily scurry off the pier into the water, go screw other crabs, drink blue frozen drinks with umbrellas and fruit in them. Would you bother to go back to the bucket and see how many of your crab brothers and sisters you could pull out before you ended up back in the bucket yourself? I'm not coming back, screw you. But I will throw you a lifeline that you can use to blaze your own path to Spiritual Freedom. I know exactly what I believe in, based on my ever expanding frame of reference. What I'm trying to tell you here is, before you jump on the band wagon because they're serving good BBQ for lunch. Do your own research and decide if what they believe, is what you believe and I believe, I believe that you can believe, anything you want to believe, just as I believe and that is my Belief. What do you Believe? LOL Under which shell will you find Jesus. Not that one, "IT" has BBQ sauce on "IT". I'm looking for the shell with blood on "IT" and that is where I Will place my Faith, Hope, Love and Charity. I'm All In. That's my final answer.

Lord, thank you for blessing me again. This recent acquisition will make an annual income for many. I am thankful for the blessings, but still empty. I know you are affording me the time to spend with You finishing my purpose for You. I pray that You guide my heart as we close out this chapter of my life. This is one book that I am soooooo...... ready to close. You have trained me, I pray that I can control my own Vanity if Your Gift is Revealed to the World. I Will need to be kept in check. ;) I Am so beautiful after all. LOL Aren't we ALL, as God's Greatest Creation?

WHEN

Oh, all of the time. I can get out of line at anytime.

NO

What?

WHEN REVEALED

Yes Lord, Your humble servant must always be kept in check. I was made imperfect for the Father's sick pleasure, but I'm digging "IT" now. Now that I understand "IT". Look Father, there's one hiding his secrets just like I used to do. They look just like Rats in a Maze. You got any popcorn, this will be fun to watch. I sure would like to see the ending before I have to go Home. Do the rats ever make it out of the maze Father?

Nathan, save your breath on that prayer. He won't answer Me on that one either. "IT" is a Promised Kingdom.

Alright, I need to get back to editing anyway.

I made it through Lord. It wasn't as bad as I thought it was going to be. I didn't remember most of it, but yeah, it was me. Mr. Hyde with Dr. Jekyll occasionally. LOL What a trip. Lord, I pray that my path will pull my crab brothers and sisters from the bucket they are in. If I haven't accomplished anything but one thing Lord. Let "IT" be a road map to a personal relationship with You. Jesus Christ my Lord and Savior. My Brother and son to One God over all Mankind.

I'm confused on how I should feel tonight Lord. Our book is done and all that is left is the final touches, including audio. Ouch, that's going to be tough. But I will be up for the challenge, after all, I want redemption in the eyes of my two lost loves. My daughter Lauren and my (2nd Wife). I'm confused because I am trying to run all of the scenario's through my head without getting excited. I am not sure how I will react to (2nd Wife) when this finally gets out. I do know I want my blood back. I want Lauren back unconditionally, but even with her we have so much ground to make up. I don't even know my own daughter. I really lost a lot chasing a materialistic God.

Alright Lord, how about a little praise for me, this has been a living Hell. Don't I get a Crown or Constellation or something?

I GODCHA CROWN
RIGHT HERE
LOL

And the constellation?

Nathan, you always did go for the sale. Sure, why not. BTW..."IT" is already named Ophiuchus, your new name in me. LOL You should have read the fine print.

LOL, all good brother. "IT" was all for You anyway. I can't say that "IT" has always been about You. I needed "Time" to grow in Faith and get past "IT's all about ME".

THANK YOU
BROTHER

No, thank you for saving me my brother. I am the brother in need of keeping.

COOL, LET'S EAT
I AM STARVED

I'm going to call my folks tomorrow and see what there lunch plans are. Let's spend the day together tomorrow, maybe even take a ride out to Leper Land and dream another dream. I pray someone will take on that project. I can not. I really believe it would heal a lot of souls on the inside and make the World a better place. A new beginning and a new generation of Gods Children, mentored under God's Laws. If God can be chipped away from our society, can Satan, now that we know we all are Satan when we become Satan?

It amazes me to think that these last few sentences will make prophetic history. So what does one say to end a book like this. Hold that portal still brother, I'm coming through.

Ian, stand still with "IT" - Pink Floyd

How can you have any pudding if you don't eat your meat? LOL

SILLY ASS

Yup, that's me at your service your Highness.

I have really been digging your poems.

LIVING WORD

Yeah, that too. Can You bless us with one more before We end this?

TOPIC?

Oh Lord, I don't know. Show me "The End" that's all folks. "IT" doesn't have to be silly, whatever You want. I'm not tempting You. I just like how Your words touch my heart.

THE END

THAT'S ALL FOLKS

Smart ass brother of mine. LOL You Gotta Love Him. He blesses OUR hearts.

**I AM THY END
I AM THY KEY
I AM THY PORTAL
I WILL THEE FREE
I WILL THEE MORTAL
I WILL THEE END
AN END TO ALL ENDS
I AM...
THY GOD
I WILL...
THEE END**

666
THE MARK OF
THE BEAST

Let's get ready to start, "The Family Feud". Today's topic: What are the top five answers to the riddle of 666? What does it mean?

Let's start with you Sally, but before we start, I need to gross everyone out with a big sloppy Al Gore kind of kiss. Give me a break, this the only gig I could get after Hogans Heroes and Hollywood Squares was humiliating.

So Sally, what do you believe 666 is?

I'd have to say the Mark of the Beast

Survey says, Number One answer. Good job Sally, give it up for her. YAY!

How you doing Mark, you big lug. How's it hanging?

Honestly, when I think about humanity it kind of hangs to the left and then when I wonder how I'm going to pay for this humanity, it hangs to the right. But I got this feeling that somehow we will be able to figure out how we can be humanitarians without it coming directly out of my already overtaxed wallet. And when that happens, I think the left side and the right side will come to the middle and we'll make one of those K Y Jelly commercials. And hey, don't worry about my age. I got plenty of the pills the drug companies have been pushing down my throat. We'll squeeze the jelly commercial in between the drug commercials.

Uhhhh...Right. So what is 666 for you Mark?

I'm going to have to go with, My Ex-Wife. She's a bitch from Hell. Wait a minute, now hold on. Can I get two. Fred can I have your answer? Fred don't talk much anyway. Cause my Mother in Law has got to have her ugly ass up on that board somewhere too.

"Survey says"
4. Ex-Wife
5. Mother in Law

Great Job Mark, I really didn't think you had a snowballs chance in Hell, but this is a public opinion poll that dictates these answers. Okay, I think we can all agree that we have no idea where this is headed but let's go to Mabel. You can take out those false teeth honey, I want to gum you right here on the set. UM-MMMM...... Mabel your looking pretty good for your age. How old are you honey?

I'll be 32 this year. I was sold into sexual slavery when I was 9 and was just released from rehab last year, but I'm doing much better.

Wow, don't I feel like such a schmuck. Mabel, honey please tell us your answer.

I believe I have earned the right to say "Predators"

Sally the survey says Predators is the number two answer, can you see it in your heart to share that number one spot?

Okay, we're moving on. How about you Davy, who's still in the Navy and probably will be for life. What does 666 mean to you?

You know, I've been aboard a ship for a very long time and we watch a lot of movies. I've always wondered what that thing on Harry Potter's Head was. Is it a tattoo of 666? Anyway, I'm going to say that thing on Harry Potter's Head.

Survey says: Strike One

Davy, did you really think the thing on Harry's head was 666?

Hey, you asked me what I believe. Screw you.

You are right Davy, I have no authority to infringe upon your beliefs. Somebody get Davy a wand and a white owl.

We are still missing one answer, maybe Clark can solve the riddle that has perplexed Man for centuries. How about it Clark, what does 666 mean to you?

Well Dick, I'd have to say...

Call me Richard please, Dick just seems to personal and we've just met.

Okay Richard, I'll go with Alcohol. Because it knocked my Richard in the dirt more times than I can remember.

Did you mean to say Dick, Clark?

No, what does Dick Clark got to do with 666. I was saying that Alcohol has knocked my Dick in the Dirt so much, but you told me not to say Dick. You Dick. Sorry, you Richard.

Right...Survey says: "Betrayers" I think the judges are going to let you have that one Clark. YAY. The crowd goes wild.

This is Dick, I mean Richard reminding you before we all go to our bonus round, that 666 is what we believe in personally as our interpretation of the signs based on our own frame of reference. A frame of reference is like an asshole, we all got one and we started building "IT" from birth.

And that no man might buy or sell, save he that had the mark, or the name of the beast, or the number of his name. Here is wisdom. Let him that hath understanding count the number of the beast: for it is the number of a man; and his number is Six hundred threescore and six.

666

The number of man. I realize that I only touched on the answer to that riddle. 666 is our frame of reference that each of us draw from. It is developed by what we see, hear, do and whether we learn from the consequences or not. Because the rulebook is overwhelming, we wing it. The rule book that I use is the Bible and quite possibly the Quaran, I am still subjecting it to critical analysis because it is not in my own frame of reference. We make up our own minds instead of following God's plan for our lives, we bump around trying to figure out what someone else is doing and may even try to take it from him.

Everyone has a Reticular Activating System. I already told you about the yellow VW and when you buy one, they seem to be everywhere. So I'll tell you about the Old Lady, Young Lady Picture. When you look at this picture, you will see one or the other. Sometimes you lock down so hard you can not see another viable option. You have made your decision and live with the consequences. Only when you accept enlightenment, do you see a different alternative.

Of our own free will. We make decisions daily and a thought process must occur before they can be made. We draw from our frame of reference that is stored in our subconscious and then instantaneously we follow our moral code. What is right or wrong. What has made me money or broke me. What made me the life of the party or the buffoon. It is these decisions that you make daily that determine who you will serve. Man or God? Your decisions are either Christ like or Anti-Christ like.

Try looking for signs. Have you ever lied in the grass on a sun filled day, a little nip in the air and studied the clouds? You can find almost anything that looks like what you seek. As a child, I saw many wonderful images. I haven't done this as an adult. It's a little frightening considering my frame of reference now from then.

When my parents picked me up from Dallas, Tx I told them I was considering editing childrens books and telling them the truth of what they have to look out for and forward to. This picture is pretty bleak right now. If you are honest about the State of our Union and the State of our World.

I wonder who he is, he must live nearby. You could have seen him everyday and not known who he was. He could be that guy right there or that guy there and those flowers are for you. NY152 – You've Got Mail

Can you see how you interpret things. You are drawn to what you seek. The Antichrist is of your flesh, he is your frame of reference, he is your subconscious, he could be your decision maker and seal your fate. The Antichrist is each and everyone of us based on our decisions.

Wouldn't it be great if everyone had a Godly frame of reference. You could let your guard down and not fear attack. Love your brothers and sisters in Christ, but be forewarned that not everyone is serving God.

Play it close to your vest and have a back up plan – Dad

I tell you these things so you will know to forgive. You can not find peace in your own heart until you forgive the person that hasn't thought twice about you, after their offense to you.

Hit me once – Shame on You
Hit me twice – Shame on Me
Hit me three times

I AM is coming after you
Do you need another illustration of His Might?

Does this shark need to come up and bite your ass before you believe me. - Jaws

Lord,
Just because I mentioned sharks, don't start sending them. I am looking forward to a cool summer here at the beach. That is if Global Warming doesn't ruin it. LOL

We mock what we do not understand – Spies Like Us

Wallace has a keen ability to spot an ambush – Braveheart

The Prophet Nathan has learned to spot Corruption.

Uh Oh, somebody has learned how to putt. - Happy Gilmore

Do not let Caesar fund these programs with your tax dollars. Let individuals that believe in what they are doing raise the funds themselves. Put the funds into a Legacy and reap the benefits for an eternity. I really just don't give a damn about the mating habits of those vicious Kenids.

Hey Al,
How about you start a Global Warming Trust Fund and put what you made in to it. It made you rich didn't it? You could have a Global Gorathon or Borathon depending on the light of the son. I think I got Ten bucks. Hell, I'd pay ten bucks to watch a monkey jack off with boxing gloves on. I will give a donation for uncorrupted findings. Don't run it through my Government for the rest of your friends to be greased with taxpayers money. We're broke and it is time you felt the pinch yourselves. I can only imagine where Nathan's Auto Sales would be if someone had given me about fifty more credit cards.

When did we give up our power as people to a corrupt Government that overwhelms us with rhetoric so we can't really see what they are up to? We are ignorant after all.

The way to make any program work is to reach the people. If you give them what they want, you will get what you want. You don't petition your government to fund your explorations and agenda. You create your concept. You market your concept and you sell your concept. If it has merit, it will sell. If not, it will die. If you still believe in your concept, revise it and enlighten us to your findings. Old woman, young woman.

Sorry to get off the subject, but you know my ADD ass. So to sum it up, 666 is our free will choosing to serve man over God based on our own personal frame of reference.

GeeZ, LoueeZ... I'm not starting out to good. I'm all over the place.

Nathanson, Focus...remember Balance. - Mr. Miagi

666 is our frame of reference that is stored in our subconscious. Our reticular activating system will draw from our subconscious every time a decision is to be made. Of our own free will, we choose to serve man 666 or God. Our decisions are either Christ Like or Anti-Christ Like. Everyone's frame of reference is different. It is based on what they have seen, heard, read or experienced. Everyone wants to believe that their frame of reference is the right one. And sometimes will go to great lengths to press themselves and their agenda at the expense of their brothers and sisters in Christ. When someone divides in the name of God, look for Greed and Power. Is it God they wish to serve or fuel their own Egos? Follow the money trail to find corruption. We must have transparency.

Just thought of this in the shower. I almost forgot it before I could get out and write it down. LOL

The Living Word speaks to different people, in a different way, at different points in time in their walk with Christ or man 666. We interpret the Living Word based on our frame of reference. Our frame of reference starts to be built at our birth. It is what we have seen, heard, read and experienced. Of our own free will we get to choose right from wrong, Christ like or Anti-Christ like. The Devil is alive and well dwelling in each and everyone of us due to the decisions we all have to make daily. The Devil is of the flesh, ONLY when you allow the Devil to become you.
   –   The Prophet Nathan

P.S.
As we have generationally chipped God from our World, we have inevitably stacked those chips in favor of man 666. Imagine being a child again. What would you see, hear, read and experience?

This is my humble interpretation of man 666. Always subject to critical analysis. Just imagine being able to sleep without worrying the Boogey Man is under my bed or in my closet. I don't have to worry anymore. I just take the Boogey out of Boogey Man and I am left with just man 666 to deal with. And he can be a vicious man 666.

IT'S IN THERE
PREGO
THE SEED OF
GOD

January 9, 2010

Welcome to Leper Land !!!

Concession stand: **ALL FREE TODAY**

Bottled water
Unleavened bread (Pita)
Canned fish

Pass out optional sack cloth robes.

Everyone that participates will receive a flat white stone with **I AM** on one side and the other side is left blank for each individual to determine their own new name in Christ.

The seven deadly sins. Videos within rooms at Fort.

Discover all of the unmentionables via video. Retrain our thinking. Show the consequences of our actions, so we can learn from others' mistakes.

Isolated posts will discover the really despicable travesties that man places on other men. PG-XIII on this place.

If you can't come to Leper Land to receive your gift $6.66 plus postage. Your own white flat stone. I AM, who are you for Christ? You will make that decision. It is your new name in Christ. Who are you really? Do you know for sure? How do you know? You will feel it on your heart when you can answer that question.

I was just thinking about having that stone in my hand. "I AM" on one side and the other side blank for only my Father, Savior and Wonderful Counselor to know. I don't want to tell you my purpose for God, I want to show you by my actions. Whether you notice them or not, it makes no difference. My God notices them and so does your brothers and sisters in Christ, whether they acknowledge your efforts or not. That's what you have a spouse for. LOL The thing that I was thinking about was the last time I kicked Austin and Dad's ass at Risk, Austin had developed a pattern of trying to figure out my mission card by my strategy and actions. But I always strategically wait until the last possible moment before revealing my Plan and unleashing my Fury of Hell and total World Domination. LOL

To the untrained mind and heart, you and I have just had a conversation about an enjoyable board game. To the trained mind and heart, you have just witnessed an inquisitive mind that wants to lap up the knowledge of a proven track record of success. So after he is beaten, he performs an analysis of the whole mission scenario. Of course, there is always the luck issue with the roll of the dice, but definitely a plan that can be learned and possibly even built upon for future games or generations, depending upon your frame of reference. This knowledge can be used for you own self-gain or it can be used to motivate your brother to achieve his own level of contentment and Glorify Our God.

January 15, 2010

The Anti-Christ is fueled by the media. What are we feeding our children with? Need a mirror? What are children being programmed with? It disgusts me and I know it disgusts our God. Why would anyone gain enjoyment from watching the sufferings of others. Dracula, what a bunch of crap that gives erotic desires.

The bad stuff is easier to believe as we all know.

Dude, I am telling you now. You reap what you sow. How are your children being programmed?

You made me! – Charles Manson

We really did make Charles, we created an environment of corruption and taboo. He manipulated these to satisfy his own thirst.

Lord, please tell me what I can do?

I think Leper Land will heal them on the inside. I know that it is always **FAITH** that heals.

Why do people think and feel this way in which causes them to do harm to your people?

Some people just wish they had never been born.
– Tombstone

Those that choose man 666 will always be there
Those that choose ME will always be here
For Eternity

Lord, I am straining to talk with you. I feel you, but why are you not talking to my heart now?

This is God reminding Nathan to shut up, shut up, shut up, shut up, shut up, shut up

I want so much to proclaim your name Father. So guide me, mold me and complete me.

Is your motivation for ME or for your own vanity? Nathan I know you. You cannot hide from ME. You are vain through and through. You must remain
STEALTH

I so want to proclaim your name Father. I so want to go in front of all of your people and proclaim your love for them.

MY LOVE LASTS ETERNALLY
I AM

Lord, I feel like I am speaking for you now. I will heed your words and not my vanity. Am I acting to humbly? I do so want to worship you in public.

Nathan, you know all of the lukewarm believers raise their hands to me in public, but they raise them to their peers they want to rule over. You cannot judge them. Who are you to judge? If their heart is in need of a lift. Show ME. Everybody else, sit your monkey ass down. It's bull shit and you know it. Praise ME. I require it. So do your ancestors and heirs. Get past the greed. See the love. I AM your Eternal God. Your Lord and Savior

I am watching Bram Stokers Dracula. Cool flick. Do you see what I mean. I think the bad stuff is easier to believe. Why are we programming children that way? Oh, I know. It's the freaking money.

Are these your words or are they mine?

Stop selling Nathan
You are over selling

Yes Lord, I know. You hired a salesman and I have a hard time turning it off.

They know. I effect everyone with everyone.
They know my Wraith

Earthquakes – Tsunami – Forest fires – Hurricanes - Tornadoes – …

Etc. etc. etc. – The King and I

I effect everyone with everyone

This is Nathan reminding Danny Glover to shut up. Start a global warming trust fund if you are that adamant about it. Don't circumvent my beliefs with your agenda that is unfounded to be true, by going to my Government and solicit your personal agenda ultimately resulting in more taxes taken from me.

You ask of Me
I ask of You

Thank you oh Sovereign Lord. You are a most merciful God, our Creator and our Savior. You are in us. We are in you. One in the same. Maybe the bad stuff is easier to believe, but we can reprogram our love for you? This is the new generation you spoke of. It will come to pass.

Lord, I pray to you. Do not allow my own set of personal issues to influence your words. I do not wish to pass my inequities, only the talents that you would give unto your people. I hope that they can learn from my mistakes. This is a guide that is long overdue.

I have given everyone Talents. They can give me the Glory or they can worship Satan. It is of their own

FREE WILL

How will they know who or what they are worshiping? Idols come in a variety of shapes and sizes, wants, desires and needs.

They know. They will always know and so WILL I

Good night Lord, I am tired and my damn finger is starting to hurt again. I love you. You are my strength to carry on. I will not rest until your message is heard. It is the Master's plan. Thank God.

Goodnight my son. Let's talk about false prophets tomorrow. I AM with you. With love and your blessings

Damn, please let me go to sleep. I don't want any awards. Okay give them to me. I will eBay them for your glory. Awards that are not truly earned are like toilet tissue. Wipe your ass with them. The one that buys it with the stench is the corrupt. Why do you deliver gifts of corruption? What is it that you are protecting? Please don't tell me that it is your own personal greed that would compromise your soul. Why do we insist on giving every child a prize? Doesn't that deflate the reward for being competitive? Why should I strive to be better, when I know you are going to give me what I want anyway?

Enough, leave me alone. Goodnight Father. I love you.

January 16, 2010

Do you know how painful it is to have the greatest Father in the world and not be able to tell anyone about it?
  − The Santa Clause II

You know why. Because they will think you're nuts. Been there, done that, stripped to my underwear and thrown in jail.

That will change Nathan. The new generation of God's people will emerge with the proper tools. Breaking the Seven Seals is just the beginning. I, Jesus Christ was sinless, you Nathan, you are ripe with sin. How can someone correctly articulate something that they have not experienced for themselves? There is an option on my peoples contract. 1000 years

209

with a world that has a controlled Satan. Write your thoughts down

Yeah, you know I know that my dumb ADD ass better write them down. Great thoughts are lost unless you do.

I really didn't think we would be doing this again.

My Last Will and Testament. The Seven Sealed, Two—Sided Scroll has been revealed. It will stun them. Now tell them your personal observations and what the Holy Spirit puts on thine heart

Lord, you know that I can get in a lot of trouble speaking my mind to a politically correct society. Even though they are words of truth, these words will hurt and hurt badly. No one likes to be told what to do or that they are doing it wrong. Wars start that way. I beg of your protection as I unveil what it is that we all need to see and what the Holy Spirit puts on my heart. We must see that it is broken, so we can figure out how to fix it.

False prophets are all around us. People want to believe so badly, they allow themselves to search for 666 and the corrupt will point out the dots. Hey, wait a minute. That's what I did. Am I a false prophet? Maybe. But I am a prophet that comes like a thief in the night bearing a gift. Sounds like Santa.

YOU ARE A PROPHET PROCLAIMING
MY HOLY NAME

Why is it so hard for us to talk about God?

Are you the anointed one?

Why do you think you are?

Is it for your own glory that you have anointed yourself?

How can you say that you are one of the two witnesses in the book of Revelations and the spokesperson for both? Who are you? What a crock of shit.

What is your interpretation of the Seven Sealed two-sided Scroll?

Why do you empower yourself enough to screw the flock?

Oh yeah, I remember now. You want the young innocent girls to anoint your small head with their orgasmic secretion.
David Koresh

BURN IN HELL

Will a real Prophet please stand up?

Is this your mission for God's glory or your own?

Take a shot, who am I to judge?

But I would not want the fate that comes with your proclamation if it is truly not on your heart.

You know I really dug how Moses raided the Temple grain. That which is good enough for God, surely won't sour in the bellies of slaves. – Moses

There has been a lot of grain stored up in the name of God for a very long time. Will the temple Pharisees of today allow God to take account and reward the faithful and damn the greedy???

Let's chat about this for just a minute. I realize that the Church is a business. Their business is to spread the Good News that

Jesus will be returning. They have been collecting in His Holy Name for an awfully long time. It is time for our Lord to take account. He has only ever asked for 10%, what is your account from your disciples for your Lord? If you have spent God's share, can you work it off? God's children are in need of healthcare and prayer. If you can not, don't blame mass exodus of the Churches on me. Nathan the Prophet. My antennas have been up since the third time I was screwed in the Church.

I'm going to see the movie Book of the Eli and see what 666 has for us.

Did you know that your decisions can be made by emotional rather than rational thought? Do you think before you act? Do you think before you speak or humiliate? Do you draw conclusions, before you have the facts? Do you think you have it all figured out? If you do, I need to talk to you. I am still trying to figure all this out and my role. No angels have appeared to me it. I'm damn sure glad they haven't. All of my words are on pure Faith and the love of our Creator.

Wait a minute, I think I see one now. Have you ever heard of the Reticular Activating System? Full credit going to Lou Tice. Have you ever bought a new car and at the time you bought it you thought it was more unique than what it ended up being. Believe me, once you buy a yellow VW Bug you will see them everywhere. It is your subconscious that is triggered to the forefront of your brain and draws your attention to what you want to see.

Note made during final edit: Do you remember when I had said earlier that I had already mentioned the yellow VW. When you read that, were you ready to correct me or just accept "IT" as fact. People will bloviate and if you do not humble yourselves to request your adversaries to please communicate to you on your ignorant level, they will steamroll your ass and you'll be oblivious to what they said because of your lack of literary intelligence and the lack of humility to admit when you don't quite under-stand something. You might be surprised how your adversary will respond when you challenge him to explain it to your poor, dumb, ignorant ass to the point of understanding. It may just be a bunch of bullshit to see if you really are awake and if not, I'm going to get this by you. I know you hate to read and your retention skills are maybe 10%, so I can expect your signature on this 1990 page healthcare bill on Monday right? BTW...did you and your Wife or is it Girlfriend enjoy the Condo at the Hamptons last weekend. Wink Wink After we cram, I mean pass this bill, what do you think about you, me and the wives or girlfriends get together and take a cool trip at the taxpayers expense, I'm sorry, I meant to say investigative research for the betterment and safety for this great nation. You need to tell me when that damn microphone is on. Next time, YOU'RE FIRED.

Do you see a connection with 666? What you see, is what you seek. Depending on how you feel will determine what you are looking for. Misery loves company. Are you one of the crabs in your family? You can stare down at a ceramic tile and find any-thing you want. So the next time you're taking a crap, look down at the tile. Do you see good things or do you see bad. You will see what you want to see. And yes, the bad stuff is much easier to believe. Unfortunately, we have been trained that way.

I am so excited to see where Hollywood wants to take us with our belief in God. It is called programming. This is where our minds are fed right from wrong, good versus evil. Which is more glamorous for you? Will God be chipped away a little further or will he be brought back into our lives? I Pray it is a message of hope.

I want to be a real boy – Pinocchio

How naïve, how easy of a target, how ignorant, distractions are very glamorous. Be careful where they lead you. Also remember that there are people that will deliberately prey upon your dreams. Remember that one. You will be so excited and they will be excited for you and want in and you out.

Play it close to your vest – Dad

We get to decide who we let into our weird little worlds – Good Will Hunting

I hate living that way. I want to be trusting. Just when you think you can let your Guard down and reveal your personal vulnerabilities, they Got you.

Just when you thought it was safe to go back into the water – Jaws

Guess what, we are living in a tank of shark's. I think Glenn Beck was right. Sarah Palin has every right to be guarded with her replies. Getting kicked in the teeth sucks. I do think everybody needs to read that book how to screw your friends and have them like you for it. It will really open your eyes to the deception that some of the most wonderful people can be using to their advantage. At least get on the same playing field so you'll be prepared for the Manipulation.

What direction are you taking your life? Have you ever been lost? When you see a sign, a sign of redemption. Even though it puts you so far behind, you know you are on the right path. A sense of relief should fall over you now. I might be on square -13, but I know I am moving forward not backwards.

Have you ever been driving along the interstate as lost as an Easter egg. Too stubborn to ask for directions until it seems all else has failed? Once you get the direction, you are relieved to find that you have been on the right path the whole time. Or you find you are miles further from your destination than you would like to imagine. First you'll be pissed, then you'll be relieved. The not knowing Sucks more then being behind. Heading in the right direction, ultimately means reaching your destination. Mission accomplished.

Are you going through life thinking that you are headed in the right direction? When you did stop for directions, the attendant screwed you out of money or something else. Did you ever think to pull out the map? Ya know you got to use your brain, don't give your power over to someone else. They could be just as lost as you are or worse. They may be out to screw you. What is your road map of life? Once the scales have been removed from your eyes, you're probably going to be pissed and then be relieved. Once you turn your life over to God, and I mean truly turn it over to God, you'll know you're on the right path and he's got our backs. When you stand with God, who can stand against you?

Sorry to break this line of reasoning up but I had to get this thought on paper before I forgot it, you know my ADD ass. My friend Brian has been working on getting his real estate broker's license while I've been working on my book and we have been tracking about the same time frame. My first book is finished and now I'm working on the second. Brian is getting his career started in developing some systems that are not being used in this area and can be very advantageous to anybody that would like to take up the path. The cool thing about this is, when you become financially intelligent, your brain starts to work in a different way. He has been coming up with some very good ideas and I suggested to him about marketing all of his endeavors. That is the difference between a person that will continue to be a self-employed person versus a business owner. I also gave him the suggestion to write down these epiphanies as he gets them. When his project is complete, all he will have to do is compile his notes to complete his Passive Income business. We have not been trained to think that way. We have been trained to either get a job or create ourselves a job, never even thought about selling our creativity if in fact it is successful. Anyway, sorry to interrupt I'll get back on my ADD track. Now where was I. LOL

Our breadcrumbs may have been gobbled up by the birds, but we have marked the trees. They have been marked in history. Are we moving forward or are we moving backwards? What direction are you taking in your own life? Have you ever been lost? When you see a sign, a sign of redemption. Even though it puts you so far behind, you know you are on the right path. Why can't we go back in history and learn from the mistakes of our ancestors so we don't continually make them again and again.

Where are we now? Freaking lost!!! How do you find the direction that you want to go? Don't you first have to establish where you are now? Audit time! How much water, food and medicine do I have. Oh Shit, not much. Mr. Federal Reserve I know it looks bleak. I just want to know how bleak it is, so I can fix it. How can I fix it if you won't allow me into your world. Your world of corruption.

You know I really don't give a damn what you think of me. I have my beliefs and live in a country that will protect my beliefs. I'll take everything up with Jesus when that glorious time comes. I respect everyone's beliefs. We can respectfully agree to disagree. You can serve any God you want to serve and I'll serve any God I want to serve. That is our rights. Who is to say that you are right and I am wrong and vice a versa? It is all up to interpretation. This is my interpretation and I'm sticking to it. Don't infringe upon my beliefs and I'll give you the same courtesy. Don't use the legal system to tear down what my forefathers have fought for, so as not to offend you. If I was in your country and I didn't like it, I would go home. If you wanted to frisk me at the airport because you have profiled me, more power to you. I have nothing to hide. My God has sat quietly while my religious beliefs have been persecuted. You won't mind if my God has a say this time would you? My God is just. My God is fair. My God is all loving. My God is all forgiving. My God gave us his only begotten son to sacrifice for my sins.

Death:
It's not really scary when you know that you have accomplished what you were here for.

What are you here for? We've been tested our whole lives by the people that placed themselves as judge and jury. Are our choices of who leads us being made by who has the most money?

I'll bet if enough money was spent you would vote none of the above – Brewster's Millions

I will attend the funeral if a free lunch will be provided. I must have a free lunch to warrant my time – Scrooge

A deal with the devil?
Mr. Pat Robertson. I don't know you, just what I've heard on television lately. This is Nathan reminding Pat to shut the freak up.

Pat, do you hear me. I've listened to you many times. Why do you tell people that I have talked to you? You have done much good and that goes a long way. But you are over stepping your power. Let me ask you one question. Are you willing to give all that you have for me? I have afforded you a lifetime of bliss. Show me your true character, by giving your God what you have collected on my behalf and in my Holy Name. Your brothers and sisters in Christ want to see your testament to Me, they've heard your testament enough.

Uh, yeah. Wow, that's a freaking challenge. I guess there will be a mass exodus of the Church after all. You're full of shit and I have been making my tithe to the Devil. Did you make the Demonic deal with Haiti? You miserable manipulator of God's word.

Final edit note: I shouldn't Judge and nor should you, but it will be fun to watch how Pat handles God's Challenge. I wonder if I will get sued? I can't wait to go before my Judge, the Judge of Mankind not the Judge of man. But if he turns his business into God's business, I would imagine his business being a wonderful hospital to heal the sick and to witness to all that seek our Lord Jesus Christ as our personal Savior.

It sure would be nice to tap into a worldwide legacy fund for disasters. I don't need to know the amounts that you are putting in the kitty. Just put it in there, because as the beacon nation, we will always be there in a time of crisis. When people are hurting and need assistance, the challenge is always placed on the 5 talent man. But the 5 talent man should not be expected to tow the line. It requires all the two talent and yes even 1 talent men to do their part as well. It is a team effort. Do you remember team effort?

Kelly has hit all the home runs he can hit. He needs help from the kid in the wheelchair. – Bad News Bears

He has a very special purpose as well. Has anyone encouraged him to find it?

Okay, I'm going to the movie now. Be back with my own Siskel and freaking Ebert Review. I promise, I have an open mind. Do you?

Well, well, well. A cross between Escape from New York and Road Warriors. At least we know how important the Bible is now. The name Book of Eli kind of threw me. I thought they had stolen my idea. – Book of Nathan

Why is it that I can't even get a good friend that understands me, to read what I have written?

They all are a stubborn people, busy in their own world. They are up to their neck in alligators, they can't find the time

Well I told him that excuses are like ass holes, we all got one – Platoon

Nathan, you are saved. You will sit by me at the throne. Your Faith has brought you here. Be patient, you've delivered my plan. Just watch. You knew this was a daunting task from the beginning. Endeavor to Persevere

Lord, I am really getting fed up. How can I make anyone listen, when I can't even influence my own circle?

I Am with you

Yeah, I know. You've said that before.

Why do you always question me? It will come. I promise. Be Patient

I am tired of waiting on you. I want it now.

Sit your monkey ass down!!! Let us smoke a while. What is your strategy for delivering salvation? You are worthy. Stop beating yourself up. I have made you this way. If it was easy everyone would do IT

Lord, it needs to be easy. Anything complex is met with resistance.

Nathan, Nathan, Nathan. Do you remember how difficult it was for you to break out of an occupation that you did not see any way from breaking free from? Have you not prospered? I will give you more if you desire. Keep the Faith

Lord, our book has not even been given a chance. It is not even available. I always think that way, always thinking ahead. I want it now. I have been rolling with the economic punches for awhile now. Thank you for allowing my finances to enable me to continue my praise of you.

I am 100% sure that you want me to disappear after this gift is delivered. My vanity so wanted to be seen. But you gave me that clip from the devil's advocate where he got sucked into vanity after defeating Satan. What a shame. I really could have been a great spokesperson for you. But I guess we'll leave that job to all of the false prophets. I know I am one of the witnesses and I know the other. I am just desperately trying to not cross you.

Question:
How does one that feels they have the solution, coming from one that is not accepted in society, deliver the good news?

Don't even think of e-mails, letters or phone calls. I am hoping the book will work.

Lord, you know that I would stand on my head and juggle with my feet to get your people to heed your warning and gift. I am considered a nut. My friend Brian says I am considered different by my peers. Not a dumb ass, just different.

I didn't say they were better than us, just different – Eddie and the Cruisers

I have isolated myself from women. I am horny as hell, I just don't want to lose focus. My heart is broken. The love of my life is lukewarm. I can't change that. I think of her all the time. I asked you for her and you gave her to me. I made it hard on her to believe in me. A check writer mentality is what most have become. How do you break through to the lukewarm Christians?

I would rather you be hot or cold for ME. If you are luke-warm, I spit you from my life. Stand. Take a stand

Stands with a Fist – Dances with Wolves

What do you believe?

What will you stand up for?

The time is now. Who are you in Christ?

TELL ME

Who are you in Christ?

Lord, how can you ask the lost who they all are, when they don't have a clue?

You know who you are
You know who they are
They will know who I AM
I AM the Creator
I AM the Everlasting
I AM All

In you I find my peace.
In you I find my purpose.

I have prayed to you to reveal yourself on numerous occasions. I am so glad you haven't. It is purely faith. If you did appear or an angel came to me, I would play hell getting anyone to believe me.

Okay, we are talking again now. I wish I had more questions. Give me some time.

Lord, I have screwed enough women to know that it is all the same. The inner beauty is what has always prevailed. I have become so educated with relationships, I feel I can never really connect with anyone again. I know all the Bullshit. The love of my life is lost and now how could I know if someone loves me or desires what I can do for them?

There is a huge difference in the physical touch. I don't want a trophy wife. I want a loving wife and a lover of yours. I want your sloppy seconds.

I've grown tired of searching for a mate that will complete me. I cannot handle that pain again. I am forever scarred.

Every lash that we both have endured, is a lesson for us to learn by. Mistakes, we learn from yours? Would you change your ways to accommodate a partner? You will never find happiness until you begin to appreciate your partner.

We are wired very differently. You cannot change the wiring unless free will wants to.

I see people in the same place I have been before. It's freaky. They will not listen, just as I would not in their circumstance. I silently chuckle when I see them trying to find who they are with materialism. What a devil's path that is.

Your checkbook will ultimately determine your fate, just as our nation will see its fate with no credit lines. We cannot sustain the present path.

Okay Lord, this is your platform. If this book is published and we have got some ears. What do you want to say?
Draw your sword from my mouth.

I am getting a bit drunk now. Hey, don't bitch at me. You selected my drunk ass.

Nathan, my son. Have another drink. You are doing just fine. In fact, let's all have a drink

DRINK OF ME
LIVING WATER

I did find it funny that you said in Revelations "Reader Pay Attention". A good wake-up call. You knew you would be speaking to someone like me.

Oh well, let me take another hit on the tree of life and I'll be right back.

Are you ready to get deep?
How about disgusting?

I am a very horny man. Why is a sexual tool accepted for a woman and not for a man? I find it stimulating, fun and different. We are the ones that are uncontrollable. Flesh light. What a difference. It sucks and will keep you out of trouble.

What do I need a man for, I've got a vibrator – There's something about Mary

I'm just like all you other Mother Freaker's. It's the man thing that keeps you from admitting that you have weaknesses. It's okay, we all have them. But we shield those vulnerabilities heavily. No one likes to be laughed at or humiliated. That is an easy target. Let me belittle you so I can feel better about me and behind closed doors, do what you do. You hypocrites. Hey, I see (Political Figure) has a boyfriend that grows marijuana. (Political Figure) I know you didn't inhale any homegrown, but did you get popped in the butt? Good for you, I am not here to judge you. But you will be judged. You are placed in a power to be entrusted. A lot of people got hurt by your lies. As I have said before, Pole Smoker, plead your case. You hypocritical bastard. It's all good. You have enough money to escape. I hope you can live with yourself. I couldn't.

You came as a lamb, you will come as a Lion. If you are coming through me, slam their ass hard enough to listen.

Disclaimer time: it's still just me. I am just getting angry thinking about it.

Joke: When I was thrown in jail, my cellmate was a huge horny man. He asks, do you want to be the husband or the wife? I really didn't want to make a choice, but I guess I'd have to choose to be the husband. Cool, Then come on over here and give your wife a blow job. LOL Come on, That's funny.

I am so lonely, but not alone. I have been on countless encounters. There is no love, so there is no love. Sex yes, no love. I found it difficult to achieve an orgasm under these circumstances. Yet I can get off almost immediately from my thoughts sometimes 3 to 5 times a day. What is wrong with me? I don't want to change it. I like it. How do I find someone that is not looking for a deal, to be honest with me about her sexual needs? Are you trapped in a relationship where they put it on you, then changed the rules after marriage? It freaking sucks.

Joke: On your wedding night you ask your spouse to put on your pants. She says they are too big. You say that's right. I wear the pants in the family. She then asks you to put on her panties. You say I can't get into those. She says and you won't with that attitude. LOL Laugh you Dickhead.

Just a thought, if we win their hearts through their stomachs and pledge to provide their daily bread, won't they go to great lengths to protect that. The world is ours for the taking. God will take his place.

Hey another note: I am a coward. I don't want to go fight and die in a war that is not supported. We already did that in Vietnam. My dad paid that price. Let's not duplicate that mistake. I'll get into it further later on, but sometimes we react when we should be listening.

Be aware, when you are finally able to make the response that you want to make, at the opportune time, it will inevitably cause regret-- You've got Mail

Hey, if any of this sounds like a bar room talk,You know the talk. It's the talk after you leave the office and you share what you really think about with a friend. You do not have to worry about your job, I'll take the hit for you. But this is what we all talk about. Speaking of bar, I could use a drink.

Okay, I'm tipsy. Let's really get in to this. I am best in this arena. Did you ever see that episode of WKRP in Cincinnati. Johnny Fever got quicker in his response the drunker he got. That was funny as hell. It was a lie, but it was funny. As I watch the news, I am ready for your bullshit. Can I get a witness. Hey, I've never tried this. Can I get a amen? Bet your ass, I won't show up drunk like the dad in Hoosiers. I've got your number and I'm sharing it with the world. By the time you read this, I'll be sober. Well, probably not, but you won't find me. LOL That's funny you stiff ass mother freaker.

Do you know why I don't use the term F. U. C. K? It is derived from an earlier time where people were persecuted and put into stockade's, spit upon, loathed and despised. It stands for:

"FOR UNLAWFUL CARNEL KNOWLEDGE".

Now are you beginning to see who was in charge at the time. Ye without sin cast the first stone. I don't like that word. It is dirty. It is foul. It is offensive. Don't use it. It represents ignorance. It represents hurt. It represents suppression. It represents death. It represents men hurting God's children. It represent the path of the insane males without restraint.

Where did you ever hear words like that, I'm going to have to wash your mouth out with soap. Hypocrites.

Not the dreaded Lifeboy. – A Christmas Story

Oh don't worry, there is no soap for you. We live in a world where you can pick up the phone and file a complaint. The ones that are being suppressed are the ones trying to teach our children values and morals and the ones that are hurtful get away with it. Is there truly a hotline for us abused children? Is it like Afghanistan? When I put my faith in you, will you pull out and leave me with my aggressors? I want to believe in you. I need to believe in you. I have to believe me. But you leave me hanging to live a life of torment. Either come or don't come at all. I have worked my deal. I am safe for now. You screw things up. How can I have faith in you when traditionally you have left?

I Am speaking to you, the oppressed. Are you ENSLAVED? Endeavor to Persevere

You can only count on the 5 talent man for so much. You must make a stand. I know that you have. I watch the tyranny. I can't wait for them to be judged, but for now it is free will. It will be bloody, that I WILL not change

Have you ever noticed the difference between fighting for something and being given something? I say thanks for the things given to me. I cherish the things I fight for. Our forefathers fought so that we may have a better life than they. Why do we act as if we have been given this right? Because we have grown into an entitlement generation. We have lost sight of what our forefathers fought for, so that we can have "IT".

Nations of the World Hear Me
Your God is not a Divisive God
Man Suppresses
God Loves

I am sorry my global brothers, the five talent nation is broke. You will have to pick up your own pitchfork and demand your freedom. I promise you, what we earn is much sweeter than what we are given.

Oh, as usual. I have deviated off the course. Back to marriage.

How many bad marriages do you know of?

Are you in one?

How can you change it and not lose your children?

I don't have a freaking clue, I failed. Believe me, when you make that jump, it will hurt you. Search your soul. Talk to your spouse. They have the same thoughts. They may still be thinking of the better deal. There is always a better deal out there. The best deal is the one that you make with each other. Find contentment and you will find happiness.

I used to bitch about the school lunch program. It just didn't seem fair for my parents. My dad told me a story about him delivering milk to an orphanage as a kid. He said they were eating better than him. He was being fed by a single mom. He was not eating well. I have since changed my thoughts. After seeing how a lot of people live, I am thankful that these kids get to eat two meals a day for free. It is highly likely it is all they will have for the day. I love the stories of my dad. He was a saver, his brother was a spender. How did that work out you might ask. I'll tell you as he told me. His brother ate every ice cream and watched every movie with his own earnings. It was a great summer. My dad stacked and saved. When it became school time. It became family time. My dad bought school clothes for both he and his brother. Man, now that has got to suck. At least he didn't have to swim through 3 miles of alligators to get to school. That's another story. LOL The fact of the matter is, when all of the chips are down, you do what you have to do. You accept it, you deal with it, you appreciate it, you learn from it and you know God has a higher calling for you. It is your family. You do for your family. We are all family. My dad now has a sense of pride for doing what needed to be done for his family. Dude, that is the character that I want to live by. Step up and be a man. I don't like the unfairness. Why should I work, while you lay amuck? It is not fair. It sucks. But I strive for better, even if I have to carry you. Don't be offended by what I call you, for you are what you are. A "N".

Why do you call me a "N"? I am your brother. I am white.

What is your point? I am colorblind. "N" seems to fit you, oh blight and sponge of our family. You bring us down. You bring nothing. Why?

I do not have an answer for that. We will have to ask a "N". Don't get your panties in a wad. This "N" is white. Maybe yellow or red. They come in all colors.

Before my brother gets pissed off at me, this was a metaphor. LOL

You don't mind me calling you a "N" do you? It does exemplify what you are.

Sorry, I went off on a tangent and I want to make a plea to everyone, that single mothers need our help. I cannot imagine trying to raise children without any help. What it must be like to have to work two or maybe three jobs just to put food on the table and a roof over their heads. In biblical times a man was responsible for the well-being of his family. When did we lose that responsibility? It is frowned upon and considered the woman's fault. That's crap. It takes two to tango. But what about the children? They are the victims in every divorce. I cannot articulate what Oliver Twist or Tom Sawyer or any of the other orphans have gone through. I am fortunate to have the greatest parents in the world. What type of a parent are you?

These single moms need your help. Don't feed them like seed to the birds. Feed them eternally with your passion legacy gift. Single moms, I am talking to you. Those of you who have found your blessings, don't forget where you came from. Those of you that are struggling, keep the faith and care for your children. It is up to you. Is there a man among you? Are you a man? Your body may procreate, your essence will nurture.

Those Chihuahuas have got some BIG balls don't they? They will chase after a much larger dog like they are going to eat him up. Their balls have to ride shotgun, because they are too big to sit in their own lap. It is like flies. They eat shit and bother people. When you have had enough, you put your blue frozen drink with the umbrella in it down and go and get the swatter. If that doesn't work, you must bring out the spray. Am I talking about dogs and bugs or am I talking about Nations? Let's try the swatters first. It seemed to work with Khadafi. Give James Bond and Rambo a call and not commit with the whole damn Army. If that doesn't work, we'll hit it with the spray. Let's try the spies like us and the like. Damn, these things are expensive and we may be more effective knocking out their infrastructure. It's working for them. But we are committed now. Peoples lives are counting on us. Can you imagine being the one that turned someone in and then your protection bolted on you? It looks as if you are ready to bolt anytime. Screw you buddy. Find him yourself. That big dog has already bit my entire family and my son and I are the only ones left. (Hey, this is a hypothetical story. You don't have to politicize it as fact, although it probably is somewhere)

I warn you, when the time comes when you are able to say exactly what you want at the time you want, you will inevitably regret it. - You've got Mail

It's regret alright and we should have the Lions share. Not for trying to right a wrong, but the manner that we took. Shit happens. You can either stick your head in the sand or deal with it. We have no choice but to deal with it.

This applies to everyone. I know numerous people that when there is a problem, they run and hide. That only makes the problem fester more. You must step up and handle your confrontations and let the pieces fall where they may. You will lose business and friends if you don't.

Have you ever seen that movie Coward of the County? You could have heard a pin drop, when Tommy stopped and locked the door. That is what the heirs of the 9/11 victims want to see. I don't blame them. Forgiveness would be very difficult to achieve. Sometimes you have to fight when you're a man.

Go ahead hit me right there, I dare you. I triple dog dare you. Okay, I'll give you that one. You hit me again, I'm coming after you.

Turn the other cheek. I am sorry Jesus, but you are pussyfooting around. Sometimes you do have to fight when you're a man. Our Father knows this, we are in the Joshua Era.

I AM instigating nothing but peace
But if the rod is the only thing you understand

I WILL smite you to the dust from which you came

Hold up my Father, haven't you given me the opportunity for World Peace?

The clock is ticking, make it fast. I Am growing impatient

Let me tell you about my mom. What a woman. She is the best. She is so concerned about me even now. How can I ever repay her? She is a lot like me. Scatterbrained and you never know when she will say something that will stop you in your tracks. My dad and I discount her, but we both appreciate her knowledge. She can put you in your place in a hurry. She is very smart in ways that are not on the surface. I love her for keeping my dad and myself in check. She is our Rock.

I am so very fortunate to have parents like this. I know very few of you have this. I am sorry. They are my family. Is your family strained like mine. The reasoning is fine, just fine.

I wanted to stop writing, but I realize that many of you do not have what I have. What a terrible thing to reach out for guidance and find that your dad gives you a snake. I cannot understand that and would never try to articulate that. I cannot. What a torment that must be to have to live in that environment. It is all around you. Man's restraint is not subject to economic boundaries. The best fail also. Restraint is a measure of a man. What kind of man are you?

I could spend a lot of time on this subject, but I feel like you have a better understanding than I could ever have. While that would have definitely screwed me up. The ones that you look to for guidance are the same ones that hurt you. Cry out. This is wrong, you know it. They know it and we will hear your cries for help.

Jenny Got moved to her grandmother's house and I liked that because it was closer for me. Jenny and I are like peas and carrots. Pray with me Forrest, Pray with me. Please God make me a bird, so I can fly far far away. Please God make me a bird, so I can fly far far away. Ouch, so sad to have to live that way. The people that are supposed to protect you are the same ones that harm you. There is a special place in hell for them.

E-mail alert, I am slamming pretty hard here. You can inter-ject any time.

You are doing just fine my son. They need a wake-up call. It cannot come from me verbally. You are witnessing my wrath every day. It comes from Faith

Yes I am. Why are you killing so many people? I know you said that it is to be, but I really don't like seeing the pain. Those poor people in Haiti. These disasters are growing in number just as you said they would. Just like birthing pains.

It is the time of the Lion
Learn from the Lamb
The Lion will take care of his own

When the hyenas took over Pride Rock/Plymouth Rock, we saw how that government was working. There has to be a great leader. One that understands balance and the circle of life.

I sure wish I could find another way to record your message. My finger is killing me. What is the most important thing to you? How far would you go? I'm bitching about a finger. WTH

I'm tired and drunk, let's go again tomorrow. You said don't be drunk on wine, so I'm hammered on vodka. If any angels did come, I don't think they could wake my drunk ass up.

Lord, you wouldn't let me sleep last night. Please, I thought I was done.

Man, I still can't get over what the false prophets say. No wonder it will be hard for me and that I must hibernate after delivery. Where was that island on Castaway. Gilligan's Island looked pretty cool, I'll go there. As long as they have those frozen blue drinks with fruit and a umbrella in it. LOL I'll be digging me some Mary Ann. Don't want any Gingers. High maintenance. Been there done that and it just ain't worth it.

Stick and move. That was my plan until I met (2nd Wife). I fell in love. I will never marry again. The pain is too difficult. This is a pain that you cannot articulate. Damn, it will make you do crazy shit. I am so glad that I live three hours away. I would be a stalker from hell. I can't help myself. I want to know. Is she as miserable as I am? I want to pray for her to recover, but I am selfish. She is the one that I love, I don't want to see her with anyone else. It makes me crazy.

I still love her and always will. Do I love my image of her or her soul? I will determine that from her own confession of love for our Father. How can I accept her back into my life? Oh how I want to. What would you expect from me? Forgiveness? Forget? I want to hear her heart. I AM is a forgiving God and so am I a forgiving Man. I can not suppress my Love. I pray that it is a true love for a life long partner, not a lust love that is not sustainable. In the meantime, I will be getting some purple putang in North Africa. Yeah, all you dudes can live vicariously through me. LOL We are insane males after all.

RESTRAINT!!!
Sit your monkey ass down and let's smoke awhile. It is what it is. You cannot make someone love you. Who's next

I know Lord, but it is hard. I compare every woman with her and they will never measure up to my dreams. Not even her, she would never measure up now. How can I solve that?

Think
Put everything into perspective. Do not go off half cocked. If she will lay with you, she will lay with another. What do you have to offer? Is she is looking for the best deal?

I do want to get some bottom land to impress her. - Sgt. York

Is that what she wants? She does want security. You wouldn't run off would you? Be honest about what you are both fixing to embark on. You are more alike than you know.

It seems like a game to meet and seduce women. I took a course and it sent shivers down my spine. I really have no idea who you are. You are drawn to a persona that I do not like. Why do you not like it? I am just not a bad boy.

I watch bad boys with some of the hottest women. WTH They are slaves to them and all they want to do is please them. I just can't figure it out. I guess I need some more books or just say screw it. I'm leaning toward screw it. I don't have a vibrator, but I have a fleshlight. LOL

I have a friend that has given up on women. I listened to him and tried to persuade him differently. I am now starting to understand his position. Why???

Let's talk about churches shall we. There are so many good churches and pastors. Peace be with them and thank you. I am not the judge for anyone. A lot of people are helped from church efforts. Just don't be afraid to examine the records and intimate details. The one that places himself as judge and jury should be ready for such scrutiny. I AM is Tired of you screwing the flock.

Burn in hell you son of a bitch. You use God's name to get your wiener wet.

I listen to the Revelations song, it causes me pain. My true love will never be. But my True Love will be Forever. My love of Christ prevails. You have caused my demise. Why do You subject me to such?

Nathan, my faithful servant. There is much for you. Be patient. You will be rewarded

Your love rewards me enough. Why do I feel so empty? You have given me everything. I have money, I have health, I have no contentment.

Balance. You must have balance. It applies to all life. – Mr. Miagi

How do I get balance?

Patience

Make Love, Not War
Love will make you

Can you take someone for your own? You are taking on a life-time responsibility. Are you sure? Love her as you love yourself.

January 17, 2010
Goooooooooooooood Morning God!!!

Are you still with me?

Always and Forever

You know the one thing that I did pick up from the Book of Eli. He explained faith perfectly. There is no audio or video. You feel it on your heart, So much it compels you to do things you ordinarily wouldn't do. Have you had a heart to heart with our Creator, our God, our Savior?

I have been thinking more and more about the antichrist. He is not of flesh until he becomes your own flesh. A very powerful adversary all the same within ourselves.

It is wise to understand your adversaries. Wouldn't you agree? – Hunt for Red October

So if our children are programmed to look for good signs, in three generations we will see your vision for us complete? You know why it is easier to see the bad stuff. It is how you're raised. It's hard to keep a positive attitude when the crabs keep dragging you down.

Child abusers will burn in hell. I don't believe there is a get out of hell free card on that one. You can take that one up with God, but if I get a vote, you'll burn in hell for eternity. You bastard.

There will be a place off to itself with the other really bad sins at Leper Land. You will be able to see the horrific sin that you have or may have committed in your heart. Even in your mind. You will see the consequences and learn from them. I hope you will leave with much more restraint on your heart and mind. You're sick, twisted, erotic thoughts compel you to do things you wouldn't ordinarily do. I hope it deplores you. I hope it makes you sick at your stomach. I hope it squashes those erotic thoughts. I know you have them. We all do.

RESTRAINT!!!

Hey that's a cool thought. We'll call it the restraint camp.

Isn't it going to be cool walking through the different lessons of Christ via videos. We will all be walking around wearing sack cloths, eating fish on unleavened bread. Far Out. Sounds pretty groovy to me. The movie Passion of the Christ will be on the big screen 24/7. A constant reminder of what he did for you. My Brother, my God, my Savior.

Thank God for the mighty beach mouse. It's a very cool drive. 22 miles on the peninsula. Many of the trees are dead from Hurricane Ivan. It reminds me what happened to Pride Rock when the hyenas were in power.

No Direction
No Balance
No Shepherd

I love that movie when Capt. Hook shoots through Peter's checkbook. Writing a check to save our children reminds me of the lukewarm check writing Christians. They want to buy their salvation and make themselves feel good about themselves. I am not your judge. Who am I to judge you. Let your heart write the check. They are the only ones that will cash in heaven.

I pray to you Father, let this book be the one, two punch for God.

The Acts of
Nathan the Prophet

Book of Nathan II
REDEMPTION

You know it's amazing when you break through to the other side. You are so aware of how silly we conduct our lives.

Status:

Buying things we don't need, with money we don't have, to impress people we don't like.

It's a recipe for disaster.

It is Sunday. A day of rest and worship. I am really digging what you are putting on my heart Lord. Please don't stop.

You know that I AM here for you
Always and Forever
Let your mind follow what your heart seeks

Free Will
Always Been
Always Be

Now I thought that quote was for faith?

Time is money. Power is money. Money is money.

Now let me get that straight – Volunteers

Fight fight fight for Washington state
brainwashing/programming

We are what we have created through free will and faith. Can you think back to your childhood. Were you the one everyone wanted to be like? Or were you the one seeking who you wanted to be like? Guess what my brother. They don't have a clue either. They are probably pretty aren't they? Have you gotten comfortable with yourself yet? It is called confidence. It is very attractive.

Chris Rock told a joke about a really fat girl. He begins to harass her. She says, oh no my brother. There is some good pussy up under there. LOL

Well, I thought it was funny. That confidence is very attractive is it not? Gluttony is one of the seven deadly sins. It will kill you. Take care of your body, it is the only one that you have. But be very careful to remember to be comfortable with yourself. Have a heart to heart with our God.

Don't give your power over to others. When you allow yourself to brood over an act of someone else, it will eat you up on the inside. Guess what, that party that you are sticking needles into is oblivious and screwed up your day or more. Forgive them, so you can receive forgiveness. There is only one that His approval is mandatory. That is our God.

How do I find my talent? Have you seen that commercial where the mom is teaching her son football, golf, tennis etc. He sucks at all of them. Then he reaches her heart with a song solo of appreciation. I am crying now just thinking of that moment.

If you are in something you don't like, strive for more. Don't be petty and blame everyone else for your situation. If IT is to be, IT is up to me. That will mean you have to put down your beer, get off the porch and get a job.

Do you want to hear a racist joke? Sure you do, you love my jokes. There were four tribes brought over from Africa. The first tribe was called the Mo Tea tribe. They were the most successful. You see them in restaurants walking around saying to the patrons, Mo Tea?

The Wee Bee tribe went into sharecropping. They go door-to-door saying Wee Bee selling tomatoes now.

The third tribe is the Moan Back tribe. They got jobs with the city. You can see them hanging off the back of garbage trucks hollering Moan Back.

The Do Da tribe had given up. They place all of their faith in someone else doing it for them. They have intelligent conversations with their peers. Do Da welfare check come on a Monday or Do Da welfare check come on a Tuesday?

You know that joke is really not too funny. That is the racist culture I have been raised in. Look at yourselves. Should I be a racist? Let's just put a fence around this community and throw peanuts to them. Wait a minute. We are already doing that. Hey, sounds like a pretty cool gig. Let me sit my monkey ass down. Hand me a beer.

This seems pretty uneventful. What else do you do all day with your time?

This is pretty much it. If I don't get too drunk, I do have to go pick up my girl at six o'clock up there at the church's fried chicken place. After all, it is her car I'm driving around.

You mean to tell me you sit around and get drunk all day while your girl works to pay your bills?

Yup, it's a pretty cool gig isn't it?

No, I don't think it's a cool gig at all. So my brother, you won't mind me calling you a "N" will you? That is what your actions exemplify.

Why are you calling me a "N", I'm white?

What is your point, it has nothing to do with the color of your skin. A "N" is someone that does not strive to better themselves and sponges off of their brother. You are a blight on your family, your community and your God. Fix yourself or waller in the slop you create for yourself and stop complaining. The peanut truck will be here shortly.

Racism will remain as long as you allow it to. Those kids need a daddy. And more importantly, they need a Father.

Look at your own life. Do you want your children following in your footsteps? Racism is colorblind. Tell me a few of your honkey jokes.

The white cop on Sanford and Son was always made out to be a blithering idiot. No one cried foul. There is no white entertainment television network and no white history month. Stop!!! Let's have an American History Month. You are creating your own divisiveness. The descendents are ready to move forward. Are You? Or do you want a check?

It is very difficult to overcome racism when you see how people conduct their lives. You should see some of the foreclosures that I have purchased. Freaking nasty. White, Black, Yellow and Green. Humans can be nasty. Do you have a family member that is nasty? How can you help him, not support him? Do not support a better standard of living at your expense. Let him rise up and take his mat for himself. Let him put down his excuses and make a better life for himself. I tell you the Truth. I AM tired of the excuses. How can you be a betterment for your neighbor? Cursed be the sponge and blight on the family.

I am getting better with interracial marriage. Just make sure you know all the ingredients. As I said, racism will be very difficult to get over, but as we have seen in our Presidential election, we are ready.

In this fight you saw two people killing themselves for their Country. I guess that is better than 20 million. When I came here tonight. I seen a lot of people who didn't like me, so I guess I didn't like you much none either. But through this fight, I seen a lot of changing. The way youse felt about me and the way I felt about you. So what I am saying is, if you can change and I can change, **WE CAN ALL CHANGE – Rocky IV**

We are trying to change other cultures that we are completely ignorant about. We have our hands full right here at home.

Just calling them like I see them – Bill O'Reilly

How's it working out for you? We cannot change racism by feeding you peanuts. We give you peanuts, so you keep us in power. You are being enslaved and don't even know it. If that is the environment that you choose, don't you deserve to be looked down upon as a unsightly, festered blight and sponge on society? Food, water, shelter, health care and freedom. You are entitled to these by the sweat from your brother, but it won't be comfortable. That's on you.

Lord, I am doinking them right between the eyes. I understand now why I am to remain invisible. Some crazy bastard might want to kill me. Please understand monkeys come in all colors. It's time for the truth. Can you handle it? I still have that mirror. I have it right here.

Look harder. Your Father is in you. - Drafiki

Simba, you are more than you have become – Mufasa

Say it again, say it again. MUFASA

The hyenas will always mock what they do not understand. There is a balance and unfortunately for us, they are in control. How do we take back Pride Rock.

Be all that you can be in God's Army. God doesn't need a draft. It is voluntary and you are already automatically registered the day you were born. You might already owe the government

$131,000 and change, but you are completely debt-free with our God. You will meet the supreme commander. Are you ready? Are you sure?

I loved it when Ramses was using the scales against Moses. Putting weight on one side for all of his supposed problems. Then Moses lays a brick on his side. That is the brick of mankind. Ramses pointed out the rash financial decisions of Moses. Raided the Temple Grains. One day in Seven for rest. Ramses is right and that is where we are at right now. The entitlements can not be balanced with the revenue unless the bricks of Mankind build our Father the Pyramid that is truly Everlasting. A pyramid built with Faith and Saved Souls. An Everlasting Entity that completes the eternal circle.

What does eternity look like? You know how tough this life has been. Imagine never reaching the finish line and enduring unspeakable hardships. I could be wrong though, quite often I am, let's examine the facts. There might not be everlasting peace in God's kingdom. But what if there is. I like my chances. How about you?

I cannot believe that we are trying to grow our economy with more government jobs. Do you understand that government is the cart and Wall Street is the mule? No wonder mules get stubborn. Look at the load we have put on. And we are still stacking.

Can you imagine what the Iranians are going through as they fight for their freedom. They want what we have. If you can't imagine, you better start trying. That is the way we are headed. Government controlling our lives.

A quick thought. Jesus, I cannot fill your shoes. You are Sin-less and I am ripe with sin. No one can fill your shoes. We all sin. It is from your grace we find forgiveness. I am the Prodigal Son. Thank you for giving your life for mine.

We have a code here son. Have your ever put your life in another man's hands, and have him put yours in his. We abide by honor and code. People die if the code is broken.

Do we get to exercise our own personal set of values?

We should have stuck up for Willie. We should have stuck up for the weak. – A Few Good Men

I don't believe that Pres. Obama understands the direction his advisers want to take us. I really with all of my heart wanted to see "Change We Can Believe In". If this is the change that we are to have, I'll pass. The first African-American President. How very cool to have evolved to this point. We need change and Obama knows it. I cannot fault him for his misdirection. It is a new direction after all. I recognize that we are in need of a direction that has only been delivered to you now. Imagine turning to God for change.

Hey that sounds like a good campaign slogan for the Leper party.

IMAGINE TURNING TO
GOD
FOR CHANGE

Unfortunately God is always the last resort. Those of you who have been down on your knees in private know what I am talking about. Have you prayed today? I had to remind myself to pray while I was wrapped up in the rat race. Now it is all I do. He afforded me the time. I promise you, if you will take the time daily to ask for direction, help, love, understanding, he will hear you if your heart is in the right place with Christ. Keep your hands in your pockets. Don't do a look at me, look at me. Do raise your hands to Him in private.

I AM
YOUR FATHER
I WILL
PICK YOU UP

Is your heart right to deserve to be picked up by the Father? We will be snatched up. I just hope I have done a good enough job for my Father so that we get to exercise the 1000 year option on the original contract.

Imagine living in a world where everyone had food, water, shelter, health care and freedom. Can you?

Hey, here's a new deal. If we do it right, it may turn into an eternal contract. After all, we were created for our Fathers enjoyment.

I can tell you truthfully it is a wonderful place to be when you truly accept the Lord Jesus Christ as your Lord and Savior. What others do, pay it no never mind. I have told you, you will be bitten. Learn from it. Forget it and continue your plight for the glory of God. What could you have done differently? Sometimes it is just best to let it go. If it comes back, then it was meant to be. You are at the fork in the road. Pick it up and run with it. God is all the gift you will ever need.

I always wondered when Dorothy got to the fork in the road, they had to make a decision and choose a path. Don't you wonder what was on that other path? They made it to the Wizard of Oz, so they must have made the right choice. Our country is choosing a path, I just don't see it merging with the right path.

Lord, did they choose the right path?

It is free will my son
It is the fork of life
Every second, of everyday

You live with the consequences of your decisions. Wow, how cool. So if you think things through and make an intelligent decision, if you get bit you kind of expected it.

Oh, good story I picked up in my DUI class.

A man is a top of a snow capped mountain and encounters a snake. The snake is cold and knows that it will not live if he doesn't reach the bottom. He pleads with the man to put him in his coat to keep him warm and take him to the desired destination. The man proclaims, but you're a snake and will bite me. The snake says, I promise you I will not. Please help me. So the man puts the snake into his coat and delivers him to the bottom. He reaches into his coat to remove the snake and is bitten. Son of bitch, you told me you wouldn't bite me. The snake replies, you knew I was a snake when you picked me up and put me in your coat. You goofy bastard.

Man, I have had some snakes in my coat. Haven't you? If not, screw you. You are a liar. Believe me when I tell you. The pain is not near as bad if you are somewhat expecting it.

Keep your friends close and your enemies closer – the Godfather

Everyone has pain
Everyone sins
Free will
I made you broken

Will you serve 666 or Him?

246

This is the coolest talent you could have ever given me. Aletheia. I can remember all kinds of shit just at the opportune time. You are feeding me Lord. Keep them coming. I promise to keep this journal of my thoughts.

I must admit, you are right. Just when I was able to say the exact thing that I wanted to say, at the exact time I wanted to say it, I inevitably felt regret. - You've got Mail

It is amazing to read through and see how my own life has evolved. Quite unpleasant actually. Believe me, when you get to decide, you will be ready to meet your maker with no regrets. He can have me anytime he wants.

This man could take us any time he wants – Crocodile Dundee II

We are on his turf and need to learn to play by his rules. We will lose if we don't.

STOP!!!
We're going to die man. If we don't do what he says, we are not going to make it. You've lost the compass. Find it!!! Assholes. - Band of the Hand

What an insightful sleeper movie that was. You see the leaders or baddies of Miami were dropped off in the Everglades to come together or die. They struggled, but when it came down to life or death, they joined together. Thus the band of the hand. Are you ready for Miami? They go back as a unit with respect for everyone's personal talents. They are met with by the man of the man. When they conquered the man, they still had to deal with the real man behind the scenes.

Right will always prevail in an open forum, but we don't know who's behind the scenes pulling the strings. Who is pulling the strings of our Government? This is a must-see. We must all band together as one strong unit and appreciate everyone's talents.

Mr. Martini, how about some music? I got to take a shower now. I want to be clean for God. It is his day. BRB

One more confession.

Well its $45,000 Forrest. Mama said a little white lie won't hurt anything. – Forrest Gump

I did have a one night stand that I did conceal in my first book. Now as I watch our icons go down, it seems important for me to cleanse and ask for forgiveness once again. The Eye of the Tiger could use some forgiveness. All he has to do is ask. Our God will forgive him, I'm not so sure about his wife.

Lord, please forgive me for being adulterous. If this seems petty to you, it is you that I am speaking to. Faithfulness to your spouse means a lot to me. It can make you crazy with all kinds of thoughts. Throw in a couple of meds and oh shit. Where is that line of reality? If you don't want to be there, cut it loose. Just don't take out your frustrations on your partner. Remember at one time you accepted each other as life partners, an a extension of yourself. Believe me, the deal you have is the best one. Work on it. If your partner refuses, cut it loose. It's better for the kids.

I have a choice, watch Obama or Groundhog Day. I already know you have to do it over and over 'til you get it right. Look at our lives. Guess I'll watch Obama.

Great speech as always. Ho Hum

We do continue to repeat history. Over and over again. Not learning from our mistakes, just creating more debt to continue. Kind of like the other fallen empires that debased their currency financing wars. That is why I'm going to buy silver with God's money, so when our currency is readjusted to precious metals, God will have a nice sum for the dream team to take over with. I will have the hard stuff, because I don't want my government to recall them for pennies on the dollar like they did in 1933. The people that abided by the government's demands got screwed. I'll tell them I threw it all in the ocean and made a wish. You calling me a liar. Screw you. How much currency is circulating anyway? Oh that's right, you stopped reporting that in 2006. I wonder why?

READ MY LIPS
NO MORE CORRUPTION

We mock what we don't understand. – Spies like Us

Knoc Sune Cowl
White Warrior – Kickboxer
training/programming
Listen
Listen while you pray
You will hear what you want to hear. Free will
Listen for Christ
What are you hearing?
You have baggage.
Check it at the door

Listen for Christ, look for the signs. They are all around you. Look for good, it prevails over evil. Many warriors have come. Listen while you train. Listen to your ancestors. They cry out to you.

Why do kids have to be so freaking cruel – Bench Warmers

I have never been in a physical fight. I've always talked my way out of it. I am a bit of a coward and don't take pain well. I would like to meet up with my childhood bully. After watching Kickboxer, I feel like I could kick some ass. The nerds you bully today, you will kiss their ass tomorrow. Not on the left side, not on the right side, but right in the middle. I still remember his name. Ahern. What a Dick. I'd like to knock his Dick in the dirt.

Sometimes you have to fight when you're a man – Coward of the County

You will call them boss, Dick Head. We do have our sweet revenge. Nerds, Nerds, Nerds.

Hold it right there coach. Say what you got to say son.
– U. N. Jefferson

Don't let the bully rule your life, make the move that I didn't. First tell the person that is in authority. You can expect an ass whipping for doing that, but you will be expecting it. As soon as you can, pick up an equalizer and knock the crap out of the bully. You will be justified if the authority was not successful in keeping you safe.

Be strong, make good fight. Remember balance Danielson. I just saved you two months of beating – Mr. Miagi

Step up and knock the shit out of them. They'll think twice next time. If not, knock the shit out them with a bigger stick.

Here's an interesting scenario. Let's just say the big guy is getting picked on by the little guy. But he wants to be diplomatic and not use the power that he has to crush the little guy. Eventually the little guy will get a shot in that could be fatal. That sounds a lot like the United States.

You could've heard a pin drop, when Tommy stopped and locked the door. – Coward of the County

Just saw the dog from Family Guy say "whose leg do I have to hump for a dry martini" LOL Funny, I wonder if our children were amused?

I want to tell you about the riddle that I mentioned in the Book of Nathan. The riddle was about Larry's son. I will exchange Larry's name for God.

Riddle:
If God's son is my son's father, what is my relationship to God?

Give up? The answer is glaringly obvious. We are all children of God. Okay, for the people that can't think generationally. You are God's son.

I AM God's son and you are God's sons and daughters. He is real and He loves you with all His Heart. Do you get what kind of Love I am talking about here? ETERNAL

**YOU ARE
NEVER
ALONE**

**I WILL
BE WITH
YOU**

**CALL ON
MY NAME
JESUS CHRIST**

**I AM
HERE
ALWAYS
AND
FOREVER**

I HOPE YOU REALIZE THAT JESUS CHRIST IS OUR DEFENSE COUNSELOR BEFORE THE FATHER.

My friend Brian and his lady friend Kim, have both told me they do not understand very much in my second manic episode. I am going to cut and paste that chapter and explain my thoughts. God was placing on my heart so many thoughts that I could not write them down fast enough. It was like a waterfall. To encapsulate the essence of the message, I was able to draw from segments of the movie clips. These were in my reticular activating system and brought from my subconscious to the forefront of my brain. I hope you enjoy.

January 28, 2010

I haven't written my thoughts down for a few days and I pray I can remember everything that you put on my heart. I want to make sure to discuss my weekend with my son, because I was trying to be a good dad and he refused to listen. But we will come back to that one.

Lord, I asked you to give me some more credibility that my mission for you is the correct mission. I am very fearful of being on a slippery slope adding words to yours. It is my desire to do your will. You gave me a very large piece to this puzzle this morning and it will be up to your people to decide. I do not normally point out the dots that I have found that have kept me on a path to persevere. I do not want to draw any more attention to myself than I have to. But I felt like this one is so enormous and so wonderful, I must share.

My sign from God. He speaks to me in different ways. I am looking to Him for guidance, not 666. It is my free will to serve my creator and not Satan.

I found this on the web written by David Ross. I will try and get his permission to use his words.

Sura 38:26 is a quote from a book or oral-tradition of prophecy. But not Muhammad's. This was in Nathan's context and was most likely attributed to Nathan and Allah both.

As it happens, Nathan had been considered a canonical prophet, worthy of a holy book, long before the Islamic and even Christian eras. 1 Chronicles 29:29 runs, "As for the events of King David's reign, from beginning to end, they are written in the records of Samuel the seer, the records of Nathan the prophet and the records of Gad the seer".

Sura 38:26, perhaps with a reworking of 2 Samuel 12 midway toward Sura 38:21-25, could have provided an apocryphal Book of Nathan, in the way mediaeval Jews and Englishmen forged <u>Books of Jasher</u>. Admittedly this is speculation. No such book has yet been found.

Lord, I had no idea the task that you have assigned me. You did tell me that I would not be able to comprehend your reach. And you also know me, when you put a riddle on my plate, I do everything to solve it.

World Peace....for eternity.

Wow, what an honor. If my book has credibility with the prophetic Islamic faith, we can all come to realize we are serving the same Father. There is only one Father. Everything after that is subject to man's interpretation and free will. I understand that my words that I am speaking for you my Father will be subject to critical analysis. As I have told you, I am ready for my crucifixion.

Lord, I am not worthy of this honor. You have said that I am ripe with sin. Why have you chosen me?

Nathan, you are not worthy. That is why I gave you a new name in Christ. Ophiuchus became you and you became Ophiuchus and you gained the talents that come with Ophiuchus. You Nathan, of your own free will, chose to serve ME your CREATOR

Thank you God, you are who I live for and you are who I Am and will ever be.

So you gave me these talents and they had been there the whole time, but I had to seek them out for myself. By our own free will, will determine whether you use your talents for the glory of God or Satan.

If we can only come together as children of God. The possibilities are endless of how we can help one another. I've asked you this before, can you imagine Peace in the World? No hunger, no disease and no wars. This has been God's plan the whole time. But our free will had to find his Kingdom on Earth as it is in Heaven.

You may believe in any interpretation you wish. I will not tread on your beliefs and I will not allow you to tread on mine. I would suggest reading the Scriptures of Jesus Christ' life. His message was of love and helping your fellow man. That is all that I am trying to achieve as well. I pray that we can all accept that we serve a higher power. I would love to be your brother in Christ, that is your free will.

As I think about this, I am reminded of the movie War Games. A computer was built to simulate military strategies. One of the games was global thermal nuclear war. The result of the game was the realization that there are no winners. If we continue to head in our present direction, this will come to pass.

I also found it interesting that the computer's name was Joshua. The movie explains it was the creators son's name. We are still in the Joshua era searching to figure out God's plan and go to the promised land. Now I have to tell you the truth. If my vision of world peace is your vision of world peace, that sounds like the land of milk and honey to me. The whole earth is the land of milk and honey. It is the responsibility of the five talent man and the two talent man to explain to everyone how to invest into themselves to please their God. As "One Nation Under God" I consider it our personal and primary objective for our Lord and Savior. We are the beacon nation and should blaze a path for God's glory.

Lord, will I see World Peace in my lifetime?

You will see One or the Other
Peace or Destruction
Health or Disease
Love or Hate
Life or Death
It is the Free Will of All to make that Choice

I Am your humble servant Lord, I will ask of your people to search their own hearts to find their talents and Glorify You with them.

That 666 riddle was tough. Who will we follow with the talents you have bestowed upon us all? Free Will and Frame of Reference.

Nathan my Son, my faithful servant. You are only now beginning to see My Vision illuminate in your heart

Lord, a smile comes across my face as I reflect back on Rocky's boss cheering him on to victory. Saying, "Go For It ROCK".

Peter was your Rock and I want to be your Rock as well. He denied you three times before the cock crowed before realizing what he had done. He Denied you. My cock is crowing over unsatisfying sexual encounters. To find balance, I must find love. My love is for you my Lord, but I yearn for a partner.

Can you tell that I am getting a little drunk. My inhibitions are lightened with drink. So are my decision-making skills. But a lot of times, I want to talk to you like a drunk at the bar. We are all lepers. We all have our problems. I pray in your time of need, you call on our Father. If you have not reached that point in time in your life, God blessed you. When you do reach that point in your life, know that He is there for you to rely on. I tell you the truth, if it were not for our Creator, I would be dead of my own free will.

You have the free will to worship any God you would like. I have put all my chips on Jesus Christ our Lord and Savior. You have seen what God does for his chosen people and you see what God can do for his chosen people if anyone stands against them. They are still misinformed, but this will be a reckoning. They want to place blame on the Romans, but it was the Pharisees that condemned Jesus. Do not condemn the Pharisees, just as I do not condemn Judas. They were all part of the plan, the Masters Plan. I have asked our God to forgive Judas for his betrayal to Jesus Christ our Lord and Savior. I have asked for forgiveness for the betrayer of mankind. I am sure my brother Jesus Christ, the only Man God to ever grace our presence will concur forgiveness. It was all part of a plan that is now being illuminated to my heart as we speak.

Lord, World Peace has been spoken of for my entire lifetime. Mostly by the beautiful bimbos at Bikini contests. How can my words change the world and deliver World Peace?

It is Time
The World is Ripe
My Time has Come

256

What do you mean by that?

You know very well what I mean
You have worshiped Satan
You have sinned an unforgivable sin
Have you asked for repentance?
I forgive you, sin no more

Okay, got a question for you. There are things that I do, that I think are sinning against you. But I continue to do them and ask for your forgiveness. I am unclear on how I can receive forgiveness for continually committing these sins.

Are these sins hurting someone?
Are these things glorifying you or your God?
Are these things embarrassing?
Are these things front page material?

If not, stop beating yourself up about them. These are the things you keep private until you allow a partner into your weird little world

Weird Little World

My brothers and sisters in Christ, I have so much to tell you. I am going to talk to you about all the things that are embarrassing, humiliating, unspoken and just downright bad. These are things that must not be censored, these are things that must be understood to conquer.

You know, I feel like I'm on the let's make a deal show. Curtain number one has shown me a way to solve our nation's fiscal woes. And curtain number two has shown me the loss of two wives, one daughter, the scrutiny of loving parents, scorn from peers and a completely unbalanced life. All for the sake of a God that I am not sure exists. I'll take curtain number two. As curtain number two is drawn, more options are put upon me. You have solved your nation's fiscal woes and can take the rewards now or you can risk it all and go for World Peace.

I guess I would always go for it. Howie Mandel would be proud.

We always go for it, that's why we are cons – The Longest Yard

I guess I will go for it now. There are so many prophets that are being suppressed, one never knows when the next one will finish the task and King David can finally rest.

Lord, I am so very turned off to organized religious groups. Why have you callused my heart for them, they do such great work for you?

The Church has not changed since the day of your Savior. I Am sending you to make retribution. The true Churches will become the facilities that not only spread my word, but facilitate my Love with Health Care

I thought the people would donate these facilities?

Nathan, are you not a business man. The Lord your God is about to take account for the ones that have been collecting in my Holy Name

I dig it. So you are saying that there is a fast track to giving your people health care?

Yes, Yes, Yes. There is always a fast track when you have the Will of your God and the needs of his people

Sounds good to me. They have been a business for God, can they be a Healer for God?

Each will search their Heart
Each will find their Heart
Each will find my Blessings
Each will live for an Eternity

So while we are above ground we need to tithe to our churches and passions and when we die, never stop?

Men with Talents
Never Rest
Men with Talents
Coach their Brother
Men with Talents
Create Comfort
Men with Talents
Have Vision

I don't know exactly how many talents I have, but you have kept me in unrest. I have tried my best to mentor, I am delivering your plan that will create comfort and I have your Vision. What Now? I am tired. I didn't sign on for the whole World Peace thing. You kind of slipped that one in on me. Lord, I am up for the challenge and any others you may place before me. Give me the strength to Endeavor to Persevere for the Glory of GOD.

Not to put anyone on the spot, but this is just about the only traction I got while trying to break through to the higher ups.

Nathan Isbell October 23, 2009 at 2:50pm
We have a mutual friend in Mr. David Walker former U.S. Comptroller and that is the reason for my contact with you. I can only assume you keep up with Davids work on the Fiscal Wake Up Tour. I really do think that I have the solution, but am

finding it very difficult to reach anyone that can spear head my efforts. I have spent five very long years working on this project and would love to get it off my plate. Please read my blog (soon to be website) www.legacywillandtrust.com and tell me why this won't work. If you don't know, please pass it on. My goal is to get this in front of Mr. David Walker.

Your New Friend,
Nathan

Legacy Will and Trust
www.legacywillandtrust.com

Smart Facebook Friend October 25, 2009 at 6:59pm
Hi Nathan -- I am not an expert on trusts taxation, but my first thoughts are:

(a) tax-exempt foundations usually are comfortable spending 4-5% of their principal each year in order to maintain the real value of their endowments, and they don't have to pay taxes. So the potential spend out from your taxable LLC would be lower still, perhaps 3-4%.

(b) I don't see a new revenue source for the government since the assets in the LLC would presumably have been either (i) been collected as estate taxes or (ii) invested by the heirs, etc.

Good luck,

--Facebook Friend

Nathan Isbell October 25, 2009 at 7:12pm
Hi Facebook Friend,
Thanks for responding to my email. I too am no tax expert, but merely look at it in layman terms. Of course the charitable organization will not be taxed, but if the total life benefit is not taxed when it is transferred into the LLC and then the dividend

checks are immediately taxed prior to going to the heirs, wouldn't that be considered a tax deferment?

Thanks for your help in advance,
Nathan

Facbook Friend October 26, 2009 at 9:22am
Yes, that sounds like a deferral.

Nathan Isbell October 26, 2009 at 9:28am
Excluding taxation, market fluctuation and governmental issues, what do you think of the concept?

Nathan Isbell October 26, 2009 at 9:32am
Have you gone to my temporary concept website www.legacywillandtrust.com or are you looking at my blog? My first contact with you only included a blog, I have since created a temp site for concept and exposure purposes only. The mechanics of the site to produce an individual a Legacy Will and Trust are forth coming.

Facbook Friend October 26, 2009 at 4:37pm
Hi Nathan -- If I understand correctly, you basically want to allow / encourage folks to leave bequests in the form of long-term annuities (to both heirs and charities) rather than lump sums. Does that get it right? Seems like a fine approach if people want to do that, as long as you can get the transaction costs down. Sounds a bit like setting up a foundation but giving very specific directions on where the money should go.

This is an important Facebook Friend.
Current City: Washington, DC
Education and Work

Grad School: Massachusetts Institute of Technology '94
- Ph.D., Economics

College: Harvard '87
- Mathematics

High School: Phillips Academy '83

Employer: Georgetown Public Policy Institute
Position: Visiting Professor
Location: Washington, DC

Employer: Council of Economic Advisers, The White House
Position: Member
Time Period: 2007 - 2009
Location: Washington, DC

Employer: Congressional Budget Office
Position: Deputy Director / Acting Director
Time Period: 2005 - 2007
Location: Washington, DC

Employer: United States Congress, Joint Economic Committee
Position: Executive Director and Chief Economist
Time Period: 2002 - 2004

Employer: Charles River Associates International
Position: Principal
Time Period: 1998 - 2000
Location: Washington, DC

Employer: University of Chicago Graduate School of Business
Position: Assistant Professor of Economics
Time Period: 1994 - 1998
Location: Chicago, IL

Mr. Facebook Friend,
I do so appreciate you responding to my FaceBook email. You get it. HooRay, Someone with Financial Intelligence gets it. Mr. Facebook, the American people and the World are begging for it. It just has to be explained in Joe the Plumber language.

"Seems like a fine approach if people want to do that, as long as you can get the transaction costs down."

Mr. Facebook Friend, I so appreciate your professional financial opinion of God's Plan. I believe you have hit the nail on the head. It will work unless people are apathetic or man places to many fees on man.

Faith, Hope and Charity. These are the key ingredients for salvaging the World that God have given to us to destroy or love as He loves us.

October 23, 2009 at 5:08pm
We have a mutual friend in Mr. David Walker former US Comptroller and that is the reason for my contact with you. I can only assume you keep up with Davids work on the Fiscal Wake Up Tour. I really do think that I have the solution, but am finding it very difficult to reach anyone that can spear head my efforts. I have spent five very long years working on this project and would love to get it off my plate. Please read my blog (soon to be website) www.legacywillandtrust.com and tell me why this won't work. If you don't know, please pass it on. My goal is to get this in front of Mr. David Walker.
Your New Friend,
Nathan

October 23, 2009 at 5:18pm <u>Report</u>
When I received your "friend" request I hesitated because I am a Liberal and we don't seem to have much in common - excepting David Walker - who I know personally. If you also know

him, why have you not sent your request directly to him via FB or his office at The Peter G. Petersen Foundation here in NYC?

I am preparing for a business trip and cannot review your website/proposal at this time. However, I suggest you write to David directly w/your request(s) and/or recommendations. The Foundation is set up to be participatory and since you are a FB friend, send him a note.

Be well. r.

Nathan Isbell October 23, 2009 at 5:40pm
I have numerous times to no avail. I will try once again. If after you read my blog you think it has merit, I would appreciate any help you can offer.

October 23, 2009 at 5:42pm Report
It will be a couple of weeks. However, if you sent the info to David a couple of times and he was unresponsive - then I would respect his rights and not press him. r.

Nathan Isbell October 23, 2009 at 5:47pm
Exactly, I did not want to irritate someone that I believe will be ultimately instrumental in launching these websites. Thanks for taking the time to read my blog. My web designer is six weeks into it, so I am hoping they will be completed soon.

Nathan Isbell October 25, 2009 at 8:34am
Hi Ms Facebook Friend,
Please check out my new videos explaining how www.lega-cywillandtrust.com will solve the nations health care woes. I still haven't heard from Mr. Walker. I would appreciate any help you can offer in getting this to him. I would like for him to tell me why it wouldn't work, so I can stop exhausting my efforts for it to be heard. I have a great career and could have easily left this alone and went on with my life. But God would not let me rest until I

had done everything in my power to present his gift. Think about that for a minute. If you really in your heart felt God had given you a gift to share with all of mankind and you didn't exhaust all of your resources regardless of the distractions of life, how would you feel on judgment day?

Thanks in advance for you help,
Nathan J. Isbell

p.s.
This has been one heavy cross to bear. I have been carrying it for five years, I could sure use some help or someone to tell me that it is the wrong cross.

Legacy Will and Trust
www.legacywillandtrust.com

October 25, 2009 at 10:43am Report
Nathan, I cannot give you the time or attention you require - and, it is inappropriate to use Facebook to press people weekends no matter what you have to say/offer. That is my advice. We are not your agents, marketers, etc. And, I did advise you I was planning to leave on a trip at this time. You have to RESPECT the time/needs of others before you can get traction for anything - no matter how good.

Signing off.

Was it a trip concerning Health Care? I tried contacting some dumb ass from the Heritage Foundation and he didn't have time for me either, he was late for a health care reform meeting.

I Endeavor to Persevere. With or without your help.

Have you met with this type of resistance in you life? It sucks. Remember I tell you the truth, the Crabs of your life will keep you silent. You must Endeavor to Persevere. Always Respectfully

Question Authority. Our Forefathers used the phrase "Question with Boldness".

Play it close to your vest
Have a back up plan
-Dad

Know you swim with Sharks
Expect to be Bitten
Learn from Mistakes
Pursue your DREAMS
-Nathan

Stoney, I Am counting on you. Get your prize by making your brother's load lighter

Lord, I Am not my brother's keeper.

That is Correct
You are
His Beacon
His Direction
His Motivator
His Decimation
His facilitator
His Judge

He is still
Thy Brother

Thyself is
Thy Brother

Love Thy Brother
as Thy Love
Thyself

Okay, now let me get this straight.

Oh shit, are your leaning again?

Well, a little, but don't change the point here. You put this worthless piece of shit on my plate to care for. He should read some books and re-invent himself as I did.

You are His Beacon

He should be coming to you just as I did. Lord, mans world broke me down to the point all I could see is Faith.

You are His Direction

I can't even get his sorry ass out of bed and when I do, I have to take care of him all day. It sucks, I have things to do myself.

You are His Motivation

I've seen him work, it sucks and he has compromised my position with my friends trying to help him.

You are His Decimation

After I had gone through all of my contacts trying to help him, I had to loan him some money just to eat.

You are His Facilitator

I just can not allow myself to get wrapped up with him again. It's a nightmare every time. He just didn't make it.

You are His Judge

How are we directing our breathen? I don't even feel like answering that question. You do it God.

Each Man is born of Talents
Each Man makes decisions of Free Will
Each Man is given a Path

Yes, that is correct my Father. But sometimes the very men you speak of are corrupted by the easy path and will not elect to have the desire for a better life over an easy life that there brother has provided.

I ask of you Nathan. What should their punishment be? You want to place yourself as Judge and Jury, so I ask you now with the Wisdom of Solomon. What should be done? Answer carefully

It is not my place Lord. I must contend with being a provider to the less fortunate. I can only try and stimulate their desire for a better life. But I don't have to make it comfortable for them.

Good Answer my loving, faithful, humble servant. Your Humility will bring you far in the Kingdom of Heaven and your brother will be with you, you will inspire Him

I remember during my pledge inauguration to Chi Phi. We were broken down with sleep deprivation and mental mind screws. My brothers will remember that it was I that said "Enough". If we unite, we have control. The authority backed down immediately and complied with our wishes. You must challenge the authority, I promise you they will back down. If they do not, know that you have the God of the Israelites on your side and devour corruption for your own salvation and the salvation of your children.

Am I defying you Lord now by being hammered on Vodka?

Nathan,
I have chosen you because you are everyone.
Strip away the Clothing
Strip away the Verbiage
Strip away the Flesh
You are I and I AM YOU

Lord, this is to much to ask of your humble servant. How will I gain credibility?

Once again you question the reach of your Lord. I warn you Nathan, don't do it again

My humble apologies my Savior. I will assume my role in your plan. Regardless of the naysayers.

What is my role in your Plan? Have I not delivered your Seven Sealed Two-Sided Scroll? Have I not fulfilled all that I was purposed for?

With Great Power, Comes Great Responsibility
Your Purpose for ME
As if I need You
Bury your Vanity
Live with Humility
You are because
I AM you are

Please accept my humble apologies Lord. I am your servant. Guide me. I will question your motives no longer.

You have laid a bread crumb trail. Expand upon your thoughts given unto you by ME. There is great wisdom for those who would listen

That is my next project Lord, but while I have your ear, I want to ask you some more questions that I don't have a clue would be relevant.

What is important to your world now?

I will make my peace with my Family. I will make my peace with my enemies. I will make my peace with my community. I will make my peace with my country. I will make my peace with my WORLD. And Peace will come to my forefathers, because we finally got it right and we can all rest in the Kingdom of Heaven. King David can rest. For the First and Last Acts of King David are recorded in the Book of Nathan. The lineage of King David will build God's Temple with the bricks of Mankind.

Hey, Just a reminder that I am just an ordinary dude. Lots of problems and sins, just like you. Would you go to the lengths that I have if you really didn't feel it on your heart? Dude, I didn't sign up for this either.

Imagine traveling across country and arriving at Wally World to find it closed. - Clark Griswold

I guess I went a little nutty.

You went a lot nutty. - Vacation

Imagine having the key to Heavens Gate and no one will listen.

I am glad I went nutty. I am red hot for Jesus. You lukewarmers keep writing your checks, we do need your support. I pray one day you can commit fully and be red hot for Jesus yourselves.

It was that connection with Islam, the Qua ran and the Book of Nathan that pieced it all together for me. My Purpose was for much more than I bargained for.

This will be the Greatest Sale of the World. I have no proof of shit. I only have Faith and a difficult to understand, book of religious parables for a compass. It's all good Jesus. We are challenging their Faith. I can dig it. I have a few mustard seeds to sow of my own.

As I read my own metaphors, I realize that the Bible was written in a different time of slang. I don't have the answers for their metaphors, just as I would not expect them to understand mine. I can only try as they would. I do know that my Savior preached love and kindness to your fellow man. That would be a great start.

This is cool, if I have your platform I can say anything that I want.

Remember, you speak for ME
BE COGNISCENT OF YOUR WORDS

Yes Lord, 1 will try. That reminds me of the ones that are in control of our children s minds. Our teachers, a very undervalued position of POWER. I ask of you truthfully, are you committed to the well being and desire of the children you mold? Be aware, everything you say is imprinted in their minds. Choose your words wisely. Our Future is in your capable hands.

Nathan, You are trying to change the World using my Words. Did you think it would be easy?

Uh......No

Duh.....No

Just Watching Sarah Palin on Fox News. She is opposed to the health care reform bill but offers no solution. Those of us that know reform is necessary will push for their own agenda. Right or wrong, they will push. I pray that the Masters plan will accommodate everyone. Please Lord, let your Plan be heard. You hired a lowly salesman. I'm doing the best that I can. Give me a break.

Nathan, I will keep you in unrest. Just as your brother David and Solomon are in unrest now. You must prevail to achieve your own rest

Cool, but let's talk tomorrow. I'm drunk.

Nathan, You have been getting drunk everyday for sometime now, what do you have to say for yourself?

Lord, I beg of your forgiveness. I am in so much torment from loss and the thought of redemption being just around the corner has caused me to want to fast forward my life to that point. These days go quickly and I don't remember much. I hope you don't mind talking to a drunk. You did hire me by the way.

Sleep it off my Son, we'll talk tomorrow

Hey, I don't give a flying fat rats ass what they believe.

Go to bed my Son, tomorrow is another day and we'll talk

Good Night Father, forgive me for my outrage.

Good Night My Son. Nathan, not even I can save you from the free will that you put into your body. I grant you health, it is your free will to destroy it

Got it. Good Night.

Gooooooooooooood Morning God.

As I was lying in bed this morning, I was reminded about a chat that I recently had with one of my Facebook friends. I don't exactly remember what her point was, but she referred to herself as a descendent of slaves. I told her that I was a descendent of slaves myself. I am a Gibeonite. The Gibeonites were spared by Joshua through deception and later were discovered and made slaves to the Levites.

So what I want to know is, what are the Statute of Limitations? Are there any Levites still around? They owe me big time, with lots of interest.

I realize my approach is laced with sarcasm. The point that I'm trying to make is, your forefathers paid a debt so that you may have a better life and strive for more, not sit around and wonder how much more you can get from the descendents of the ancestors that enslaved your ancestors. You are still being enslaved by not striving for more on your own merit. You are enslaved to poverty of your own free will. Stop blaming your situation on someone else and take responsibility for your own free will. There are still barriers, I pray that they all come down with time. It is your personal responsibility to Endeavor to Persevere.

Excuses are like ass holes, we all got one – Platoon

The Parable of the Three Rings

Gotthold Ephraim Lessing
An uneasy peace ruled in Jerusalem. Saladin's victory against the Crusaders had cost the Muslims dearly, both in the loss of troops and in the depletion of the royal treasury. Saladin was resolved to rule with civilized humanity as far as possible. But it

was an uneasy peace, with Jews, Christians, and the newly victorious Muslims all suspicious of one another.

Thus when Saladin requested an audience with Nathan, a leading Jewish merchant, the latter was very apprehensive about the Sultan's motivation. Nathan was known far and wide not only for his successes in commerce, but also for his skills in diplomacy and negotiation. Jews, Christians, and Muslims alike called him Nathan the Wise.

Nathan's suspicions were well founded, for Saladin was indeed looking to replenish his exhausted coffers with a loan or a gift from his wealthy Jewish subject. Too civil to openly demand such a tribute from the peace-loving Nathan, the Sultan instead masked his request in the form of a theological question.

"Your reputation for wisdom is great," said the Sultan. "You must have studied the great religions. Tell me, which is the best, Judaism, Islam, or Christianity?"

"Sultan, I am a Jew," replied Nathan.

"And I a Muslim," interrupted Saladin, "and between us stands the Christian. But the three faiths contradict one another. They cannot all be true. Tell me the results of your own wise deliberations. Which religion is best?"

Nathan recognized the trap at once. Any answer except "Islam" would offend Saladin the Muslim, whereas any answer except "Judaism" would place his own integrity under question. Thus, instead of giving a direct answer, Nathan responded by relating a parable to Saladin:

In the Orient in ancient times there lived a man who possessed a ring of inestimable worth. Its stone was an opal that emitted a hundred colors, but its real value lay in its ability to make its wearer beloved of God and man. The ring passed from father to most favored son for many generations, until finally its owner was a father with three sons, all equally deserving. Unable to decide which of the three sons was most worthy, the father commissioned a master artisan to make two exact copies of the ring, then gave each son a ring, and each son believed that he alone had inherited the original and true ring.

But instead of harmony, the father's plan brought only discord to his heirs. Shortly after the father died, each of the sons claimed to be the sole ruler of the father's house, each basing his claim to authority on the ring given to him by the father. The discord grew even stronger and more hateful when a close examination of the rings failed to disclose any differences.

"But wait," interrupted Saladin, "surely you do not mean to tell me that there are no differences between Islam, Judaism, and Christianity!"

"You are right, Sultan," replied Nathan. "Their teachings and practices differ in ways that can be seen by all. However, in each case, the teachings and practices are based on beliefs and faith, beliefs and faith that at their roots are the same. Which of us can prove that our beliefs and our faith are more reliable than those of others?"

"I understand," said Saladin. "Now continue with your tale."

"The story is nearly at its end," replied Nathan.

The dispute among the brothers grew until their case was finally brought before a judge. After hearing the history of the original ring and its miraculous powers, the judge pronounced his conclusion: "The authentic ring," he said, "had the power to make its owner beloved of God and man, but each of your rings has brought only hatred and strife. None of you is loved by others; each loves only himself. Therefore I must conclude that none of you has the original ring. Your father must have lost it, then attempted to hide his loss by having three counterfeit rings made, and these are the rings that cause you so much grief."

The judge continued: "Or it may be that your father, weary of the tyranny of a single ring, made duplicates, which he gave to you. Let each of you demonstrate his belief in the power of his ring by conducting his life in such a manner that he fully merits -- as anciently promised -- the love of God and man.

"Marvelous! Marvelous!" exclaimed Saladin. "Your tale has set my mind at rest. You may go."

"Sultan, was there nothing else you wished from me?" asked Nathan.

"No. Nothing."

"Then may I take the liberty to make a request of you. My trade of late has brought me unexpected wealth, and in these uncertain times I need a secure repository. Would you be willing to accept my recent earnings as loan or deposit?"

The Sultan gladly acceded to Nathan's wish.

And thus Saladin gained from his wise Jewish subject both material and spiritual benefit, and Nathan the Wise found a safe haven for his wealth and earned the respect of the Islamic Sultan.

- Source: Abstracted from Gotthold Ephraim Lessing, *Nathan der Weise*, a drama in five acts (1779). Events leading up to Nathan's telling of the parable are depicted in act 3, scenes 4-7. The parable itself is contained in act 3, scene 7.

You have heard from the Jews and the Muslims. They have a ring, I have only my Faith. I AM Christian. - The Prophet Nathan

I AM proud of you my son. You have taken your place finally. I will guide your thoughts as I have and you will put my words on all hearts that would listen

Take your place Stoney. Make our world a better place and claim your prize. Your Fathers Praise.

Good afternoon Lord. I realize there is no way I can give all of my thoughts to your people. It is a never ending waterfall.

Nathan, why have you not considered this your job? I have satisfied your financial requirements, yet you creatively avoid Me. You now know My vision. Why are you hesitant?

Lord, you have placed a tremendous amount of responsibility on my heart. Yes, you have shown me how to deliver your message. But I do not know if I can. Who am I?

ME DAMN IT, Nathan get your act together. Take your place. I have a lot invested in you

Why do you continually come to me in a drunken state?

We have talked all day, yet you have written nothing down. What do you have to say for yourself?

I'm scared Lord. I'm scared for using your words. I'm scared that you have not given me any visual or audio signs. I am not sure I am on the right mission. But I am sure I am on the right mission.

Nathan, all I have asked of you is to write your thoughts down. You cannot change the world that you live in. It is the free will of your peers that will change it. I like your idea for the back cover of this book. Please recite it for ME once again

God, please grant me the **SERENITY** to accept the things I cannot change,

The COURAGE to change the things I can

And the WISDOM to know the difference.

– Your Humble Servant and Brother In Christ

ALL MEN

Nathan, tell your Brethren why you chose that prayer for your own thoughts. This book is about the Acts of Nathan the Prophet after all. TELL ME

Lord, because I am a broken man. I am heart broken, lonely, addicted and yearning for the truth to be told.

Next time, tell me what you really think. LOL
Tell the Truth as you have observed it
Don't be shy
Don't be embarrassed
Don't be intimidated
Remember, I have your back
Who can be against you

I don't like it when you call me out on my problems. I know who I am and you know who I am.

STOP!!!
I know who everyone is

I know their every thought
I know that they worship 666
I know that they worship ME

The question is...
What do you see? How do you conduct your everyday lives? Do you cleanse your soul by going to Church on Sunday and making sure everyone notices your presence? What do you do on Monday through Saturday? I am not your judge. You are your own judge. Just remember, when you meet Jesus, drop the bullshit. And Pray that you have dropped to your knees in private long before that time comes to pass.

We are going to get around to those dirty subjects My Lord. I am just finding some creative avoidance myself. Are you insisting at this point?

Why a fig leaf?
Why clothing?
Why embarrassment?

Forgive me Lord, my drunkenness has caused me to forget what you have told me.

I have had so many vodka moments. You are telling me so much and I am not a faithful servant. You have put your faith in me and I have put my faith in you, but I am inept. I am flawed. Please make me the witness that you so desire. I am so screwed up.

Nathan, it is not possible for you to encapsulate the entirety of my message. You will need the infrastructure of a team. Your team will show another side of you. Let those without sin, cast the first stone

Yes Lord, but I do apologize for my shortcomings for you. The thoughts that you are putting on my heart are for the betterment of mankind.

I am completely blank Lord. I have failed you once again. How can I possibly show your people your vision of world peace? It has been a fantasy dream of our society for as long as our generation has been alive. Every hot chick that has ever posed in a bathing suit has always opted for world peace. A very novel request, but one that has not been achievable until now.

Lord, I know I am getting ahead of myself. But I am in that frame of mind to interview you. I am struggling with the concept of me being your messenger. You have shown me over and over again, that I am speaking for you. I am still questioning myself. But if I am speaking for you, I want to make the most impact that I can for your glory.

Talk to me. I beg of you to talk to me. I have prayed and prayed and prayed. Please allow your humble servant Nathan to deliver your message without bias.

Nathan, you are my humble servant. I am speaking through you. My people will heed your words because they are the truth. The truth is in everyone's heart, their minds will explore the consequences

Lord, you have not given me a staff or anything that would exemplify I am telling the truth. They will need more proof.

Proof, proof. How much more proof do they need? You have shown them the Father's plan. They all see how it can work. When you bring your God into your life, All is Good. Love me, as I Love You

You know Lord, I have not even gone through the second manic episode, but I must talk to you now.

I need your guidance. I am lost.

Follow the breadcrumbs of your past. Many will have been eaten by the birds and the corrupt. Follow your heart, your mind will fill in the blanks. I AM with you

January 30, 2010

The Buddhist say we create our own heaven and hell here on earth. This is very insightful, because the whole earth is the land of milk and honey. Of free will we can choose 666 or God. If God is eliminated, we are responsible for our own demise. These wars won't stop until the earth is no more. However, God's option is to choose love for your global brothers and sisters in Christ. World Peace.

Many cultures have artifacts portraying men with large penises. We giggle with embarrassment and miss the message being conveyed. The message from our ancestors is that this head does the thinking and directs our decisions. This head destroys lives. Without restraint, this head destroys you. Our ancestors wanted to make no mistake in conveying this message, hence the size of the organ. We missed it with the shame. Further discussion later. This is a big topic. Pardon the pun. LOL

As you are diagnosing my disorder/gift. I procrastinate to do, then when done, I procrastinate to follow through. If I ever do, I have already moved on to another thought.

Please understand, the most creative minds will provide the most comfort. But their thoughts go unfulfilled. We need a thought board, so everyone can participate in the process. Maybe other creative minds are good at following through. What a winning combination that would be. Will you marry me? LOL

Watch the "Thought Board". Many people will become rich, it may be you. Do not be afraid to post your thoughts. You won't do anything with them anyway at this point. But you may gain new inspiration to follow through. All any of us need is encouragement.

**A BROTHER
DOES NOT
SCREW
A BROTHER**

**I
FEED
OFF YOU
YOU
FEED
OFF ME**

**YOU
INSPIRE ME**

**YOU
COMPLETE ME**

**I LOVE YOU
MY BROTHER
IN
CHRIST**

Forrest

Yeah, Bubba?

You just lean against me and I'll lean right back against you. This way we don't have to sleep with our heads in the mud. - Forrest Gump

So many times I have procrastinated in picking up this project. My God gave me signs of encouragement. So I endeavored to persevere. You will see signs. You will see signs. You will see signs. Which signs are you looking for? 666 or God. Why is the bad stuff easier to believe? Is it the path of least resistance? Is it harder to be good?

When we Weave a Web
We become Trapped in What
We have Created

Look at the life you have created for yourself. Is this what you envisioned that you would grow up to be? How can you aspire to change it? If you do not aspire to change it, be content with it.

I wanted to be a magician.

What are you now?

I run a syndicated porn operation.

Well, I guess you're amusing people in a way. - Mr. Deeds

Please understand my disorder/gift keeps me in constant unrest. My first book has not even launched and I cannot contain my excitement for our Lord and Savior, so I am writing a second book. I thought my purpose was to salvage my country and then I was led to salvaging my world with world peace. I cannot imagine what my third book will be about. LOL Moses, King David, King Solomon, Jesus, Muhammad and I, will stay in unrest until God has his kingdom here on earth as it is in heaven.

How am I doing John? Who are the 24 elders? No, do not even think about putting that on my plate. I'll find out when I get there. And I'll find out who's leg I have to hump to get a dry martini. LOL

This is Darryl and my other brother Darryl. - Newhart

I can't wait to meet my other brother Nathan the prophet. I am convinced he was King David's son, who else would have the balls to scold a King unless he was your dad.

You know he would never kill his son. Or would he? Be careful to not overplay that right. They are your mother and father and warrant your respect always.

Unfortunately, you do have to respectfully question their authority when you are in the process of building your core sense of values. Always refer to the Father for advice in this arena. And keep your damn mouth shut, so you do not offend the ones that gave you birth. They deserve your respect and Love. Just understand that their frame of reference may be limited and they are not the mentors that you are looking for to fulfill your purpose for God. Love them and honor them, but understand there is but one Father, theirs and yours. Abide by His rules.

Umpa Umpa Dumpa Di Doo. I have a riddle waiting for you.

If you will listen you will go far. - Willy Wonka

WOW WOWSIE WOW WOW WOW!!!
Can we really achieve WORLD PEACE?
It is a very clear vision now.
It is my God's vision.
It is the fulfillment of Moses's vision.
Do you really think these cats knew about Wall Street?
If they did, how could they explain it?

BIRTHRIGHTS
DESCENDENTS
LINEAGE
NUMBERS
12000 X 12000
144,000

I can just not emphasize this enough. Can you just imagine if the "We are the World" fund raiser had been invested? Can you just imagine the starving children of Africa receiving their daily bread and we don't have to reach into our own personal budget. Their fund is creating jobs for us all.

Can you feel it?
Exercise the Demon
Repent and Thou Shalt Be Saved
 - Pet Detective

I do love being right. LOL

I just did an intensive study on Islam. Well maybe not that intense, I'm lazy after all. I watched You Tube Okay. I wrote all their research down and I am procrastinating to type it in this book. I promise, it'll be in here. Some very cool stuff that ties us all together under ONE GOD and ONE GOD ONLY. This is why my vision is so clear. But I feel like playing some more. For now.

Lord, give me some more clips to tell them about.

Go to your Second Manic Episode

Your no fun. I am still procrastinating.

Let me tell you about Creative Avoidance. LOL My dad has been in the market to buy a car for over two years. Why do we pick the fly shit out of the pepper?

Because some do come from a frame of reference to play it so close to the vest, that it infringes upon their ability to take a risk. Unfortunately, I see this generation moving into just that type of arena. Recession, Depression, what does that really mean? The hole we fall into may be inescapable.

You can't bench press your way out of this one. - Jingle all the Way

And we can't borrow or create money any longer.

Remember when the Prince from some Bogus country was courting Ellie Mae Clampett? He had piles of his country's currency, but it was used as the napkins at the Clampett's feast. "The thing about Possum is, it's just as good the next day." LOL

Waste not, Want not.
I thought every child was taught this. I was wrong. When you move into the Depression era, you will learn this lesson the hard way. Have you ever heard of leftovers and have you ever cooked up a crockpot full of beans and fed everyone three meals from it. You better wise up. I always used to hear the starving children in Africa story. Then I would say, here, send them this. This is what I refused to eat. You know what, they would gladly take it and be so humble and gracious. It will be all they have for the week.

I have been meaning to tell you about the movie War Games. I may have already mentioned it, but this is what happens to me when I drink. I will repeat myself over and over and over again. LOL now where was I. Oh yeah, the machine was built to discover there was no winner in nuclear war. WOPR

Do you remember in the karate kid, when they were discussing Pearl Harbor. Daniel talked about the American loss and Mr. Miagi reminded him of the Japanese loss. Then he says " WHY WE SO STUPID".

Are we really that stupid?

No, but sometimes you have to fight when your The Man.

I'll ask the perceived "Axis of Evil".

What is it that we are doing, that would cause you to provoke us to the point you give us no choice but total annihilation from God? I AM Christian and accept my brother the Jew to be Gods Chosen people. I do not begrudge my Brother, I love my Brother as I love you my Muslim Brothers. Just as Joseph forgave his brothers for their unrighteousness. We need to forgive each other and live in Peace and Harmony in this Great World our God has given unto us.

If our leaders continue to use God as their divisive instrument, it is for power, money, greed and CORRUPTION!!!

Ask any Dad who has lost a son. Ask any Mom who has watched their child starve to death.

The Government is to keep us safe. Period. The rest is up to us to control. We The People.

God will have His Government over Man or Man will destroy themselves. It is free will. It is the antichrist we presently chase. I want more.

I wrote the book on wanting more. The question is, how much more?

I want the fairy tale.

Tell me Kit, who does it ever happen for?

What, you want a name? How about Cinderfreakinrella. - Pretty Woman

A single shoe
can change
a Life - Cinderella

A single Book
can change the
World – The Holy Bible

You know Lord, I am having a hard time with this Prophet gig. Speaking for you is treading on a slippery slope.

Dammit Son,
If not You
WHO?
You are Ophiuchus
Be Strong like the
LION

Cool, I just like to keep my defense shields up from those that would throw rocks.

Stay Invisible My Son
Your Vanity is not of your
Control

Simple request folks. My vanity abounds and I would love to be a visual spokesperson for our God, but it is not about me, it is about Him. So I can not.

Do not Worship me, for I am merely a Man. - Pet Detective

Do not pursue this Man
He has done what I have asked

**What have you done for Me
Lately?
GOD
ALLAH
YAHWEH
So sayeth, the twenty four Elders**

Hey, I'm still looking for that drink and where is the can?

VANITY – The Devil's Advocate

Look at that nut that got his family to lie about a child being in a runaway balloon.

How did that work out for you?

As I told you I believe I am a descendent of slaves. A descendent of the Gibeonites. I don't really know, but it makes for a good story line. Do you remember that movie that the butler listened to his employer and made wise investments himself. No one knew. Not even his daughter, who was impressed with materialism.

Being a servant to the Levites was not a bad gig. They were in the Know. They were fed, watered, sheltered, cared for, but did lack freedom. But gained companionship.

Treat your employees as you yourself would want to be treated. They have lives just as you.

**Compensation is Warranted
When the Warranted Is Due
The Warranted Is
Not Entitled**

J. O. B.

Get one and be wise and patient. Strive for more on your own efforts. If IT is to be, IT is up to me.

If your not first, your last. I lived my life by those words.

I must have been high, drunk or both when I said it.
Talladega Nights

Not everyone is first, we are all part of God's Team. So Let's "SHAKE -N- BAKE".

Be Mindful of Words
Impressionable Minds
Live by Your Words

Not everyone is first and we all don't get a trophy. I will try harder next time. I want a trophy.

How did you get a trophy for that piece of shit you built?

Oh, I just got one for showing up.

Really, no wonder. Congratulations, your project exemplifies your motivation.

Duh, thanks. Didn't you get one, they are over there on the table.

No my Brother. I don't want one of those. I want what I earn. It makes me feel better about me and motivates me for more.

I think I'll continue to strive for more just because I feel better about it and I know my God wants me to have an abundant life that I create for myself.

SECOND MANIC EPISODE "THE CRAZY STUFF" REVISITED

I felt the need to explain myself. When I was in a full blown manic state, a waterfall of thoughts were coming over me. The only way that I could encapsulate the essence of the message was to sample from my subconscious and bring to the forefront of my brain something that will help trigger the thoughts. These are my breadcrumbs so that I can revisit and tell you my thoughts.

*will denote new additions.

I AM

I AM contacting you now.
Is Help really on the way?
Check out the front page of USA Today October 9, 2007

*This article was my first exposure to the Fiscal Wake Up Tour Challenge.

I have the remedy.
I am ready.

666 – important dates?

Riddles:
27 coins
What happened to the other dollar?
Two men Two doors
Larry's son

*I believe I have told you about all of these except the 27 coin riddle.
Riddle 27 Coins:
You have 27 identical coins, except there is one that is slightly heavier than the other 26. You have balancing scales

to work with. You are allowed to use the scales three times and three times only. How can you be 100% sure that you can identify the heavier coin?

I recently ran into my old Physics teacher from High School. I told him that this riddle had stuck with me, he couldn't remember it. One more reason for teachers and mentors to pay close attention to what you tell your kids.

Anyway, do you give up?

Take three stacks of nine. Put one stack on each side of the scales and one not included on the scales. If they are balanced then the stack not on the scales has the heavier coin. Obviously, if one side is heavier on the scale, take that stack. Proceed with the same process two more times. 3 – 3 – 3, then 1 – 1 – 1. I'm not real sure why that stuck with me.

I am gay – Kevin Kline

*Just watched this movie where the school teacher was coming out of the closet and the ones of authority were trying to suppress him. The town loved him and accepted him for who and what he is. Just as the Father accepts all of His Children.

If I could just get some bottom land – Sgt. York
I figured those guns were killing hundreds, maybe thousands, so I had to stop them guns.

After Sgt. York got what he wanted, I heard he returned back to the bottle.
You sure learned a lot up in those hills Alvin.

*Sgt. York was trying to impress his girl with materialism and all she really wanted was him. I guess we have been trained that for sometime and everyone suffers the consequences of be driven for more and more and more.

Sgt. York found Christ and truly wanted to follow scriptures. He had to do a lot of soul searching to go agin the bible by killing men. He found his peace when he realized that to keep the peace, some men would die. But peace would save many more than would be lost.

The demon in the bottle can get the best of us. Be Careful. What is your bottle?

It must be nice to always think you're the smartest one in the room – Broadcast News

*This is a simple case of old lady/young lady. Be careful you do not become so smart that another alternative becomes blind to you. Your opinion is based on your frame of reference. Have you really seen, heard and or experienced everything? Take the salve from thy eyes. Your brother is pretty smart too.

If you could express yourself right now, I know that you would do a better job than I – Hook

*Peter was addressing a group of grown orphans that Granny Wendy had taken in and cared for. He was saying that words are just not enough for the Love and Appreciation due to her. If we give Love, we get Love in return.

Simba, you are more than you have become – Lion King

*I hope this one is self explanatory. Inspire for more out of life. It is what you make of it.

Young lady / Old lady – Shallow Hal

*This pictures illustrates our frame of reference. We draw from our subconscious and make our decision. Be open minded, there are always alternatives. Who will you serve?

Fire, Fire, Look at what I have created – Castaway

*God creates everything. Man utilizes what God has given us to create comfort or misery. We are an innovative group of God's children. Don't suppress us any longer.

World Peace – Miss Congeniality

*You slipped this one in on me. I accept the challenge. Wouldn't it be great to see World Peace in our lifetime. I am hopeful that it doesn't take three generations to see this prophecy fulfilled.

Loaded gun – There's something about Mary

*Refer to the letter to insane males.

Rape, Pedophile, Institutionalize – Shawshank Redemption

*Can you imagine being trapped in an environment that you have no control over and someone is continually hurting you. Then you grow in this environment being your norm and become terrified to break away from it. The story ultimately represents the pursuit to endeavor to persevere and claim your own Redemption.

Republicans and Democrats – Heat Miser and Mr. Freeze

*I love this Christmas story. The two bickering brothers and getting nothing accomplished. It took Mother Nature to straighten her boys out and it will take God to straighten us out.

Island of Misfit Toys – Lepers

*Who can't relate to one of these cats. We're all screwed up in some form or fashion. Or are you a liar? I'm a Nathan in the Box and I will be heard.

I wish I had $1 million – It's a wonderful life

*If it is to be, it is up to me. Don't tempt your God and make it a wonderful life whether you get the million or not.

My people want freedom and I go to see that they have it – Braveheart

*Are we ready to pull together as One Nation Under God and receive Healthcare from our Creator?

You make me want to be a better man – As good as it gets

*Lord, you inspire me to be to be a better servant.

You complete me – Jerry Maguire

*You will never be complete until you accept the Lord Jesus Christ as your personal savior. He is our mouthpiece to God.

Scooby Doo ending – Wayne's world

*I sure am praying for a Scooby Doo ending. Look at the mess we have made for ourselves. God's Plan will work.

Fake charities – The Jerk

*There is always someone pandering for gifts. If you can create it, market it and sell it, by all means we want to hear

your idea. Don't by pass the people and go to Caesar with kick backs and back room deals for them to buy into your own wealth building agenda with our money.

Ability to smell an ambush – Braveheart

*We must become aware of our surroundings and frame of reference. There are people serving man 666 and their attacks can screw up your little world. Be mindful and ready, not paranoia. This is no different than being a cautious driver anticipating their fellow drivers moves. Have forgiveness in your heart, not forgetfulness. Learn from your mistakes, start with the first one, you will repeat it time and time again until you do. Lovingly counsel those you see that are lost, in PRIVATE. DON'T INSIST they hear you. Plant your seed and see on which path it will land. It is always of our own free will. I ask you for the truth, are you the one that is 666 to your brother? Here, need a mirror?

Run for it Marty – Back to the Future

*What is it Doc?

It's the Libyans, I stole their plutonium and sold them a canister of used pin ball parts.

Whether we realize it our not, we have been trained to fear our Global Brothers. Guess what, they are getting the same brain washing. If we do not overcome this prejudice, it is going to land us in a War that has the potential to destroy this beautiful planet our Creator has given unto us. Be fruitful and multiply. I just can't remember the part about being divisive and destroying one another. Our One God has a different plan. It starts with the first step to a 1000 yr journey of a Satan free world. God's Government, God's Treasury, God's Kingdom here on earth as it is in Heaven. God's Temple will be built with the bricks of Mankind. I pray that you live in Freedom and can be a part of it. Your God wants you to have Freedom. Believe me, there is no kitchen table in the World that's wants Nuclear War, but some World Leaders are pushing to the point of NO CHOICE. Stop Them and Free yourselves.

Opinions are like assholes, we all got one – Platoon
Two camps – Hate and Love

*And the opinion of the arrogant, vocally robust continue to rule over God's people. You will abide by their opinion or you will be shot. Do you really think that is how our Creator wanted it? If you are in the Hate Camp, I beg of you to give the Love Camp a try. If we don't start loving one another, we will destroy one another. I am asking each and everyone of you, what can you do to help create World Peace?

Turkish prison – Pain, Guilt, Customs, Cultures, Homecoming – Midnight Express

*Pain – The punishment that he endured in prison.
*Guilt – What had he done to his Loving Father?
*Customs – Unfamiliar with customs that caused more pain.
*Cultures – Everyone has a different frame of reference based on what they have seen, heard and experienced.

*Homecoming – Any Father welcomes home their Son. Just as our Father will welcome us regardless of what we have done. Just be careful with those unforgivable sins. I just don't think there is a get out of Hell free card on those. If you don't know which ones they are, Pray. You will know.

Golden goose – Jack and the Beanstalk

*This is probably the best lesson in patience and greed. If you had a Goose that laid you golden eggs everyday and would lay golden eggs for your heirs for an eternity, would you kill it to get the eggs inside?

*If you had an heirloom that produced you a passive income check and a passive income for your heirs for an eternity, would you cash it in?

Fame – Failure - Rebirth and Wiser – Rock Star

*How is it that you can strive for so much out of your life, but when you get it, you don't know how to handle it? Don't be a rags to riches to rags story. Educate yourself while striving to achieve your dreams. Once you achieve your dreams is when your true character will emerge. I ask you to reflect on the role models of your life that you believe that God would approve of. Now, emulate them and strive to emulate Jesus Christ our Lord and Savior. Your shortcomings will be forgiven with a simple truthful request. Forgive me Father for I have sinned...........
Thank you for your Grace Lord.
Amen

Wizard of Oz – TD Jakes

*KNOWLEDGE – COMPASSION – COURAGE HOMECOMING

Will we ever get educated and see the World for what it is. A Gift from our Creator?

Will we ever gain Love for our Global brothers and prevent famine, disease and suppression?

Will we ever gain the Courage to do something about it?

Will we get to see our Savior do his biggest miracle yet and achieve World Peace in our life time? That's a Homecoming that I can only articulate, but would love to experience. How about you?

Will work for food

*We have all seen these signs. I heard a sermon where the preacher made a comment about it not breaking the family budget to give them a few bucks. You just never know when you might be saving someones life. Jesus says, when you give to them, you are giving to me. A few words of encouragement and prayer will suffice. As much as you would love to do more, you must remember they are Lepers as we all are and they may cause harm to your family if you embrace them to much.

666 # of a man?

*I am still working on this riddle at this time. It was a tough one.

Get your credit score up to 666 and you have a right of passage as a man
Rituals – Roots

*I don't think this is the 666 solution, but while we are here let's talk about credit. If you intend to borrow, you must intend to pay it back with interest. Be very careful with credit. Materialism could easily become the God that you serve. Been there and done that. It is a miserable World believe me. You have to get on that treadmill of life because you have no choice.

I owe, I owe, so it's off to work I go. This is a noble work ethic, but be careful not to allow your materialistic dreams to destroy your contentment dreams. You will save yourself a lot of sleepless nights.

Can I get an big Amen on that one. Whewww.... what a nightmare.

Betrayal – Patrick and Terry

*I have forgiveness truly in my Heart, for I know the only way I can receive forgiveness of my transgressions is to forgive my transgressors. That doesn't mean I have to forget.

Hit me once, shame on you. Hit me twice, shame on me. Hit me three times, I am coming after you.

The Two Headed Beast is what holds us captive, it can be slayed. This is the struggle that every Man contends with. - Restraint

*Refer to the Letter to the Insane Males

The market needs more money for continuity. God's Legacy Trust LLC will create a new foundation.

Question for you. How many generations will it take for God's Plan to create a foundation in our economy? A propagating income stream is just that, it's builds upon itself. It would be nice to know that I am investing into something that has a foundation created by God's people that can never be touched. It will seal an eternal marketplace.

Real-life knowledge – Back-to-School Rodney Dangerfield

*Didn't you just love that part where the professor was trying to teach about business when he didn't have a clue of the real world. I remember attending a Sunday school lesson and the teacher begins to tell us that he is not an alcoholic or

addict or any of these other problems. I just thought, well you need to sit your monkey ass down and let's hear from someone that has experienced Leprosy and by the Grace of God and their own free will, freed themselves of it. I don't need you to damn me. I need you to inspire Me.

Lower-priced tuna, That's American man. Schooner tuna, the tuna with a heart. – Mr. Mom

*It always amazes me, when the chips are down we all pull together for the betterment of our neighbors and ourselves. I believe the chips are down my brothers and sisters in Christ. But this time it is Global.

Lord, please help your humble servant to inspire his Global brother. Until we reach out Globally, we will never see what are Creator had intended for us. The land of milk and honey. The whole planet, it is what we make of it.

If our World was a football team, would you say we're having a winning season? – Heaven Can Wait

*Let me see, we have wars and rumors of war. We still have hunger, disease and suppression. We have dissension and corruption amongst ourselves and our Global brothers. I'd have to say, just a personal opinion mind you, that 666 has a major league lead. But I know our God is the comeback Kid. When there is Faith and Hope, Our GOD is unstoppable. Now get out there and win one for the One God, he is everlasting. We all are his children. Heat misers and Mr. Freezes alike. Muslims, Jews, …..................... and Christians alike.

We don't care what the other teams are doing, we want to do the right thing. If the porpoises are getting caught in the nets, we'll charge an extra penny per can to save them. We'll be on the porpoise team. We'll advertise "Would you pay an extra penny to save the fish that thinks?"

I want it now daddy – Willy Wonka and the Chocolate Factory Impatient – No Discipline – No Guidance – Uneducated - Greed

Hold up signs during clips like Wayne's world, cool

*I was just being silly here. You must become as a child to connect with our Lord and Savior Jesus Christ.

I was rushed through my mortgage closing – Ignorance

*Every decision you make will serve Man 666 or God. Think before you react. The consequences could cause you great harm or joy, be careful with your decisions. They could last a lifetime. For those of you that don't realize it, that's a really long time. Maybe even eternal.

Do you know how easy this is for me? – Good Will Hunting

*Pulling from my frame of reference that was built from what I have seen, heard, read and experienced is easy. Putting it all on paper is the hard part. The truth can always be found in our past. But generation after generation we think we know more than our parents. We need to wake up and wake up now. If our God doesn't destroy us first from frustration, we might end up destroying ourselves of our own free will. I mean really, how much does our Father have to do? I asked him that question and ran right into a brick wall with his answer. Do you remember? What Nathan, do you want another disaster? Not no, but Hell no.

Why we so Stupid. - Mr. Miagi

303

Stay free mini pad joke

*There once was a midget that was on the wrong path of the Lord. He was put into prison for his transgressions to his fellow man. While he was there he found the Lord and started reinventing himself with knowledge. By the time he had served his time, he was ready to make it in the real world. He became very successful and when he ran into a fellow midget inmate, he discovered his pal had not been near as fortunate and was on the run from the law again.

This inspired the successful midget to build a half way house to build confidence and hope amongst his midget brethren. They were educated and could enter the work place with a completely different attitude. They were there to do God's work. Let me tell you brother, your days go by a lot more pleasant with a Godly attitude. The joke was that he named his half way house, stay free mini pad. Wah, wah, wah. Kboom...Ching

Build businesses for the lepers and halfway houses
Hope of going home serving humble pie
Pie – Michael

*Midgets or Lepers, we are all children of God. Give your leper brother a chance, but keep your antennas up.

He smells like cookies – Michael – vanity

*This is simple. Are you doing what you are doing for the Glory of God or the Glory of yourself amongst your peers?

What do you do when your real-life exceeds your dreams?
Keep it to yourself – Broadcast News
Corruption brought on by Envy

*It is so easy to enjoy the success. Be mindful, your brother could be having a terrible day and be envious of your success. When it is your good day, ask your brother about his day. If it is bad, be empathetic and wait til your brother is having a better day before sharing your own good news. Remind him of the everlasting good news about our Lord and Savior. God has a plan for everyone's life, the pitfalls make us stronger to witness for our Lord. Inspire your brother, I can not say this enough. If you don't inspire, you will carry your brother.

He 'aint Heavy, He's my Brother.

Brother you know I was just thinking after my chat with our God and Creator. He says if I inspire you, I won't have to carry you. How can I help my brother to strive for more in his life? What can I teach you? Brother, I am sorry that my taking the easy approach and just giving to you has decimated your desire to want more for your life. Brother, I can no longer continue to carry you. The load on the mule has reached it's breaking point. If I can't inspire you, we both are going down. Tell me brother, what motivates you? What are your dreams? What are your goals? Yours are different than mine, but I appreciate how they compliment each other.

I was saving up for a Husband – It's a wonderful life
Generosity – Compassion – Racism

*This is our History. It is, what it is. Let's learn to accept it and appreciate the lessons from it. It is time we all joined together and appreciate what all of our brothers have been through. It is also time to stop using it as a crutch.

I've got a Golden ticket – Legacy Will and Trust – Willy Wonka

305

*Yes I do. But what a struggle to be heard. Not even ole Slugworth was around. No, if it is to be, it is up to me. Losing everything for my God was a little extreme and I would have preferred having a partner on this journey, but this journey was for me and me alone. I'm Crazy after all. I chose God.

Feed tuna mayonnaise – Night Shift
Creativity – realized failure - QUIT
How much will it cost your family?
Bipolar disorder
How much does it cost us, to not let you create?

*You know, you can't make chicken salad out of chicken shit. But someone thought it would make great fertilizer. Encourage your children to follow their dreams. Be aware, they may see a different dream than yours. Are you shoving your dream down their throat. This dream can bite back. Don't alienate yourself by running your child's life. Be a part, not the focus of their lives. We have to learn from our own mistakes, learn to plant seeds. I would recommend listening to Lou Tice's series of tapes. Very informative when raising children. You can feed life into your child or death, just any mentor can.

Would you hire a leper?
Let's all take our masks off and put on a new one
Mask – Jim Carrey

*We all want to express ourselves in our own unique way. I only ask of you to look at yourself in the mirror and honestly ask yourself if you would hire you, to manage the integrity and money of your own business? I pray it works out for you. If it doesn't, refer back to the mirror.

Funny how when he puts on the Mask, the real person inside emerges. Is this what intoxicants do? Hows that working out for you?

*It hasn't worked out to well for me. Everything I have ever done really stupid, I was drunk. But you probably have a lot more control over your addictions than me. I pray we don't hurt anyone before we kill ourselves.

Anyone who challenges
You're going to lose – A League of their Own

*With God on our side, who could be against us? That's right, your own frame of reference stored in your subconscious that makes the decision for you to serve 666 or God. You could actually be against yourself. I wonder if that qualifies to be called "Shooting yourself in the Foot"?

Let me just stop you right there, before you say something you will inevitably regret – You've got Mail

*When you say or do things in a rash manner, you will ultimately second guess yourself and a more thought out decision could serve more beneficial for all concerned. Think things through very carefully, then live with the consequences.

That's the gift that keeps on giving – Christmas Vacation
Legacy Will and Trust

*Yours and God's Legacy will keep giving to the Earth and the inhabitants thereof. Your heirs will come to know the Lord by witnessing His Healing Power. God so wants to heal His children. His Earthly Entity will do just that with the bricks of time and mankind. Legacy Will and Trust – "Growing God Back Into Our World One Generation At A Time".

Not everyone thinks like you Patrice.

Oh yes they do, they just don't admit it. – Coming to America
Narrow Minded – No understanding of Cultural Diversities

***This is a great illustration of how our frame of reference
dictates our behavior. It is so easy for us to think we were all
raised the same and in the same type of environment. This is
what causes us to be so narrow minded. It is hard to see others
views when our own views are the only right approach that
we can see. Before acting on anything important, console your
family and friends. Respect their opinion and make up your
own mind. You will be the one living with the consequences.**

We must be getting close, I'm getting a hard on – Top Gun

***What can I say, I'm an insane male. I am a Leper. I have
restraint over the beast.**

October 16, 2007

Financial Intelligence Required

Before I except my clinical bipolar diagnosis, take my meds,
suppress my creativity and slip into a lethargic state like the rest
of the kids on Ritalin. I would like someone with financial intelligence to tell me why this won't work.

Will someone please answer these questions? Can legacy will
and trust: feed the world - stop drug abuse with quarterly screen-
ings for non-prescribed medication - keep the stock market from
crashing – Answer my 11-year-old stepson's birthday wish to
bring prayer back to schools – show the world we want peace
through the teachings of Jesus Christ – not to mention a check
from God's Legacy Trust for their daily bread – profile everyone

that wants free services – such as healthcare and food – will this help to stop terrorism by knowing who is here?

Cut through all of the political spin? Start healing people on the inside with mental counseling? Why did the 14-year-old kill himself for God? Did his teachings from home not match society? Put God back into our hearts? Change foreign perception of the United States and God. If not the present generation, possibly the future generations that are receiving Legacy checks from God? Stop civil liberties unions from pandering to the sensitivities of other cultures and beliefs, while sacrificing what my forefathers fought for? Stop global warming? Just kidding or am I. Put your money where your mouth is. Let everyone know that God loves us so much he sent his only son to save us. We crucified him and it set us on the wrong path? Set us on God's path?

Anonymous Christian/African-American

Set up a global warming trust fund, so I don't have to pay for you to chase rabbits.
Don't you dare ask Caesar for another red cent.

I worked real hard for this Louie – Trading Places
Trust

*We all work hard for our money and expect our Government to frugally keep us safe and headed in the right direction. It is past time we start headed towards our past and once again become One Nation Under God, Indivisible with Liberty and Justice for All.

Movie – kids get wrapped up in their class instructor while he was illustrating how easy Hitler had it. Can we rally behind God? The insignia for God's Legacy Trust LLC means healing. Red Cross – Jesus has left, but the blood remains. Gold and Purple Serpent – Temptations – Sin

*This instructor conducted his own campaign to see if he could rally his students into doing things that they wouldn't have done had it not been for brainwashing. When you rally people, you can really get people fired up into going along with the vocally robust. Be careful you don't find yourself rallying behind something you really don't understand. You could be supporting something that could actually be harmful to you. Beware of large overwhelming things. Their intent was to overwhelm you to keep you from being enlightened to the real hidden agendas. If it is too difficult to understand, it is corrupt.

Escape – Indian – One who flew over the cuckoo's nest

*Do you ever just want to get off the planet and sit on the sidelines for awhile? Do you remember when Maverick disengaged from his struggling wingman? He needed time to assess the situation. I promise you, make time everyday for our Father. Have a heart to heart in private and you can put your life back into perspective. Now that you realize 666 is what you choose to serve and not an outside influence, you can begin to see a new beginning for your life in Christ.

Let Caesar have what is Caesar's
15% Federal 5% State
Let God have what belongs to God 10%

*This sounds fair to me across the board. Let the rich keep more and I promise you, they will create, give, love and nurture more. I always thought if the movie theaters would keep their concessions reasonable, we wouldn't have to smuggle in our own goodies. I know in my heart, if they were reasonable they would make more money and provide a better entertainment environment. Unfortunately this exemplifies our tax structure here in the United States. People are still smuggling their candy in and our Government is passing out Joo Joo

Beans to anyone who didn't plan well or work for it at our expense. The rich want to be fair, the corrupt rally the people for their own self gain. This should be what we strive for. A flat tax structure. No monkey business. Cut and Dry. Then budget around it.

I don't know about you, but when I needed to get my budget in order I sat down with my bills. Looked at how much was coming in and how much was going out. We are in an oh shit moment like we have never seen before. What is the first thing we do? Cut up credit cards. Move money around to get the best interest rates. Pay off the smaller balances first, then move to the larger ones. We do not create anymore debt and we tighten our belt by making cuts to unnecessary expenditures and strive to make larger payments to our debt. Debt free and Financially Free. That is the place to be baby.

So tell me, should any business or Nation for that matter have a different strategy? I can only speak for myself, but giving me more credit cards was definitely not the right direction. I needed someone to ask me, can you live without the country club for awhile? All the way down to eating beans and wieners. Let me tell you, when you're debt free, those are some damn good beans.

You must understand, we have been trained to consume. If we stop to consume, our machine breaks down. We need to learn how to consume, so that what we consume does not consume us with debt.

I did not want to bore you with numbers again, I was looking at the $10 million illustration for the starving children in Africa. It says, if in 1985 $10 million was collected and put into a feed the world Legacy trust fund yielding 10% annually, the African 2008 Rice budget would be in excess of 1.5 million that costs the taxpayer zero dollars. That's a lot of rice that we didn't have to ask for a donation for.

After the $10 million was spent and not invested back in 1985, what is the Rice budget today? How are we going to pay it so people don't starve? What better way to stop the war on terrorism, than by winning their hearts through their stomachs. Win with love.

How much does the Jerry Lewis telethon fund have in their account? How much would their Rice budget be? Or will we need another boring Telethon to feed today's need.

*I wasn't ragging on Jerry, he's a great man for all his efforts. But I do have to wonder what the balance would be if all of that money had been put into a Legacy fund. Wow, what would the disbursements look like today? How many jobs would be created by the funds being invested into our economy and the charity surviving on half the profits for an eternity?

How many examples of how God's Legacy plan works do you need? Money may be the root of all evil, but it can solve a lot of problems. When your money works for all of us, rather than us working for money. At present, we spend more than we have and the marketplace has caught up with us. Can we leave our future generations a bill or a check. The time for change is now. Or we could just leave it to our dogs. I can only hope they have more financial intelligence than the current recipients.

When the government pension plans go bankrupt, will that wake us up? Probably not, that generation will be dead.

*If a pension is unsustainable for civilian businesses, shouldn't they be unsustainable for Government. Jump on in, the water is just fine. We can't take away what we have

promised, but we can let it die out. We can't abandon what we started in Afghanistan and Iraq either. How can we be trusted with information if the people are afraid we will pull out. Can you imagine how they are being threatened. You know the Americans will leave and when they do, I will torture your child if I hear of you turning any of us in.

October 30, 2007

To: David Walker
Re: Fiscal Wake Up Tour Challenge

The answer is compounded interest. In lieu of increasing the inheritance tax, allow taxpayers to use their death benefits to open an LLC. This LLC will be invested into the US stock exchange. The monthly yield will be reinvested 50% and 50% disbursed to the taxpayers heirs. This creates a new found income stream that can be taxed forever.

Our arrogance makes us think it is trying to communicate with us – Star Trek IV
Cultural Diversity-- Ego

*It's all about me. We all conduct our lives by what's in it for me. If our mindset would change to what's in it for my brother, our World would completely change. Remember, when you give your brother what he wants, you get what you want. I know this will be hard. You must have faith in your brother, but keep your guard up. You don't know who he is serving.

Such Decadence – Moscow on the Hudson

*We are a generation of entitled people. We don't look upon what we have, but what we do not have. Our brother

313

has it, why don't I? Brother can you spare a dime, now give me your wallet. Income Tax, Death Tax, Sales Tax, Breathing Tax....................................... ETC.ETC ETC How does our Global brother perceive us? What would they give to have what we have? We are sooooo Entitled.

Happy learned how to putt – Happy Gilmore
Focus – write what I want to say

*Have you ever put together a project that comes with pieces and instructions? A major pain in the ass the first go around, then you realize if you had to do it over again it would only take you a fraction of the time. Your life is a project as it forms your frame of reference. Everyday new pieces are allowed to enter at your discretion. You must focus on what you allow to enter and accept what your brother has not.

Exchange info for a transfer – A Few Good Men
Discrimination for Legacy

*Are you trapped? Jenny didn't have to live with her father anymore, she moved in with her grandmother. You must be discreet. You must find the person that you most trust. Not necessarily clergy. Been there, done that. When you make your move, close that door and another will open for you. Forgive your transgressors so that you do not dwell on it. It will eat you up on the inside if you do not forgive. You never have to forget. Our Father is very sorry that He has to allow man 666 power over man 666. I will pray for you that you are able to pull yourself out of that trap with the help of our God, family and friends. God will have His vengeance on your behalf at Judgment Day. This is the unforgivable sin. Preying upon the helpless.

Problem first – Discrimination
Solutions second

*I have come a long way in judging my discrimination frame of reference. How ignorant I have been. It should never be by the color of ones skin. It should be by each individual actions that encompass their essence. Now, judge yourselves. What do you exemplify to your brother?

Drawing for a month-long cruise, one ticket per person, one dollar. That is your permanent number, maybe this is the number you need to get goods and services or this is the antichrist. I don't want to be the antichrist.

*All of us are the Anti-Christ when we accept him into our decision making process. Be quick to listen and slow to respond. Our decisions are now the history. How does your history read? Christ like or Anti-Christ like. Pray for forgiveness and forgive your brother.

You don't tug on Superman's cape. You don't piss into the wind. You don't pull, the mask off the Lone Ranger and you don't mess around with HIM – Jim Croce

*If I am to be kept silent by my judges, I can not fulfill my purpose for God. Seek out your purpose for God. Be very careful. Is this your purpose for Him or for You? Step out for our God and you will be judged by your peers and you will be judged by your God. Who is your real friend when you are all alone in the World? Who will never leave you when you are at the lowest point in life? Who will forgive you? Who will love you for who you are, no, who you really are behind the mask? Oh, be sane about it. The crazy shit didn't work out to well for me. LOL

I don't know who I am
I don't know who I am supposed to be
I do know, I am more than I have become. – Lion King

315

*This is what I was seeking. Nathan, you are more than you have become. Who are You? What do you do for the betterment of your neighbor that creates wages for you to fulfill your contentment dreams? What is your purpose for God? Is this too deep for you to think about? Are you too busy fighting the rat race? If you seek, you will find. The signs will be unbelievable to your brother, but your brother is not your judge. He just places himself as judge. When you know who you are, what you do and your purpose for God, you will achieve an abundant life. It is our Fathers promise.

I am on the verge of a nervous breakdown.
Without a backup plan and God to talk to, I cringe.
Would prescribed medication erase the line of reality and cause me to do something I ordinarily wouldn't do? I think so.

Hold on way a minute, let me put some God in it. Ooh Aah

If this plan doesn't work, I am as crazy as a run over dog. Check me in. No prescribed meds please. On second thought, I'll have the buffet.

I feel your pain – Million Dollar Baby
Parental Alienation Syndrome

*Who knows you more intimately than God? Ask Him to relieve you of your pain. It will be your faith that heals you. Don't tempt thy God to heal you for your belief in Him. Trust that our God has given your brother talents to heal you with the gift of health care that He so desires to facilitate for all.

Anyone willing to give up birthrights for one lump sum. I want to know what he is going to do with the money. He may be a prophet.

Special Ed is for Goofy screws – Island of Misfit Toys

*I am a Misfit Toy. I don't fit in with my circle now. I hibernated while searching for my purpose. I was socially inept. I just wanted to tell everyone what I was going through. They looked upon me as crazy and weird. I prefer to be referred to as different. In fact, I like being different. I believe our God makes us all different and most yearn to be the same. Conformity is a powerful tool. If I am different because I profess the Lords love for me is true, what does that say about what we have conformed to. I believe our God wants all to be different for Him. He is the goal post, He is the finish line.

The Starving will Sing
Rub a Dub Dub
Thanks for the Grub
Yeah God!!!

*I don't know why this little humorous prayer stuck with me from my childhood. It always seem to piss the older people off for some reason. I guess it would be better if it read the starving will work for food.

A horny man is a dangerous thing – History Channel
Men can not be trusted to adopt. Heterosexuals have a hard enough time restraining from perversion. Homosexuals will cross the line of morality and a child should not be subject to such. Lesbians can procreate on their own during a one night stand, but their perverted make up is totally different than a mans and I believe they make fine nurturing mothers. Neither should be allowed to adopt.

I ask our Father time to fix problems. Give me the strength to make them heed.

Do you want Hank? – Me, Myself and Irene
Vulgarity – Two personalities – Good and Evil – Angel and Devil

*Hank is the character that stands up for himself to the extreme. He is invincible in his own mind. Years of being meek will sometimes make you emerge to something you want to be to address your transgressors. You can let your hatred build up to such a point that you lose your compass of reality and do things you wouldn't ordinarily do. You give your power over to them, when you allow it to eat you up on the inside. God will grant you the Serenity to accept the things you can not change. The Courage to change the things you can and the Wisdom to know the difference. Just ASK HIM!!! Search your heart for your answers, He is answering you now. Don't let your frame of reference allow you to remain narrow minded.

Exercise the Demon – Pet Detective
I know I am right!!!

*I love that dance he does after he spills out the solution to the dilemma at hand. Can you see me dancing right now for our Father. I know I AM right.

Sean Hannity is the Heat Miser
Alan Combs is Mr. Freeze
Bill O'Reilly – I am too much.

Hannity and Combs, I liked the show better with the two opposing positions. I didn't agree with either of them all the time, that is the beauty of debate. Bill and Rush, what can I say. You are too much and I love you for it. Keep us unbiasedly informed.

All I am saying
Is give peace a chance – Billy Jack

*World Peace. Wow, I never thought that would be my mission for God. The Holy Spirit was leaving me clues without me being aware at the time. Jesus told us, "I have so much

to tell, but you can not handle it all at this time". We have to be baby stepped into awareness.

I love the girl that screams out obscenities, so he takes her to a ballgame – Deuce Bigelow Male Gigolo
She gets your attention, doesn't she? Does God need to scream out obscenities to get your attention?

*Say what you want, colorful metaphors in an awkward setting will grab your attention. This manner of speech fills space for the ignorant to expand upon their point. God doesn't like it and I try to monitor it and will fail from time to time. I just want to be cognoscente of it so I may attempt to curtail it. In this book, I am speaking to the masses and I am on their path of understanding. Just as Jesus witnessed to the sinners and tax collectors, I witness to the masses because I am one of them. I'm not witnessing to the perfect people. Who am I to witness to you, you are sinless and perfect. It is the hypocrites that are not witnessing for God. Who do you call a hypocrite? "Before picking the speck from your brothers eye, remove the log from your own."

Is it too much to ask for a roof over your head and food to eat – George Bailey
Anyway my father didn't think so.

Is it too much to ask for free medical care? – Nathan

We are Hungry
Are we Worthy
Before the Word Thy God

*If you plan to demand the 5 and 2 talent men to pay for it, YES, IT'S TOO MUCH TO ASK!!! It is not too much to ask of our Father, who yearns to heal us and dwell among us.

319

Thank you for my Mother and Dad.
You did real good Momma—Forrest Gump
He made his peace with God – Lieut. Dan

*Honor thy Mother and Father. Make your peace with the Father.

It is hard to chill, when the devil blocks my purpose.

All things are possible for those that believe in our God through Jesus Christ, his only begotten son.

My title is Wonderful Counselor for I serve a Wonderful God!

*Once again, I am wrong. I am not the Wonderful Counselor, the Wonderful Counselor is the Holy Spirit. I am merely a humble servant of the Lord. How arrogant of me.

Lord, please do not lead me to temptation. Cleanse my soul.

I'm not worthy – Wayne's World

*I really struggled with this one. Who am I to think I am a Prophet. The definition of Prophet is one who speaks from God. It pays little and yet costs plenty. I was very reluctant to assume this title. It was when God spoke to my heart and said "if not you, who?" Then he says to assume my role. Okay, I've said it. Nathan the Prophet. Everyone get your stones ready to end my blaspheming mouth. I did get my first blasphemy call out. It is in the facebook section. I guess the next words for me to listen for is "Crucify Him".

Self-Esteem – Weird Science

*If there was a topic that would tempt me to write yet another book, this would be it. Unfortunately for me, I still suffer myself.

Bumper stickers:
Are you following Jesus this close?
Normal people frighten me
On Fire for God

That's the thing about that line, they keep moving that little sucker – Broadcast News
The Line of Reality – Over prescribed medication

*I have witnessed a rash of meds that are circulating as recreational drugs. I'll be the first to tell you, knock yourselves out. But what concerns me is that I am seeing people around me that are dying from their experimentation's to escape from reality momentarily. I must tell you that I am very naive in the arena of drugs. Cannabis is my only exposure until here recently. I know my personality and I know that if I like it that much, it will kill me. So I choose to refrain. I did recently try some focus pills while partying. I really didn't pick up on anything except I controlled the conversations and it made my ability to achieve an erection impossible. I didn't like them, thank God. If it is not from my Father, I don't want it. Recreationally speaking that is. I have witnessed people doing things that they would have never done had they had their senses. I am just picking up on this because I was usually inebriated at the functions that I was attending.

I have learned shorthand with my Aletheia.
I can bring a whole story to you from a small clip of a movie. I have the ability to draw from movie clips, the answer for most quandaries and direction of how I want to take my own life. Are the movies that are being produced today exemplifying the message that we want our children to lead their lives by?

321

I'll be home for Christmas, if only in my dreams.

I am Jim – Taxi
Aletheia

***More than I really wanted to admit for most of my life
now. I really have gone through life in a drunken stupor.
When you put your life on display by writing down who you
are, the truth can really hurt. I want to live the rest of my days
happy and sober. I pray that I will not have the pain in my life
that sent me there in the second place. The first place was for
curious recreation. The second place is for depression.**

You want me on that wall
You need me on that wall
You want TRUTH
You can't handle the truth – A Few Good Men

***After you take your own personal examination, you will
have to accept which truth is you. It may sting to reflect on
your life. Where you have been, where you are at and where
you are going. All paths to God are good, but you have to ask
yourself are you on a God path?**

My name is Sue Seer.
Excuse me, what is your name?
Her name is Lucille – Volunteers
Dialect – Speaking in Tongues
not Yibbity Yibbity Yah Yah Yah Praise God – Can I get a
A-A-A-AMEN!!!

***I read in the bible that speaking in tongues must be able
to be understood and conveyable to others, otherwise it is gib-
berish. Speaking in tongues is dialects and languages. I'll give
you an example. When we came back from Japan, my dad
had a dream to build a farm on the land he and my mom**

322

purchased before we left the states. We lived in the sticks and I can remember trying to get directions from a redneck. He said you go right past the big "Tire" and it's right there. Tire, what the hell are you talking about. After a lengthy communication battle I was able to interpret his dialect as Tower. Man speaks in tongues to man. The Holy Spirit has a tongue all His own. He speaks to your heart if you will listen.

Once Solomon gained all the wisdom. He gained all the greed and lusts of this world. He made a mistake.

*I can not begin to imagine what God put on Solomon's heart that compelled him to build our God a temple. King David was told that it was not his place, but the place of his seed. Did Solomon make an assumption that he was the seed to build God's House? It is no longer standing. What do you think? His entity is in the minds, bodies and souls of all of His children that will help facilitate his Kingdom here on earth. The bricks of Mankind. It is eternal.

What have you learned Dorothy?-- Wizard of Oz

*Self-reflection. This is the perfect time to have "it" all about you. Ask our Father for His help in figuring out your daily dilemmas. Think things through and search your heart. If you worry, examine the worst case scenario for that particular situation. If it turns out better, then you are lucky. If it is the worst, you can now better deal with it. Now decide if there is anything you can do to alter the situation for a better outcome. If not, deal with the consequences of your actions and learn from them. This is a great portion of your life that you can submit to your frame of reference. The lessons that sting the most are the ones easiest to remember.

Acts 17:31 I don't want to pick a date

1 Thessalonians 1 – 5

Hebrews 10:27 give me the faith that will seal my salvation, Lord
please Lord

Matthew 24:40 I have been warned

So shall it be written, So shall it be done – the 10 Commandments

2 Thess 2:1-4 Jesus has got my back
1 Tim 4:1-2 everybody's got their own agenda
2 Peter 2:1 – 3 not a good job to be in, if your heart is not right with God

Wooganowski-- Duh Woogie – There's something about Mary
Nathan – Duh Nathan the Prophet

*Was I saying that to you or myself? I'll let you be the judge. You're so good at it.

Knowledge of Nathan – ask Gene

*After work I would proceed to poison myself with alcohol and would always find someone that is going through some trials and I would start to try and help them with their problems. Gene would get a kick out of it and labeled it "The Knowledge of Nathan".

Only pierced never a broken bone,
I remember that proclamation.
What a dumb ass AM I.

Know your place, he that would sit at the front, shall sit at the back.

I will build your temple, Lord
Not filled with the riches of Solomon
But filled with the technology of this culture. Here we will use it and beat the devil at his own game – Media
Your temple will be called Leper Land
Your Grace will heal your people
Faith – Always Been, Always Be

But what about graduation?

When you can take pebble from my hand, time for you to leave – Kung Fu

Wow, how naive
We need a halfway house
Roof – Food – Clothing – Medical care – Job – HOPE!!!

Your name will grace many businesses and anyone who scorns at the lepers will answer to you. Who am I to judge. I am a leper.

? Six eyes = eyes 2 + sunglasses 2 + bifocals 2

*I'm still working on the 666 riddle. Write your quandaries down.

I chased every devil
I was ill prepared
I have faith
I have strength
I am saved

That's the way uh huh, uh huh. I like it uh huh, uh huh

144,000 songs
Man, where is Brian Wilson when you need him

Lord help me
Give me the sales pitch
I need to convince:
drug companies /alcohol /tobacco/
government/Caesar

The system can be tweaked and everyone can live a better life. Give unto Caesar what is Caesars and give unto the Lord what is the Lord's.

I have cast my net to the point the Lord is blocking me. I will cast no further, I will be content with whatever he gives me. For I know I have, truly given it my all. Without crossing the line of sanity.

Dear (2nd Wife),

I am not the Cook
I am not the Maid
I am not the Landscaper
I am spending time with our Father
I am sorry that disturbs you
I love you, bear with me
Nathan

I am sorry for calling you bitter. The devil has jumped on you. A Godly woman. I pray God, Please remove the scales on her eyes – I cannot turn the light on to her heart.

Performance – Do you want your God to dance? – Jerry Maguire or will you dance for your God and Creator

*Are you a rebel or conformist? Either can be good or bad depending on who and how you serve. Ask yourself, for who's Glory will this serve.

Maybe I am the Lone Wolf McQuaid?
Because I am tired of teaching and not being heard – Seclusion – but I love people and I want to share

I refuse to roll up in a ball – Yo Adrian

*Since the bad stuff is so much easier to believe, we allow ourselves to fulfill our own prophecy. You have to find yourself in order to be comfortable with yourself. Might I suggest Astrology. Look up your sign and your new sign with Ophiuchus interjected. You might be surprised the characteristics that your sign says. Emulate the ones that fit your persona for the Glory of God. The more you reinforce who you are to yourself, the more you will become that person. The question is, who do you want to become? Come out of your shell and take your place. Do not allow self-confidence to hinder you from the abundance our Lord has promised you. You got a problem, let me tell you about mine. Everyone has problems and many great books can help you to pioneer your way out of the weeds. Read, evaluate, execute and live with your decisions. To do nothing is a decision that you will have to accept as your own.

Am I going to serve time, for spending time with our Father?

Stop dragging/Dragon me off course Devil, I want to go to Leper Land

Why can't a parent be a friend? What is it we are hiding? Does the devil have a secret?
I bet he does. Gootchy Goo

I hope the Terminator doesn't get me. Is he the boogie man we have heard so much about?

Trust – Deception – Humiliation – Media – Drugs
The devil's mission statement:
DEATH

Nathan the Prophet
Wonderful Counselor
Servant of God
"A Godly Man"

I will once again, write a check for all that I have for your people.

Hey Deeds, can you use $1 billion?
Sure, why not – Mr. Deeds

*I took the money of course, I'm not crazy – Arthur

Two signs that let me know that it is acceptable to receive 10% from my work only, the concession stand.

The hole that I dig, becomes deeper and deeper. I hope it turns out like Shawshank Redemption. The Latter part of course.

*I am at the point of no return and I have nothing else to lose and I have all to lose. I have faith that I will have my redemption.

Waz Up T. D.

I heard you

888 or 800 – I am not answering that one – that's a bill collector

Okay I get it
You want me to start writing again

The cruise ships will unload and reload giving everyone who seeks it, the Good News

I get it now – Bill Murray Scrooged

*Love, Empathy, Compassion, Action. How we treat our brothers and sisters in Christ is how we should be treated. I ask you, are you ready to be judged by your actions?

People from near and far will come
Listen – Field of Dreams
It will shock them
I know the truth, can we do anything about it?

*Build it and they will come. Daddy, you don't have to sell the farm. They will come. God's people yearn for a Shepard to look after them. I have built your Everlasting Earthly Entity Lord. I pray that your people will come and join in your Gift and allow you to dwell among us and in all of our hearts.

I confess, the legal ways of our society and culture, don't work for me.

I have a get out of jail free card. Do you have one Jack? – Harrison Ford Movie

Oh well, I didn't think about that. I just wanted to serve our Father.

Act appropriately before our Father and you will be a Pro in his eyes.

We need housing for employees/lepers of Leper Land

329

Buy all Martyn Woods For cruise raffle

Porpoise – bottle nosed dolphin – Purpose

*I must fulfill my Purpose for God or live in unrest eternally. Lord, strengthen me. Yours is the only approval that I seek. The only approval that will free my heart. The only friend that I have ever had. Lord, how can one express their love for another individual for something that is based on Faith?

I HAVE NO
TROPHY
I HAVE A
CROWN

CROWN YOURSELVES
BEFORE OUR
FATHER

JUST AS I
YEARN FOR ACCEPTANCE

I
THE SON OF GOD
THE SON OF MAN
AM IN UNREST
JUST AS MY BROTHERS
DAVID AND SOLOMON

I WILL
HAVE WHAT MY FATHER
HAS PROMISED

AN EVERLASTING
ENTITY WHERE I CAN DO

MY BEST
I WILL HEAL YOU
MY BROTHER
JESUS CHRIST YOUR
SAVIOR LIVES
MY HEART LIVES
GODS LEGACY TRUST
IT IS MY LEGACY TO YOU
YOU ARE THE
KEEPER
OF MY
HEART

I HEREBY
YOUR LORD JESUS CHRIST
FORGIVE YOU

What the Hell? Lord, we have sinned so much. We need a cleansing. We need the angels to come to us. We need you to show your wraith.

WHAT SHALL YOU
HAVE ME DO?

Alright, if your going to play the smart ass bullshit with me, I'm going to do it with you. I want to see World Peace before I die. Ha Ha. Like that is ever going to happen.

WHAT ELSE???

Are you shitting me here?

ASK!
YOUR MASTER
HAS BECOME YOUR SLAVE
TELL ME

Lord, I'm drunk, you know that. Why do you compel my heart now? Why do you ask me when I AM incoherent?

YOU CHALLENGE ME
I CHALLENGE YOU

THE FATHER
OUR GOD
ASKS OF YOU
OF YOU OUR GOD
ASKS

AM I
NOT YOUR FATHER
AM I
NOT YOUR GOD
AM I
NOT YOUR SAVIOR
ARE YOU
NOT MY SERVANTS
ARE YOU
NOT MY CHILDREN
ARE YOU
NOT MY CHILD???

Damn, when you put it like that I have no other choice but to serve you my Lord. But I am just one man. What can one man do to reach your people in their present state? They will never listen to me Lord. They will listen to you oh Lord. Speak through me oh Lord. Please speak through me. Lord, I do not know how you can sum up your presence now in our lives, but I ask you to do just that.

I AM
THY SON OF GOD
I AM

332

THY SON OF MAN
I AM
THY GOD
I AM
THY HOLY SPIRIT
I AM
THY HEART
I AM
THY SAVIOR
I AM
THY BROTHER

THY BROTHER
IS ME OR
I AM MAN
666

Porpoise:
The first thing God showed me
God's beauty – man's existence
This is our Legacy, embrace the lepers. We are people just like you.
You discriminate, he does not – KNOT

A knot becomes tighter
with every tug
A knot becomes larger
with every loop
A knot becomes
a foundation
A knot accepts
My Divine Plan
You are a knot
for ME
or Not
Pray I even accept

your Knot
You Knot Head
Ask not of thy God
Be thy Knot
for thy brother
Be thy Knot in my
Everlasting
Earthly
Entity
My heart is in
Knots
My Grace
Forgives your
NOTS

Book title
"If I were" Nathan the Prophet – Wonderful Counselor – Servant of God

"If I were" a Murderer
Thanks O.J.

Wait til you see the movie, your kids are going to love it – Marty Back to the Future
Something has got to be done about your kids – Doc

*Dude, let's take a little trip in the time machine to see what Doc is talking about. Our kids have become entitled to what their brother has worked for. How can we sustain this with just one flux capacitor? The load that we have already put on it has weakened it Globally. If it dies, it will be considered a hoax from the beginning. The nay sayers said it would never work and now they can gloat. Ahh... but there is another vision. Everyone gets their own flux capacitor so that they may travel through time and inspire their heirs to strive for more and not rely on their brother for their existence. They

are inspired to pick themselves up and say "If IT is to be, IT is up to ME".

Your children need for you to be a parent and occasionally, they need a doctor.

You are resting me for being a servant of the Lord. Why can't I be forgiven for my mistakes? Are you crabs in a bucket? Ask Ralph.

80/20

Can you overlook the 20 and be content with the 80
Multi-lesson – stay with me now

Fed 15%
State 5%
God 10%
Can you live with 70%? X_____

Peace and Love 100%

Your Temple will be filled with Bling Bling – Technology
So when you demonstrate your powerful hand, only the treasures of this world are lost and human life is spared and your temple can easily be rebuilt by the people of this World.

*Leper Land

Your earthly entity Gods Legacy Trust LLC will be built in the same manner the Great Pyramids were built. With the life long efforts of your people. Everyone is a brick in Gods Entity. Some used and some not.

They are just like cats, they can be trained, but it requires a tremendous amount of patience. No one really owns a cat. No one really owns a human.

Look up the definition of patience – ask Brian

You are enough to hold public confessions of faith
Don't forget planes and airstrip
But a performance is not necessary
Show your pride with the sign, the sign of God.
Do not erect or worship the sign
Conceal it in your heart
Reveal it in your wave
Love your fellow brother, we are all looking for different cheese stations – Who Moved My Cheese
I hit the Mother Lode
Good News – I share – I am not greedy.

I have been given ADHD and I like. Now that I know what ADHD is. How dare us for suppressing the future prophets for the devils glory, because of ignorance and greed.

Ghost of Christmas Present opens his curtains – Scrooge

*Don't tell me what is behind your curtains, I am not your Judge. Tell our Father what is there. He already knows and waits for you to confess to Him. Ask for forgiveness and control over whatever demon you allow into your own life of your own free will.

I am one of you. Our forefathers are speaking to me. I went through life in a drunken stupor – stupid lost child. I have Aletheia – learn - unforget. Beware of false teachings, getting kicked in the teeth sucks.

Take off your masks. Lie down in a bed of snakes. You will be bitten. It really hurts don't it. Know that your salvation relies on your perseverance to never take your eye off you're creator. God, the one and only, your choice, he is always with you. He loves you unconditionally. Regardless.

I am becoming what I am meant to be.
Damn the torpedoes, I am coming in.

Ice has the lead. Okay you guys, I'm coming in.- Top Gun
The arrogant, vocally robust are responsible for the demise of the Knights Templar and Jesus Christ.

*"Weapons of Mass Destruction". Someone has to take charge and sometimes mistakes are made. We can all play armchair quarterback after the fact. After the attack of 9/11 I can assure you that anyone of us would have had our antennas up for future attacks. Hindsight being 20/20, a different approach may have served less costly. I'm still digging on the whole 007 thing. But we are where we are, so let's finish it and save our Global brothers from tyranny and oppression. By the way, I am proud to have been a citizen of the U. S. under President George W. Bush. He made me feel safe and I believe he did what he was compelled to do for the safety of all.

That whole "I am" thing works in real good. It is in the script. Imagine that.

*Wait til you see "I WILL" LOL

Use your imagination and dip into the pool of Bathsheba? Cleanse yourself for yourself, not for the approval of others. Vain – Pain

337

*Ask yourselves, is your expressions of love for our Father or for your neighbor? I can not judge what is on your heart, only the Father and you can. Don't be fake.

Experience the past, so that you can articulate it. They have a purpose too. We are still paying a debt. What is the balance? Check please.

*Fallen empires debased their currency funding wars. Hmmm... sounds like a pattern here. Currency has always been readjusted to the value of precious metals. I'm afraid we will have to adjust the value of precious metals to the amount of currency that is circulating this time. It is a beacon that must be used to determine which way we are going. It is our financial compass, never to be creatively altered again.

I had to become a commercial real estate investor to have the vision of your Temple.

Is the Indian in the commercial still crying over man's existence and harm done to our environment?

*That commercial is Classic. I still remember getting a tear in my eye as well every time I saw it. I saw this man appealing to his brothers and sisters of this planet. I did not see him pandering to Government with back room deals for funding. If you ask of your Global brothers and sisters for something that is for the good of all, then you receive much more than Caesar could ever afford to give you.

We have lived in Solomon's World long enough. Let us dwell in your World Lord. This one will do just fine. Just tweak it a bit. You've GOD mail.

Six dollar bill
The metric system may be easier, but I never got it.

I don't get it – Big
GRUMPS – Star Trek
Scary Revelation

*Once we have something embedded into our brains, it can be very difficult to see anything different. I loved that episode when the Grumps were the people that were diseased and possessed. The children hid from them and dreaded the day that they themselves would become one. Grumps was short for Grown Ups. We forget our childhood dreams and become Grumps.

Okay, I am starting to feel good God. Give them to me

Separate Leper Camps
How low can you go
Can you go to Da Flo
But Nobody Know
But You and
God

Poppies will make them sleep – Wizard of Oz
Ask your forefathers
There is no place like home – Immigration

Have you seen my home?

*Yes, I have seen your home. It is beautiful and I love to visit there as often as I can. Why do you come here when I want to go there?

**FOOD
WATER
SHELTER
HEALTHCARE
FREEDOM**

screw You, screw You, screw You
Who's next – Coming to America

*I believe Jesus told his disciples to kick the dust from their feet of any town that would not listen to them. My approach was a little different.

Good Ship – Good Crew
Hoo Ray for ME
And screw YOU – Dad
Play it close to your vest and have a backup plan.

*Unfortunately my dad is right. I never wanted to believe that. What's in it for me? That is what we have become.

Rocky Marciano was how old when he beat Joe Lewis's ass?
How old is your God? Can he be our Rocky? Because it sure has been Rocky and Rolly so far.

Okay okay, I like the place, but these damn bugs are eating my ass up. I'll wait in the car.

*My first introduction to Leper Land. The mosquitoes were terrible, we'll need the help of the Purple Martins, not green martians.

Don't waste your time on me, you are already the voice inside my head.
Come – Learn – Leave – Spread – You're holding up the line
Shit or get off the pot – Nathan

*Lord, I pray to you. Please allow Leper Land to happen. I believe it will absolutely change lives for the Glory of God. I ask of no recognition or reward Lord. This has never been about me, but about You my Lord and Savior. Your people

are hurting on the inside as well. Please Lord, use Leper Land to speak to their hearts and heal their souls.

Be prepared to leave the bad lands most hurriedly. Age is a factor here. Wait till they really need The boogie man. Be trained to spot him, ADHD. Help him, he is a future prophet wanna be.

Some make it, some don't. But how do you know before you try. Are you willing to bet the family farm?

Go ahead, try to draw the sword. If it is not you, have a back-up plan and live a wonderful life. Some will enjoy what they do. Some will strive for more. Cursed is the man that holds judgment over the starters and lagers. We need each other. There is plenty of shit I don't want to do. But to the person who is striving for more while picking up my shit, I pay you the respect that you deserve. Just a little bit is all I need, I have a plan and a backup plan, so watch out Devil. I am coming to get YOU.

Murdock, I'm coming to get you – Rambo II

*Have you been betrayed? I have been betrayed by a friend and a Minister. It HURTS!!! I have never been be- trayed by my God. Trust in Him, for He is the only one that will never leave your side.

I guess dipping in the ocean and lake was theatrics on my part. It is too damn cold to get wet. Is this the line of judgment we must all use. The code didn't work and the machine did break down.

Exercise good sense
The nuts are the ones that must perform
You, our God knows who you are
He always knows – A Christmas Story

*The greatest inventions start off as crazy. Some call them crazy, I call them creative. Pursue your dreams and never let anyone drag you down.

We should have stuck up for him, it was not his blame – Shame to carry

We're suppose to stick up for the weak. We're suppose to stick up for Willie- A Few Good Men

*Weak in mind, spirit, body and soul. Be blessed and thankful for the talents God has given unto you. Use your talents for the betterment of your brother, not to his detriment. What is it that you gain by doing such. Your brother is weak. He needs a HAND UP, not a HAND OUT.

I'll never know how much it Cost
To see my sin upon that Cross
I'm giving it all to you

Man this shit is so good, I think I'll buy my own tape-- TD Jakes

Answer: All in your Heart
Not in your pocket book. Give til it's comfortable. Put it in God's hands

Sorry, I can't pick up hitchhikers to Foley. You might be the devil.

I wouldn't have minded so much, but your slobbering dog would soil my interior.

Excuses are like assholes, we all got one – Platoon

Use them wisely

Hot Tub Time:
My fingers hurt – Nathan

Isn't the ocean beautiful?

I keep ending up at Point Clear, not Point Clear Alabama.
Point Clear?
Probably not, it isn't for me either. Try this:
Let there be no misunderstanding
I AM is the Father
Jesus is the Son
Nathan is the Humble Servant
The Holy Spirit is all of this shit floating around us keeping
score with consequences.

I see my footprints in the sand, I am is still carrying the load.
Try this:
Ban nothing, we need Judas
But if you want a check from God
You must be Clean

Quarterly drug test
Healed because it was detected
Don't suppress God's gifts to heal the nations any longer

***I prayed about this and I just don't want man to use
"IT" in any way to suppress man. Maybe "IT" would be best,
if man suppressed with Love.**

Don't forget us misfit toys, we want homes too.
Boo-hoo boo-hoo not another Christmas
Nobody wants us

Well you thought you were better than everyone else and you
kept secrets. How can we trust you? What have you been waiting
for? My 10 acres and a mule ain't showed up yet – DD

Answer: they ain't going to show up. Where did you lose your faith?

I ruined you by making you boss. Everyone is not supposed to be boss, it is their decision.

* Joke: A handful of buddies went to a hunting camp and when they checked in they rented a hunting dog. They chose a dog named Salesman. He was the best dog they have ever witnessed. It was a great trip. The next year the buddies decided to do the trip again and wanted that same dog. When they arrived they requested Salesman to be their dog of choice. The owner replied that he didn't think they would enjoy the trip because he had changed Salesman's name to Manager and he hadn't been worth a shit since.

I need a physical exam. I hate smoke, leave that woman to God, hurts my lungs, but I like it up until I am done.

For ME – Ricky Bobby

*What do I have to lose. I have lost everything. All I do is for Christ. When you have a purpose, you have a beacon that will always keep you in check with your life.

Not the Planet of the Apes
How silly we are to laugh at other cultures because of our own ignorance – Borat

*We Mock what we do not understand. Our frame of reference dictates whether something is funny or weird. How can you possibly have the frame the reference of people from different cultures? It is very different from your own. It is your arrogance that makes you think you are right and they are wrong.

Cancel the party
Tell them I don't feel good
I don't give a shit
I am Hobnobbing
With the Almighty
I'll bring a note
This is beginning to look Eerie
I will check in Monday
But I will not be silenced, 911
That was easy
I have taken the path of least resistance my whole life.
One more round – Rocky V

*When you have something worth fighting for, the odds make no difference. "Give me Liberty or give me Death." A man with his back against the wall and has nothing to lose is a very dangerous man.

Never give up
Help is on the way
Am I the help?

Are you the coconut that will pay full price Nathan? If you are, I didn't want to miss you. Car business.

What is a fair price? Tell us, don't make us barter in the street. We want to support you without getting screwed. Tell us what is fair and we will pay it.

Lost books of Nathan
Good news, I just found it – ask Brian

A. R. K.
Acts of Random Kindness – Evan Almighty
I can dig it. Who goes first Nathan?

*Acts of Random Kindness is what builds our ARK's. You will build a financial ARK for yourselves and for our God to heal your brother and allow Him to dwell among us for an eternity.

Mr. Mom – the job sucks
and needs nourishment and appreciation

*Until you try this job, you just can't appreciate it. Your spouse has been home all day waiting for your arrival so they can have a intelligent and meaningful conversation. You arrive home tired and demanding. How has that turned out for you?

Step up – be a man in what ever capacity

Women respect your Men

We are an extension of each other

WILL > TRUST > GOD

What can I say, it is his patent – Nathan

What's up in Leper Land today – Cool Breeze – Doc Holiday

*Have you ever been convinced that if you could just get the one thing that you desire most, you would be fulfilled and content? Once there, you realize that it may have not been what filled your heart after all and you yearn to go back to a different place and time. Always strive for more my brother, but keep your antennas up to what makes you and your significant others happy. You might end up celebrating on your own.

I need a holiday

If we took a holiday, could we have some time to spend together – Madonna

Can you handle this Jerry?
Sure Rick > File 13

*We all have our own agenda. Slow down and see your brothers. He really may be able to bring something to the table. If you smite him for his efforts, you've trained him with negative reinforcement to keep his mouth shut and do as he is told. He will keep his mouth shut in your presence and curse you behind your back. He will not be an instrumental part of you achieving your agenda and will secretly hope you fail. God has given us all different talents. Watch for your brothers, they may be greater than your own.

Don't become too big, you will have no rest.
Make your judges accountable, you allow the Dragon to pierce my body, but not my heart and soul? Nathan

Hey, I am just working with the tools you gave me.

What was the name of that movie that was the counterpart to X-Men? All of the heroes had bizarre talents. Pee-Wee was the fart man. I guess with my gift Aletheia, I am able to articulate life's experiences through my own life experiences as well as through the eyes of our forefathers via movie clips teaching us right from wrong.

Thank you Father – what a wonderful gift it is
your humble servant Nathan

Fishing – Hunt for Red October

*Making Memories. When you spend time with your family, you are making memories. Take a moment after each true

setting with them and determine if you have left the kind of memory in their mind that will resonate with them for a lifetime. You still have time to correct it if you can recognize it early enough. Correct yourself in their eyes. There is no shame for making mistakes, this is how we learn. There is great shame by allowing mistakes to fester.

Youth > Trust > Mentor

How could you know?
I didn't even know. - Vinnie Barbarino

*The only way to know your purpose for God is to look for it. "Seek and ye shall find." Once you find it ask yourself, is this for His Glory or mine? Your heart will reveal the answer to you and only you. Do this for your God's approval and not your peers approval.

I like the fasting thing, but I am getting kind of hungry – Nathan

Whoops, I am not supposed to let the cat out of the bag. – Bulimia

*It is amazing what self esteem will make us do to ourselves to please others. You need to get comfortable in your own skin. Everyone is beautiful in their own unique way and God wants you to love yourselves as you love Him. You are a beautiful child of the King and He loves you with all of His heart.

Jolly Roger – Buddy
Shattered dreams hurt
If you bet the farm
Have a backup plan

Are you willing to lose all that you are because you are convinced you have the answer?

"GO FOR IT"

If not, sit down and shut up. I can't hear the real movers and shakers, don't be scared and don't leave me hanging.

No no, these are important, these are papers, not Gook Shit – Platoon

*What one disregards as unimportant, others regard as crucial. Why do we regret throwing out what others treasure and love? Even to the point of envy and desire. What you once considered worthless, now has worth to you through the eyes of someone else. Be very care what you disregard. This has meaning in everything in life, you fill in the blanks.

After You – you are a true friend
How big of a boat can you Captain, Gene?
Training

*Gene named his new boat "After You". A true gentleman is not hard to spot. A slick hustler however is. Guard your heart until you see theirs. It is good to let your guard down, just know who you reveal yourself to.

Sample it all, find out what you like. Strive for it. Your God wants you to have an abundant life. You do know your God wants that don't you? Have a plan for your goals, learn from my mistakes and the mistakes of your forefathers – Nathan

666
Don't look for signs
You are being tempted and giving in to temptation.

Why don't you just come on down? King of the Jews Ha Ha Ha

*How many times did I tempt my God? Every time. Every time I prayed for proof and deviated from Faith.

I need no visual miracle, but I pray you reveal your plan and all of my efforts will pay off.

Let me publicly confess your undying love to all of your people.
Your deeds will carry more weight than your words. Heal us Lord – Nathan

Sorry to be such an argumentative #$%&, but I have a list of questions that make you go Hmmmm...-- Nathan

It is not for you to know. Even my son Jesus didn't know the hour of your Savior.

I hate cliffhangers. Does this one turn out good? – Nathan

For all that trust in the Lord

I went blank – Nathan

*I believe this was the first time that I recognized that the Holy Spirit was actually speaking to my heart. Even then I did not hear Him. I was still pursuing my own agenda and not allowing God to fulfill His through me. Everything was too much about me and I could not hear Him.

Do you hear their cries for help? After their busted, be active for God
Drug Companies
Right Track, Wrong Tools
Didn't God give us 12 fruit bearing plants to heal the nations? Yes, I know I read that somewhere.

Where is the compass? Find it – Band of the Hand
I don't want to eat an alley cat. Care for animals as they care for you

*The spiritual compass is the Bible and the Gospel of Jesus Christ. The financial compass is precious metals. Both can be used as your compass so as to never get off track with our Creator or our budget again.

Don't lose sight
Your father loves you more than any animal. Be aware. How hungry are you with the treasures of this world that animals should needlessly sacrifice their skin off their back literally, so you can impress. How sad.
Image – Dances with Wolves

Dead carcasses rotting, what say you?

Is it that damn cold? – Nathan

*We were all appalled by Cruella De Ville. A dog skin coat after all is cruelty to animals. Where does one draw the line?

I'm not taking a test
You take the damn test
Here are my notes.
Screw you – Nathan
Oh God – George Burns

*I always thought it was kind of funny that the religious leaders tempted God by demanding proof via a test. You are the only one that can test your own Faith. One thing I can tell you for sure, your Faith will be tested and tested greatly.

This is real fun and I am laughing my ass off, but most of the shit is serious.

How can I count on my brother to do his part?

***You can only count on your brother if you inspire your brother.**

We're going to Leper Land till you get it.

Will I have to keep swearing after I am found out?
Yes, dammit George – Marty Back to the Future

You tell me people, which Nathan do you want?

Something for everyone – Bourbon Street

It's me – it's me – it's Earnest T.

You can come in
You can come out
M*A*S*H – Frank Burns lock up

***The accuser becomes the accused. Beware that men will rally men to destroy men when the agenda of man becomes more important to a man than to men.**

Who is the nut?
Depends on the spin – O'Reilly

Wife called 4:04, guess I will submit, put on my game face and probably get drunk on wine. I deserve it. Oh shit! I can't get drunk, you might come tonight. I'll pace myself – Moderation.

You are the only one I can talk to Lord. Not even my Godly wife. Find forgiveness in me Lord. The devil is very powerful. Let me give them your new tool Lord. That will be in your favor and honor.

Let me just stop you from saying something you will regret later wife – You've got Mail

*A quick wit, sharp tongue and lack of empathy will place you in an apologetic situation quickly. Be mindful of your words, you never know who is listening. Words hurt and can last a lifetime. You can apologize for them, but you can never truly take them back. Be quick to ask for forgiveness and not allow them to fester.

I would feel bad for showing my ass if she has planned a early surprise birthday party. If not, it's okay. I shouldn't show my ass anyway.

I don't give a #$%&
They are here for free food and drink and to lap up to you for donations – Back-to-School Rodney Dangerfield

*Have your heard "you are what you eat". You also are who you think. If your thoughts are negative, your personality and actions will follow and visa versa. Your self talk is who you will become. What are you telling yourself? Does your self talk personify who you would like to be? It will personify who you are. Who do you want to be? Take control of your thoughts and be that person that you want to be. No one is stopping you, but you.

Oh hell no, I'm not taking that, oh yes you are, Mama needs a nap.- Childrens Motrin

How was your day dear?
Oh just another day of carrying the sins of the world on my shoulders kind of day.
How about you?

Please forgive me Lord, my forgetfulness has cost us another thought. My antennas are up.

But they are damaged, forgive me Lord for my sins.

Is this what people with Alzheimer's feel like. I don't like it. I want to go home, where it is safe.

*In a manic state of mind, it is like being in a cloud without all the white stuff. At every turn you just don't know what will surface. I began looking for signs and would find them pretty easily. By the time I was through looking for signs of the world that are much bigger than me, I was lost in my immediate world. Thank God for GPS.

Please fix my home. I was just watching La Bamba. Don't envy thy brother for their talents, develop your own if even for yourself. Then love your brothers success, yours will come in a different way and all will appreciate your talents for you.

I will deny you tonight, under protest, forgive me Lord. I love my wife.

Forgive me Lord. I will not deny you again. I know three times damn. Although my hand is sore, my heart soars. I respectfully request Coco – or heir and Holy Terror or heir. Coco – Chocolate Lab – Companion - Loyal, Holy Terror - solid white German Shepard – Bodyguard – Sight Dog.

Will you gouge out my eyes Lord?
I say I have suffered long enough, Father I have had enough strict discipline.

Andrew we won't except 2nd Pl. – Breakfast Club

*Man, are you one of those assholes in the stands demanding perfection from your child? It is good to gently push and plant seeds, I call this inspire. When your children find themselves, they will push themselves. Your job becomes encouragement and patience. Remember this, if you push hard enough, you will inevitably be pushed back. I ask you this, if your child becomes so beat down that instead of lashing back, they lash at themselves like the failure you have instilled in them. How does one receive forgiveness from someone that has taken their own life as their only means of lashing back to their authority?

We do not train to be merciful here,
Mercy is for the weak – Karate Kid

*Ask for mercy when mercy is truly deserved. Give of mercy freely, but observantly. You may ask of God anytime. You can ask of man only so many times.

No discipline Johnny
Is this the Johnny I've heard so much about?
Give me some Johnny jokes baby.
Here's Johnny – Shining

*Where did you lose your Faith? Are your thoughts in control of your life or are you in control of your thoughts? Your mind will go wherever you want it to go by your own free will. When you sense your thoughts and life are out of your control, give them to the Wonderful Counselor that Jesus promised to send to us all. He is in me and He can be in you if you allow Him to become you. Satan is in me also and can easily become me. What say you?

Where do you lose it? Where is the line? What would you do with no lifeline? Call God

355

I must be conscious of every decision I make for fear of re-percussions. I played drums hmmm...

Party On Wayne – Party On Garth

*Decisions come with consequences. Evaluate your life and you will realize that you are where you are, based on the decisions you have made and you are living with the consequences. It is your bed, you made it, you lie in it.

I do not rely on people to sustain me. Therefore I speak my mind. Sorry if I offend you. But you know I am right. Please don't take me yet Lord.

O Tay I got sumptin to say --Buckwheat

*Lord, I pray to you that all I do is for You. I pray that I am accurately doing Your Will. How can I be sure? Where is the proof?

YOUR FAITH
WILL DELIVER YOU

If you thought you were the person that TD Jakes is looking for, considering you don't work there, how could you get to see the Wizard? I know in my heart. He is not behind curtains.

*The Wizard is a phony and a liar. God and Satan are the only ones that can pull your strings. What strings hold you captive? What strings give you strength? God is not behind curtains, 666 is, with corruption and greed. By the way, TD is not a wizard. He is a messenger just as I am and you can be.

How long will you allow the devil to suppress my tongue?
I hate to put God on a deadline, but I am checking in on Monday, November 12, 2007. The devil drove me to drink. He is driv-

ing me crazy. I hope the medication will help get rid of him. Rather than sedate my Christianity and build my tolerance.

Why do we lie to our doctor? Secrets
Mafibachev – damaged, but delivered

*Mafibachev was the only living heir of King Saul and had been dropped at birth. He was lame and uncared for. King David wanted to honor his friend Johnathan, by making room at his table for the last living heir of King Saul. The point to the story is, we can all be damaged and still be delivered to His table. Those that would be first, shall be last if even invited.

How can I fix it, if I don't know what is broken. – Heartbreak Ridge

*How can I know what is broken, if you will not allow me to examine IT. This statement deals with so many things in life. You can go through life with your mask on shielding your vulnerabilities and never live your life. Finances, Heartbreak, Addictions, Self Esteem etc... Only you can determine what is broken in your life. What is preventing you from enjoying the time that God has given you on this planet. You get just one shot here, you better make the most of it. On your death bed, what words of wisdom would you give to your loved ones. That sounds perfect, now name your LLC that, so all of your heirs can be inspired for an eternity.

The truth shall set you freedom – Braveheart

Once I am discovered, I will no longer be able to move about you, to find out who you really are. The Mask will come off. The freaks come out at night. Heh heh

People are truly like cats, they require patience, they have tremendous tenacity. And even when we think we own them, they refuse to be owned. – Slavery

I hate the dating process, to find a mate with our masks on. Who are we? What are our motives? Are you as trapped as I am? How can you plan your escape and escape to where?

Can you go home?

Fortunately for me, I was born in a loving home. I can come and go as I please. I have rights as long as they don't offend anyone. When did the Lord's words begin to offend you? Did you do a self-examination to determine if the problem is within you? Take off your mask, it has blinders.

Girls Gone Wild – sorry dude, you offended the wicked and they framed you. Right to free speech or not, you're screwed.

*"IN YOUR FACE". My brothers and sisters in Christ. This is not a good approach in pressing your rights and beliefs on others. You create animosity amongst your peers and you will need to keep your guard up. They will one up your "in your face" mentality. This is what (Thing One) threw in my face, saying I had crossed the line and offended him. All the while his husband (Thing Two) was crossing my personal space. Don't use your rights or your minority classification to stick my nose in it. You are infringing upon my rights and I'll knock you down. Just as the cops of Panama City did it to that poor bastard that sits in jail now.

Secrets weave a web. Too many secrets will trip you up during confrontation, especially if you are pandering for approval, votes or love.

I have the right answer. Follow me. You follow Drafiki, he know the way – Lion King

The answer is the circle of life. How will we leave Pride Rock? Plymouth Rock? Will our heirs be equipped with the teachings of Jesus Christ or the Devil?

*The Circle of Eternal Life.

Will our generation continue to do nothing to replenish what we have consumed, except procreate new consumers? What will our generation leave the World? At the present time, it looks like a big fat Debt.

Remember, remember. Go to the rulebook – Bible
All of the answers are written down.

But the rulebook is too damn long. Do you have it on CD? Yes. Well can you keep me entertained. I guess I am so lazy. I want to learn by watching a movie or playing a game. Although, you'll play hell getting anyone to play.

Who will lead us Lord?
I cannot
I am a drunk
I am a addict
I am a sexaholic
I am impatient
I have lost my tolerance
I am tired of working a flawed system

But I still have a DREAM!!!

If this prophet thing is my new gig, I can dig it. I need someone to take better shorthand than I.

Make sure everything is accurate, so you can use my words against me. I screw up – I am human.

*Mistakes are a natural part of learning. Save yourself a lot of heart ache and learn from the mistakes of your fore-fathers. Our Country is in great need to go back in time and learn from some of the most brilliant men our Country has ever known. The conglomerated efforts of those that manu-script-ed the Constitution of the United States is mind bog-gling.

If I didn't make any mistakes, how would I know if it is right?

Grow from Love – First Wives Club
How can I grow, when you're screwing my husband you de-ceptive bitch.

*Who can you trust? I just don't have an answer for you on that. I have major trust issues myself. I will have to put to you that I don't know. So many things I have been able to express to you, but when it comes to love, I am inept. All I can tell you is that it hurts. Does it hurt less not taking a chance and resolving to loneliness. I don't know right now my brothers, but it is looking rather bleak for me right about now. I can endure no more pain. I can only trust in Christ. He will bring to me a soul mate that will share my thoughts and desires.

**LOVE AND YOU
SHALL BE LOVED**

**LOVE ME AND
YOU SHALL BE LOVED
FOR ETERNITY**

I know who I am

I know my purpose

I am Nathan the Prophet - Wonderful Counselor – Servant of God

Can you dig it?

Ha Ha Ha

Go home nut

Run Home Jack – Hook

*The Wonderful Counselor. I thought it was me because of the thoughts the Holy Spirit was putting on my heart. I must take my place as a humble servant of God. Period. I give full credit to the Holy Spirit that Jesus promised to send back to all of us. Are you listening to your heart? He is speaking to it now.

Mission Statement

Rectify all inhumanities man places on himself with the word of The Lord God Almighty!!!

KISS

Keep It Simple Stupid

*I have tried to make it as simple as I can. His plan is arcane, but blatantly obvious once you get it. If it were easy, someone would have answered John's query years ago. Who is Worthy to break the Seven Seals of the Two-Sided Scroll and reveal God's Last Will and Testament? I am not worthy, I am merely a humble servant of the Lord. But Ophiuchus is worthy, he is a humble God of Medicine and a servant of the One and Only True God. All anointment's come from God and only God. My sinful nature does not allow me to accept this Honor. My rebirth in Christ does. I gladly accept the tur-

moil, agony, pain, heartbreak and Love, Forgiveness, Salvation, Peace.

Rock the boat, don't rock the boat baby, don't tip the boat over.

QUESTION AUTHORITY

*I can not emphasize this enough. Educate yourselves and do not allow someone to bloviate over your head. You are as smart as you want to be. Now take your role in society and be accountable for yourself and keep others accountable for their actions.

If they Look like shit
   Smell like shit
   Walk like shit
   Talk like shit
They're probably full of shit or a duck.

*It is not to hard to identify what you are dealing with if you will open your eyes. I can tell you my brother, Love can put a pair of Rose Colored Sunglasses on you that will make it very hard to see the flaws. Use these glasses for the betterment of your relationships or take them off so you may pursue life without regret.

Life and the money game

Age
25 – 34	First quarter
35 – 44	Second quarter
45-- 54	Third quarter
55 – 65	Fourth quarter

Game Over or Over Time?

*There is only so much time for you to build your Financial Ark. I was told about investing a portion of my wages years ago and I even did it for a time. It seemed such a long process that I became bored but persistent. You can get wrapped up in your own financial world and find yourself trapped if you are not sniffing for new cheese. I ask you again, if you were hurt tomorrow, how would you pay your bills? You must have an income to sustain life. To have a life, you must have an income that does not control you. Always be thinking, how can I do what I do, that is for the betterment of my brother and I don't have to do it. I just get a check.

When will we make time for you my Father? Your creation is beautiful that is a genuine compliment, not meant to stroke your ego. My excitement for my reward has diminished by the pain I am in enduring.

*There is very little room in our lives for Christ. Their was no room at the Inn when Jesus first entered this World and it hasn't gotten any better since. Please do not tell your Savior on Judgment Day that you just couldn't find the time. "The Cat's in the Cradle and the Silver Spoon, little boy blue and the Man in the Moon. When you coming home Son I don't when, but we'll get together then Dad. You know we'll have a good time then." We all are the prodigal children of God. Jesus Christ is our Brother and Savior. He gave His life for you and I. How do we give Him thanks?

How to Win friends and influence people versus how to screw your friends and have them like you for it. You decide.

*If you want a book to help you manipulate your brother, this is it. If you want a book to help you to inspire your brother, this is it. It is our choice how we use knowledge to our benefit or detriment.

363

How many prophets have been silenced by our own igno-rance? Were they burned at the stake?

*Step up and take a stand for your God. You will be chas-tised, scorned, beaten down, humiliated and LOVED. Who are you trying to please anyway?

I want to be Sniff
I want to be Scurry
Sorry, I am not an animal. Deal with the hand you have been dealt. It will work. I am convinced.
I want to be HIM – WWJ D.
I want to be Ha – Naysayers
Who moved my cheese?
God, I crave your cheese – Nathan

*Brothers and Sisters in Christ, I tell you the truth. You better keep sniffing, because things will change in your life. Are you prepared like the Boy Scout. Life is ever changing and how we deal with it is how we are measured by God. Have a plan and have a back up plan, but always respect His plan for our lives.

Lord, why show me these things and not allow me to change them. Are these the things that must happen or can happen.-- Scrooge

*Why Lord?

I AM...
AND
I WILL...
YOU ARE...
AND
YOU WILL...

Give us a Scooby Doo ending – Wayne's World

*It doesn't always turn out the way you would hope. In fact, more often than not, it turns out the opposite. These are the experiences that form your frame of reference that you carry with you for your entire earthly lives. Be open minded and forgiving. Your brother is a dumb ass and you are a dumb ass for not inspiring him. We can carry him no longer. My dumb ass has to inspire my brother's dumb ass, so God can fulfill His promise. God promised Jesus Christ an Everlasting Earthly Kingdom in His Holy Name. Do this for Me and I will establish your Kingdom forever. Dude, He gave His Life for mine and yours. I am in a forever debt to my Savior. What can I do for you Lord? I am your servant to command. Pleeeeeeeeeeeeease... tell me and ease my pain.

Would the book sell better titled:
Nathan the prophet, the Messiah, the Savior, the One and Only, the Almighty, the One to tell you all is well in the World, Go Ask Oprah.

*Probably Go Ask Oprah or Dr. Phil. Let me turn the volume up on this one. GO ASK GOD!!! You can never get personal with them, so get personal with your creator. He loves you and wants to hear from you. He's not going to give you a better parking spot or a million dollars, but He will provide for you. Ask of Him and you shall receive.

This is something I must articulate, because I will never experience it. He has made that point quite clear. Our Father who art in Heaven, Hallowed be thy name. Thy Kingdom come, thy Will be done. On Earth, as it is in Heaven.

*I can only start it with the Will of our Father in Heaven. Revealing your plan is all that I can do Father. I await further

instruction, but grow weary from all I have been through and put my family through. Let my loss be humanities gain.

Let the name of Moses be stricken from everything and replaced with the name Ramses – 10 Commandment's

The significance of removing the name of Moses, is the attempt to remove his memory from our hearts, minds and future generations/History. The Egyptians always thought of things generationally and how over time, anything can be erased from history. Our society keeps chipping away at our belief that we are "One Nation Under God". How many more generations will it take, for us to be so politically correct that there is no room for God in our lives? Just as there was no room at the Inn for Jesus Christ, there will be no room in our hearts for God. Who is this God anyway? Didn't his name used to appear on the U.S. Currency that was debased to the point of Worthlessness and Extinction?

If the U. S. economy fails, it will be a direct reflection on Judea Christian Principles and Capitalism. The two are intimately intertwined. I just have to wonder what the schools will be teaching my Great Grandchildren when or if that happens. I have a vision of that, but I'd prefer not to share with the class on this one.

*I think I will share in this book. They will be influenced by cold blooded leaders of our past. Mao, Che, Hitler, Stalin etc...

Sign, sign, everywhere a sign. Do this, don't do that, can't you read the signs – dumb ass

Are the signs right?

Don't follow them and see where that gets you.

Your son verbally challenges what he hears on TV. Do you think he should be checked out? – my grandmother's inquiry to my parents

*My training and programming began at an early age. I am glad that I challenged what I heard on TV or anything else for that matter. Always respectfully question authority.

Her name escapes me, probably because my dad's brother robbed me out of my check – Legacy.

If it is killing you, why do you continue? I got a secret.

When you find out who you are and your purpose for God, you are the only gauge to compare yourself with. Until then, emulate people you want to become.

WWJD – no, I never wore one. I thought it was hokey at the time

Homosexuality --
He might not be okay with it, that's on you. But I am okay with it – Nathan

Well I am glad to know that you are okay with it. You pompous ass – (Thing One)

I heard about water purification ridding the saline for potable water. You are probably on the wrong track and you need some stoned kid in a garage to figure it out. Bill Gates gave us Windows and made more money than God. Do you need some more names. That would bore my ass. I get the point. Do you? We better catch that kid before he sees the wrong doctor.

*I wonder what the percentage of gifted children are having their inspirations and dreams being sedated to conform with the supposed NORM???

This is a letter to future prophets. Wow, is this my first time to prophesy?

Hey you, lazy procrastinator. Put down that pipe and listen. If you're going to go through life medicated. Then bring something to this world that can help your neighbor.

1. Write your ideas down
2. reread number one – thanks Mr. Miagi If done right, no can defense. Crane technique.
3. 30 hours on tape lost to the devil. Are these the lost tapes of Nathan? Ha Ha Have a credible source easily accessible to you, I am working on this path for you to examine your work. A Think Tank.
   4. If this is a pain in the ass for you. Shut up and get a job. Hit the pipe when you can relax and be with your Father.

I know I'm laughing my ass off too.

If I am made in your likeness, your a goofy bastard too. I love you God. Where have you been all my life? – Nathan your humble servant

I love where this is going, keep them coming
And the hits keep rolling in

Let's roll
Let's sample a little of the hearts of heroes. The man that sticks out to me is that football player that gave up all of his future for his country/people/family/God.

How easy it is for God to fall to the back of the line. Even for me. I'm sorry Lord. Help me keep you first in my heart, not always in my words. We got business to take care of and we're moving on up to that deluxe apartment in the sky-- the Jeffersons

You made me a poor reader. Was this your deal with the devil?

*Our brains work in different ways. It appears that most people would rather have a root canal than read a book. I must admit, I fell into that category until I had to reinvent myself at the age of 42. I do retain information better by hearing it on CD or playing a game, but my best retention is video. Discover your best way to get information and educate yourselves. If IT is to be, IT is up to me. Do you want more in life? Learn more. No one is going to give it to you. You have to be thirsty for it. It is Living Water from our Father and a history of mistakes by our forefathers. Learn to follow the rule book and save yourselves a tremendous amount of time and grief. It is so easy to be so involved in life and miss it completely. You can slip into a state of ignorance just because someone has awarded you a diploma. Believe me, you don't know shit yet in your life. You are not the Scarecrow and immediately have the knowledge to lead men. It takes a lifetime to develop your frame of reference, make sure it is the frame of reference that you desire.

The devil goes up to Georgia. But if I lose the devil gets my soul. This is when you spoke to me Lord. I want my fiddle made of gold. You let the people decide. I'll take my blessings from the rabble – It's a Wonderful Life. I already have yours.

*Well Mr. Potter, you warped twisted old man, I will take my blessings from the rabble that you call cattle and I call men. We are the most charitable people when we see something we believe in. We will help our brother. We will inspire our brother and yes if we have to, we will carry our brother.

And I believe you keep your promises.

*Lord,
**Thank you again. You are so blessing me in my life. I have
never been so blessed in all of my life. Financially and Spiritually, but I am still lacking in love. Were you sending me a
message through the Genie in the Movie Aladdin? We can't
pray to stop Death and we're on our own to give our heart to
whoever we want to of our own free will. Cool, I always wondered why you never answered that prayer. A prayer that I
have prayed countless times. I understand now Lord, You are
a great God. The one and only God over all men.**

I have a picture of Ralph in my Bible. I have not paid any attention to it, but I knew it was there.

I just looked at it. His arms are outstretched. My first thought
was, where to now? My second thought was, is this it? The lot is
straight, the cars are cranked, this ought to do it. Where's all the
people?

Ralph – are you ready?

***I've been searching my entire life for what it is that I do.
If you do this and this, you will get this. Not necessarily my
brother, making a go of it on your own can present some very
turbulent times.**

Get ready, get ready, get ready – TD Jakes

How do I get a book deal? Somebody has got to think this shit
is as funny as I do.

***Anytime you try to be creative you will meet with resis-
tance. You will have people that are envious, non-supportive,
judgmental and absolute saboteurs of your dreams. Not only
will you have to deal with other people, but you will have**

plenty of hurdles just trying to figure out the process for doing something you want to do, without being screwed by people preying upon your dreams. You might want to get you some soap on the rope when you enter into this tank of sharks. I promise you that you don't want to be bending over to pick anything up in this arena.

I do – failed commitments, please take off the mask.

10% in the bucket ought to do it. It worked for me, but what do I know, I'm a leper.

*Before you make any life long commitments take the time to know the facts before you leap. It can be a leap of faith or a well thought out plan. Have faith in your God, do a fact finding mission on who you decide to give your heart to. A broken heart will mend with time, but it sucks.

Man these cigarettes are killing me. You got to die of something, I guess. My son wants me to quit smoking, so he can spend more Quality time – ask Austin

The amount of time concealing my secret world, would have been better spent with him. The devil is robbing me.

*Cigarettes and alcohol have robbed me of a lot of my life. I don't want to be this person, but I am drawn be the bright lights of advertising. Smoking is so glamorous isn't it? NOT.

Humans are not logical – Spock

Whoever said we were – Kirk

*Why do we do things that we know are bad for us? The only answer that I can come up with is, we're stupid.

You don't own me – First Wives Club

Look at my mess, I need help.

Help – I need somebody – Beatles

Help, I've fallen and I can't get up.

*Who picks you up when you fall? Who has your back under any circumstance? Who will you turn to when your family and friends turn from you? Have you taken a personal examination? Listen to all that would give advice, then make up your own mind. You are the only one that will live with the consequences of your actions.

I've always liked Stephen Wrights style of humor. Dry and sarcastic.

You know that feeling you get leaning back in your chair right before you lose your balance and bust your ass? I feel like that all the time – Steven Wright

I feel like I have fallen and can't get up – Nathan – Age

Honor your Mother and Father even when they're ignorant. My parents are far from ignorant concerning smarts. With God, I don't know. I have been ashamed to ask. Forgive me Lord. My past times don't make me the best Witness for you.

That one hurts

*Yes, my sinful ways have made it difficult for anyone to believe in me. How can I tell someone about what has happened in my life with our Father, when they only see the person I present on the outside. My outward presentation may resemble yours, does my heart?

(Thing One) was the first to call me Holy Roller – I kind of liked it.

*Just imagine, I am thought of as a witness for God. Who am I Lord to proclaim your Holy Name?

LEPER FOR GOD
OR
LIAR FOR MAN 666

I am surely to be blind, because women are gorgeous in all shapes and sizes.

You know there is a God – Coming to America

*It's a good thing they are beautiful, there might be a price on their heads. LOL I have to wonder if people use these talents to get what they want? I wonder if they use them so much, they become the crutch of survival? Remember, beauty fades and you're left with what is between your ears, not your legs.

Was the Shock God a Prophecy?

Because I am enjoying screwing with people and being the invisible Mario.

Dog, I feel your pain. Refer to Mrs. Doubtfire for your forgiveness. Are we really brothers from a different mother? I use the N. word all the time. Maybe it's time to turn a new leaf. Stop picking the fly shit out of the pepper. You are imprisoning your own people.

*When will we be able to put racism aside and focus on the heart of the individual? We may have to ask the wise 'ole owl on that one. I feel in all my heart that we can, how long is the question. I can say, if you look for the small stuff, you remain small yourself. Did you hear what he said? Yes, how do you want or do you want his head on a silver platter? Get over it and strive for your own self worth. You are giving your power over to a bigoted moron. I've been there, I'm guilty. Please forgive me my brother, I was a finished project of what my

frame of reference evolved to by what I have seen, heard, read and experienced for myself. Can we pick up the pieces together and put Humpty Dumpty together again? Would you take the blood from your brother to heal a loved one? How do you know what color person it came from? It all looks red to me, it looks just like the blood spilled on the cross. The blood of Jesus Christ runs through all of our veins. He is our brother and God is the Father. It is time my brothers in Christ. The compass of life includes everyone and everyone is called to fulfill their own purpose for God. You will have to find it for yourselves, but I can assure you that it does not include color coordination. Save that for your shoes, belt and hat.

God doesn't like you. I don't like you. You are users of this system. Ask (Thing One), he loves to tell this story. How he gets over on his peers, so he can be first at the table. He is the one that should be last, if even invited.

*Well I don't think (Thing One) will be interested in telling you, so I will. I may have already, but it sickens me enough to tell you again. When (Thing One) and (Thing Two) go on their cruises, (Thing Two) says he is handicapped and in need of a wheelchair. They are the first to get on board and the first to get off. (2nd Wife) chuckled with them and enjoyed the story. I cringed in my chair and wanted to blast their selfish, inconsiderate asses. So I guess I was already getting prepared for the ultimate blowout confrontation with me and the Thing 1 & 2 Clan. My fuse is long, but when I blow, there aren't any survivors including myself. Blow the bomb by the way, I don't want to get any Thing excited. They look for anything on the Gaydar. Why do we go along to get along? You must exercise your own set of principles and values. Would you have giggled with them or do what I wanted to do? Or maybe you're saying to yourself, hey that's a great idea. Yes my brother, (Things) will always be among us and it is not limited to the (Things). Anyone may qualify to be a manipulative asshole.

This is the song that never ends, it goes on and on again my friend – Nathan

*This song does go on and on my brother. Accept who you are and accept your brother for who they are. You may not condone it, but who are we to judge our brothers. They will be judged one by one by their actions. Their consequences are still pending and looming over head until that day. Treat your brothers the way you wish to be treated.

Your silly, no your silly. Are you having fun with this One Life the Lord has given you?

*You must become as a child to understand Christ and where you are presently at in your life with Christ. Our brother Jesus Christ knows exactly who we are. There is no mask that He can not see through.

I am looking for signs – ask (2nd Wife)
I am headed to the pass
Had to write it down before God.

*We all look for signs depending on what we are looking for. You will find those signs. It is justification or creative avoidance.

**You know, I don't have a clue what this is about, but the line headed to the pass. We are all headed to pass. What we pass is the question.

I am not organizing all this shit, so you can forget it.

We can send it in as the babblings of Nathan. Read by the author – nope, I don't want that job either. A ADHD stupid screw.

Whitey/Stony can you get my bag. Nathan's version movie with Hank – Jim Carrey – him carry

Someone please help me carry this CROSS.

*As bricks of Mankind, we can erect our Creator an Everlasting Entity. Who will help Jesus with His Cross? You are forgiven by the blood of Christ. The Father promised He would establish His Kingdom here on Earth. I just didn't realize it would be a continuation of Christ's work, healing the sick and witnessing for our Father who art in Heaven.

No wonder God did not allow me to reach Wikipedia.

Is this the video game that alerted the bad guys – trailer park – Alex

The last shall be first, respect your brother

There were sure enough warnings even for my ADHD ass

*How do you know if you are the one? How do you know that you are not if you are not willing to look? Do not look to your brother to shape you. Shape yourselves in your own image of God. God has given you talents to help your brother. Use Jesus as your guide and you will never fail. All pitfalls will be looked at as learning phases in life that will mold a better or worse you. Look at every hardship as an opportunity to learn. I can not tell you why some things God allows to happen. I do think He allows man 666 to make it happen. Mourn from your loss, cry out every tear. Now pick yourself up and become better from it. These can be some of the most influential moments of your life. Learn from them and put your Trust in God. There is always a reason, many take years to understand. Some it is not for you to know at this time. You will eventually be given the answers you so desperately seek. God has a plan and man 666 will alter it. Many of His children come to Him way before they were supposed to. You

can not change that, rejoice they are in the loving arms of our Creator and you will join them again.

You said my torment would get greater. It is true, like birthing pains. I must get this out. Number one: your plan or number two: the devils plan. I'll take curtain number one. dumb ass, jackass

*Lord,
Forgive me of my thoughts. I am so ready to be done with this so I may enjoy my life as well. People are so ignorant and unfeeling that it has made me really not give a flying fat rats ass whether they comply or not. I just want to heal from my torment and be done. I have wanted to put this back into your hands so many times. But you kept on pushing me and pushing me. What more can I do Father if your people will not listen?

ARE YOU FINISHED?

Not yet my Lord, I am getting close I hope.

YOU DO YOUR PART
I WILL
DO MINE

I WILL focus on the end result, not the interim. Does the end justify the means?

I AM
ETERNAL

YOUR END IS
YET...

I WILL...

Not a mistake of mine, but a mistake of culture

run home Jack
      Jack ass – Happy Gilmore Adam Sandler Movie
run home Jack ass
Good advice. How's it working out for you? He loves you.
Forgive my damaged antennas.

***At life's bleakest moments you can rest assured you have
a home with our Father. Your brother will try to prevent you
from coming and you will be tempted. Remember, "There's
no place like Home, there's no place like Home, there's no
place like Home". Our Father welcomes us with open arms
and a fatted calf. His door remains open, it is you who close it
to Him and to yourself.**

I want one of those remotes
Click? First a boat, a loan again. Where do I start God?

***When did we become so entitled that we think we should
immediately have what our parents have worked their entire
lives for. CREDIT... Wow, that's an impressive salary you are
making there. Based on my projections you can afford much
more than you currently have. Great, where do I sign? They
must know what they are doing, they let me have it with my
signature. How could I have anticipated these hardships I am
living with today? Well it was all there fault for giving it to
me in the beginning. They should have known I couldn't afford this if there was any hic cup in the market. Remember,
I wanted less and you said I could have more. Well you can
have it back, I didn't like it anyway.**

**Screw you, it is time to step up and take responsibility
for your own actions. We all make mistakes, now learn from
yours and don't make them again. If you are a repeat offend-
er of anything, doesn't that make you look kind of stupid? Do**

you feel stupid the moment you get busted? The excitement may build in anticipation of a thrill, but the consequences suck. If you were in a third world country they would cut off what you offended with. Ouch, what were you thinking?

That payment is going to eat you up – my first toy – 74 Corvette While I am trying to sell.

*Now that I think of it, that was my one toy. I never had another one, I could never get over the debt to afford it. I was already living way beyond my means. For those that are to smart for me, that means you are spending more than you make and facilitating your lifestyle with credit. Just as it is unsustainable in our Country, so it is unsustainable in your own household.

Materialism is a whole chapter. A very long chapter. Let them play the game. It explains it better than I. I am tired again. I wrote the President again – predictable – Forrest Gump

*Unless you are fortunate to pay cash, materialism will keep you on the rat race treadmill. It can become a night-mare if you aren't careful. It is a nightmare that will rob you of your life. I can't emphasis enough to monitor the payment books you are willing to live with to pacify a need to impress others.

*Robert Kiyosaki is my hero, he has a game called Cash-flow. It is a must have for every household. It's entertaining and extremely educational for the financial intelligence that I spent a lifetime seeking. I loved monopoly, had I been given this game at that stage of my life there is no telling where I would be today. We all learn in different ways, but I believe there is no better way to learn than trial and error. Can I em-phasize this point enough. Jesus you tell them.

*My children, what Nathan says is true. Search you heart for your mistakes and learn from them. Ask the Wonderful Counselor, the Holy Spirit to guide your thoughts. He is all around you, accept me and the Father into your heart and you will find direction. I promise you.

Where is Lieut. Dan, Gene?
I've got money now. That's good. One less thing to worry about.

*"I think he finally made his peace with God". Everyone has a financial noose around their neck. If you can ever be in a situation that this noose is loose, it gives you time to reflect on life and really take the time to step outside the box and look inside. You have a decision in front of you when you finally exit the rat race and enter the fast track. You can continue to strive for more or you can learn to live with a level of contentment that you are personally comfortable with. Let me warn you, the quest for more can become addictive. It can be the worse drug you have ever been exposed to. You can be so wrapped up into achieving your dreams and lose them at the same time. Always measure your costs to your gains. It can be very illuminating to you to know what direction you are taking your life. I can show you how a financial statement works and so can my 14 yr old son, but I can not show you a balance sheet of your life. That is a fill in the blank form for only you and God. In your life, what are your assets, liabilities and passive love?

Worry will kill you faster on the inside – cancer? It will drive you insane. Don't worry, be happy. Our Father loves us. Enjoy now. You will be going home soon enough. Which house, it's up to you.

*Lord,
I want to come Home. I am ready. I understand your heart for me. How can any Father not allow His children to learn

from their mistakes? If the mistakes were blessed, we would become entitled.

*If I give you a fish and bread today you are most appreciative. If I give you the same tomorrow you are justified to receive it for your time. If I do not give you a fish and bread on the third day you feel cheated out of your entitlement. How can I wean you from your brother when you keep Caesar in power? God is good and so is your brother. Tough love is called tough for no other reason than it is tough. So tough it out. That is why I left you on the mountainsides wanting more. I planted my seeds and I wanted to see if you were fertile ground. I AM here and I want what our Father has promised. I want to dwell among you and heal the sick.

*I'm wondering if we can get it at all. I'm sick of trying. I'm disgusted at what we have become. I wouldn't blame Him for allowing us to destroy ourselves, we really are not worthy to receive His Grace. No wonder Moses threw the tablets to the earth. Stop the party just for a second and change gears. The party can continue, just allow the bridegroom to join in. He so desperately wants to party with you. He can have you, I'm sick of you and I'm getting another drink. Something with an umbrella in it. LOL Screw you.

I don't have a clue what the Lord will have me write next, but I feel good. Da Na Na Na I knew that I would, so good – Nathan/ Little Richard

*I'm getting there again Baby, I'm listening to a little K C and the Sunshine Band. "That's the Way UH Huh UH Huh I Like It"

Richie Valens flight
Pray that your plight is not in the winter – somewhere in the Bible

*Man, I was in a completely controlled manic state of mind for seven months. I didn't fly with my friend Bill during that time. He had just gotten his plane out of the shop and I just felt something bad. I think that this will resonate with anyone that has ever dodged a bullet. Although the trip went safely, I feel better not going and endangering the others. Sometimes you just have to follow your gut. It wasn't my time and I didn't want to make attempts to make it my time. I thank the Lord for not taking my brother from me. I would be lost without Him.

I am driving my brother, like Michael the Archangel. Plus I don't have to worry about going through detection devices. I need my medication. You Bastards – Braveheart

*You Bastards is right. Okay, I use what our Father has put on this earth to heal the Nations and our physicians have something that will help my back pain. But if I use what my Father gave me, I can not use what man has for me unless I buy it on the black market. That's screwed up and what creates corruption. Let me have anything I want and keep me in check with laws. I will learn from my mistakes, but you make it so damn attractive to want what I can't have. You Bastards.

My image of living in the U.S. as being the best place to be, has been a little shaken. I am proud to be an American. But this sucks. Have we really defeated Long Shanks? I am tired of the scraps from his table. SEC? Security Exchange Commission

Okay is that what you call it now.

*My country is the Greatest Country in the World. I love my Country. I do not love what my Country has become. See me as the Indian crying over the pollution, but my crying comes from corruption and greed. But this little Indian is pissed and I am willing to fire a few arrows of my own. I will

fire them with the Will of God so their impact will resonate in many more hearts than a single arrow. We have had enough. Make us safe!!! and get the hell out of our lives. Stop force feeding us things that will line your pockets. If you think it is important, if it is, then others will think it is important as well and won't mind supporting it. Start a trust fund that will facilitate for generations. Just keep your freaking hands off my check and let me support the things that I believe in. You will find much more blessings that way. I ask you this, are you more apt to tip more for humble service or required service? If you have never worked in this industry, let me tell you that it is how we feed our family. You work hard for your money and I work hard for mine. If I have served you well, give me my due. That is all I ask for everyone.

I want my SEC – Gator Growl – Go Gators – Smothers Brothers
The little Faggot got his own jet airplane
The little Faggot he's a millionaire

You have got to be kidding Yo Yo tricks for my drunk ass.
    Taste Great!!! Less Filling!!!
I admire you for sticking it out. But you suck, for this stage environment.

*How do we witness to our brother? Are we shouting scripture into his ear? He is deaf, mute and blind. Now what do you do?

ALL THAT WOULD
HEAR
SEE
FEEL
SMELL
TASTE
... ME NOW

I WILL
GIVE UNTO YOU
WILL YOU
GIVE UNTO ME

*I am down my Lord, my Savior. Draw your blade to my sinful heart. I beg of mercy for not only myself, but my stupid ass brother that I love and will always care for. He is my brother Lord. He is your brother as well. Please forgive all of us, for we are a sinful people and by your Grace we are a forgiven people.

Lord help me reveal that you can be all things to all people

Let me close the greatest Sale of my life

World's Greatest Salesman
That is what we really are. The devil has many tools in his bags. We all are distracted and attracted to see whats inside. Don't give up Santa Claus. I like him. Teach your children about their check – they will receive on their 18th birthday – Nathan. Sorry kids, compounded interest needs time to mature.

*Man, I am so digging this bread trail that you left for me. I had no idea that I could deliver your words via movie clips. But that is your gift to me Lord and I thank you. If I can tell your people something that they would live by, what would it be Lord?

DO NOT TEMPT THY GOD
THY GOD DOES
NOT TEMPT YOU
MAN TEMPTS YOU
WITH YOUR OWN
DESIRES

Use judgment please, of course take care of the orphans. That is where you will find him and you are not quite ready – Maturity

*Are we not all orphans in some degree or fashion? You may have a mom and a dad, but do you have a Father? I love my mom and dad, they are the best. They were instrumental in developing my frame of reference and I am blessed to have a healthy one. I pray for all those that are not as fortunate to focus your love to our Creator. He has His arms open to you. He knows you can not forget and He knows you can prevail any circumstance that confronts you. He also knows that you have become scarred. These are the scars that can control your life or the scars that can shape your life for Him. With all pain comes healing. It hurts now, but my brother it will guide you to achieve what you were meant to be. I know, your life sucks and it shouldn't have turned out this way. Ditto my brother. So it sucks, what now? Brother, envision a new life for yourself. It is never too late to re-invent yourself. How many years will you pass out shopping carts at Walmart because you have to? Pass them out because you want to. It makes all the difference in the world when you love what it is you do. Love your brother as your brother loves you. Our Father wants us to love each other. Just as brothers quarrel, we are still brothers and when the chips are down, we come to the aid of our brother.

I am trying not to sin like my forefathers did. I don't want to wait 40 years, if I can even make it that long – Nathan

*Don't kid yourselves. We have all sinned just like our forefathers did. What can we learn? I had to have this drilled in to my thick skull, Google you questions, evaluate opinions and determine your own thoughts. Make up your own damn mind. Get it.

*Who has more answers? Google or God?

*Answer: It depends on your frame of reference.

I want an Umpa Loompa now Daddy – Willy Wonka

*Are you pacifying a situation? You are creating your own nightmare, I promise you. They do grow up and you will reap what you sow. Invest time now or misery later. Your children need guidance and they need you to give it to them. They look to you now, not later. Stop!!! stop your damn life for just a moment. What are you doing to mentor your children for a better life? Hey, if you are going to support them for the rest of their lives, then I'm not talking to you chumps. I am talking to the folks that want their children to become all they can, without any restraints from man. Do not be the facilitator because you have money or addictions to the future of your children.

But that girl has a fine ass. Girl, you look in so good, somebody ought to sop you up with a biscuit – Coming to America

*Are you pretty? Wow, you have got some shit to deal with and you don't even know it because you are blessed with beauty. When you find yourself crying to a cabdriver about not being loved, but fulfilling a gold digging purpose, you will start to yearn for real love. Biff will always screw Buffy and they will portray the perfect life. We will all idolize them and not know the true story behind closed doors and they will not permit you in until it is to the breaking point. I tell you the truth, the prettier you are, the more screwed up you are. I can not even imagine having to fend off every shark that wants a piece of you. Hell, for that matter, I want a piece of you. At least for the night. After I search your soul, I may find there is no beauty inside and that is the beauty that lasts. Here's the weird part, the person that could make you the happiest may be intimidated by your beauty. Men and Boys listen to me, make the approach. The Studs and Geeks are doing it and

accepting rejection. I have a real hard time with this one as well. I do not like to do the walk of shame, but as my friend Bill has pointed out, you can never strike out or hit a home run if you are not willing to step up to the plate. Ever wonder why some of the most gorgeous women are with the most opposite of mates. It is because they had confidence and you did not. You may even be subjecting yourselves to a lifetime of misery due to it.

Cover-up Nikki, you never know when there are N's around
– Band of the Hand

*This is a bad ass movie, I hope you can watch it. It is so exemplary of the Man being in control of the streets. I have to ask you, how much are you worth? Understand, I want to do all the things that you don't. You are my slave for the night and all I want to know is how much? How much is your soul worth?

Nikki – ask Prince or whatever sign he is

My guess is less is more, but not with clothing

You don't have to be a stick in the mud though

Don't let the latest fashions drive you $$$
Just cover your ass

*It amazes me the differences in price for the same article of clothing depending on where you shop. It also amazes me to watch people pay an exorbitant amount of money to inflate their egos. I understand completely, I've done it. Now that I am above it, it seems so ridiculous.

I wrote a book about myself. I know everything in it, but I don't have a freaking clue what is in it. I have five original tapes in a sealed federal express package mailed to my parents. Can I start the bidding at $1 million for God's Legacy Trust LLC.

*I wish I could find that FedEx package. I'd like to hear what is on them as well. I was in a complete manic episode praising our Father. I hope. LOL

I wish I had $1 million – It's a wonderful life

*Wish and dream all you want. Pray for the things that are important. Genie, you've given me everything that I have asked for, so why am I so empty?

PURPOSE
YOU HAVE ONE
PURPOSE
SEEK YOUR
PURPOSE
I AM
YOUR PURPOSE
YOU WILL
YOUR PURPOSE
WILL YOU
SEEK MINE
I WILL
BE YOUR PURPOSE
PRAISE ME
AS I
PRAISE YOU
YOU ARE MY
CHILDREN
YOU ARE MY
PURPOSE

*The Lord our God looks to us to fulfill His own Purpose. He wishes to see us seek our own for Him. Why is this so hard, don't we see the same things in our own family. There are always lost sheep in any family. How we welcome them home is what is at question. My Father kills a fatted calf, my heart can only pray to be that forgiving. My Father welcomes you home and so must I. Sulking only caused me to miss the party and celebrate your homecoming. You are my brother after all. Father forgive me, but I will still need to examine his heart. I will have forgiveness in my heart, but awareness in my brain. Time will heal all wounds. All wounds that are clean. The scars will always remain as reminders my brother. Just as the hands, feet and side of Christ will act as a reminder for us to forgive our brother, look for the scar and not pick the scab. Let it freaking go. Forgive Him.

This money is for you God. This buds for me. Your grace is enough for me. The things of this world, given to us by you. All natural?

*If you ask your Father for a fish, do you think He would give you a snake instead? Yet when we ask for the fish that our Creator has given us, man suppresses it and gives us a snake (alcohol and cigarettes). These are much better for you because we make more money on them. Man creates corruption, when man suppresses anything from man. Man should be allowed to explore anything he likes, as long as it doesn't infiltrate over into another mans space. Caesar, keep us safe with laws governing the people that would kill themselves and their brother. Do not push my brother, my brother will push back. Let me inspire my brother. My back has been turned to my brother, you have shown me something else. The eyes in the back of my head. Even after I have turned my back on my brother, He is still my brother. I will always care for my brother. I will keep a close eye for my brothers rebirth in Christ. You can't fool me, don't even try. I see your heart.

This is a pain in the ass, but it requires more labor. The lepers are coming, the lepers are coming – ask the Tinman

They are from the school of knowledge – they know what it is to really eat an alley cat. Third world impoverished countries suck. Let's fix this. As the beacon country, One Nation under God.

They really "Will Work for Food", not entitlement.

*People of the Global World UNITE! "We Are The World, We are the Children" we are all children of the same God. He has many names, but He is the same God. The one Creator of the whole Universe. Jesus Christ is the only begotten son of God and He is my brother and my Savior.

I am looking at a fat ass (Yeah I checked it out., I'm only human) white girl with a black baby. Where is that babies daddy?

*"That's just my babies daddy". Catchy tune, here's another racial joke. "What is the most confusing day in the Hood? Fathers Day." It is sad that racism still continues to exist. But I ask you, how close do these songs and jokes hit to your own home? They are color blind by the way.

If you love them, okay. Interracial marriage – but make sure you read all of the ingredients on the back.

*Hell, you better read all of the ingredients regardless of the race issue. I mean really, you are committing to one another for the rest of your lives. This is huge if you have intentions of following through on your commitment.

What is black and white and red all over? – a newspaper

Forget the color, know your mate.

Can they be made accountable? Not by your power, don't even try. Only through Jesus Christ can you understand the Father.

Let's do something different. Let's go to church. Maybe they were just fixing to call me or maybe they are still waiting.

I am waiting for the National Enquirer to come put this angel out of my misery.

*I loved that part of the movie in Michael when the reporters realized that they would have a killer story about an angel. They started dancing and singing "Thank you Jesus, Thank you Jesus". I just have to wonder if we give thanks and praise to the one that is pulling the strings of your life. We curse Him when things don't work out, do we praise Him when they do? Something tells me that we become prideful with our successes and give the praise to ourselves. Let's just see how far that will get you. You will have your face to the floor sooner or later begging for mercy and Grace. I pray it is not to late for you when that time comes.

We have no homosexuality in our country. Ha Ha Ha Iranian Leader
Our ignorance – they are in complete control – control freak – let them decide – let God judge – step back nonbelievers.

*It is statements like this that allow me to appreciate the diversity of my cultural up bringing. Let me tell you this, this man is more familiar with the Bible than 99% of the fundamentalist Christians. It is because they are taking it as the battle plan of God to over throw what they have achieved with their own tyranny. Do you remember the part in Borat when they realized they were staying in the house of Jews? They were terrified because God has allowed the Jews to kick ass with much smaller numbers. The only times the Jews got their own asses kicked is when they didn't take the time to

consult God for guidance. They are God's chosen people and as a Christian Gentile I do not begrudge them that honor. They have suffered for generations and I say give them their due. I love you my Jewish brother in Christ, I pray my Muslim brother in Christ will accept and believe in you also. In order for us to save all of our own asses, we must unite as brothers under one God. Hey, I'm digging the whole Muhammad thing. I haven't finished reading what it is he has to say, but I have an open mind. Do you? I want World Peace in my lifetime.

All we are saying
is give peace a chance – Billy Jack

*This puzzles me, does it puzzle you? We send our children off to war and they come home in a box. They die with Honor, but they are gone to our Father. Our Father is not ready for any of His children via wars, but receives them with open arms. It is man that manipulates God's word to fulfill their own agenda.

If you don't know how hard it is to be heard, you are probably dead. Another one bites the dust and another one gone and another one gone, another one bites the dust. Heh Heh

*Even with the technology of today, it is almost impossible to be heard. Keep your faith my brother, our Father hears you and will bless all that you do for Him. He is the only one that you need concern yourself with. If it is for His Glory, then screw everyone else. You do what you are compelled to do by the Holy Spirit.

If you are looking for the devil. He is on the front row.

*Time and time again, I am faced with the dilemma of witnessing to the unbelievers and the convenient believers. I

think I would rather break bread with the unbelievers, just as Jesus chose to eat with the tax collectors. I don't want to hear what you think I want to hear. I want to hear why do you not believe in your hearts. Keep your tithe if it does not come from your heart. Screw you, God doesn't need any tithe that does not come with blood, sweat and tears. He will have His, will you have yours is the question. When you give to our Father, give with your heart and your soul will follow. Now you know that your tithe will go directly to help your fellow man, not to the payroll of the Church. I get pissed every time I pass a Church parking lot and see it empty. There are only cars on Sunday and Wednesday nights. What a wonderful health facility these Church's would make. You want to talk about bringing the word of Jesus Christ to the unbelievers, you start healing their children and they will believe. Oh yes, they will believe in our Father.

I must be on the front row – commercial

*When I search for help, I do not go to the front row of the Church any longer. I go direct to the Almighty, I have a bat phone that I use. I'm still working on the Bat Signal in the Sky for everyone to see, but I will leave that to Jesus. If He wants to come on a surfboard with fire balls shooting from His ass. I can dig it. But for now, I will just believe that He is coming back through me. I just hope that I can be the Lion that God wants me to be. I damn sure have a sharp tongue and I will cut you. My only request is that if His words cut you, can you change your behavior? Dude, I'm not talking about becoming Holier than Thou. That's the shit that turns everyone off from the get go. I'm talking about being real and when you need to make decisions you ask yourselves WWJD. Would my brother Jesus Christ have a drink with me. Abso – freaking – lutely. He is cool. God sent Him to give us some guidance and brother do we need some right now. I still want to know who's leg I'm going to have to hump for a dry martini in Heaven. LOL

I wouldn't mind a N like Colin Powell for a Father in law. Overcome racism. It's hard to get all your people to overcome ignorance. Then we can identify the N's from the rest of the colors – and heal them. What color was N anyway? shimmer 666 felt

*Dude, let me ask you a question. If one of you aspires for more and achieves it, why do you want to drag him back into the bucket with you? I saw an amazing thing with the election of Barack Obama. I want to believe, but I don't want anything that he does, or I do for that matter, to be shielded with the veil of racism. I ask you, if I can not make an attack of my opinion without it being regarded as racist, isn't that in and of itself racist to my beliefs? I don't give a flying fat rats ass what color he is. I'm concerned with the well being of all my Global brothers in Christ. Today he is black and tomorrow he is white. Will you do your Uncle Tom bullshit on the days he is white. OH, you can't tell those days apart. Then sit down and shut the freak up and listen to what the man is saying. If you are a brother looking for more from your brother, rather than contributing your part. Screw you "N" I hope you suffer immensely.

Answer mailbox
had you going there didn't I. You lucky devil – skunk

Who do you think is the devil?
My name is nobody – Henry Fonda

*The devil is in each of us with the decisions we make. Make a difference in your life and the lives of others. It is your decision who to serve. I choose to serve our Creator and His Son Jesus Christ. Man is a mother Freaker and I will not follow in your footsteps, but the footsteps of Christ. I will carry

my sin infested body and beg for His Grace and forgiveness. He will carry my love infested soul to our Father. I wish to hear a not guilty plea from my Father. You may pass to the Kingdom of Heaven my loyal and faithful servant.

My mom is first to call, one o'clock one hour grace period, from high noon

Mom, I didn't know it, but I am a writer.

But you hate to read.
Yeah, but I did what I had to do to reinvent myself. To pick myself up from the mire. Somewhere along the way, I met God. And we are going to see the Wizard. If it is the last thing I ever do. Auntie Em is sick and needs God to heal her.

*God is behind curtains until you wish to see Him. You don't need an appointment and you don't have to beg anyone to talk with Him. I tell you now, fall to your face and proclaim your love and dedication to your Creator by yourself. Do not tell your brother what you have done, keep this in your heart with Him. He will question your motives if you blab about what you have done. Is your praise for Me or for yourself?

I didn't know I was supposed to be looking for a prophet. If a prophet crawled out of your ass would you know one? Prophet Nathan you dumb ass.

*A prophet has crawled out of my ass and I am so glad. How in the Hell could I know I was a prophet until He gained control of my thoughts and written words? I didn't want to accept this Honor, I just wanted to fix my own world, but He had a different plan for my life. I had to lose everything to accept Him. I pray you don't have to endure this pain. I have nothing else to lose, I have no where else to go, I have no one else to love. Therefore, I will thrash you with your own lies

to yourselves. We live and die by our own words. Lord, I am hesitant to really let my tongue loose, I ask for your guidance and will allow you to become me. Speak to me Lord, speak to my heart.

I AM
THAT I AM
THOU ART
I AM...
OR
I AM NOT
I WILL...
OR
I WILL NOT

Here's a sign

I sat in front of a boat named Promised Land II no shit. And a humbled man says, I can only dream to rent one.

*We are renting our time from our Father. We are on a short term lease and there is a buyout clause in the contract. In order for us to purchase our place in Heaven, we must reinstate birthrights and fulfill God's Vision to our everlasting existence. Trust me my brother, God enjoys watching us. He wants to see us live an abundant life that includes abundance for your brother that he gains from your inspiration, not your brow.

Ask of your Father, you shall receive.

I am a coon ass
Not a dumb ass
I am a dumb ass with ADHD
Coon ass with my senses

Crazy like a fox
What did a coon ever do to you?

Momma used to just scare them off with a broom – Forrest Gump

N joke, do tell – Wild Hogs

First Dr. – I can take off that leg in 15 seconds
Second Dr. – I can take off that leg in 10 seconds
Third Dr. – that ain't shit, I can take that leg off in 8 seconds

Mame that Coon. (Name that Tune)

*Look inside yourselves. Can you be crazy like a fox? Just when they think they got you down, you're coming up. How much tenacity do you have my brother? Don't show me your crutch, I'll shove it up your ass. Show me your desire to be more than you have become. That is when I will give you a hand up my brother. You become what you want to become,. What do you want to become? What are you willing to do to get there? I promise you no one is going to knock on your front door and give it to you. You must find out on your own who you are, what you do, your new name in Christ and who you are in Christ. When you arrive, I want to be the first to congratulate you. It is a feeling and accomplishment that can not be articulated. I may have not gotten all the merit badges and gold stars, but I don't give a shit what you think. I only give a shit what my Father thinks. He is who I have to answer to, for all my sins. I will wear a crown for my efforts and if I have failed Him, I will wear a crown of failure, but be rewarded because I have done all that was in my power to deliver His Gift as I understood "IT".

Public Schools
try this maze

in > ========= out

Can the system be dumb-ed down any further? I remember listening to a talk show and this very smart young lady from Calif. had married a man from Virginia. Somehow their intellect was gauged and the woman realized that her husband had gained more knowledge than her, while scoring substantially lower in grades through their respective school systems.

*Shall we accommodate the ignorant at the expense of the gifted? Who will determine who is ignorant and who is gifted. If you have only one gauge to determine this, I say that it is you who are ignorant. Our Father made everyone with a different brain to interpret and learn in a different manner. It is up to us to determine what our purpose is. Don't discount me because I do not conform to your archaic teaching principles. Explore the minds of children that seem to be off somewhere else. They are dreaming about the future or what could possibly be for lunch, so don't coddle their ass, Just Watch.

All of this soldiering/learning is bull shit – Heartbreak Ridge

*Why do we not teach our children financial intelligence? Are we training them to be consumers so the wheel of progress continues? I would like to have known this little tidbit that had been omitted from my 16 yr scholastic curriculum. A lot of my mandatory classes were bullshit to me at the time because I didn't want to be well rounded, I wanted to be rich.

Hey, is watching chicks ass a class? it sure is. The technique can be a real problem. – Rape – Pedophile – Incest – SHITHEAD College

*We hold class daily 24/7. Let those that have restraint enter the pearly gates of Heaven and those who do not, burn in Hell for an eternity.

WWJD
The Wonderful Counselor can pass the buck

*The buck has been passed to you by the Holy Spirit, what are you going to do with it knowing that He is watching your every move?

You can reach me on the Bat phone, but don't bother me unless it's important.

I'm enjoying the second half of my life. Scooby Doo

*I will disappear my brother in Christ, for this is not for my Glory, but for the Glory of God. Please do not chase me for a story. I will give all that my Father asks of me in due time. Let God be the Icon that we serve. Now and Forever.

A lot of doctors are us ADD goofy folks. We don't have time for petty things like paying bills. We're too busy trying to heal the world. - Dr. Nathan

*I must admit when I was wrapped up with the Father, I really just didn't want to screw with anything else. They did seem so petty in the grand scheme of things. When you aspire for greatness, you may forget where you came from. Always keep God in the forefront of your mind and you will be successful if only in His eyes.

I hereby award, by the power vested in me, by the Wonderful Land of Oz – U.S.- Knowledge/Truth

To you Lion – Courage and Knowledge

To you Tinman – Compassion and Knowledge

To you Scarecrow-- well, you already have been given knowledge, but you can have all of the rest of the shit the others have.

Dorothy – What have you learned?

If I told you, you would laugh. So I'll let the scarecrow tell you.
You're screwing up – Nathan

*I am the Scarecrow. I have knowledge, compassion and courage. My God has blessed me with all when I went searching for them. Jesus help me out here. This is so you.

KNOWLEDGE
COMPASSION
COURAGE

YOU ARE WHAT
YOU POSSESS

IF YOU DO NOT
POSSESS IT
IT WILL
POSSESS YOU

Hey, this whole cussing thing has got to stop.

Dammit George, not yet. – Back to the Future

Adm. I've noticed your use of colorful metaphors since we have been on this planet?-- Spock
It is the only language this culture understands if you want to be heard – Kirk
Star Trek IV

They Ignant
Do you understand Ignant – ask a Louisianian

I do apologize for my language. It is totally unnecessary, but in this case it is necessary. I hear how you communicate to one another and I know how you emphasize your positions. I am empathizing God's word so that that you will listen this time. Do you realize you fill in your statements with these colorful metaphors because you don't possess the knowledge of the Kings English. It is difficult to express yourselves when you don't have the words as part of your vocabulary. So you either bloviate or discount your message with cussing to get what you want.

I met a man walking up from the beach with all the fishing gear, he says he forgot his bait. What bait shop do I use? I like the discrimination idea, that always stirs up the N's and they stir up the Honkeys/Donkeys.

And somebody gets paid.

"Shake Down"

*Do you realize that every time you squeal it enables others to profit from your misfortune? They are not there for you, you dumbass. They are there for themselves to see how much they can get out of it. You may get some coins, but you further institute racism. You may say to yourself, as long as I get Minezese. This way of thinking has got to stop. When you get from others, you inevitably rob from your future. The manipulators of society will answer to God for their evil ways. Good Luck (Thing One and Two). I wouldn't want to be answering for my decisions if I were in your shoes. You're Screwed. But hey, you went through life screwing others, so it is only fair that you get screwed in every orifice for eternity. You will beg for death to come and relieve you of your torment. Death will never come, for you are experiencing death, you Bastards.

Let's follow the money/memory trail

Give them a get out of jail free card and watch them work your magic.

*We serve an all merciful God and He is very forgiving. How many times must you be forgiven? If faced with Life or Death, would you beg for mercy? You know damn well you would. Why would you even want to put yourself in that situation? I just don't know how merciful our Father is when you reach that point of no return. This is our proving ground for our Father. Have you proven yourselves to be worthy of receiving our Savior? If you are blessed enough to receive forgiveness from your brother, DO NOT go back in your ways. Your ways will inevitably hurt someone and you will not be able to enter the Kingdom of Heaven. In fact I think that it is only fair that the burners get turned up on your account. I'm sorry to be such a judgmental brother, but I'm sick of your ass.

I am at the beach. I just had an epiphany. Maybe I will be able to see God do his work. My big head is blind and my stiff drunk head has no conscious.

Sex before marriage, I concede you are right. Ask Amy and Andrew or is it Jack and Jill?

Jack fell down and broke his crown, Jill came tumbling after

*My brothers and sisters in Christ. I wish I could give you guidance in this arena, but I have failed myself. I can only tell you what I have learned from my mistakes and they are plentiful. I hate to say this because it goes against God, but I know that hurt that comes from divorce and it is a pain that no pill can cure. There is no broken heart pill and there never will be. You may numb yourself, but your heart is still bloody. All I am saying, before committing to one another, know one another. If this means living together, then I think that this is better than "that's just my babies daddy". Once you know

each other, you won't be comfortable in your soul before you proclaim your love for your partner before thy God. This is a proclamation not to be taken lightly as it seemingly is now. It is for life and don't commit to anything for life unless you are sure in your heart. You just don't understand the hearts you will break based on your decisions.

The man is the head, take your place.

Not here, in the ring. You only fight in the ring, Tommy Gunn. – Rocky V
Devil, this is the ring you've been wanting – Media

*Are you man enough to claim your role in society? That remains to be seen. Do you only fight for life when you are paid? Can you fight for life with no recognition? Can you take yourself to the position of head of the household? You have many that rely on you, can you accommodate them? If not, then don't put yourself in those situations. Don't even go there, but if you do, be a freaking man and live with the consequences of your decisions. Be a man or check your balls at the door, you wimp of a man.

We all thought you wanted a diamond ring. Brought to you by De beers-Commercialism – Materialism

*Stick that diamond as far up your ass as you can. That is how much good it will do for you. How many carats is your heart? Maybe a carat meter is needed in your relationship. Talk to your spouse about everything, even when you know she or he will not be interested, but emphasize the things that are important to you. I can't and don't want to keep up with the insignificant bullshit, but I do want to hear what you have to say about the things that matter to you. Be careful in your selection of what is important and what is not. When Peter

403

cried wolf, the town came running. When Peter cried wolf for the third time, he was eaten and no one cared.

Lord, are you pissed?

*God, Hope and Charity. If you were to give our Country a grade, what grade would you give it? And Why? I think I will answer my own quandary. Let me see, how to grade, how to grade. I'd have to give our ancestors an "A". As time has passed and we have chipped God from our frame of reference, the grade began to slip. Presently I would have say a "D+" that is trying to be a "C", but is studying the wrong material and will slip to the "F" failing category very soon. We exiled from tyranny with great determination and now we have failed our ancestors and our God. Good News, we can rectify this situation. It is not to late to do so. God's Divine Plan is birthrights, it always has been. Now you know why the Bible put so much emphasize on them in the life of Esau and Jacob. No wonder Isaac was so upset. He had failed our Creator in passing along birthrights. He didn't know the significance either. He was doing what he was instructed to do. God probably told him something like, you don't understand these things I tell you now. It is not for you to know. It is your purpose for your God to do as I say. Your descendents will comprehend or they will self destruct. I remember when my God was telling me that I do not possess the comprehension to understand His reach and that I would see at His direction and timing. I continue with blind faith after losing all that I am in this world. I will endeavor to persevere for my God. His Kingdom will reign or I Will die broken hearted, just as I believe our Savior Jesus Christ died. My brother and your brother loved us so much he sacrificed Himself for our sins. Our Father accepted Him in to His Kingdom and promised Him an Everlasting Kingdom on earth. Gods Legacy Trust LLC. What say you?

404

Chill a little – my fingers hurt

*I can't begin to tell you how mentally straining putting together God's Gift has been. I am a procrastinator and a world class student of creative avoidance. I was in contact turmoil challenging myself, is what I am doing for Him or for me? I have put it down and I have picked it up. The discouragement was immense, especially with no support group that could understand. All I have is my Father, the Son and the Holy Spirit Jesus promised to us all. There is no way that I could have continued to pick myself up. My God picked me up and has been carrying me for over five long years now. I am so thankful He did. I may have taken the coward route and killed myself had He not. Please don't misunderstand, He did not literally pick me up, He lifted my heart to do His Will. It gave me purpose, it saved my life. If you have no purpose in your life, how do you occupy your idle time? "Go ahead and die and decrease the surplus population" - Scrooge My purpose for the longest time was to be rich. That's all I wanted and willing to do anything to get there. I was serving the wrong Master and I even sacrificed my first born to him. What I wouldn't do for a time machine right now. Can you learn from my mistakes brother?

Have you ever seen the shimmering of the sea?

*Our Father has created many beautiful things for us to enjoy. Take the time daily to appreciate all that you do have, rather than ponder on what you don't. If you envy what your neighbor has, do you envy the payment book as well?

I love the water, it is a wonderful gift.

*All Gifts from God are magnificent. They are tools to solve our problems. Man suppresses some and manipulates others for his own self gain. Use the tools of our Creator to

405

invent things that will bring comfort to your neighbor. It is those creative minds that continually get suppressed that pisses me off. The most brilliant minds will go unheard without the proper forum to express themselves.

I cannot reproduce the thoughts. They are from you Lord. Do not allow my tracks to be covered. I've carried the worry of the world long enough – Mercy – Uncle Nate

*This cross that you have given unto me Lord is challenging. I have struggled long enough. I need help from my brothers and sister in Christ. I need your help to fulfill Prophecy. I need to hear you pray to our Father. I need for you to pray for me.

I AM
AND
I WILL

*Thank you Father, I know you will always have my back, but can your people believe in you?

YET...

Sorry Shauna, for not being a part of your life. I can't wait to hear if you have the shining.

*The shining is the ability to truly allow the Holy Spirit to enter your heart. Your mind, body and soul will follow what is on your heart. Don't tell your neighbor with words, tell them with your actions. Cursed is the man that plays a giving man as a chump.

Past a leper on the way to the men's room. He was disgusting, perfect for the movie.
I said, how's it going?

3 seconds pass
It's going well.

*Don't we turn our heads in disgust over the lepers of our society? I think I caught this one off guard because no one had spoken a word to him in weeks. I warn you, love the lepers, but be aware they are lepers and may be serving man 666. All I am saying is serve them, but keep your guard up.

Fine, we are just fine. The lie of the devil – ask David Walker

*We are not fine. Just as no one really wants to hear what's growing in your butt, they don't want to hear our country is headed to bankruptcy. Our country has something growing alright, a catastrophe. If we do not heed God's Divine Plan, we will self destruct. "Socialism is great until you run out of other peoples money". -Margaret Thatcher.

To think I actually thought this leper might rob me and take my wallet. I only have a dollar. Perfect for the script. Hey, I guess we now know what happened to the other mother freaking dollar. Riddle: three men check into a hotel.

Answer: Nathan God it.

*Riddle: Three men check into a hotel, money is tight so they share a room. The manager tells them it will cost $30 dollars for the night. Each man gives $10 and goes to the room. Soon the manager becomes aware that he has charged too much, for the room rate was to be only $25. So he gives the bell hop five $1.00 bills to take to the men. The bell hop gives each man $1.00 and sticks two in his pocket. If each man has now paid $9 dollars and 9 times 3 is 27 plus the two the bell hop stole makes $29. What happened to the other mother freaking dollar.

I'll try Lord, but I will challenge you on the blame game. You made the serpent.

Grace, Ahh it feels so good.

Plead your case you pole smokers and bush biters. He loves you. Arthur, the Bach Family will always Endure and we will Endure this. But know this, your kids could be future prophets.

*I believe I have beat on the (Things) enough. Do understand that our Father loves and forgives you, He is just displeased as any dad would be. But honestly, there is no telling what your loins could produce. The world may miss out by your decisions, but these are your decisions to make alone.

Where are my accusers? Where are the ones I have touched?

Will they speak for me or deny me?

It's looking real good or crash and burn – Maverick

*I will have my accusers and I will have my believers. I have been instructed to deliver His Gift and not hang around to gain praise or pain. This time you will not even have the opportunity to kill the messenger. This messenger has learned from my predecessor and God has shown me how to escape my crucifixion by controlling my vanity.

If we infringe on the rights of the movie companies
    screw 'em
It's coming anyway
Who heads up the Supreme Court anyway?
Let him tell us there is no Santa Claus. – Miracle on 34th St.

*Who places themselves as judge and jury over our lives. Let them tell us there is no God.

Birth of the Leper Party.

Let's see, who do I pick, Nathan?
I've always liked newt1162.

Yeah, but that was your porn handle good buddy.
You asked.

*Porn is here now, in our past and will remain in our future. It is just one of those things that man desires and man will have, even if corruption is necessary. Think of the things our Government suppresses from us, does it not breed corruption?

What about his vice? I don't have a clue let him decide. But I already know I like his wife. She will do great things.

I can hear it in her – Braveheart

*You can inspire or decimate with your words. It is truly amazing to watch someone that you have encouraged by touching there heart in a way that they want to emulate what it is that you see in them. You breathe life into them or you breathe death to their curious spirit inside.

Come on baby light my fire

*Way to go Newt, your wife is a hottie on the inside as well as out.

Good news, I found them. I got them right here.
Look harder – Lion King

*Look harder, look into your soul, what does your heart tell you? Your heart is the hot line to the Holy Spirit. He begs for you to allow Him to enter it.

This is the living Word of God with animation. It has been here the whole time. Let's connect with every tribe, every nation. Lets freaking do it.

*To be a World Power in the eyes of God, we must become our Global brothers keeper. We can not afford to be their keeper with the wages you earn in life, but at your death you may bless whoever you would like for an eternity. God will not be pleased until every man has food, water, shelter, healthcare and most importantly Freedom.

We keep saying it "Let's Roll"

I love that commercial of a room full of do nothings. Pick it up, right Bill?
Somebody has to have the vision and pick it up, so that we all may have direction. What direction is our world heading in right now? as we speak? It's pretty frightening.

*Some are born to lead while others are born to follow. If you place yourself as the leader, be prepared to be questioned and embrace scrutiny, your life may depend on it.

These are science fiction stories about the second coming of the Lord. Dammit George, you have to cuss or they won't hear you.

Okay, it will be a great freaking movie. Wait about bringing the kids Rated PG XIII.

*Book of Nathan coming to theaters soon. LOL Hey wait a minute did I just prophesy? I guess if it doesn't come to fruition, I am not the prophet I thought I was. We'll just have to wait and see. God has all the time in the world, my days are numbered.

*"I would have liked to have seen Montana"
– **The Hunt for Red October**

*I pray to see your miracle before thine eyes meet you.

**THY EYES HAVE BEEN OPENED
YOUR HEART IS ON DISPLAY
YOU HAVE SEEN
IF ONLY IN YOUR
HEART**

*Yes Lord, I can see your plan, but will your people.

*Hey Bro, the Father has already answered this one. Are you finished yet?

All of my shit can go on eBay for sale. This should start God's Legacy Trust LLC. Deal?

*All that I am and all that I will ever be is for you Lord. My heart writes a check that will only cash in Heaven. Lord, please accept all that I have. I won't be needing it where I am going.

The devil got all my mail.
I hope the one with the loudest trumpet got my e-mail – Oprah

*Guess not.

Can you hear me
It's okay, we're safe now

Come out, Come out, Wherever you are. Warriors, come out and playyyyyy – Warriors

*Do not be surprised when the guilty rally men against you to cover their own misdeeds. The easiest way to avoid your failures and misdeeds is to shift blame to another party. When will you take responsibility for your actions?

Greed-Draggin
Cultural Diversification – Blood Sport – Roger Moore thief, air balloon, can't lift treasure

*Men will be men. All men are tempted by greed. All men can justify it to man. The question to ask yourself is, can I justify it to my Lord? How much is enough? How much can you carry? How much will you lose while attempting to gain?

Leo it's okay, you can go home to your family – Lionheart

*Even the most unmerciful can have mercy when they can see your heart. It is your actions that reveal your heart for all to see. Have you analyzed your actions? What do they portray to your brother? More importantly, what do they portray to your Creator?

Children, I have candy and sweets and it is all free today. S/ Chitty Chitty Bang Bang
Say shoe city as fast as you can, over and over again. A new song combo sample.

*Our children and ourselves are so easily tempted. Have you heard there is no free lunch? The only free lunch is the lunch that our Lord gives us. Lord give us our daily bread so that we may praise you eternally.

Can you supersize me for $.39. He loves you. He wants to heal you. Hey, I like it. A God tax. Let them pay until it's comfortable.

You healed my baby, thank you Lord Jesus Christ. Thanks are necessary, can you pass that bucket. No not that one. God's bucket.

*Praise of our Father is necessary my brother. He has only ever asked for 10%. I implore you to fulfill your financial obligations to our Creator, He only wants to give it to your brother by healing his pain.

I kind of wanted to go home, but you're not done. It is 3:28 is five o'clock okay?

You are home. Don't you love it. Watch the Purple Martyns.

*How good is your sense of direction? Mine sucks, thank God for GPS. How do you formulate your sense of direction if you don't follow a map? You can always follow your foot steps, but what about new destinations? If you are ready to walk in the foot steps of the Lord, there is a beautiful road map in the Bible.

Why are you coming home half drunk?

I ran out of money. Shit, get off my ass. I am spending time with our father. Who's Yo Daddy?

Is the Harley Davidson doing it for you? You missed your chance Terry. I'll bet you will work your skinny little, floor flushing ass off now, won't you? Tell me, will you serve me? How much do you need?

*Please forgive my wicked thoughts, your betrayal was all part of the Master's Plan.

I guess we don't have to reinvent the wheel after all. The lepers will fulfill all of your needs. Costa Rica sounds great, but how

413

about Prichard Alabama. How about N. O. not no, but Hale N. O. Dem sum crazy fukas ober der.

My wife bought dinner for the family on vacation from serving the renovation needs in New Orleans. A dinner seemed the least she could do for the fearless warriors that forge into harms way armed only with the Bible, Faith and Love for other human beings.

Give me the tools of the devil. They work pretty good God. Are you hearing me my Father? Can you tell I am scared shitless?

*What are the tools of the Devil? I would have to say the seven deadly sins. I have experienced them all and now I can articulate them and learn from them. The reason these tools work so well is they have a tendency to be hidden within our hearts. Your mask says one thing and your heart says another. Remember you will always follow your heart, good or bad and your mask is your manipulator. We mask our heart because that is where we are most vulnerable. The heart is where we carry our scars.

His word gives me comfort. I will hear sounds of war and wars to come. These things must come.

Is must a scroll down option?

Yes, I would like to see everything on the menu.

Do you want the buffet, the whole Enchilada, the whole ball of wax?

Well, you got your work cut out for you don't you? --NEWT '08

Oh man, he is a Republican. No, I am a leper and I am sick and I leave among you.

You know God knows his shit. When he makes me mess up words like live. It truly is the living word.

*Newt/Mitt '12 I'm so sick of the squabbling of the two parties and I believe everyone else is also. We need a party of truth, by the people, for the people. Will God live among us or leave us to destroy ourselves? I think the ball is in our court on that one. I will do all in my power to fulfill His Last Will and Testament.

It will take centuries, hopefully, to dissect all of this shit.

Hopeful Prophecy

How 'bout it monkey
Are you ready to Tango or Rumble?

*Are you ready to inspire your brother or are you ready to kill your brother. Any government that instigates war in the name of thy God will be defeated. Ask yourself, would your God condone killing your brother. He condemned Cain for slaying Abel. Are you getting the point? You have to question anyone that would have your children come home in a box and your children sending others home in a box. Look outside the box and see what we are doing to one another before another life is taken. That life may be your own.

Be afraid. Be very afraid.

*"The only thing we have to fear, is fear itself".
- Dr. Martin Luther King Jr.

The signs are off the chart.

*666 You will find what you seek and interpret it in the way that suits you.

We have seen what man could do. Holy shit, did you have any idea Batman?

*To the Bat Cave. LOL I could use a drink.

Iraq – Freedom

But what about the bullies?
Do what you got to do. I got your check and your medicine.

*How does one truly gain appreciation for freedom when they live with intimidation? I ask of the intimidators, what compels you to intimidate your brothers? Are you yourself intimidated? What is your purpose for God? I don't believe it is to kill your brethren in the name of Allah. Do you really believe that is what Allah would ask of you as your purpose for Him? Start by questioning authority, you will probably be shot, but your brothers can now see the intentions of their leaders. They will see the truth. How many of you will they kill for seeking the peace and harmony that Allah has promised?

How are your children, by the way?
Good, you call U. S. if you got a problem. Other than that, I'm ready to take my monkey ass to the house.

*It is time for you stand up for yourselves. Our men and women of the uniform have families too. Your independence can be achieved if you will fight for it. Our forefathers fought and died so that we did not have to live with tyranny and so can you. We are still fighting the same fight today.

Forgive me Lord, for I have sinned. I role-played immoral sex and we laughed.

Devil screws the Lamb. Ha Ha Ha

Isn't that what's happening every day in our lives?

*It's time for the lamb to start watching his backside, for there is a devil in each and everyone of us. Now that you know who the devil is, you can be on alert to look for him.

You are a sly old fox God. It makes for a great script.

*I reflect all that you have put me through to mold me as your witness. It is funny as hell and I could have never orchestrated it myself. The Lord does work in mysterious ways.

It was not I who was sleeping, but my brother – Platoon

*So it was your brothers fault. Let me ask you this, if you were alert, would you have alerted the rest of us to the danger? After all, your brothers are dead and you can not change that now. I suggest you remain alert and not rely on your brother. Your brother is untrustworthy after all. At least that is what you tell me all the time as you shift blame to him.

Excuses, Excuses –WAKE UP – I Am Coming...

*I pray for that glorious day my Lord. Use me, your humble servant anyway you desire.

I am aware of the serpent now. I will put my foot upon the head of the scorpion. And splat. No more problem. This is for you Zodiacs @#$%&'s

*Wow, I couldn't believe what I was reading when I went searching in this arena. It started with my birth date and ended with my new name in Christ. Check out what Nos-

tradamus has to say about Ophiuchus, it will blow you away. Ophiuchus, the God of medicine, master builder. Now examine my purpose for God. The final piece to the puzzle came to me the other night and solidified to me that I am fulfilling my purpose. Sir Isaac Newton and Nostradamus had a scientific perspective of God. I have a sociological perspective, it is what I have seen, heard, read and experienced. I was compelled by the Holy Spirit to write it down. I must admit, I'm thankful that my God has given me the financial ability to focus on His Plan. This computer is a hell of a lot easier on my fingers and I can express myself more freely. LOL

Sorry for the sin, can you have the Martyns come and take care of the pests/devil?

*Martins eat thousands of mosquitoes, maybe the Angels can take away the devil in each of us. My demon is alcohol and cigarettes, please Lord free me from them.

Draggin / Dying
their / your tongue

*At first when I saw this I said Nathan, you must have been high, drunk or both when you wrote this. I stared at the words for some time. I found what they say to me. Can you search your heart and find what they mean to you? I see a multiple of possibilities.

**Looked again with sober eyes and see: your tongue dragging, they are dying. Sorry for the delay folks, but "Here I AM to Save the Day". LOL

Jackass

Okay, how do I contact Time Warner Books? Is the owner a devil? – Ted Turner

Maybe Jane Fonda wants some salvation? Surely her father did. Ask him, he is a nobody – My name is Nobody

*Again I profess this is a must see movie and insert which role you would like to audition for. An Old Lion disappears and a Young Lion emerges to take his place. It truly is the circle of life.

Are you embarrassed to ask our forefathers questions? I don't blame you. In every environment I speak of God. They want to stone me, so I did it for them.

*Why is it so difficult to discuss our Creator with our fellow man? It is almost like an oh shit moment, here we go again. Jesus this and Jesus that, have you found Jesus yet? I will confess, I was the same as you my brother. I didn't want your pamphlet and I didn't go to your church. Dude, I escaped to church to free myself from my (First Wife). Now if the Lord isn't moving in mysterious ways, I don't know what mysterious is. I would get my head right and go and listen. I wanted to know what was going on, I wanted to be able to hold an intelligent conversation about something I did not understand. As I gained understanding, I quickly realized the same peers that I felt embarrassed about not knowing the Lord, didn't know shit for themselves. It was all a show and where to go for lunch.

Ahh, the tree of life
Frick you and your little dog too.

Futuristic stories, you are a riot.

You can call me Joe. I helped Nathan. Joe Fox, just Joe – You've Got Mail

*This is a message to the players. Play all your want, but until your heart is broken are you really ready to play the game. I am ready, watch out, I'm coming out. Your Savior's heart is broken. Can we bring Him back to life? Can we allow Him to dwell among us? Can we build His Kingdom here on earth? His entity starts with one brick of mankind. Lord, I have laid my brick for you. Show me Lord, show me. Show me your merciful power. Speak to their hearts as you have spoken to mine.

All y'all can have the peace prize, I want that God Reward.
Catch Lucky, he's got Lucky Charm's. They're magically delicious. It wasn't gold, you jackass. It was medicine and food.

*The Lord thy God wishes to heal us. Stop chasing rainbows, He is right in front of you. Oh man, does He love us. I'd have said screw it long before now, but not Him. He has patience and all the time in the world. Please, I beg of you my brothers and sisters in Christ. Lets fulfill Gods Last Will and Testament and then lets strive for World Peace. Only then will your King be at peace. Let us rejoice and let Him rest.

Am I Doinking you yet? Pay attention Stoney – I Love Ya

*Love this episode of Everybody Loves Raymond. He was illustrating to his wife what it would be like to live across the street from his mother and doinked her on the nose. When the Holy Spirit enters you, He will doink you on the nose until He gets you to fulfill what your purpose for God is. You have to be seeking it, it will not just appear. You must search your heart.

Who will be the first to present their idea before the Lord? The Lord will grant you your patent. Thank you for sharing.

*Hey, I'm talking to you. Pay attention. Your idea is freaking brilliant because it will better your neighbors life. "Just

Do it", just freaking do it. You already know what to expect, but your God urges you to fulfill your task for Him and for your brother.

You can plead your case to the court most high.

*Anyone may enter the pearly gates by simply accepting Jesus Christ as our Savior and acknowledging He rose from the grave to be at the right hand of the Father. I want one of those crowns He promised. I'm special and I want to be special for my God. Use me Lord, I am yours to use. If what I have done for you my Lord is wrong, then I kneel before you and draw my own sword for you to make judgment on me. My soul is yours Lord. My body is yours Lord. My mind is yours Lord. I give my heart to you my Lord, because my heart is the most precious thing to me. I want you to be the keeper of my heart. Please Lord, accept my humble offerings to you. I give you all that I am. Are you crying yet, I AM.

I am selling.
I like both my heads, even though one is badly beaten. It is time to masturbate or are you the apprentice baitor? Let's go fishing, I'll tell you all about it.
Thanks Dad – Boys
Thanks Mom-- Girls

*Let's be for real here. Do you really think that your kids will one day wake up and understand sexuality? If you are lacking yourselves by the lack of knowledge, then educate yourselves by reading the books of someone that proclaims themselves an expert. Beware, always make up your own mind on anything you do. You are the only one accountable for your actions. Now teach your kids before they learn lessons in life the hard way. The hard way sucks, but can be avoided with proper guidance.

Whatever, you gauge your child's faith and direction. Step up and be Parents.

*Is there a Man among you? Step up and assume your role or waller in your self pity. Are you a Man among Men? Are you a Man of God? Show me your Heart.**

SHOW ME
THY GOD
WISHES TO SEE
YOU DANCE
FOR THY
GOD

Who will fill in my pieces Lord? Will you come again or is this time for keeps?

*Nathan, my brother. You are doing great, keep up the good work for our Father. All of the pieces are coming together through you. My humble servant and brother. Your heart is pure. Your mind is clear. Your body is clean. Your soul is mine.**

*Thank you Jesus for being my friend, brother and keeper of my mind, body, heart and soul. I am yours.**

Smoke the day's last cigarette, trying to make it through

*We are all trying to make it through my brother. There will be pitfalls and triumphs. You are being tested. Yes, our God is observing everything that you do. Yes, especially the nasty stuff. He understands how your mind works. He knows every decision that you will face and He allows you to answer of your own free will. He gives you consequences for your decisions. He is patient to see if you are Christ like or Anti-**

Christ like. When you meet Jesus my brother, He is the greatest of defense counselors. He is the apple of our Creator's eye. Convince Him that you want forgiveness.

HELP ME
HELP YOU

I'm avoiding conversation, but Father, I Love people too

*I wanted to be with you Lord. I was not ready to share you. I needed my special time with you. I needed my space with you. I needed to hug the carpet with my face down to you Lord. I need to here your judgment now Lord. I must know now while I am still here on earth. Your humble servant must know if I am serving you in the manner that you approve of. My peers don't approve of it, but screw them, I need your approval. Am I tempting you Lord? That is not my intention. I just want you to speak it to my heart Lord. Speak to my heart.

FORGIVEN
SAVED

Don't let me die with a broken heart Lord. Your people do not know where to turn.

Show them the TRUTH, Oh God

We are hungry. We are ripe. Don't let me be the sacrifice. I still have my marbles, they've been freeze-dried like Buck Rogers or is it Roger that?

*In the History of Mankind, we never have been as ripe as we are right now. It is time for our Lord to Harvest. He is among you to take account on how you have been managing what He left you in charge of. Show your God what you have done with that you were entrusted. Will you bury your talents or use them for the benefit of your brother and God? When did God tell you to stop investing your talents? Leave your heirs, charities, passions and God an inspiration note from your heart, to be delivered to their heart for an eternity.

Dew Circuit
Break Out
We are the Dew, move over.
Let U. S. Dew what we Dew Best
　　　SAVE

*Shit, another Vodka moment. Let's study this, I don't have a clue. Can you see it? "IT" is there. Let your reticular activating system draw from your subconscious. Focus.

SAVE
AND BE
SAVED

*You turkey, I wanted them to think about that one for awhile. LOL I love you God.

Can you afford not to be in good hands? – God

*Give us our daily bread Lord. Give us World Peace or Give us DEATH!!! It's just too easy. Open your eyes my brothers, it's just too freaking easy. It is of our own free will that we live in peace or destroy ourselves. Our God will start over again. We will not. Can you feel His presence? He is here right now. He is your brother. Accept Him into your heart NOW!!! Now deal with your transgressions, your brother only knows you as you. Your God knows you for you. Seek His approval only. Be strong like the Lion. Hear me freaking ROOOAAARH. God is on my side, so screw you. Somebody has to pick it up where Jesus left off. What a guide huh? What an awesome Man God, the one and only begotten son of our Father. I don't have healing powers like our Lord. I have builders talents and I aim to build a temple of Mankind for our Lord to reign over for an eternity. He will heal us. Let me be the first brick Lord, what an honor. Heal us Lord. Love us. Forgive us.

Sprint ahead. I am in an epic tale, if I rescue Zelda. Can I win?

*What are you in a hurry for? Live your life day by day. Take time to cherish what you have in your life. Those that follow my words will live, those that don't will wake up and realize they missed "IT". It is too late now. If I only had a time machine, the things I would do different. You can not replace time, so use it cautiously. Yesterday was a memory and today we will make some more. What kind of memories do you wish to make?

Wife asked me to go to parents. Audubon here I come.

*The Exodus of Nathan, the birth of Ophiuchus.

September 4, 2009

Waiting on the world to change-- new song

One step at a time – Jordan Sparks
Thanks to God for that one. I needed to remind myself of the definition of patience.

*Happiness and contentment have been achieved
-The Cone Heads

*I don't know about you, but I am so glad to be out of the second manic episode. Wheeew... That was long and painful. To recapture the essence of the Holy Spirit was mentally stressful. I am blessed to be given the talent of Aletheia, I just

followed my breadcrumb trail. No birds will eat your trail if you write it down.

   *So shall it be written
   So shall it be done. LOL I love that one dude.

LETTER TO:
INSANE MALES
PG XIII

February 2, 2010

Ground Hog Day
Let me guess, he will see his shadow and we will have six more weeks of winter.

Well, we need to pull him out a little early and have a little chat about the things that make us hide.

Cool, it gives me more time to finish this book.
I am looking forward to Spring Break here in Paradise.

Ophiuchus Means:
Some Men could be saved in Judgment
By a Savior... A Physician

Greek Mythology
Asclepius
The Healer
One to cure the sick
And Insane Males.

Ophiuchus and 2012
Ophiuchus will appear
Center of the Milky Way

This only happens every 26,000 years and is represented in Nostradamus' paintings. Ophiuchus will come and of our own free will, we will accept Him or deny Him. Just as we make those decisions for our Father. Just as we made those decisions for our Lord and Savior, Jesus Christ. Examine closely the message of Jesus Christ and the message that Ophiuchus is bringing to you. All I do is for Christ, for I know that is the way to the Father. My Creator. My God. Our God.

Look Man,
If you want me to take you for training tomorrow, then we're going drinking tonight. -Kickboxer

I'll need a few drinks to loosen my tongue and lose my inhibitions on this topic. I want to talk to my fellow insane males. I am just like you. My little head has directed my thoughts my entire life. You have to get hold of it. I do mean that metaphorically and literally.

Brother, I am going to talk to you about what everyone is uncomfortable talking about. I got my sex education from a ripped Hustler Magazine I found while dumpster diving.

Girls are given a body book in their adolescent years. It simplistically explains how her body works. I don't know if there is a boys book or not, but there should be. Believe me, we are the ones with the seven horns.

I will do my best to share what I have seen, heard and read. I am no expert in this arena. You can refer to some great books like the Sex Starved Marriage by Kevin Leman.

I also highly recommend the Five Love Languages by Gary Chapman. These love languages should be talked about during your dating cycle to see if you are compatible with your potential lifelong mate.

If you are like me. My little buddy was making all of the decisions for me. My number one love language is Physical Touch. I want to know how often my potential **LIFE LONG PARTNER MASTURBATES**. Believe me, it will save you both years of misery. Did you giggle? I bet you did.

You women that screw your mans brains out and make him think that this is what he has to look forward to for the rest of his life, are only sealing your own fate for a miserable, unfaithful, heartbreaking experience.

Know the ingredients of your potential mate. Girls, accept the fact that Boys are driven in this way. Talk about it without embarrassment and both of you make wise decisions on how you want your life to be effected. It is always free will with consequences.

I heard that Jewish women screw their husbands brains out so they don't have to contend with those thoughts while at work. Now that's a great partner. I'll do my part in this relationship and I won't even drink at you in disgust.

Guys, remember. The women are in control of all the vagina. Somehow it is accepted that a woman use a vibrator.

What do I need a man for, I've got a vibrator. - There's Something about Mary

Men are very visual and watching this act is erotic. Why is the reversed role revered as unmanly and weak. We are the horny bastards. It is this suppression that will cause men to explode. It's terrible to carry a rusty load around and feel weak for masturbating. It can cause a man to do things that he would not ordinarily do. F.or U.nlawful C.arnal K.nowledge. Rape. You throw some booze and dope on that fire and brother, you have got yourself a blaze. A blaze that will cause a man to do things that will destroy his life and the lives of his victims.

Can you just imagine living in a household as a child and having a pedophile for a parent and the other parent condone it. That will screw your head up. What kind of frame of reference is this child going to take to adulthood?

If I had to take a guess, that would probably be one of those unforgivable sins. But hey, plead your case before your Lord and Creator. Better you than me. Good Luck you sorry bastard.

That is all I have to say about that. - Forrest Gump

Men are creatures of sight. The Porn Library is full. We can screw any shape or size with a fleshlight or our fist. Take out your sexual frustrations here, not by harming any of God's children.

To the sluts that have humiliated themselves before thy God. We Salute You. After extensive research into the porn industry, it's huge by the way, I have discovered that the library is full. It was purely research by the way. LOL NOT. Once the clothes come off, we are all really the same. You look just like your Grandma and Grandpa. We don't need to see your naked ass take a rooster in your mule. You have been Warned.

Ask for forgiveness and sin no more. - Jesus Christ

I don't want to see my daughter or any family member doing this. Can you imagine if one of your friends points out to you, your Grandma getting poled on the internet? Not a very prideful moment to say the least.

Oh my brother, you've got baby batter on the brain. That stuff will screw you up. - There's Something about Mary

It absolutely, positively will. Of your own free will. Be careful going out with a loaded gun and pouring intoxicants into your body. The consequences can last a lifetime.

I know someone that a one night stand cost him $247,000.00 in child support. Ouch, I guess he should have taken the gun and left the cannoli at home. - Godfather

I sacrificed my first born to the God of Materialism. A Sin that I carry and beg for forgiveness. In my heart, I know my unborn child and my God forgive me. My mistake and naivety caused me to commit Murder. I so wish I could go back in time. There is no telling what I have destroyed.

Therefore I, a prisoner for serving the Lord, beg you to lead a life worthy of your calling, for you have been called by God. Be humble and gentle. Be patient with each other, making allowances for each others faults because of your love. Always keep your souls united in the Holy Spirit and bind yourself with peace.

We are all one body, we have this same spirit and we have all been called to the same glorious future. There is only one Lord, one faith, one baptism and there is only one God and Father, who is over us all and in us all and living through us all.
Ephesians 4 : 1 – 6

And further, you will submit to one another out of reverence for Christ. You wives will submit to your husbands as you do to the Lord. For a husband is the head of his wife as Christ is the head of his body, the church. He gave his life to be her Savior. As the church submits to Christ, so you wives must submit to your husbands in everything.

And you husbands must love your wives with the same love Christ showed a church. He gave up his life for her to make her holy and clean, washed by baptism and God's word. He did this to present her to himself as a glorious church without a spot or wrinkle or any other blemish. Instead she will be holy and without fault. In the same way, husbands ought to love their wives as they love their own bodies. For a man is actually loving himself when he loves his wife. No one hates his own body but lovingly cares for it, just as Christ cares for his body, which is the church. And we are all his body.

As the Scriptures say, a man leaves his mother and father and is joined to his wife and the two are united into one. This is a great mystery, but it is an illustration of the way Christ and the church are one. So again I say, each man must love his wife as he loves himself and the wife must respect her husband.

Ephesians 5 : 21 – 33

Desire to please me, as I desire to please you. Obligatory sex sucks. Do you Love me, as I Love you? If I have not done my part in this relationship, tell me. Do not manipulate me to get what you materialistically desire. Manipulate me to create a family environment that we can both be proud before our Father. You are in control of what I desire. Use it to the betterment for our relationship with God and each other. Your head is much smarter than my little head, which does the majority of my thinking. I am the head of the family and I will hunt for the well being of my family. That is my part financially. I will nurture you and help you. That is my heart and Love for you. All I ask in return is that you do your part and make me feel desired. I must have love from a partner. I have love from our Father, but I must feel His warmth through you. A partner is what completes us. Without one, you can enjoy your lives as you chose, but will never really achieve the balance in your life that you secretly desire.

I have witnessed a shift in paradigm. The man hasn't taken his place, so the woman has assumed the role. Are you the man of your family? No, not because you have a penis. Are you a real man, provider, educator, protector and Godly.

I remember you. You're the kid that got the trophy. How has your life turned out? I have always wondered.

Well, I am kind of in between jobs, but my wife has got a real good one over there to the Piggly Wiggly.

Congratulations. Your life exemplifies your motivation.

Duh, thanks. I guess.

Stupid is as stupid does Mrs. Blue

I Guess – Forrest Gump

You my fellow brother in Christ. Let me tell you about what God wants for your life. I want to share the secrets with you, so you too may enjoy an abundant, joyous life serving the one true God. The God of Abraham, Ishmael, Isaac, Jacob, Esau, Joseph and his forgiven brothers, Moses, Muhammad and my personal favorite, My Savior Jesus Christ. Thank you Christ for dying on the Cross, so that I may be forgiven of my Sins. Man struck you with every lash. Man strikes himself with free will. Who will we serve? 666 or God. There is no "None of the Above" option on this multiple choice question.

**SERVE GOD
OR MAN 666**

**LIVE
OR
DIE**

OF YOUR OWN

FREE

WILL

Our Lord thy God has spoken.

So shall it be written,
So shall it be done. - The Ten Commandments LOL

Sorry for the chuckle, I just couldn't help myself. I am who I am. And I accepted my responsibility when I accepted the Lord Jesus Christ into my heart.

The point is, God doesn't have to destroy us with disasters. We will destroy ourselves. If that is the path that we choose for ourselves. Believe me when I tell you my Brothers and Sisters in Christ. Every kitchen table in this world is searching for the answers. And the answers are definitely not coming from expanding Government. We are blessed to live in an only somewhat corrupt nation. In Other Nations, the people don't have a snowballs chance in hell of ever seeing a change. At least not without bloodshed and revolt.

Where would this nation be if the South had been triumphant? Would the Men of color stand up and revolt? You bet your ass they would. They revolt now for entitlements, as do all colors looking for handouts from their brother.

My fellow countrymen, I am William Wallace. I am not ten feet tall and shoot fire balls from my arse. But what I see here today are my brothers willing to die for something we have never had. FREEDOM!!!
Braveheart

Rah Rah Shish Cume Bah Go Aladdin
Jafar Jafar He's our man. Not.
Genie of the Lamp

Just think of the Tyranny in Nations of the World. They each have their own Pharaoh with a hardened misguided heart.

Who'd have thought I, a Leper, would be chosen. Do you think you are chosen? Give it a try, accept Jesus Christ into your own heart. See how it works out for you. I tell you the Truth, we are all Lepers or Liars.

It is through your faith, that you are healed. - Jesus Christ

I chose Him and He chose Me. I chose Him over every obstacle and Giant in my Life. I Am Hurt, but I Am Blessed. One head badly beaten.

CONTROL THE
BEAST
BETWEEN
YOUR LEGS

RESTRAINT
IS THE
MEASURE
OF A
MAN

YOU
WILL FACE
FINAL
JUDGMENT

ALL MEN

I'm digging on the option in the New Testament Covenant from God to his people. 1000 yrs of Satan being imprisoned and God's people living an abundant life serving Him. WORLD PEACE!!!

If we can make this Heaven on Earth, maybe we can even cut a deal after the 1000 yrs. Maybe Gad the Seer will write a book or maybe we won't need any more miracles to stay on God's Plan for our lives. We have finally learned from our mistakes and this is the

CHANGE
THE WORLD
CAN
BELIEVE
IN

You know I'm drunk now. But I can't emphasize enough to you to exercise your Demon and not hurt any of God's children. I promise you, there is no get out of Hell Free card on this sin. You can beg for forgiveness all you want. You will burn in Hell. I could be wrong, quite often I am, if we could only examine the facts. Please, you be sure and tell us how it worked out for you. Inquiring minds want to know.

Hey I don't know this for sure, but if I have a vote, you mother freaker, it will be an eternal death for you. You were entrusted as an adult to conduct yourself in a proper manner before your God. You chose 666. I, Ophiuchus, find forgiveness very difficult in my heart. I can not forgive you. It is not my place. You must throw yourself on the mercy of God's Court.

Trust Me, Jesus is a great defense counselor. I've spoken to the Judge and He is a very open minded God.

Before I introduce you to our Lord and Savior, I want to ask you one thing.

Were your decisions made for God or for Man?

Okay, thanks. You can go in now. Just a little tip for you. When he asks you why you didn't repent.

Don't tell him that you never heard you were suppose to.
He hates that and will always come back with some shit about "wasn't it written in the Acts of Nathan the Prophet" or some other shit like that. Believe me, if you haven't accepted our Lord

Jesus Christ into your heart at this point. You're Screwed. LOL But what do I know, I'm a drunk.

George saved the druggist that day. We all make mistakes and we all deserve a second chance and a third chance and a forth chance. Just remember, your family is only in for so many chances. The last chance is yours and God has got your back.

I wanted to put this in the loneliness category, but I am inspired now.

I AM
ALONE

ALONE
AM
I

ALL
IS
GOOD

GOOD
IS
ALL

I AM
WITH THE
FATHER

FATHER
WITH THE
I AM

Damn, I think I'll send some of these into Hallmark, maybe they will accept one or two. LOL

I loved how the town came together and really enjoyed Mr. Deeds poems. They were shitty we all know that. Just the love felt in the room by people that were there to support one another, rather than tear one another down. Is that just for small towns? Can we bring it to Miami? Can we bring it to Washington D.C.? Can we bring it to our World without constantly reaching into our pocket?

YES WE CAN

Damn, Obama. You had some good shit. Let's try a loan modification on your slogan.

Hmmm....
Let me see. God you pick it.

**IN
GOD
WE
TRUST**

Your killing me. You know I'm a nostalgia buff. Isn't that the main slogan on our currency that our forefathers fought so hard to preserve?

You know, I'm thinking of what I can cleverly say to you to make you think and understand. The drunk in me wants to tell you exactly what I think of you.

The Christian in me wants to reach down in the bucket and save one more crab.

Every time I ran back to find Bubba I kept hearing: Help Me Forrest, Help Me. I had to find Bubba, he was my very best friend. - Forrest Gump

Friends, how many of us have them?

Do you know what will tear your heart out like nothing you have ever experienced before?

It is better to have loved
and lost
than to have never loved
at all

Yeah, whatever. The pain is excruciating, I need a pill. I am still in Love.

How do you sever it Lord? How do I let it go? She said she didn't love me. She said she wanted to forget she ever Knew me. These are things that I can not forget. I certainly forgive her, but I expected to be released from my commitment to her when she released me and I released her in my heart.

**I KNOW
THY PAIN**

**I KNOW
THY PAIN
ALL TO WELL**

**YOUR
HEART BREAKS
AND YOU SCAR**

**MY BROTHER
I CARRY SCARS
FROM EACH OF YOU**

**FORGIVE ME
FOR COMING AS A
LAMB**

**LOVE ME
FOR COMING AS A
LION**

**I AM
THY SAVIOR
I WILL
HAVE MY KINGDOM
I WILL
HEAL MY FAMILY
BY FAITH
IN YOUR
FAMILY**

I know you are not asking me to become a celibate Priest. I am out on that one, my brother. I am not even a preacher. Nor will I ever be.

I'm not a golfer, I'm a hockey player. - Happy Gilmore

I promise you, you will not be seeing me doing some bogus Benny Hinn slap you on the head shit and healing you.

Hey Benny,
You've been collecting quite the bounty. Give account to the Lord so that he might heal his children. Gods Legacy Trust LLC.

**THANK YOU
NATHAN**

THE
STUDENT
TRAIN
THE TEACHER

OF YOU
THAT HAVE COLLECTED
IN MY
HOLY NAME

I AM
HERE
FOR ACCOUNT

You know guys, I don't think he is really pissed. Well, yeah he is. But we can wiggle our way out of it. The message is you sons of bitches took the money and didn't invest it into God's people so that the money collected would flourish. So now we are still in the same freaking place we were in yesterday. WTH

THE CHURCH
MY BRIDE
MY LOVE
MY HEAD
MY ONE
TALENT
TEAM

SHOW ME

Shut the hell up, I'll handle this.

Lord,
Forgive Us of our Sins
We really are stupid sons of bitches
We don't learn from our mistakes

442

We continue to follow Man 666
We continue to defy you
I ask you Lord
Place the Sins of Mankind
On my Shoulders
I feel I have carried it long enough now to accept it.
If these dumb ass mother Freakers can't believe
What about the masses that do?
Please don't destroy your beautiful creation
For the denial of the few
You hear our hearts oh Lord
There are many of us that still believe.
Take account, please Lord.
Take account slowly.
I'm digging Heaven on Earth.
I can't wait to get there.
But I'm enjoying the ride.

How was your day?

How was your day?

How was your day?

How did you let God influence your day?

Did you witness to someone that you knew needed it. Or did you coward to the fact that you are a Leper yourself? Who are you to counsel me? You are my best counsel. Let those of you that can share from experience, shed light on the things that I, Ophiuchus, can only articulate.

Oh Lord, I'm really drunk. What can I tell your people that I won't have to apologize for tomorrow? How well do I know that routine.

NATHAN
YOU ARE SO WELL
VERSED IN APOLOGIES.

APOLOGIZE
FOR
MANKIND
CAREFULLY

Dude, that is deep.
Let me hit the tree of life for enlightenment and I'll be right back.

Okay, if Nathan the Prophet can scorn King David, (because he was a son) I Nathan the dumb ass will scorn God. (because I am his loving son that has witnessed mankinds evil deeds to one another)

Lord,
You left us a rulebook full of riddles. Very few will take on the task to interpret and solve them. I realize that you did this so they would become timeless. But a qualifier about the slang of the time would have helped.

DID I NOT TELL
YOU ABOUT TONGUES

Well, that was an easy one. Dialects and slang.

How did we get here Lord? Why are you allowing yourself to divide us? We all know that there is but One God. Your Father, Christ my Brother I AM a son of God, as are You.

Okay, stop the lovey dovey stuff. I still want to know how we got to this state of the world?

FREE
WILL

Thanks, you're a shit load of help. No, I need something that I can sell. Give me some more inspiration, something that will grab someone's attention. Front page shit.

FREE
WILL

Lord,
You're boring as Hell. But I can always count on you to be the same today and forever more. You are my Rock Jesus. My every thought is of you. My Brother.

I can't wait to meet you Jesus. But we're going to have to liven your ass up. I'll teach you the hustle, if I can still remember it. If not, I can always refer to politics.

Hey, wait a minute. Isn't this the chapter for the insane males?

How do I get off on such tangents?

I'm sorry,
I am sorry,
I am truly sorry,
I am truly very sorry,

I'M NOT SORRY!!! AH HA HA HA

Pee Wee Herman

I liked the dude. You just can't go around beating your meat in public. Exercise the Demon and exercise restraint.

Don't come in my mouth. What, we're in a nice restaurant. - Andrew Dice Clay

Hickory Dickory Dock.
This Bitch was sucking my cock.
The clock turned Two
and I blew my Goo
So I dropped her off
at the end of the block.
– Andrew Dice Clay

Little boy blew,
Hey, he needed the money.
– Andrew Dice Clay

Let's talk about prostitution. Seems it was around during King David's day and still here today. So if it is going to be here of our own free will, shouldn't it be safe? Let me ask you a question. If you knew for a fact that an insane male had his sexual frustrations relieved by one of these women and it effected his thought process and he didn't harm your wife or child. How would you revere this profession then? Would you welcome the tax? I wouldn't want this for my daughter, but I would want her safe. I pray that she will strive for more using her brain and not her body. But as a dad, I would be a nervous wreck to think she was hooking on the streets. I won't preach until you're ready, just call me and let me know you are okay. You are my child and I will always Love you, regardless of the choices you make for yourself. I AM here with open arms. I WILL be your Father.

Best 'lil Whorehouse in Texas

"ALL THE SINGLE LADIES", "ALL THE SINGLE LADIES". Cool song, do I have your attention?

"You can ring my Beeeeeellllll, ring my Bell"

446

You have power. You have control. Manipulate as you always do to get a happy family environment. The man may be the head, but you are the Rock.

Okay, my Bar room buddy. Let's talk.
Don't worry, I always get the bad eye
this time of night.

Hit me with your best shot. Fire away.

**GO TO BED
NATHAN
YOU'RE
DRUNK**

That hasn't stopped you from talking to me before.

True. Ask Of Me

I hate when you put me on the spot like this. I prefer to ramble until you put a thought on my heart.

OKAY!!!
I'll ASK.
I WANT YOU OUR FATHER, TO ESTABLISH YOUR KINGDOM HERE ON EARTH AS IT IS IN HEAVEN. I WANT YOUR GOVERNMENT TO RULE OUR LIVES IN YOUR GLORY. I WANT FOOD, WATER, SHELTER, HEALTH CARE AND FREEDOM!!!

I WANT WORLD PEACE

Do this for us Lord and we will never need another miracle again. Your Kingdom will be established here on earth and every trip to the doctor will be a learning lesson about you. Jesus Christ our Lord and Savior.

Nathan
What do you ask of thy Lord?

Dude, I don't think I can make it any clearer.

Do you want
another Disaster?

Duh, No. Don't I feel like a schmuck. I always forget that it is free will that will destroy us, not God.

Nathan, don't you think you need to go to bed?

No, I'm good. I'll call a cab. I do only have to crawl in bed after all.

I am glad you are taking precautions when you poison yourself

Lord, I am so ready to give up the poison.

Point???

I guess I am not ready after all. I am in Unrest mode.

I will continue to take every lash that man has laid out for me. It is of my own free will that I die at the hands of Man.

How many times do I have to tell your dumb ass. Those cigarettes and alcohol are killing you

I know Lord, but Pinocchio has got more than a stiff nose.

What does that have to do with the tea in China?

Don't tell me that Nathan has to become your teacher once again. You know. The little head thing.

I know what you are talking about Nathan, I was just screwing with you

So, So, So. You're just a regular guy huh?

**NO
I AM
THE MAN**

**THE MAN
WOULD BE
PRUDENT
TO BE
HUMBLE**

Sorry Lord, I think I was getting a little cocky with drink. I am sorry.

Please don't avoid my call. You know I am broken. You know I will sin. Please Lord, always give me your Grace.

Can you hear me now?
Can you hear me now?
Can you hear me now?

Nathan, How can I resist. You're such a goofy bastard. LOL LOL LOL LOL LOL LOL LOL

Lord, my humor has gotten me places and gotten me out of places. It is a gift that you gave to me.

Use it to our Father's Glory. You must reach as many people as you can. Our Father's net will catch all that is needed to provide for everyone

Hey, I know you. WILSON!!! - Castaway

Hey, I know you. Is this the first time I have spoken to you Jesus?

BUSTED!!!

I have been talking to our Father and making praise for you.

Go back and read your own words my Brother. When you speak to the Father, you are speaking to me

So He don't hear shit, unless it goes through you?

That is correct

You must be one hell of a counselor by now?

You Can't Know

I guess.

Stupid is as stupid does Jesus.

Nathan, you are in a different league now. The Crane Technique no longer will work when dealing with Masters. You must focus on Balance. The force of All Men will come through to you when you fight for right. Listen, did you ask Drum. The drumbeat of every heart calls out to you to endeavor to persevere

I'm good, I just don't like it when my brother gets that way with me. I get a little pissy.

What the hell did he say that promoted you to be pissy with Him?

I hate when you call me out. I have nothing to be pissy about. I love you my brother.

Before I go to bed Lord. I want you to tell me what you think of me. Please TELL ME. I gotta know.

What the Hell
How much reassurance do you need?

I wasn't talking to you Brother. I was talking to our Father. I don't want to step on any toes, but sometimes I just want to go to the top.

Nathan,
I AM the top.
You are doing adequate

Adequate from you Lord is unsatisfactory in my eyes. I will try harder. With you by my side. I know that we can convince Mankind to believe in you, the Son of Man, the Son of God, just as we all are.

Is this a big trophy Jesus?

World Peace. Yeah, what do you think?
You are a goofy bastard

No Lord, I am not goofy. I am overwhelmed with your Grace. Lord, since we are such great buds now, are you coming back soon?

I AM
HERE

I AM
THERE

I AM
EVERYWHERE

I AM
WHO YOU
SEEK

I AM
IN YOU

I AM
THE HOLY SPIRIT
TAKING
ACCOUNT
WITH
CONSEQUENCES

I AM
666

I AM
GOD

I AM
FREE
WILL

Can you talk to me without giving me parables? I dig them, but sometimes I just want you to belly up to the bar and you give it to me straight.

I'll have what he's having. Him Lock is it?

Ice Water – Top Gun

Sober up Nathan,
I Am talking straight to you now

Working on it...

You are my Beacon Brother, but you're just too damn good.

SHOOT FOR
THE MOON

YOU WILL
LAND AMONGST
THE
STARS

Lord, you know I like these conversations. It truly is like Father and Son.

Preacher, we all love you Preacher..
I Love You. - Pale Rider

Then came a Pale Horse and it's rider was Death.

Let's talk about the death tax. I do not know the ins and outs of these laws. I can only speak from a Joe the Plumber outlook. I do know that the Death tax is outrageous and I do know I saw some nut from Washington trying to justify receiving all of our life long efforts and leaving the heirs nothing. She says "the heirs didn't earn it". I say to you Caesar, you didn't either. It is my birthrights, what claim do you stake in it? Oh, that's right. You have a 48% stake in it.

I will tell you the truth. The Rich will find loop holes and the Poor will once again get screwed because of knowledge and the lack thereof.

I suggest to my fellow countrymen, no tax on the initial transfer to your LLC. After all, it is with your life long efforts that we invest into our economy for the Hope of a brighter future. Then let Caesar get in line with the rest of us for his check and budget according to the success of our marketplace. Sounds like Caesar should be rooting for God's Dream Team. Just as I and you.

Can you picture the arrogance of our elected public officials. They work for us. From the bottom up. I think of Napoleon in the movie Bill and Teds Excellent Adventure. What an arrogant Dick. No, No, No. This is how we're going to do it. I see her, I see the Old Lady. There is no Young Lady. Hey, I am the one screwing this snake. You just hold it's head and shut up.

When you're done relieving yourself at the expense of my Grandchildren, can we examine that parable again?

What parable?

You know, the 5 talent, 2 talent and 1 talent one. You know how the 5 and 2 talent men prosper, then they ultimately bury what they earn. But not before the 1 talent man gets his cut, which is almost half and looking for more. How the hell did this happen. The 1 talent man (Government), the one that brings absolutely no source of revenue to our country, how the freak did he out maneuver the 5 and 2 talent men?

**POWER
GREED
DEALS
MONEY
EGO
CORRUPTION**

Duh, I'll take "D" for all that I have Alex.

Ok, folks. Nathan is going for it. He is risking all that he has for God. The silver of Judas.

The correct answer is "D"

ALL OF THE ABOVE

Oh Joy, I knew I was right. Alex, tell me. What have I won? I'm so excited.

Ding Dong.

Hang on someone is at my door.

Can I help you? Do you have a check for me?

Yes sir. This is Darryl and my other agent Darryl. No relations. We're with the Internal Revenue Service.

Mufasa – OOOOOeeeee Say it again

Internal Revenue Service. We're here to do a check, not with a check. We'll need to see all of your tax information for the last 10 years of your miserable, pathetic life. Darryl seize that computer and Darryl seize all his banking accounts. Do you have any valuables like precious metals?

No, I threw my silver in the ocean and made a wish. Screw you.

Sounds like what happened to Winthorp – Trading Places

Question for you? Does this sound a lot like the KGB? I guess we'll have to ask a Russian. I have just never witnessed this before in my country and in my lifetime.

I GOT NO WHERE
ELSE TO GO

I GOT NO WHERE
ELSE TO GO

I GOT NOTHING

I'VE CHANGED
SIR

I'VE CHANGED

- AN OFFICER
AND A
GENTLE MAN

Alright Mayo, get up and we'll see if you have changed. I am glad to see that you see it takes a team effort to reach a common goal finally.

GOD
IS THE
MAN

MAN
IS THE

GOD

CAESAR
IS
MAN

MAN
IS
CAESAR

God is ready for his Government to rule and establish his Kingdom here on earth, just as it is in Heaven.

I AM
LONELY

LONELINESS

How many of us stay in a relationship because of the fear of loneliness? What have you done for the relationship to be in it's present state? What can you do to make it better for both of you? I promise you, your partner does not want to start over anymore than you do. Talk to each other. Respect each other. Love each other.

If your partner is unwilling to participate in making your lives better together, unfortunately we do have to make very difficult decisions. Lonely is better than miserable. If you are miserable try to change it. If you can not, then you are not doing your family any favors by staying in the relationship. A life without a partner, is no life at all. How well do you know your partner? I tell you the truth, the pasture is not greener and you will find someone just like the one you are married to now or worse. Make the most of your original decision. Make the most of your marriage.

I can not emphasize enough to you to know your partner well. Be honest about your weird little world. We all have one. Make life long decisions with all of the facts.

Women:
Remember your husbands crippling sexual needs. Privately, treat us like the babies we are.

Men:
Remember your wives must have appreciation, assistance and support. Love them as you love yourself. Put on your rose colored glasses my brother, for you will never have anyone more beautiful than a wife that loves you for who you really are.

Beauty will fade my brother. The heart remains the same. You can not change your spots and you already know your partners and your own. The discovery process sucks, do you really want to do it again?

Life is like a box of chocolates, you never know what you are going to get – Forrest Gump

You are never alone when you accept Christ into your heart. Relish in the alone time that you have with your Father. Do not dwell on what you do not have, but what you have. You are a child of the King. No one can take that away from you. It is of your own free will who you will serve.

MAN WHO HAS
FRIENDS
CAN BE ALONE

MAN WHO HAS
GOD
CAN NEVER BE ALONE

A servant of the Lord is not a bad gig, my brother. It is the best job I have ever had and he is blessing me. Monetarily yes, but more importantly, spiritually. Our checks do not cash in heaven, but our life long efforts will produce checks for the Salvation of our World for an eternity.

Brother, being lonely sucks. Forgive yourself, forgive your transgressors, forgive your authority, forgive your world and most importantly, forgive your Father for putting you to the test of WORTHINESS

See Lord, I like it when you talk like that. I understand. All this mustard seed crap is to hard to follow.

Nathan, that was a parable. Disect every phrase. My brother, our Father's words are Living Water

461

What do you mean by Living Water?

HE THAT WOULD
DRINK OF ME

WILL LIVE
ETERNALLY

Okay, I got it. What about you? I have to ask you this. Have you ever been on your last ...... and search for answers? Rich or Poor. Intelligent or Ignorant. Beautiful or Ugly. Confident or Shy. Athletic or Nerd. When you go to your knees and your face hits the floor in private. That is when you accept Jesus Christ our Lord and Savior into your heart. An unbreakable bond. Believe me, He's your only friend when you reach this point in your life. Your supposed friends will diss you like garbage. Of your own free will and God who strengthens you, will you pick yourself up from the mire and strive for more or start sucking on the Government tit at your brothers expense.

Since I have no audio or visual, my Father touches me in a way that let's me know He is with me. I get a tingling sensation on the left side of my head and sometimes it can run through my entire body. I would expect your sensation to be unique to you. Watch for it, it is there. If your heart is truly with the Lord. Who do you have to prove yourself to, this is all done in private. Have a heart to heart with our Lord, you will never be the same.

I asked my Lord for the Intelligence of the Scarecrow, the Compassion of the Tinman, the Courage of the Lion and a Home for our God here on Earth.

But that is probably a pipe dream. Since your frame of reference will not allow you to see past your own self gratifications. Your heart is calloused with failures. You've lost more than you have won and refuse to try again. Just as the Jews Endeavor to Persevere, so

462

must your God. He will have his Temple or our World will destroy itself. The Temple will be built of the bricks of Mankind.

Let me explain something. The task master wants you to make bricks with no straw. The one talent man is relaxed in the shade with a blue frozen drink with an umbrella in it watching the Hobble doodle worms hump. It's great research, had to go to Copenhagen to actually get a real grip on the worms grip. But it was definitely good use of taxpayer dollars, I can assure you. That little rascal could solve Global Warming and save the planet.

Let's all hump. Make mine a vodka martini, shaken not stirred.

What the hell are you talking about Nathan? You do need help? This will save the planet as we know it. That worm has the semen of the God's.

Okay, sounds good to me. Lets set up a Hobble Doodle Worm Legacy Trust and you market your research and ask for donations.

But before I go, tell me this. Can legacywillandtrust.com create a propagating, everlasting, taxable income stream? Also, can God's Legacy Trust LLC fund all of God's Health Care Centers? Last but not least. If we all serve the same Father, can World Peace be achieved. I sure would like to see it in my lifetime.

**I AM
INTERESTED
IN THIS**

**YE WITH
AN ALTERNATIVE**

**STEP FORWARD
AND BE
HEARD**

463

I would love to hear it as well. I will subject my concept to critical analysis. Will you subject your critical analysis to critical analysis? Be prepared. I 'aint taking no bloviated bullshit. I've got your number. I know where you live. I know your most intimate details. LOL

Are you hammered Nathan?

I had a little drink about an hour ago and it went straight to my head. I'm tired and I want to go home. Boom Boom Boom. - Jaws

Nations of the World. The 10 talent team is tired and they want to go home to their Loved Ones. It is up to you to take your country back. I promise you, your Lord will be on the side of right. You may die, but isn't that better than to have your children live in a World of Tyranny? You know right from wrong. Search your heart. It may be from your blood that your blood has a better future than you. Be that generation that stands up. The United States has got your back and so does God. God has given the United States a little lesson in GIVEN FREEDOM and EARNED FREEDOM. You must take what is yours of your own free will and live by the consequences. Stay home big brother, unless I have a bully with his foot on my head, I'll handle this myself. We became the police of the World when we began searching for ways to protect ourselves. Let us learn from our mistakes and successes. History is a great road map. Our God never changes, nor do we. It is of our own free will that we live in the environment that we are presently standing.

Hey, aren't you going to congratulate me on my house closing? I thank you Lord for blessing me with my daily bread.

You're getting more than bread my Son. You're getting Salvation. Ask and you shall receive. If your heart is right

464

with the Lord, No request is unreasonable. When you do the will of the Lord, you will be blessed. You will be blessed**

How about blessing me with some more Vodka, I just ran out.

Hello Nathan,
Are you ready for some Vodka moments?

Yep, Hic cup.

Riddle me this, riddle me that. Who's afraid of the big bad bat? - Batman

Who is this big bad bat Lord? I will be prepared for him.

Nathan, you're shitfaced. You couldn't hit the side of a barn. Sleep it off while I talk to our brothers and sisters

Cool, it's on you. I think I'll have another hit while you give the next lesson.

Child of God. Tell me. What has Nathan not discussed with you? How can I reach your heart? You know you need me. You know I love you. Please believe in me and love me as I love you and our Father

I so want you to have a better life. I so want you to have an abundant life. I gave you a brain. Stop being a scarecrow and use it. Life is for the taking. Train yourselves to strive for more. Do you want a trophy or everlasting peace? Peace comes from within first, then from without. We are so without Peace right now. How can I make my Muslim, Jewish and Christian brothers make peace and realize we all serve the same God.

Don't forget about the Russians – Patton

Alright, Buddhist, Hindu, Morman, Pentacostal, etc, etc,etc, etc, etc, etc........................

Why are we fighting about who has the best God, when we worship the same God?

Nathan, I told you to go to bed. I'll handle this

You can be such a shit sometimes.

Brothers and Sisters of my Fathers World. I desire praise. I will take your praise of Me and invest it in you. I will be your Beacon. I will be your God. I will be your Shepard. You never need worry again. I will heal you. I will love you. I will nurture you. I AM and I WILL

So what do you want me to do, tell them I WILL sent me?

Go to sleep Nathan, you drunk bastard. We'll play tomorrow. If you're sober

Nah, Nah. I like these talks, they are my favorite of all. You have me spit out everything that I have heard, seen and experienced. I am experiencing you my Lord, right now as we speak and I want to talk about it.

I'm your Huckleberry – Tombstone

Talk to me Goose – Top Gun

Talk to me GOD, Talk to me.

You need some inspiration.

You are right. Mr. Martini,
How about some music.... - It's a Wonderful Life

Lord, I am reminded of the Star Trek episode where the people of higher learning were able to mentally and telepathically controlled the midgets. Are we in that same state with the ignorant? Will the ignorant become educated or will we the intelligent, provide comfort for all mankind?

Let's have some midget tossing and have some laughs.

Brother, is not your brother a midget, a Leper? What do you gain at the expense of your brother? Your brother is a Man among Men. Inspire Him. He has talents you have never seen. Do not mock what you do not understand. Encourage and Inspire. He may see the Young Lady and you may see the Old. You must all see our God. The One God of all Children of God

Jesus, you are the man. I couldn't have hic cup said it any better myself.

Nathan, there is a Seagrams vodka cooler in the frig. Go and get it. I'm busy here

You can be such a turkey sometime. I love you my brother. I am hammered, so I think I'll sit this one out. Is it a grape or green apple? I like them both.

Enjoy my brother, let me have the platform. Our Father sent me to pay for your sins. I have accomplished my task. But I, like Abraham, Ishmael, Isaac, Esau, Jacob, Joseph, David, Solomon, Moses, Muhammad and Nathan are living in unrest. Until our Father's Plan is implemented, we will have no rest. I tell you the truth, it is what your ancestors died for. Birthrights, it is the key to everlasting Salvation. It is the Masters Plan, It is your Fathers Plan, It is the Plan of Mankind if Mankind will continue to be Mankind

You're so damn deep. What the hell does all of that mean?

Sober up, you'll figure it out

Yeah, yeah. My alcohol problem. I am only sedating myself because I feel like I get closer to you Father.

Write that one on the wall at your next A. A. meeting you great justifier of addictive personalities

You can be a dick sometime when you're right. But you are always right.

So who is the Dick and who is the Dicked?

I guess it depends on the frame of reference of the person making the decisions that effect other peoples lives.

Miagi have hope for you Nathanson. Or should I call you Ophiuchuson?

Miagi, you have given me great wisdom. I AM still earning my God Given Name. I AM still considers me adequate, which is better than inadequate I guess. I have to make my Father proud in order to assume the role of Ophiuchus and be deserving and worthy of that Constellation.

Just think, if with the Lord's help I am successful and establish God's Kingdom here on earth as it is in Heaven. I'll be recognized in the Stars of Heaven. Dude, that is so much cooler than Hollywood. It is infamy.

RECOGNITION
FOR THY
BROTHER

IS SWEETER
THAN THYSELF

How's that, you're speaking into my bad ear. - It's a Wonderful Life

What are you telling me here?

ENCOURAGE
THY BROTHER

YOU HAVE HAD
YOURS

LET HIM
HAVE HIS

ASSUME
YOUR ROLE

LET HIM
ASSUME HIS

IF YOU
DISOBEY

YOU WILL
CARRY
YOUR BROTHER

I think I got that one. But what do I know, I'm just a drunk. Are you saying that if we don't inspire our brother and neighbor, we will ultimately have to foot the bill for their expenditures?

DUH

You're such a smart ass. I can't wait to give you a wedgie.

Hey, what chapter is this anyway?
I think I have gone off on a tangent again.
Where are those breadcrumbs?
Lord, how should I label these ramblings of the truth?

"IT'S IN THERE"

PREGO

LOL LOL

**YOUR GOD
ENJOYS A GOOD
LAUGH
AS WELL**

Sounds like a good corporate sponsor, there you go God. We can use all the help we can get until God's people no longer hurt. Hurting sucks. Have you ever Hurt? Have you ever been Hurt? God Heals. God Loves. God Forgives. God is Eternal. God is Judgmental. Rut Roe so much for the rah rah session. If that is your choice of your own free will.

I'm tired and drunk, I'm going to bed now.

**SLEEP WELL
MY SON
TOMORROW
IS ANOTHER
DAY**

**LIVE
LONG AND
PROSPER**

Live Long and Prosper. You're such a dick sometime. LOL I love you my brother. I will try and sleep, just don't keep giving me thoughts. I have to crawl my monkey ass out of bed every time to write it down. How am I doing? Lord. Can you hear me now?

**WHO IS
THE DICK**

**THE DICK
IS YOU**

**OF YOUR OWN
FREE WILL**

**GOOD NIGHT
MY BROTHER**

**I
LOVE YOU**

I Love you too, Lord. GOD Night. Good Night.

February 5, 2010

That was fun. They may think I am crazy, but they need to heed your words.

Above all, you must understand that no prophecy in Scripture ever came from the prophets themselves or because they wanted to prophesy. It was the Holy Spirit who moved the prophets to speak from God.

–   2 Peter 1 : 20 – 21

If you love me, obey my commandments. And I will ask the Father and he will give you another Counselor, who will never leave you. He is the Holy Spirit, who leads into all truth. The world at large cannot receive him, because it isn't looking for him and doesn't recognize him but you do, because he lives with you now and later will be in you.

   –   John 14 : 15 – 17

Jesus replied. All those who love me will do what I say. My Father will love them and we will come to them and live with them. Anyone who doesn't love me will not do what I say. And remember, my words are not my own. This message is from the Father who sent me. I am telling you these things now while I am still with you. But when the Father sends the counselor as my representative and by the counselor I mean the Holy Spirit, he will teach you everything and will remind you of everything I myself have told you.

   –   John 14 : 23 – 26

But I will send you the counselor, the Spirit of Truth. He will come to you from the Father and will tell you all about me. Then you must also tell others about me because you have been with me from the beginning.

   –   John 15 : 26 – 27

Two men will be working together in the field, one will be taken, the other left.

Two women will be grinding flour at the mill, one will be taken, the other left. So be prepared, because you don't know what day your Lord is coming.

Know this, a homeowner who knew exactly when a burglar was coming would stay alert and not permit the house to be broken into. You also must be ready all the time. For the Son of Man will come when least expected.

Who is a faithful, sensible servant, to whom the Master can give the responsibility of managing his household and feeding his family? If the Master returns and finds that the servant has done a good job, there will be a reward. I assure you, the Master will put that servant in charge of all he owns. But if the servant is evil and thinks, my Master won't be back for it for awhile and begins oppressing the other servants, partying, and getting drunk, well, the Master will return unannounced and unexpected. He will tear the servant apart and banish him with the hypocrites. In that place there will be weeping and gnashing of teeth.

- Matthew 24 : 40 - 51

But now I am going away to the one who sent me and none of you have asked me where I am going. Instead, you are very sad. But it is actually best for you that I go away, because if I don't, the counselor won't come. If I do go away, he will come because I will send him to you. And when he comes, he will convince the world of its sin and of God's righteousness and of the coming judgment. The world's sin is unbelief in me. Righteousness is available because I go to the Father and you will see me no more. Judgment will come because the prince of this world has already been judged. Oh there is so much more I want to tell you, but you can't bear it now. When the spirit of the truth comes, he will guide you into all truth. He will not be presenting his own ideas, he will be telling you what he has heard. He will tell you about the future. He will bring me glory by revealing to you whatever he receives from me. All that the Father has is mine, this is what I mean when I say that the Spirit will reveal to you whatever he receives from me.

– John 16 : 5 – 15

Story of the Three Servants

Again the Kingdom of Heaven can be illustrated by the story of a man going on a trip. He called together his servants and gave them money to invest for him while he was gone. He gave five bags of gold to one, two bags of gold to another and one bag of gold to the last, dividing it in proportion to their abilities and then left on his trip.

The servant who received the five bags of gold began immediately to invest the money and soon doubled it. They servant with two bags of gold also went right to work and doubled the money. But the servant who received the one bag of gold dug a hole in the ground and hid the Master's money for safekeeping.

After a long time their master returned from his trip and called them to give an account of how they had used his money. The servant to whom he had entrusted the five bags of gold said, sir you gave me five bags of gold to invest and I have doubled the amount. The master was full of praise. Well done my good and faithful servant. You have been faithful in handling this amount, so now I will give you many more responsibilities. Let's celebrate together.

Next came the servant who had received the two bags of gold with the report. Sir, you gave me two bags of gold to invest and I have doubled the amount.

The Master said, well done my good and faithful servant. You have been faithful in handling this amount, so now I will give you many more responsibilities. Let's celebrate together.

Then the servant with the one bag of gold came and said, sir, I know you are a hard man harvesting crops you didn't plant and gathering crops you didn't cultivate. I was afraid I would lose your money, so I hid it in the earth and here it is.

But the master replied, you wicked and lazy servant. You think I'm a hard man, do you, harvesting crops I didn't plant and gathering crops I didn't cultivate? Well, you should have at least put my money into the bank so I could have some interest.

Take the money from the servant and give it to the one with the 10 bags of gold. To those who use well what they are given, even more will be given and they will have an abundance. But from those who are unfaithful, even what little they have will be taken away. Now throw this useless servant into outer darkness, where there will be weeping and gnashing of teeth.

– Matthew 25 : 14 – 30

FOR THOSE WHO HAVE
COLLECTED
IN MY
HOLY NAME

I AM
HERE TO TAKE
ACCOUNT
WITH MY
EARTHLY
ENTITY

You know, if you spent what was God's not helping God's children. You know, that 10% while running your businesses of spreading God's Word, a Noble cause I might add. You can be redeemed. Ask God if your Church could double as a Healthcare facility. We need all we can get for all of Mankind to rejoice in our Creator's Love.

A personal plug for Christian Life Church and all Churches that came to the relief efforts of their brothers and sisters in Christ. The Hurricane Katrina victims Thank You and so does our Father.

- The Prophet Nathan

The Final Judgment

But when the Son of Man comes in his glory and all the angels with him, then he will sit upon his glorious throne. All the nations will be gathered in his presence and he will separate them as a shepherd separates the sheep from the goats. He will place the sheep at his right hand and the goats at his left. Then the King will say to those on the right, come, you are blessed by my Father, inherit the Kingdom prepared for you from the foundation of the world. For I was hungry and you fed me. I was thirsty and you gave me drink. I was a stranger and you invited me into your home. I was naked and you gave me clothing. I was sick and you care for me. I was in prison and you visited me.

Then these righteous ones will reply, Lord, when did we ever see you hungry and feed you? Or thirsty and give you something to drink? Or a stranger and show you hospitality? Or naked and gave you clothing? When did we ever see you sick or in prison and visit you?

And the King will tell them, I assure you, when you did it to one of the least of these my brothers and sisters, you were doing it to me.
   –   Matthew 25 : 31 – 40

**I AM
IN YOU**

**YOU
ARE
IN ME**

**INSPIRE
YOUR BROTHER**

OR CARRY
YOUR BROTHER

YOU ARE
YOUR BROTHERS
KEEPER

I will inspire my brother. I will teach my brother. I will watch my brother's back. I will heal my brother. I will Love my brother unconditionally and He will Love me.
- The Prophet Nathan

February 7, 2010

Super Bowl Sunday

um, ooh, aah,eee, Oh My, Oh my God!!!

Can I take your order?

I'll have what she is having.
–   When Harry met Sally

Laugh you moron, let's have some fun on our Father's Day.

Introduction of the 401 K plan. Okay, I'm going to tell you my observation of the Defined benefit and the Contributed benefit plan. I remember this new savings plan that the Government had just approved. You could invest a portion of your paycheck into the marketplace and avoid paying tax on that money until you start to draw it out. The thought process was that during your working years your income would be higher than your retirement years. Not exactly a very inspiring goal, but made sense to a lot of people. So you would be in a lower tax bracket when you begin to draw out your retirement nest egg.

The shift from Defined to Contributed sounded good to the businesses that had employees on Defined benefits, because anyone with any sense could see that benefits guaranteed for life are not sustainable for any business. They come right off the bottom line and if any of you have ever owned your own business, you know how important that bottom line is. It is where the owners of the business determine whether they get to eat or not.

Dollar cost averaging is what was preached. Makes sense, sometimes you buy high and it is averaged out when you buy low. Things were humming along pretty good until the Crash and people saw their retirement funds cut in half. I just have to wonder if the stock market prices will continue to stay up when the barrage of baby boomers start to collect at the age of 70.5 when it is mandatory for you to start to draw it out and pay taxes on it.

As a businessman, it would be so easy to see how there would be no way to sustain such a wonderful entitlement package to our employees. We are witnessing many people that have put all their faith into a defined benefit package and are now being told they will have to take less than they were promised. If you don't have it, you just can't pay it. So sorry.

My question is: If the 5 and 2 talent men recognize these entitlement packages are unsustainable and Congress has passed a bill that will help us out, why then is the 1 talent man still on Defined benefits? Why are the employees of the 1 talent man making on average almost twice what the employees of the 5 and 2 talent men make? It is time for the 1 talent man to tighten his belt like the rest of us. I was always told what is good for the Goose, is good for the Gander. Does that only apply to sex?

Hey, I was recording a deed the other day and the clerk made an interesting comment. She said that she took a cut in pay and more employees were hired that were not needed. Interesting, is that our way of stimulating economic growth? Grow more 1 talent jobs at the expense of the 5 and 2 talent men.

I could be wrong, quite often I am. Let's examine the facts. - How to Win Friends and Influence People.

But what do I know, I'm just a Leper. I think I'll apply for that cushy new job with the 1 talent team. I would love to have the job deciding who gets to see the Doctors first. I will make almost twice what I was with the 5 talent man and after only 20 years I can retire with a guaranteed pension for the rest of my life. Of course, I think it goes without mentioning that I will make a fortune in under the table deals. So how bad do you want your wife to have that brain tumor operation? Is it worth $666 to you?

Warden, I really need this contract. I can not compete with your army of free labor. My wife made this cake for you. I think you will find it tasty, especially on the bottom. Hint Hint – Shawshank Redemption

When I left for Sacramento, those tin pans were all but whipped. There is a Marshall named Stockburn. He will uphold any law that pays him the most, if you know what I mean. Now I've reasoned with you and bargained with you. Preacher or no preacher, those tin pans have got to go. - Pale Rider

Geronimo spent 22 years in jail despite the deal to be returned to his family. We have gone back on so many deals. Who got the worse deal? The Africans that were enslaved and brought to a foreign land. Or the Indians that were murdered and driven from their land. We paid off their taskmaster and gave the Indians Casino rights. We reneged on the 10 acres and two mules deal. It reminds me of Longshanks, he paid off the Nobles with more titles and land at the expense of their own people. Greed. How much do I need to pay you to sacrifice your soul and screw your brother when you arrive in power? Did you know that the Indians were not allowed to worship their proclaimed One God in the manner that they so chose? I certainly am glad we have evolved from that barbaric law.

February 9th, 2010

Lord forgive me, I have chosen of my own free will to allow 666 to enter my life once again with alcohol. I jeopardized my entire life and what you have been doing in my life, by drinking and driving. What if I had been hurt or worse, what if I hurt someone else.

Lord it was a very difficult Christmas this year. Officially losing my soul mate. I know what excuses are like. Please put it so deep into my subconscious that my auto pilot doesn't whip into the liquor store. This has been my Demon my entire adult life. You have given me everything and I continue to serve the bottle. Give me the strength to get through this, I know I will be so much better off without this Demon in my life.

I can't even flirt with it. You know flirt with it. I'm only going to drink wine. That didn't work. I'm only going to drink beer. That didn't work. This is my Satan. What is your Satan? Can you control your free will and serve God or are you so far gone there is no going back? Are you a Prodigal Child of God. I am not your judge. I've got enough problems of my own. I pray that I will serve myself, by serving the One and only God of all Mankind. Good Luck to you, I pray that you can make it through. Please pray for me as well. This is not what I want for my life and I know it is not what you want for yours either. I am creating pain for myself to soothe pain. I think they call that, shooting yourself in the foot.

DOOBIE DOOBIE
SMOKE A
DOOBIE

On each side of the river grew a tree of life, bearing twelve crops of fruit, with a fresh crop each month. The leaves were used for medicine to heal the nations. No longer will anything be cursed. For the throne of God and of the Lamb will be there, and his servants will worship him.

- Revelations 22 : 2 - 3

I really don't understand why you will not try and discover the benefits of what our Father created to heal the Nations. Yeah, there's a lot of good medicines we have discovered. They really do make your back feel better. So if you get the squirts or vomiting that is normal, but if you see signs of swelling in your brain. Discontinue use and report to your doctor immediately. Let's mix up what the three wise men deemed more valuable than gold. What the Egyptians valued so much they transplanted trees from Ethiopia. What the Pharisees perfumed the alter with for enlightenment.

I want to know why the wise men brought Gifts of Frankincense and Myrrh that were considered more valuable than gold. The gold was for food, water and shelter. I want my God's Gift. I want those medicinal qualities researched for the Health of all Mankind.

Did you know that Frankincense contains THC, the same stimulant in cannabis? It is known as a depressant and is mildly hallucinogenic. Did you know that Myrrh was used as some sort of embalming ointment? Did you know that there have been discoveries made of enormous medical value concerning treatments with cannabis? Would you be pissed if you found out that something that would have saved your spouse or made them more comfortable was available, only suppressed due to greed and corruption. Why can't we mix our creators gifts in the sink and see what we get.

First you gave me a wink and then you said you would mix it up right here in the sink. I closed my eyes and held my nose. I took a drink. I didn't know if it was day or night. I started kissing everything in sight, but when I kissed a cop at 34th and Vine. He broke my little bottle of "Love Potion #9".

Hey pharmaceutical companies, are your hands tied to greed or are your hands being tied to greed? These chemicals that you are peddling are erasing the line of reality for people. Get God's tools, so you can give God's people what they need for their health.

1. Frankincense
2. Myrrh
3. Cannabis
4. Cocaine
5. Opium
6. ???
7. ???
8. ???
9. ???
10. ???
11. ???
12. ???

You will find the rest of these in primitive cultures and in Stoney's garage.

Our Father gives us a fish and man suppresses it and gives us a snake. This is so much better for you because otherwise it would cut into my sales. (Alcohol & Tobacco) It doesn't have to cut into sales. Men will always kill themselves of their own free will. But Men will always crave what they don't have and inevitably corruption emerges like a mustard seed. More strain on over populated jails as it is. It is medicine from our Creator and it is our choice to how we heal and nurture our bodies or destroy them.

I will tell you this, the DUI school I went to worked for me. The system works, just tweak it a bit. If I want to get hammered and not jeopardize the well being of anyone else. Screw You. Can't you see that I want to kill myself? Why else would I over do it? I can't get what I want, so I am running amphetamines through battery acid and getting high with that. I know these sores on my face are due to the acid being rejected by my body and burning through my face to escape. But it almost fulfills that empty feeling I have inside, until the crash.

Brother, I know that feeling. It is a feeling of unfulfillment. I know you are searching. Search no further, the Lord is begging to come into your life. He has watched you every second of everyday. He has pity and Love for you.

**I BELIEVE
IN YOU**

**CAN YOU
BELIEVE
IN ME**

**PICK YOURSELF UP
GO HOME
CREATE A NEW
AND BETTER
HOME!!!**

You can only pray for your Brother, it will always be of their own free will to make their decisions. 7 X 70 Yes, you are your brothers keeper. Love him and be his beacon and mentor. He is lost and can be found. Do not push, for you are sure to be pushed back. Let them know they are welcome home as Clean Men. Give them Hope. Give them direction. Let them go. Pray

My dad would make fun of my grandmother for the amount of pills she was taking. He would act like he was injecting something into his vein and then do a dance twirling his finger around. He regrets doing that now, now that he has a chest full of pills.

We mock what we do not understand. - Spies like Us

Something tells me that there is a chest full of pills for everyone, because we truly are still just practicing on the lab rats we call humans. It is a practice and we are learning from mistakes. Doesn't it make sense to go to our Creator first, to examine what He has given us before we start scraping battery acid samples.

I promise you. Man will find all the medicine we need, if we will search for those other seven plants and discover the hidden qualities of all twelve.

Maybe the professor from Gilligan's Island will give us a hand. All they had to work with was the island. He kept finding stuff, didn't he? I still think he was a Munich. Ginger never could get a rise out of his hidden low self esteemed ass. Could she? He was smart, but he was shy.

Let me tell you about shy. I sound like Forrest Gump. It sucks. When you finally convince yourself to make that move and you are met with negative reinforcement, how you deal with that negative reinforcement will dictate all of the days of your life. Do you remember when George McFly hit his bully. His life changed forever. He did not have Malice in his heart, but a sense of what is right and he wanted to protect what he loves.

**I LOVE
MY FAMILY**

**I LOVE
MY NEIGHBOR**

I LOVE
MY COMMUNITY

I LOVE
MY COUNTRY

I LOVE
MY GLOBAL BROTHER

I LOVE
MY WORLD

I LOVE
MY GOD

MY CREATOR
I LOVE

Brothers, we are so close. We are so close to achieving all that God has planned for our lives.

He waited until you were completely primed and ready. You have locked down and there is no one else right for you, except this guy that stood you up. I so wish you would take another look at what has been around you this whole time.

Brinkley, Brinkley.
Somewhere over the Rainbow.
I so wanted it to be you.
- You've got Mail

What are you watching?

Bert and Ernie. - Forrest Gump

So let the training begin. His Momma taught him well and he listened.

Oh I'm glad I remembered this. I told you that I was going to talk to you about my efforts to mentor to my 14yr old son. It didn't pan out to well. I remember when my dad came to me about the birds and the bees speech. I shut him down because I was embarrassed. I'd like to go back in time and kick my own ass now. How do we become so smart at such a young age? We don't. We just build a frame of reference upon what we see, hear and experience. Our own reticular activating system that will enable us to make it to the top. I will do it for myself, I do not need you.

Seems to me that all of the biblical stories I have heard, always show the child learning from their elders. I have to wonder if the child has found new elders in the media. It is however, the best Pinocchio draw ever. FAME

How can I be a mentor to my son? I drive a 300k mile Honda. Which I will put on another 700k, he just doesn't understand. It is a love that comes from nurturing. If you take care of your things, your things will take care of you. If you allow your things to control you. Your things will take control of your decisions. How many payment books do you have?

Step up on this chair. I don't want this one to go over your head. If you buy on credit, you get a payment book. They really suck. Have you tried making a payment to a dream account? Make those payments into your own account and avoid the interest and I promise you, you will treasure what you buy. Bring cash or silver with you to count out what you are spending. Count it out slowly. You will appreciate your dream more when it comes from the sweat of your brow, rather than instant gratification and a payment book.

Have you ever been to the casino and you buy different color chips? The color of the chip determines what league you are in.

Let me think of some tribes.
This will be a new joke if I can pull it off. LOL

The Given Tribe:
They are the tribe of the lucky sperm club that didn't have financial intelligence. So for free drinks and liquid courage, they have Given up their birthrights. They had no value, they had been Given their whole life.

The Cruiser Tribe:
They bought cool rides with their new found wealth from their Father's brow. When the cruising ride was over, they had no map and went right back to being lost.

The Misguided Tribe:
These are the people I feel most sorry for. I am one of you. I looked for guidance from authority and my authority was no more equipped to govern than I. If you do everything right, things are suppose to work out for you. NOT. When we become God's people, you can use that as your guiding light. But for now, just know that you're on your own and everyone is trying to screw you. Especially our Governmental authority.

The Disillusioned Tribe:
Nah, I 'aint believing it. Surely no one of color would become successful and turn his back on us.

I know black men that I dearly love. They told me they would not work for black men. They said they look for ways to screw their employees. I am not throwing a blanket over everyone here. I am just saying, how can your race come up from bondage, if you continually treat your brothers like slaves. Are you the new taskmaster? Lepers or Liars, remember.

The Fukdat Tribe:

It's too damn hot outside for all that bullshit. Besides, my needs are being met by my family and government. LOL

The Pooler Tribe:

After I drop my girl off to the Church's Chicken, I use her car to check my traps. Yolanda looking good, Tyrene looking fine. I think I'll stop by and see Morisha. It's all good. I got til five o'clock to pick up my girl. Are you the car pooler or the poorer of mind, body and soul?

PICK YOUR
MONKEY ASS
UP

DAMN YOU
TO HELL

WOMEN
DAMN YOU
TO HELL
IF YOU
ACCEPT LESS
THAN WHAT
YOU'RE WORTH

Let me tell you about me when I was a business owner. I wanted to make money. I would give Ralph and DD cash because it was flowing out of my ass as I perceived. If I had been taxed and scared. They would get nothing. Believe me, we do not all work for Scrooge. Your employers want you to live an abundant life as well. There must be some rewards to take on the responsibilities of others lives. Being the boss is a pain in the ass by the way. What are you going to do for me today? Wah wah. You're fired. I'll do it myself.

You can't fire me, I'm with the Union.

Holy Crap, do you mean to tell me that an organization that was once highly revered for making stands for human rights, has in fact turned this power into a crippling factor to conducting good capitalistic business? How the Hell did that happen?

Don't tell me: Greed
                   Power
                   Money
                   Corruption

JUDGMENT
DAY
ALL MEN

I knew John Kennedy personally and sir, you are no JFK.

The zinger heard around the world and splatted a Quail with a direct hit.

If the glove doesn't fit, you must acquit.- Johnny Cohran

It's amazing how a fancy jingle can draw our attention and allow us to join in a crowd that we don't have a clue about.

Try this on for size.
I know my God personally and you sir are no God, you are a Son of God or Son of Man 666.

Mr. Martini,
How about some music...

This is your chance, what will you confess on Judgment Day? I have confessed my sins and my God has forgiven me. I can not tell you the feeling of repenting of your sins. It is a feeling of yours all to your own. I can only tell you how I feel. I am not afraid to die. I am sure that I have done what the Holy Spirit has put on my heart. I can't wait to meet Jesus. I would like a little more time on earth as we know it in Heaven. But if my Savior wants me now, I am ready.

I don't know why God calls up his children earlier than we think He should. Who are we to question God? Always replace your grief with the Glory of God. He has a plan for everyone, it is up to us to find our own purpose for Him.

I pray Lord, reach everyone's heart and let them follow their hearts to serve you and only you. Now that we know what 666 is, allow us to suppress him for 1000 yrs as promised. I believe when your children realize the boogey man is in all of us and you,

Jesus Christ, is in us as well, we will start to live a life like you intended us to live.

Tell me Lord, in your words, how do you want us to live?

You're not talking to me tonight. Why?

I AM thinking. Give me a break

Lord, I know that it is a difficult question to answer with a short answer that your people will understand. Please try.

LOVE THY SELF

LOVE THY LOVED ONES

LOVE THY NEIGHBOR

LOVE THY NATION

LOVE THY WORLD

LOVE THY GOD

Dude, you are so deep.

**Nathan, you can not comprehend how deep I go.
I AM the everlasting. I AM and I WILL**

I have to tell you, I am digging on the I WILL stuff. It is kind of like someone that tells you how great they are and you wait to see or question them. The World is ready to see you again Lord.

Gods Legacy Trust LLC

GODS LEGACY TRUST LLC

MY EARTHLY ENTITY

**I WILL
HAVE MY EARTHLY ENTITY**

**I WILL
HAVE MY KINGDOM**

**I WILL
HAVE MY GOVERNMENT**

**I WILL
GLORIFY THE WORTHY**

**I WILL
BE YOUR SHEPARD**

**I WILL
HAVE MY WAY**

Thank you Lord, you are so wayyy cool.

What about those things we do that we question if they are really sins? So we continue to do them.

**ASK
HEART**

Sometimes I'd like to slap the crap out of you, tell me the truth.

**WHEN YOU SLAP
ME**

**YOU SLAP
YOURSELF**

So you are saying by continuing to do the things that we know are sins, we are willing to accept the consequences of our actions on Judgment Day.

**NO SHIT
SHERLOCK
LOL**

**OF YOUR OWN
FREE WILL**

Lord, tell me our fate. I know mine. What is Mankind's?

**SERVE MAN 666
OR
SERVE GOD**

A little more Lord. I can not comprehend your Grace.

**DESTRUCTION
FAMINE
DISEASE**

OR

**LOVE
HOPE
FREEDOM**

**OF YOUR OWN
FREE WILL**

Lord,
I am not sure why you selected me, well yes, I guess I do understand. The lowest of the low can relate to anyone as long as they are willing to be beat down by the other parties ego. Once

you get through beating on me, examine what I am saying for our Lord and Savior.

Screw You. - Hank

We all have a Hank in us that is being suppressed. What I and your God want to know is, when are you going to take a crap in the front lawn of injustice?

I WILL
MEET YOU

I WILL
JUDGE YOU

I WILL
FOREVER
LOVE YOU

I AM
YOUR
FATHER

Yes you are and I am your son. I am ready. Father, have I pleased you? Am I more than adequate? I'm not looking for a Dudley Doo Right Badge, just reassurance.

HOW ABOUT A
CHESTER PIN IT ON
LOL

You're screwing with me tonight. It's all good.

Nathan, what is it that you want from thy Lord that I have not already given unto you?

A strong enough voice to proclaim the Master's Plan and achieve World Peace.

DONE!!!

I AM...

AND

I WILL...

Luke, I am your Father. - Star Wars

**I AM
YOUR FATHER**

**I AM
YOUR CREATOR**

**I AM
YOUR SAVIOR**

**I AM
YOUR CONFIDANT**

**I AM
YOUR LOVER**

**I AM
YOUR FORGIVER**

I AM is my best friend. - The Prophet Nathan

**I WILL
TRAIN YOU**

**I WILL
NURTURE YOU**

**I WILL
SAVE YOU**

**I WILL
LISTEN TO YOU**

**I WILL
LOVE YOU**

I WILL
FORGIVE YOU

I WILL is who I have been seeking. - Nathan the Prophet

His WILL be done here on Earth as it is in Heaven. Now that you know what God's WILL is, I challenge you to read the bible again with that understanding. The Living Word will take on a whole new meaning. His WILL has been kept a riddle and now it is revealed. What WILL we do with it?

ASK OF ME

YOU WILL RECEIVE

When your heart is right with Christ, it is like the Crane Technique. No Can Defense. - Karate Kid

I WILL
FEED

I WILL
WATER

I WILL
CLOTHE

I WILL
SHELTER

I WILL
HEAL

I WILL
HEAR

I WILL
FREE

Genie, I FREE YOU.

Quick, tell me something to do.

Ahhhhh, pick up the laundry.

NO, NO. Oh, it feels so good to be FREE. - Aladdin

ONE WORLD
UNDER
GOD

My Brother, I Love You. Let no one separate you from the Father in Heaven. He sent His Only Begotten Son to pay for our Sins. He sent me His Servant, to right the wrongs of Mankind.
– Nate the Child
because I Love you my Father

MY WILL
WRITTEN

MY WILL
DONE

So Shall it be Written
So Shall it be Done
– The Ten Commandment's

Sorry, couldn't help myself. Damn I love that line. LOL

FACEBOOK LETTER TO: (2ND WIFE) RESOLVEMENT TO LOSS

Nathan Isbell March 5 at 2:28am

I know you said you were not interested and didn't have the time, but I'd sure love your opinion as a Christian friend. One that I trust. http://tablemanners.biz/nathan/and also http://tablemanners.biz/god-legacy/They are both still a work in progress. I have to get them finished so I can have an attorney review them before we launch our radio talk show campaign. My publicist said because of God, we can't get on secular radio. Can you believe that crap. Says it will offend advertisers. So we are taking the approach of a public service announcement and slipping God in under the radar. LOL What a shame that this world has no room for God. I have so many stories to tell you about this whole process. I would have quit a long time ago, had it not been for the signs that the Holy Spirit kept giving me. These signs may be a little spooky for you. Just keep one thing in mind. It will take God to fix our mess and that will come with a little spooky. LOL

(2nd Wife) March 5 at 6:25am

Nathan, as you know, I read a lot of books and one thing in common with all of them is the fact that the author does extensive research to back claims made especially by God. I hope you are doing research with all of this stuff, otherwise it might not be taken seriously. This is a lot for me to absorb, it takes me back and I don't know if I can do that at this time. Who is this publicist and what is he or she getting out of this?

The bible says if you have no love, then your words are just clanging cymbals. I know you have lots of prejudice and you are very sarcastic when it comes to people, you judged my entire family, maybe you should work on your love walk with people around you, God is more than all of this. He is love first! The bible says faith, hope, love but the greatest of these is love. Be careful about all of this. I'm sorry, but I don't think people are going to be accepting of this without back up from the bible or history books.

Nathan Isbell March 5 at 8:35am

It is difficult to back up faith. I don't know if I can back up the Holy Spirit moving me to do what it is that I do. Yes, I have done an enormous amount of research. Try reading the book as if you don't know me. It may help you to see that my purpose is for Christ and Him alone. This purpose came before you and stayed with me after you. It will haunt me until it is complete. I may get laughed at and egg thrown in my face, but I almost think that that is the way it is suppose to be. I pray that you don't think that I am doing all of this for money. God has met my financial needs and then some.

(2nd Wife),

I have been looking for that expert for over five yrs now that can tell me why legacywillandtrust.com won't work. Why do you think it won't work? I'm not being sarcastic, I really want to know why you think it won't work.

(2nd Wife) March 6 at 7:01am Report

It's not difficult to back up faith it all has to be backed by the bible.

You do what you feel you need to do, Nathan, I hope it is all that you say it is. I told you my thoughts on it years ago, I don't think people will leave their money that way. Maybe some super rich person with no heirs, but for the most part, people will leave all of their money to their family all at once.

Nathan Isbell March 7 at 3:33pm
(2nd Wife)

I respect your views and they are noted. My view is different from yours. I think that once people understand Eternal Salvation through Birthrights, they will understand thinking generationally. T.D. says that it is time we begin to think generationally. We just haven't had the means to do so. My humble opinion is that people are searching for something to have faith in, why not let it be God and reveal Gods Plan.

I have heard your comments and they are duly noted. I just have to complete my purpose for God and I just can't help myself to but to let you know that you have disappointed me in the your ability to recognize that someone may want to step out for God for the betterment of Mankind. I know this is Grandiose, but I also know that it is driven by the Holy Spirit. I will be heard and my concept will be subjected to critical analysis.

As I have told you before, please someone tell me why this won't work. Your answer is Apathy. Apathy is not the answer that I was looking for. Apathy can be overcome through Faith and Hope and especially when there is a Shepard to look over us.

You asked me to give up my Passion for Christ when you asked me to leave legacywillandtrust.com alone. I sacrificed my soul mate, my wife, my first wife, my daughter, my respect from my parents and etc.... Can't you see that I am trying to fulfill my purpose even though it may be arcane for you?

It is all good. I now see that I really never knew you at all. I really thought I did know you as I witnessed your generosity of money, just not of time or empathy. It is lukewarm, maybe you should take your own advice and review your walk with the Lord.

I have resolved to the fact that you never loved me and I am not sure you can rebound from your childhood to accept the fact that someone loves you and is deserving of your love. I understand that your frame of reference will not allow you to think of anything grandiose. I was impressed with your lofty goals to help single moms, you were never really passionate about it enough to make it happen.

(2nd Wife), I want to thank you once again for coming into my life as painful as it was for you. I promised God to always do what I could to look out for you. He is blessing me now. Ask of me and I will do what I can to help you. I will always love you. I fell in love with a (2nd Wife) that I am not sure you can resurrect. If this is the (2nd Wife) that you are and have become, I promised God to help you in anyway I can. I asked Him to make you my wife and I would forever take care of you. A promise is a promise. Especially when your God is blessing you.

Take Care (2nd Wife),
I WILL always love you.
Nate

(2nd Wife) March 7 at 4:26pm Report
Nathan,
I am really sorry that you feel that way, and you are making me out to be this awful person. I look at my walk with The Lord on a daily basis. I repent, and surrender constantly. I am a single mom with 2 kids to take care of all on my own, with NO ONE to help me or give a damn, I have a heart for single moms, but unfortunately, I am one. Right now, my ministry is my children, I would be remiss if I left them home alone to go work with other people. That is not the order of God, I am a mother first, then I have to work to support them and then most of the time, nothing is left. you are a very critical person, you always have been. thanks for the money, it will help me with my medicine. If you think you never knew me, then so be it, I am who I am, and I haven't changed, just a little more worn out from all the mess. Take care, and I hope all of your dreams come true.

(2nd Wife) March 7 at 4:32pm
Oh, and you are right, I probably will never recover from my childhood, are you happy about being right about that? I wish I could have had someone love me right, don't say it was you, because it wasn't, you did all that you did for sex, never really for me, you had an ulterior motive, always, you wanted something in return, always. I'm alone and I am working on all of my shame issues, and if I never recover, I never recover, but I will die trying, I don't want to be like this, at least I look at myself and know I need to change, you deny your mental illness as if it doesn't exist.

507

Stop throwing stones. It is my opinion, I don't think your idea is from God or will work, why do you have to attack me because I think that? Stop judging for heavens sake, if you are a Godly man, you wouldn't judge me so harshly.

Nathan Isbell March 7 at 4:47pm
I do not judge you nor have I ever judged you. I AM in no position to judge. I AM a sinner of sinners. I give a damn about you and the boys. Yes, sex is my primary love language that you could never fully understand. You never really got it that it is that important and how I was so prepared to do everything in my power to have a great life with you and the boys.

We both have our walk with Christ. I am choosing to get what is on my heart off my heart. Once I have done that, I have fulfilled my purpose for Him. My sorrow comes from that you are my soul mate and you never loved me and can never believe in me. I WILL forever be alone.

My next step is to hire attorneys to review my sites and make sure that I am free from litigation.

Nathan Isbell March 7 at 4:54pm
Oh, you changed. You changed big time. There is a (2nd Wife) in you that I fell in love with. The (2nd Wife) that initially came to Foley. Everyone met that (2nd Wife) and fell in love with her as did I. Finances became an issue and buried that (2nd Wife). The (2nd Wife) that I knew was fun loving and was passionate about Health Foods and God. Where did you give up your Faith? It is so puzzling to me that you can hear my words of Faith and my Passion for Christ, yet you do not hear me. You wanted a Godly Man and I AM making myself vulnerable for God, yet you do not hear me nor does anyone else. The more the resistance, the more I felt like I was on the proper mission for God.

Nathan Isbell March 7 at 5:06pm

I am so sorry for everything that I have ever done to you to cause you pain. I must fulfill my purpose for God. Pray that I am successful, I WILL always take care of you if I have the means to do so.

Nathan Isbell March 7 at 5:22pm

You are my true love and lost. It is a pain that I must endure for a lifetime. I chose God. I pray that you can one day see that. (2nd Wife), I WILL not preach to you. I AM not worthy in your eyes because of my past transgressions. I AM not sure of my purpose, but it makes sense to me. I must get this off my heart and try to establish Gods Earthy Entity and Government here on earth as it is in Heaven. It is the Holy Spirit that puts this on my heart.

My God has said unto me:

Dammit Son,
If Not You,
WHO?
Assume Your Role.

I love you (2nd Wife), but I love our Creator more.

Nathan Isbell March 7 at 6:27pm
(2nd Wife),

I will always love you. The resistance is expected. HONESTLY, I just pray that you can hear my heart before the rest of the World hears it. It would be to late to salvage any love for one another at that point. We will definitely be doing a Take Care forum. And I WILL take care of you. It is my promise to God.

Nathan Isbell March 8 at 8:42am

This will be my last letter to you (2nd Wife). I do not want to bother or harass you again. Now that you have read my book, fully understand the concept and know the essence of my heart, you have stated your claim and judged my belief in God. Your claim is that it will not work due to apathy and you do not believe that God is moving me to do what I do for Christ. I AM a false prophet in your eyes. I AM so glad that we don't burn witches at the stake anymore, I'd be so toast right now. LOL

A prophet speaks from God, it doesn't pay anymore. Yet it costs plenty. My next book will be titled Acts of Nathan the Prophet. If the Bible is a prophetic book, my books will fit into prophecy and history. You can not see past who I AM in your own eyes. Believe me, it works and you will see. Sooner or later.

There was an ulterior motive to finishing this project and I AM so glad it was there. I wanted the (2nd Wife) that I fell in love with back. Yes, even after the kicks in the teeth at Christmas I could not get past her. I really thought I could break through and save her, she has been through so much and worthy of being loved and taken care of. She will not relinquish command of her destiny. The years and men have callused her heart. Now that you see my heart and I see yours, you are not the woman I thought you were or that woman is in devils chains with scales on her eyes. Bitter. The girl that I fell in love with must not exist anymore. I would have thought a Godly woman would have had pride for her partner, that he is compelled to step out for God. I need a supportive partner as I try and complete my purposes for God. I thought after these websites and book that I would be done. I was enlightened to an even more grandiose goal. I really didn't sign up for it, God kind of just slipped it in on me since I will have the floor on His behalf. World Peace. I AM praying to be heard by people that don't have apathy in their hearts , but a sense of I WILL for my GOD. The One and Only GOD. My comfort comes from the fact that Jesus faced the same adversities with his loved ones and surroundings.

This will enable me to get past you. I so need to get past you and move on with my life. It is difficult to get past someone when you have love. I AM glad for you that you never had love for me. I kind of wish I had known that earlier, but it was all in the script. Your tongue lashes stung and ripped the worse.

Good Bye, Good Luck, Take Care,

Text me if you need something. I WILL do all in my power to keep my promises to God. Even overcome heartache. I WILL let you go now (2nd Wife), so that I may begin to truly heal.

Nathan
because you have seen my naked soul and you do not Love what you see.

P. S.
I want to thank you once again for coming into my life as painful as it was for you. You were a large part of completing my purpose for God and I WILL be forever grateful. I just prayed that you would be a part of it. You can't always get what you want, but if you try sometime, you just might find, you get what you need. Love the one you're with. I AM with GOD. I AM SAVED.

(2nd Wife) March 9 at 7:16am Report
I don't know what you're talking about! Tongue lashing, that was (1st WIFE), you were always the one to cut me off at the knees with YOUR words. We would talk about that too. You have twisted everything. I was as kind as I could be, to the point of oppression and despair, I was miserable but didn't say it cause I didn't want to hurt you!!!!!!!!! You can twist the past up as much as you want, it isn't truth, I tried and tried to make it work, I kinda wish you would have told me you wanted to be the "prophet Nathan" before too, ya know that's kind of a big deal. Oh well! Sorry you have pain, but like you said, you chose God, make sure it's Gods voice you are hearing and not the devil or yourself, the bible says to test the spirits.

-

511

Nathan Isbell March 9 at 9:28am

(2nd wife),

If I had known what my purpose was at that time, I'd have told you. I had to go searching for it. Yes, prophet Nathan. The title doesn't pay any more, but costs plenty. Now everyone can laugh at me. It's Okay, there is but one that I must prove my worthiness too. I didn't ask for this, but I am proud that our Father selected me to deliver His Gift. Again, it is very arcane. One that is delivered a Gift from the Holy Spirit might anticipate it being arcane. Take Care (2nd wife), I am finally past the (2nd wife) that I fell in love with. She doesn't exist. Now I can find balance.

I am meeting with attorneys today to cut a deal for them to review my websites and make sure that I will be free from litigation. I am anxious to hear if they think I am sick, crazy or a prophet. Maybe you can't see my purpose because you worry too much about what other people think about you. Your name is off the blog by the way. I hope you are not so incognito when Jesus comes. You might miss him if you have not prepared your lantern with enough oil.

Above all, you must understand that no prophecy in Scripture ever came from the prophets themselves or because they wanted to prophesy. It was the Holy Spirit who moved the prophets to speak from God.

2 Peter 1 : 20 – 21

If you love me, obey my commandments. And I will ask the Father and he will give you another Counselor, who will never leave you. He is the Holy Spirit, who leads into all truth. The world at large cannot receive him, because it isn't looking for him and doesn't recognize him but you do, because he lives with you now and later will be in you.

John 14 : 15 – 17

Jesus replied. All those who love me will do what I say. My Father will love them and we will come to them and live with them. Anyone who doesn't love me will not do what I say. And remember, my words are not my own. This message is from the Father who sent me. I am telling you these things now while I am still with you. But when the Father sends the counselor as my representative and by the counselor I mean the Holy Spirit, he will teach you everything and will remind you of everything I myself have told you.
John 14 : 23 – 26

But I will send you the counselor, the Spirit of Truth. He will come to you from the Father and will tell you all about me. Then you must also tell others about me because you have been with me from the beginning. John 15 : 26 – 27

(2nd Wife) March 9 at 10:02am Report
Good luck

Nathan Isbell March 9 at 10:29am
Thanks (2nd wife). I hope you can see it come to fruition. It's all about God having an earthly entity through which he can heal his people. I'll never understand why you can't see that. I guess it is because of your hate for me. Maybe one day you can truly forgive me. This has been a very strange ride for me also. Remember, I am not doing all of this for a ministry, politics or money. Quite the opposite, I am doing it all for His Glory. He is blessing me so much right now and has given me the time to finish this. The Acts of Nathan the Prophet is awesome. Full of wisdom dealing with everyday life. It is what I have seen, heard, read and experienced in my lifetime. It is my opinion and observation. It is my script.

Good Luck to you too. I pray that business picks up for you.

(2nd Wife) March 9 at 10:34am Report

Nathan, STOP twisting, I never once said I hated you!!!! Stop it. What glory is God getting from this, please tell me

Nathan Isbell March 10 at 1:48am

But now I am going away to the one who sent me and none of you have asked me where I am going. Instead, you are very sad. But it is actually best for you that I go away, because if I don't, the counselor won't come. If I do go away, he will come because I will send him to you. And when he comes, he will convince the world of its sin and of God's righteousness and of the coming judgment. The world's sin is unbelief in me. Righteousness is available because I go to the Father and you will see me no more. Judgment will come because the prince of this world has already been judged. Oh there is so much more I want to tell you, but you can't bear it now. When the spirit of the truth comes, he will guide you into all truth. He will not be presenting his own ideas, he will be telling you what he has heard. He will tell you about the future. He will bring me glory by revealing to you whatever he receives from me. All that the Father has is mine, this is what I mean when I say that the Spirit will reveal to you whatever he receives from me.

John 16 : 5 – 15

Nathan Isbell March 10 at 2:21am

(2nd wife),

I am unveiling what the Holy Spirit has put on my heart. At every expense in my life. "All that the Father has is mine" including the solution to the Worlds largest riddle.

Then I saw in the right hand of him who sat on the throne a scroll with writing on both sides and sealed with seven seals. 2And I saw a mighty angel proclaiming in a loud voice, "Who is worthy to break the seals and open the scroll?" 3But no one in heaven or on earth or under the earth could open the scroll or even look inside it. 4I wept and wept because no one was found

514

who was worthy to open the scroll or look inside. 5Then one of the elders said to me, "Do not weep! See, the Lion of the tribe of Judah, the Root of David, has triumphed. He is able to open the scroll and its seven seals." - Revelations 5: 1 - 5

When the spirit of the truth comes, he will guide you into all truth. He will not be presenting his own ideas, he will be telling you what he has heard. He will tell you about the future. He will bring me glory by revealing to you whatever he receives from me. All that the Father has is mine, this is what I mean when I say that the Spirit will reveal to you whatever he receives from me.

Nathan Isbell March 10 at 2:42am
(2nd wife),
I am fulfilling prophecy by creating His earthly entity.
Gods Legacy Trust LLC

Jesus came to establish His Kingdom, & His Kingdom differs greatly from what people expect.
Many today hold out hope that Jesus will come back to earth & establish an empire, the glory & splendor of which has never been seen before – and that the Jews will be the prominent people in that kingdom.
But that is just not the case!
Were there any clues in the OT that Jesus' Kingdom would be different from what people expected?]
III. HIS KINGDOM WAS PROMISED
A. God promised through Nathan that the Kingdom of Christ would last forever.
2 Sam 7:12-13 (God's promise to David) – When your days are fulfilled & you rest with your fathers, I will set up your seed after you, who will come from your body, & I will establish his kingdom. 13 He shall build a house for My name, & I will establish the throne of his kingdom forever.
1. If this prophecy applied only to Solomon, then it was unfulfilled, untrue & impossible.

515

2. But this prophecy is primarily about Jesus Christ (a descendent of David & Solomon), & the kingdom over which He would reign.

3. His kingdom, like Solomon's, entailed the building of God's house, the church (Quote Matt 16:16-18; 1 Tim 3:15), not a physical structure, but a spiritual house made up of living stones (1 Pet 2:5).

4. And Jesus promised to be with His kingdom "to the end of the world" (Matt 28:20).

B. God promised through David that the Kingdom of Christ would be governed from Heaven.

Psa 110:1 – The LORD said to my Lord, "Sit at My right hand, till I make Your enemies Your footstool" (Matt 22:41-46).

Mark 16:19 – So then, after the Lord had spoken to them, He was received up into heaven, & sat down at the right hand of God.

Nathan Isbell March 10 at 3:35am

I sent you some more clues, but God has decided not to send them. Once again technology robbed me of the Holy Spirits thoughts. I can only summize that He wanted you to follow some dots on your own.

Take Care (2nd wife),

I WILL always love you and care for you.

The Prophet Nathan

"BATTLE"
OF FAITH

Pastor Facebook Friend is asking: so Church - do we have to tell people we are Christians or do they ask us why we are not like everyone else??
Yesterday at 8:29pm · Comment ·LikeUnlike
7 people like this.

Facebook Friend
no I dont believe we should have to tell others we are christians are actions should set us apart from the world. they should be asking us why we are different and we should be living the life that makes them want the peace, joy, and love that we have
Yesterday at 9:01pm

Facebook Friend I always tell people I'm a Christian, but usually it's after they've come to me and told me that I'm "shining" or "covered in light." They always see something different about me. It is very humbling to experience this so often. I know its God, and I'm so glad He shows Himself to people this way. But again, it is a very humbling thing for me.
Yesterday at 9:14pm

Nathan Isbell
Who's approval do we seek? I would like to say Jesus, but I'd be lying for everyone. Jesus is such a second thought in our lives. I had to just try and remember to pray. Now that Jesus is in my heart I have to remember to work. John, answer me this: define Christian as opposed to Muslim and Judaism. I have been searching for a very long time, so don't bloviate my ass. I have found some real clues and I am searching for more. The time is real near, no shit. Forgive me of my language, but my God and I have had a little chat and He told me that the only way to reach His children is with a few colorful metaphors. You can quote scripture at them all you want. You have got to belly up to the bar and really talk to them if you want to reach them. I guess that is why the Holy Spirit is on my heart so much. I have been ministering at the bar for a long time. Drunk as shit. I find it very amusing that

518

God has chosen me to deliver his message. But very prophetic. I didn't ride in on a mule, but I am such a sinner. Who else would reveal Gods Last Will and Testament? The Vessel and the Lamb. The Seven Sealed Two Sided Scroll. Have I told you what 666 means? Before you even start to question me, I warn you. I am who I am and I know who I am. I know my new name in Christ and I know my purpose for God. I can spell it out with detail. Don't question me, question God. I speak for Him. It doesn't pay me anymore, but costs plenty.

The Prophet Nathan

Yesterday at 9:20pm ·

Pastor Facebook Friend @Nathan - God said not to use such words...so I would seriously consider who you were talking to. God does not change, nor does He lie.

As to my bloviating - I will say what I deem necessary to convey the message.

As long you as you still consider yourself a sinner, then Jesus truly has no part in you - for once you are cleansed, you cannot be dirty again unless you willingly choose to walk in filth.

As far as you speaking for God....He truly doesn't need you to - Jesus rent that veil so we did not need someone to speak to Him for us.

Whose approval? God's. Please tell me who said anything about approval? I am asking about how we show Christ. Do we have to tell people because our actions do not show it, or as Facebook Friend said, are we asked why we are different and then have to explain it? One is arrogance seeking acceptance. The other, humbleness seeking God's face.

Additionally, being drunk is something Jesus says not to do. As you proclaim His name as your Savior...why would you flaunt that in His face? Remember, He is our Savior AND OUR LORD. You need to understand what Lord means.....

And finally, as for me or anyone else questioning you, I leave you this: if it looks like a skunk, smells like a skunk and walks like a skunk - I have no need to ask it if it is a skunk.. Just observing and listening tells me much more than a battery of questions that can be danced around and upon.
Yesterday at 9:58pm

Facebook Friend 2
Let me tell you a sad sad story. I was away from the Lord for many years, I worked and there was a woman at work I didn't even know she was a Christian, she was nice enough etc. but never heard anything about Jesus or her religion. I was floored when I got saved and found out not only was she Christian but a Pentecostal preachers wife! Talk about hiding it under a bushel?
Yesterday at 10:04pm

Facebook Friend
Nathan, if I may while you're waiting for Pastor's response: I don't think Christians believe we are seeking Jesus' approval. The first thing we learn when we are saved is that we are not worthy of his love, salvation, or approval. That's what makes what He has done for us more awesome.

And He's not a second thought in my life. Nor many other Christians I believe. I live every moment of my life with the immediate awareness of Jesus' presence, living by His word, and seeking His forgiveness when I know I've erred.

God can use the foolish things of this world to confound the wise. But it seems doubtful that He is using you in the method you describe. Your methods seem more like a mockery of God. The people you are ministering to know what a Christian looks like. What makes you think they're listening to a drunk?

God's word admonishes us to not to be drunkards, or use foul language, so it is doubtful that He told you to use "colorful" language. Every knowledgeable Christian would know better.

There are plenty of ways to deliver God's message to people without engaging in sin to do so. That type of behavior when evangelizing or ministering simply mocks God. And who would trust the "prophecies" of a drunk? In fact, such behavior diminishes the deity of God by making the assumption that God is "cool with it." God is due much greater respect than we give Him. This language, and other casual worship behaviors remove God from His thrown, and attempt to humanize Him, making Him more like us. which He is not. God demands and expects far more respect than this.

I walk in the office of prophet, very humbly, and with great fear. I don't have to call myself a prophet. God reveals it when I speak, and when I speak, my words fit the Biblical qualifications of a prophecy. They edify, exhort, or comfort. Anything other than that, I check myself numerous times through prayer, and I seek confirmation of the information before I speak. To do otherwise is to be operating out of the flesh. I prophecy with fear and trembling, because if I speak out of God's will, and people are harmed or misled by what I've said, then I am accountable to God for what happens to those people. A prophet is a spiritual warrior,and a protector of God's people. Be sober. Be vigilant. These are the words I live by as a prophet.

It is your own confession that you are a drunk. Who believes a drunken prophet? I don't see believing that anything you say has any value until you sober up and learn the whole word of God!
Yesterday at 10:10pm

Facebook Friend 3
Amen, anyone that believes they are a sinner and preaching the word of God is delusional or WORSE! In the first place Jesus

Christ should and is my first thought and my first consideration in all things. Without Him I am nothing, there have been encounters in my life with hypocrites, but I don't really think anyone has ever said "I'm a sinner, (which is to say I am going to hell) let me tell you all about God! Let's see the number one thing that you would truly know if you KNEW anything or understood completely what you are reading in the bible would be that Jesus Christ died for you and if you accept Him and His FINISHED WORK at Calvary, then you Believe and are saved if you repent and ask Him into your heart, turn and surrender your all to Him, so that He can complete the work in you to make you Righteous before a Holy God. Nathan you are spouting what you have read and what you have heard others say and teach without BELIEVE-ING. So your words are empty and fall on deaf ears probably. The bible says that the one that knows more, more is expected...Hell is gonna get really hot and miserable, better think it over, and what's more, what ever force inside you is driving you to do this can be conquered by THE BLOOD OF JESUS CHRIST!

Yesterday at 10:19pm

Facebook Friend
Nathan, to answer your question about the difference between Christian, Muslim, Judaism:

Judaism is a religion that teaches belief in the one true God, the same God that Christians worship. This religion doesn't accept Jesus as the Son of God and the Christ predicted in the Torah (the first 5 books of the Christian Bible). They are still waiting for the arrival of the Christ. The Jews are God's chosen people, born of Abraham, of whom God said his descendents would fill the earth. Christ came to them first, then to the Gentiles. Judaism is the history of Christianity before the physical arrival of Christ. (He's all over the Old Testament).

Christianity is founded in Judaism, but Christ, the son of God, came in fulfillment of the law, giving a new commandment, and establishing His place in the Trinity, which before Him was not fully known, though it had been revealed in Jewish scripture. Christianity is the only religion that teaches irrefutable truth. Christianity teaches that salvation is not by works, but by God's gift of mercy.

The Muslim religion is false. Allah is not the one true God. Islam teaches things that are in opposition to each other. Both cannot be true, so there is false teaching in the Islam religion. Islam teaches that good works over bad bring reward. This is false. Although Islam has some similarities to Christianity, it is a counterfeit gospel that cannot stand when the facts are checked.

I hope this answers your question, which was actually a bit vague. I'd love to tell you more, if you can be more specific in your question.
Yesterday at 10:43pm

Oblivious Facebook Friend
The best compliment I get is I KNEW YOU WERE A CHRISTIAN! Praising God for his will and grace!
Yesterday at 10:56pm

Pastor Facebook Friend
@Oblivious Facebood Friend - excellent response. It is awesome to see someone jump in and nail it!

@Facebook X - you betcha. That is the whole point of this discussion....

@zLukewarmer - you got it - praise God for your insight.
Yesterday at 11:06pm

Fondly Facebook
Men should see the Lord in us..and covet' to be like us..admire..us for surely we are different!!..just like the above..it is

never a struggle for my colleagues to automatically tell em that ..i am a woman of God or as they fondly call me..a girlfriend ' of Jesus.....

15 hours ago

Nathan Isbell

When Jesus comes as the Lion, I believe he will be cussing mad. I try not to cuss when witnessing, but I choose not to witness to the choir. I choose to witness to the masses that will only hear you when there is use of colorful metaphors. As far as a drunk, I find it a way to slip in under the radar and witness to the folks that need God the most. 10 hours ago ·

Nathan Isbell

I'm not looking for a ministry or politics, I just want to get what the Holy Spirit put on my heart, heard. The Lamb approach fell on deaf ears. 10 hours ago ·

Facebook Friend

Nathan, you put yourself and those you think you are ministering to in danger. There are many who will say Lord, Lord, did we not minister in your name and cast out demons? And Christ will say, depart from me, I never knew you. It isn't if we know God. It's does God know us? When God looks at you Nathan, what does He see? If you don't believe he sees a misguided drunk and a fool, then you are deceiving yourself. Clean up your act and represent God in a way that honors him, or you won't reach anyone.

10 hours ago

Facebook Friend

No, not on deaf ears. The words fell from the lips of a drunk. So nobody chooses to listen.

10 hours ago

Facebook Friend

And any voice that tells you to use foul language and get drunk, is not God and is not of God. It is demonic Nathan. Clear and simple. You need deliverance from this so you can see God's real truth.

10 hours ago

Nathan Isbell

That's the beauty of this country, we get to choose to believe in whatever we want to believe in. Stone the drunk, he is blasphemous. I have always submitted to what the powers that be say. Now I have educated myself and respectfully question authority. Who among us can determine what God's real truth is. It is all their interpretation and who questions their motives. First there was God. Then Man. Everything after that is subject to mans interpretation.

9 hours ago ·

Facebook Friend

Nathan, you ask who can determine what God's real truth is. Everyone who reads the Bible, because God's truth is in the Bible. It is irrefutable. It doesn't involve interpretation, it is spelled out clearly. You are following the same line of thought that every misguided soul follows by choosing not to believe that the word of God is of God and truth.

I hear the weariness in your voice. I know you are frustrated because no one will listen to you. Well, I'm listening. It's just that I hear what is behind your words. I recognize the lies that have infected your faith and are dragging you down into despair. God doesn't do that to His people! God lifts us up, encourages us, and fills us with love. He would never leave us to feel alone and abandoned, apart from the Body.

We should question authority, and test the spirits, but we are clearly directed to submit to authority. Without a strong, truth-

525

knowing authority over us, we are subject to deceit that will lead us to think we do not need any authority. And that is not God's way. Authority is our protector, not our persecutor. You say, "everything is subject to man's interpretation." You may think that, but that doesn't make it true. As scripture explains... all things are subject to God, and His Word clarifies everything, separating truth from lie, and flesh from spirit.

9 hours ago

Nathan Isbell

Facebook Friend ?, thank you for listening. I can not begin to match you or anyone else with religion. All I can say is that the Holy Spirit has put a gift upon my heart and I must share it before I go to meet Him. I am doing all in my power to deliver his Gift. Would you like to know what His Gift is?

http://godslegacytrust.blogspot.com

I am a Sinner and I am Saved. My websites are almost complete, then off to attorney review. All I am trying to do here is to get people to reinstate birthrights and allow our Creator to take His place here on Earth with an Earthly Entity that will bless us all with the Gift of Health Care and an understanding that God dwells among us now.

As far as scripture and the Truth. It is major league up for interpretation. That is why we have wars. How I interpret a parable will come from my frame of reference and yours will be different from mine. That is why God spoke in parables. To reach everyone's heart with their own frame of reference. Of our own free will, our decisions are either Christ like or Anti-Christ like.

9 hours ago ·

Nathan Isbell

I have cleaned my act up many times and will do it again. I know that I am on the wrong path sometimes. Unfortunately, the path that I am on sometimes is very crowded. You can not reach the ones on this path shouting from your path. Because people on my path know that people on your path are hypocritical and judging. I ask you, if you truly felt like the Holy Spirit put something on your heart that would benefit all Mankind, what approach would you take? Mine has been a little crazy and I have lost everything once I turned to God in a red hot manner. My ending has not ended up all too happy like Bruce and Evan Almighty. I have carried this cross for over five yrs and lost everything, but God has lifted me up and blessed me the finances that afforded me the time to finish His work. It is almost done. Everyone will be able to go online and create themselves a Living Will, Will and Living Trust FREE of charge. This will establish a propagating, everlasting, taxable income stream that will create jobs, pay for socialized health care, rebuild social security, combat the national debt, fund charities and passions and subsidize our heirs incomes for a lifetime.

My publicist says my concept is Brilliant, yet arcane. Finishing the website will be the way to reach the masses, he says.

My attorney says the concept is great. He liked the fact that our life long earnings would be better served invested rather than squandered by our financial intelligent inept heirs.

My website designer can't wait to finish the sites. He wants to be the first customer. He wants to create himself a Living Will, Will and Living Trust free of charge.

Do you have a Living Will that will determine who will pull the plug on you if you become incapacitated?

Do you have a Will that will determine who will get the '74 Pinto Wagon?

Do you have a personal Foundation that will bless all of your heirs for a lifetime?

Most people die intestate. I am trying to change this for the Glory of God.

9 hours ago ·

Facebook Friend

Nathan, I don't talk religion. I don't care at all for religion! I talk the Word of God. That and that alone is enough for me. The word says that even in the last days the elect of God will be deceived. I check myself constantly against the word of God to make sure that I am in line with His truth. If I don't, I become vulnerable to the lies and deceit of the devil. He is cunning, and quite able to appear like or sound like one of God's own. But he is a liar. I'll look at your blog, and I will pray for you, but I am offering you a hand to draw you into the body, into the light. If you remain out there alone, you are too vulnerable to stand. I am stronger in the Word and in the Lord than anyone I know, and the devil can still get to me. He brought me to near destruction not long ago, because he was subtle, and he found a place to enter. God has taught me well that if the devil can get to me, he can get to everybody else. Everybody Nathan. If you really do have a message to deliver (and believe me, we all do) then you need to be surrounded by strong Christians - strong in the word, strong in the true spirit of God. You need them to keep you covered in prayer, and you need them to keep you on track with the truth of God's word so you don't start going the wrong way. I've person- ally witnessed pastors turn into cult leaders. I've seen innocent souls stolen by the darkness. I don't want it to happen to you.

9 hours ago

Facebook Friend

Nathan, I do have a will. I do have a living will, and a trust. I have no children of my own, but I have made financial provision for the children of those closest to me. I established all of this years ago.

How I pray though to leave them a spiritual legacy, far more valuable than money.
9 hours ago

Nathan Isbell
I have determined the only one that I need is God. He has been with me every step of the way. If I am wrong, then it is on me to plead my case before my Creator. My defense attorney is Jesus Christ. All that I do is for Christs Glory, not mine. Many will not like the manner in which I witness, but much more will connect because they are on the same path as I.
8 hours ago ·

Facebook Friend
Nathan, do you not see that you are on a path of "the blind leading the blind?" You say many will connect because they are on the same path as you. That doesn't make sense. They are on a path of destruction - all unsaved are. So you are telling me that you and all those unsaved people are all on the path to destruction. Or don't you realize what you just said?
8 hours ago

Nathan Isbell
I love the fact that you would like to leave a spiritual legacy. You will name your LLC and it will be printed on every legacy check ever disbursed for eternity. You can put what ever inspirational words you would like to be remembered by.

Mine is "From the Estate of Nathan J. Isbell - Endeavor to Persevere"
8 hours ago ·

Facebook Friend

YOU, you say, have determined... that is flesh speaking. That is not God. God is coming back for the Body, not pieces of the body scattered here and there.

8 hours ago

Facebook Friend

Nathan, to leave a statement printed on checks that (by the way) won't be dispersed for eternity (since eternity as we know it is coming to an end) is not leaving a spiritual legacy. Helping people find God, and teaching them the word, showing them how to have a personal relationship with Christ, that is a legacy. This earth will pass away,and everything in it, but the word of God will endure forever, and His spirit will be forever, and we will be with Him forever, in eternity. That is what matters.

8 hours ago

Facebook Friend

God doesn't contradict His word. He doesn't say one thing and do another. And He doesn't tell us to do anything contrary to His word. He certainly doesn't want us so focused on a mission or a calling that we stop looking at the one who gave us the mission/calling. I've known too many people who are so focused on the "mission" they stop looking at God. God leads the way. When you take your eyes off of God, and focus on anything else, you are operating in the flesh and not the spirit. We must be guided by the spirit and truth. And the truth is found only and irrefutably in the Bible, the anointed word of God. If one does not believe the Bible, then one does not believe in God. Because the Bible is the only evidence we have of His existence. And it has stood for thousands of years without being proven wrong.

8 hours ago

Nathan Isbell

I am on a path with other sinners. The masses. I am very well aware of what I do. My decisions are always Christ like except

530

when dealing with the honoring of my own body. I have of my own free will elected to destroy it. The torment that I have been dealing with not being able to deliver Gods Gift has caused me to want to fast forward my life to the life that I know God has promised me. This is not a good plan and I don't recommend it. It is just what I am doing.

God is not coming back for the body. The body is sin filled. You are either a Leper or a Liar. God is coming for the soul.
8 hours ago ·

Facebook Friend
You will know them by their fruit.
8 hours ago

Facebook Friend
Nathan, hear the one true God speak, not what is speaking to you. Go past that, cry out JESUS HELP ME, Save me, forgive me. Find yourself a spirit filled man of God, he can help you meet the one true LIVING GOD...no this imitation that is talking to you. You are on here seeking, God is calling to you Nathan, not with words, He is pulling at your heart. Run to Him Nathan. Humble yourself as a little child...Abba (Father) waits to save you and free you from that which is perverting the Gospel of Jesus Christ.
8 hours ago

Facebook Friend
That isn't God Nathan. God would never tell you to sacrifice yourself this way. The torment is because it isn't from God. Torment is from the devil. Not God. God gives us good things, not bad. He would never do this to you Nathan. He would never do it to you!
8 hours ago

Nathan Isbell
Does one believe the bible is complete?
8 hours ago ·

Facebook Friend
Girls, with all due respect, please back off and let me talk to Nathan.
8 hours ago

Facebook Friend
Nathan, I have not, and I will not preach at you. What I am doing is reaching out to you to share truth with you. I understand what is happening to you. I know that you don't have to be destroyed. I know that you and those you are trying to reach can be rescued from this path of destruction. That is the perfect will of God for all of you. But if you don't trust me, if you don't trust someone who can share the truth about God with you, then you will perish. And God will weep, and I will weep, because you are His precious beloved. He says to you, "I know the plans that I have for you, to prosper you." God would never bring destruction to one of His own. Never! Do you believe me Nathan?
8 hours ago

Facebook Friend
Okay. I'm sorry too Carol. I've been on with Nathan for a while, and I'm genuinely concerned for him. He doesn't need to be rebuked or preached at. He needs prayer and understanding, and much more.
8 hours ago

Nathan Isbell
I am still counting on cashing in on the 1000 yr option in the contract. So if it ends in 1000 yrs so be it. Let those at that time plead for a new contract from God. I am looking at now. And now looks rather bleak. We can either bring God into our world with His own Earthly Entity to heal the sick and dwell among us or we can destroy ourselves through wars or entitlements.
8 hours ago ·

Nathan Isbell

When you get tired of kicking the drunk used car salesman, tell me this. My interpretation of the Seven Sealed Two-Sided Scroll in the right hand of Him who sat on the throne will work and bring Salvation to us all by allowing God back into our world and lives by allowing Him to heal the sick.

8 hours ago ·

Facebook Friend

Nathan, God tells us that we are in this world but not of it. We are to resist the carnal things and live by His spirit in us. That's the great thing about God. He doesn't dwell outside of us telling us what to do and punishing us when we don't. He dwells inside of us, he lives through us as we yield to him. That's where we get the power to repent and live holy lives. We can't do it in our flesh, but only through His spirit living in us. There is always hope in Christ, not darkness, not bleakness. This is why I believe you are not hearing the true voice of God. These type of thoughts and beliefs are from the devil Nathan. Not God.

8 hours ago

Facebook Friend

Nathan, I have not been kicking you. I'm sorry you feel that way, and I apologize if anything I've said really makes you believe that. I've been sincere in my desire to help you, to see your suffering transformed into the glory of God. How can God give you a message that interprets the end of days when He has told us no one knows, on earth or in heaven, except the Father? And why would he give you so heavy a thing, when you cannot even carry in your heart the small things of God? Please, come reason with me. I told you, I'm not preaching at you. I'm sharing what I know about God. I've been at it for 40 years, and I do know what I'm talking about. Please.

8 hours ago

533

Nathan Isbell

PLEASE, Please, please... tell this drunk, foul mouthed sinner, used car salesman and Prophet of the Lord why the concept of the scroll that the Holy Spirit has put on my heart won't work. I am only trying to complete His mission of having an Earthly Entity that all can praise Him and receive His blessings for an eternity or as you point out, whenever He elects to take account.

http://godslegacytrust.blogspot.com

8 hours ago ·

Facebook Friend

I am unconcerned with end time details Nathan. They won't matter until it is too late for them to matter. God has shared information about the end times with us, not so we may be distracted by the need to interpret them, but to be warned by them, that we might start living rightly in the here and now, before the end times come and destroy us. And I say this as the prophet that I know I am. Anything and everything, if it doesn't line up with the word of God, it is not of God. That is a truthful fact.

8 hours ago

Nathan Isbell

Apathy is not the correct answer. I may be the lowest of the low, but my Faith has brought me to this point. If I could only have someone with financial intelligence tell me why this won't work, I would shut up and go away. But alas, no one has been able to rebuttal my claims of the Seven Sealed Two-Sided Scroll.

Who am I to be able to reveal the scroll? I am a sinner that has experienced the seven deadly sins. How else could one articulate what they have not experienced for themselves?

8 hours ago ·

Nathan Isbell

Not even Jesus could break the seals for He was sinless. It is from His right hand that I took the scroll to reveal to all His Last Will and Testament.

The Prophet Nathan

Subject to Critical Analysis

8 hours ago ·

Nathan Isbell

When you have read the Vessel and the Lamb. Let's talk. I am no match for you in theology. Remember, I'm a drunk, foul mouthed used car salesman. But I am financially intelligent and a servant of the Lord.

7 hours ago ·

Pastor Facebook Friend

@Nathan

"As long you as you still consider yourself a sinner, then Jesus truly has no part in you - for once you are cleansed, you cannot be dirty again unless you willingly choose to walk in filth."

@Pastor Facebook Friend.

You claim that because I proclaim myself a sinner that Jesus has no part in my life. Are you proclaiming yourself to be sinless after accepting Jesus Christ into your life? According to my bible that I read, there was just one sinless one. The hypocrisy that some born again believers live is the standard at which the unbelievers stake their claim in unbelief. Because we have been saved, does not prevent us from being tempted and the unbelievers are always there to point it out. We are all Lepers or Liars, even after accepting the Lord Jesus Christ into our hearts.

7 hours ago ·

535

Nathan Isbell

We can only strive to be Christ like. We will all fall short. Shoot for the moon and you will fall amongst the stars. Not a bad place with Christ.

7 hours ago ·

Nathan Isbell

This is the simplest that I can make the concept. Why do we continually feed the charitable birds their daily bread. They will be back tomorrow for their rations. We must plant our charitable seeds for the charitable birds to harvest for an eternity. Just as we must plant our life long earnings for God to have His Earthly Entity to Heal and dwell among us.

7 hours ago ·

Nathan Isbell
@Carol
Examine my fruit and subject it to critical analysis.
http://godslegacytrust.blogspot.com

@Elizabeth.
I have no audio or visual claims. It is what the Holy Spirit puts on my heart that I must deliver before my own Judgment Day. I chose to lose all that I am to follow what my heart has compelled me to do through Faith and Faith alone.

I am as lost as any sinner until someone can prove my/His theory wrong. If no one can prove it wrong, then I must continue to Endeavor To Persevere for the Glory of God.

My flesh tells me that what the Holy Spirit has put on my heart is right and the Salvation of Gods people.

Anyone care to rebuttal? Don't focus on me, I'm a drunk. Focus on Gods Plan. The Vessel and the Lamb. It's a lot shorter than the 2000 page health care reform bill. Just imagine, Gods

Earthly Entity healing the sick without Government intervention. That is the God I serve. The all loving, healing and forgiving God.

6 hours ago ·

Nathan Isbell

Let him that hath understanding count the number of the beast: for it is the number of a man; and his number is Six hundred threescore and six. Here is my humble interpretation of 666. 666 is our frame of reference that is stored in our subconscious. Our reticular activating system will draw from our subconscious every time a decision is to be made. Of our own free will, we choose to serve man 666 or God. Our decisions are either Christ like or Anti-Christ like.

6 hours ago ·

Nathan Isbell

Michelle, the bible is a prophetic book and many prophets will come in the name of the Lord. I wouldn't have come had He not given us a Gift. There are lost books of the Bible, who is to say that this prophetic bible was not sending messages to the prophets of the future. Google the Acts of Nathan the Prophet. It is the title of my new book soon to be released. It is a book of what I have seen, heard, read and experienced in my lifetime. The Holy Spirit of Truth compelled me to write my thoughts down. I am a sinner, but I am trying to be as Christ like as humanly possible. I will fall short, but by the Grace of God, I will be forgiven for my shortcomings.

6 hours ago ·

Kara

quoting my wonderful husband " correction is wasted without showing him the way to changing his heart". I SMILED when I heard this, my husband used to think this when he was drunk and high in the bar. The real testimony would be from my husband. If your friend would like to discuss any of his theories with someone who has lived this out and now leads a huge youth organization for Christ I am sure we could arrange this. Correction is only received if the person is open to it, but what wonderful rally of brothers and sisters in Christ. We are all on such wonderful journeys with Christ, it is quite an adventure.

6 hours ago

Nathan Isbell
@Kara
We are all on wonderful journeys with Christ and they are very personal based on our own frame of reference. We get to decide who we serve. It is the arrogant, vocally robust that imprison Gods people by pressing their beliefs and suppressing our own.

Tell your husband congrats from me. I pray that I will be able to free the demons that destroy me once the Masters Plan is revealed.

Jesus said, bring my accusers forward.

Now, Ye without sin, cast the first stone.
6 hours ago ·

Kara
I do appreciate your zealous desire Nathan and am excited to see what god does with your life keep digging and looking for your answers in the good book and only the good book. Ask the lord to show you the answers not confirmation on being right. Real change comes conviction from Christ not judgment from peers. I like to be right but I pray that god takes those walls down so that I can hear his will, not my will. I tell my children sometimes we can want to sooo right that we are doubly wrong lol. This is not necessarily about you but about me. Keep seeking Him and He will show you. Watch the substances they tend to get in the way of our listening. Dig deep sir, he will show you! With Love Kara (Secret Society Ministries)

6 hours ago

Nathan Isbell

Thanks for the kind words Kara. This has been a struggle for me for over five yrs now and I lost my loved ones when I turned to God. It is way past being right. It is Redemption. Everyone will soon see how Gods Earthly Entity will heal the sick and He will dwell among us. I have a concept website up and the functioning site will be coming soon. Check it out.

http://legacywillandtrust.com

Because I have stepped out for God, I am considered crazy by my peers. My publicist says arcane and brilliant. My attorney says great concept, need to find out if it is legal. My web designer wants to be the first customer for a FREE Living Will, Will and Living Trust.

5 hours ago ·

Pastor Facebook Friend

ok...a lot has gone on since I hit the hay.

@Nathan: Jesus came to cleanse us from our sin. Either you buy it or you don't. I do. Either you are a new creation in Christ Jesus or you are not. I am. Jesus said we will do as He has done, and He has walked sinless. We can too. It is within our ability. To say it is not is to make our Jesus out to be a liar. And seeing as how God does not lie....

You used one of my biggest peeves and a great weasel word "interpretation". There is no need to interpret the Bible - it has already been interpreted. All we need to do is read it. The quagmire of personal interpretation, yada yada yada, was brought from the enemy to cause division amongst the churches. Paul warned of it several times. Read it - it is all in his letters.

The bottom line is simple: when you do the wrong things for the right reasons - they are still wrong. I minister not to a church

539

crowd, but the lost. The homeless, the drunkard, the drug addict, the murderer, the adulterer, the homosexual, the fornicator - I do not run a weekly church. I travel to where they are. I do not have to become as they are to minister to them. I only have to bring Jesus for that to occur. As Paul said" that I may be all things to all people so long as it causes them not to stumble"....you are reinforcing a sin state by proclaiming Christ while intoxicated, Nathan. Those people are looking for deliverance from that bondage to alcohol...you are perpetuating it.

And yes, you are not accountable to anyone but God. You might want to fully consider that statement. Because if you humble yourself before men, then God will have no need to humble you before Him....but if you choose to maintain your "I only answer to God" stance, then when God sends those to walk alongside you in counsel, you have refuted Him....and that leaves you NO chance to avoid being humbled by Him directly. I am not sure that is a walk you honestly wish to make.....

As far as the whole "scroll from the right hand of God" trip... what you have written does not line up with scripture thus far. The Bible warns us about that as well.

We will continue our prayers for you Nathan...
5 hours ago

Pastor Facebook Friend
oh, and just so you know - I do not consider myself without the capacity to sin...but it is a choice I make when I do. I am no longer a sinner....I am now a saint, in lockstep with Christ.

"It is the arrogant, vocally robust that imprison Gods people by pressing their beliefs and suppressing our own. " If your beliefs are Scriptural based, then no one would have the ability to stand against them, for the Bible is pretty simple and very clear.

Our salvation is between us and God, His Word is not individualized, it is a standard for all.

5 hours ago

Nathan Isbell

Pastor Facebook Friend, thank you for your service to the Lord for witnessing to the Lepers of this World.

How can you line up scripture to something in the bible that has not yet been revealed? I contend that I have revealed Gods Last Will and Testament.

I stand ready for critical analysis for my revelation. I have yet to hear anyone refute my claims.

I claim: legacywillandtrust.com will establish a propagating, everlasting, taxable income stream that will create jobs, rebuild social security, fund passions and charities and provide legacy checks to all heirs for an eternity.

I further claim that Gods Legacy Trust LLC will fund the physicians, nurses and staff at Gods health care centers.

Drunk or not, that is my humble interpretation of the Worlds Largest Riddle.

I would rather face my Creator knowing that I have done all in my power to reveal what the Holy Spirit has put on my heart. Until someone is able to refute my claims, I must Endeavor to Persevere for the Glory of God. I will always respectfully question authority.

Tell me where you think I am wrong.
5 hours ago ·

Kara

Well put Pastor Facebook Friend, What a stir during the night huh I couldn't help what was read during the last 14 hours lol ultimately your original thought says it all, as leaders we are constantly adjusting our behavior to be "above reproach" therefore we are not questioned on who we stand for...it is obvious in all things (a constant process). I tell all of our bands that it isn't right, but we are judged by your actions by the world and on a bigger scale Christians are judged by the same standard, people are always trying to debunk words and beliefs. The heart is the key, change comes from the inside and the flesh then starts to follow.

4 hours ago

Pastor Facebook Friend

something about "add nothing to this nor take anything from it" rings in my heart.....

You are begging for an argument, Nathan. Why not just walk in love and be humble.

4 hours ago

Nathan Isbell

Do not ministers interpret parables to convey the message that Jesus Christ was ministering? The whole book is interpretation of the Truth.

4 hours ago ·

Pastor Facebook Friend

No. Ministers use parables as allegories for their teaching. If they are interpreting the Bible, then they are in danger of satanic influence.

4 hours ago

Nathan Isbell

Pastor Facebook Friend, add nothing and take nothing away resounded in my brain as well. It's a good thing for me that the

Book of Nathan is one of the lost books of the Bible. If you will examine what it is that I am trying to accomplish for our Lord and Savior, you will realize that I like my chances on Judgment Day. I have established Him an Earthly Entity in Gods Legacy Trust LLC and fulfilled prophecy. God waits to see what we will do with His Last Will and Testament. God healing people through His people. Is that so bad?

GODS LAST WILL AND TESTAMENT BOOK OF NATHAN Then I saw in the right hand of him who sat on the throne a scroll with writing on both sides and sealed with seven seals. 2And I saw a mighty angel proclaiming in a loud voice, "Who is worthy to break the seals and open the scroll?" 3But no one in heaven or on earth or under the earth could open the scroll or even look inside it. 4I wept and wept because no one was found who was worthy to open the scroll or look inside. 5Then one of the elders said to me, "Do not weep! See, the Lion of the tribe of Judah, the Root of David, has triumphed. He is able to open the scroll and its seven seals." - Revelations 5: 1 - 5

Pastor Facebook Friend, I am having a little trouble with the simplicities and clearness on this passage. Can you explain it to me?

I am not looking for a fight, I am looking to be heard and complete my purpose for God.

This ends with the same results that I have experienced for over five yrs. No one can refute my claims and I am discounted for my beliefs. I only have my Faith and Gods Word.

As far as the interpretation issue, we can always agree to disagree. I will not bother you again. Jesus shook the dust from his feet when his closest of people would not accept Him.
The Prophet Nathan

Pastor Facebook Friend

The book of Nathan is Apocryphal, just like the others. Maybe relevant, perhaps a good read, but not scripture.

Nice try on the whole "shake off your feet thing", but you sir, have not the authority under Christ to do so. Jesus walked in purity before the Father, sought not to exalt Himself. Jesus did NOT shake any dust off His feet, sir. He instructed the disciples to do so when they went out proclaiming HIS GOSPEL - not something apart from it. Again - His Word says not to do the exact thing you have done.

The book of revelation was written in such a manner as to evade the guards on Patmos. If John the Revelator had come out cleanly and said what he saw, the book would have been torn asunder and lost forever. As for the clearness and simplicity of the passage you posted - it is BLATANTLY simple. Just read it.

Lastly - you are not bothering me - I do not mind steering you back to His Word repeatedly. For it is in His Word that you will find truth. Please understand - Mohammed came to the Judaic Council with "another Gospel"....and we see where that has led.

You follow your heart, and seek God. He will reveal all things in His due time.

about an hour ago

Nathan Isbell

I have read it over and over again. I still need your help to figure it out or have my own interpretation of it. It really is just not simple and clear to me. I ask again of you, how do you explain the seven sealed, two-sided scroll in Revelations? It is "BLATANTLY" obvious to you and arcane to me. Please share with the class.

Nathan the Prophet

1 Chronicles 29:29 Now the acts of David the king, first and last, behold, they are written in the book of Samuel the seer, and in the book of Nathan the prophet, and in the book of Gad the seer,

2 Chronicles 9:29 Now the rest of the acts of Solomon, first and last, are they not written in the book of Nathan the prophet, and in the prophecy of Ahijah the Shilonite, and in the visions of Iddo the seer against Jeroboam the son of Nebat?... See More

I ask of you, if an Earthly Entity was created for God to bless his children with the gift of health care, would that not be considered the last act of King David and Solomons lineage?

May Allah Almighty guide us all to the truth. Ameen. May Allah cause us to destroy our egos. Ameen. May Allah guide us if Christianity be the truth. Ameen. May Allah guide us if Islam be the truth. Ameen.

This sounds pretty open minded to me. But what do I know, I'm a drunk.

Sura 38:26 is a quote from a book or oral-tradition of prophecy. But not Muhammad's. This was in Nathan's context and was most likely attributed to Nathan and Allah both.

As it happens, Nathan had been considered a canonical prophet, worthy of a holy book, long before the Islamic and even Christian eras. 1 Chronicles 29:29 runs, "As for the events of King David's reign, from beginning to end, they are written in the records of Samuel the seer, the records of Nathan the prophet and the records of Gad the seer".

Sura 38:26, perhaps with a reworking of 2 Samuel 12 midway toward Sura 38:21-25, could have provided an apocryphal Book of Nathan, in the way medieval Jews and Englishmen forged

545

Books of Jasher. Admittedly this is speculation. No such book has yet been found.

I understand that this is arcane to you. I first thought my purpose for God was to fix the fiscal woes in our Country and I wrote Gods Last Will and Testament - Book of Nathan. I didn't realize until I had started my second book that my real purpose for God is World Peace. Acts of Nathan the Prophet - Book of Nathan II.

Pastor Facebook Friend, I ask you to open your fundamentalist Christian eyes and see that all I do is for Christ. I just can't understand why Christians have a hard time with that. I couldn't convince my second wife either. Stop focusing on me and focus on what the Holy Spirit has put on my heart. It is our Salvation.

I did find it interesting that you used the term "apocryphal". My reticular activating system went right to work on that one. Drawing from my frame of reference which is ever growing. Remember my interpretation of 666. Yes, I am interpreting. I'll take this up with God whether it is satanic or not on Judgment Day. I don't require man to tell me what is Satanic and what is not. It is their interpretation and they won't be holding my hand when I meet my defense counselor, Jesus Christ our Lord and Savior.

By the way, I am a recovering Alcoholic. Have I been slurring my words. LOL

Pastor Facebook Friend
Act as you wish, and you are right - you are the one who will face God on that day - and man, you will have a LOT to answer for.

I have no issue with my being a fundamentalist Christian. God says that is what we should be. However, you have a serious issue - for you are quoting TWO Gods....and now have two masters....
39 minutes ago

Nathan Isbell

There is but one God and Man has elected to name him in various names. God, Allah, Buddha, Yahweh etc... Let me ask you a question. Would you have invaded the camps of Geronimo and killed Indians that were worshiping in their own way that did not comply with yours? My problem with fundamentalist Christians is that they can not see that we all serve the same God. If it does not fit into their little brochure it does not exist. Sir, I ask you. Do you confine your belief in God so as to infiltrate the beliefs of others that are worshiping the same God. If I do not light an incense right according to your laws, do you condemn me? Sir, I ask of you. Who are you to condemn anyone of their belief in our Creator in our own private way?

Man, by judging me and my belief in our Creator, you have a lot to be answering for. Who the HELL are you to judge me?

I quote the only God that has spoken to my heart. I quote the same God of Moses, Abraham, Ishmael, Isaac, Esau, Jacob, Joseph and his forgiven brothers, Muhammad and my all time favorite Jesus Christ our Lord and Savior. So I guess I could be misconstrued into quoting for the one and only God that is not up to mans interpretation. Our Father who is in Heaven.

I also missed the part in the bible that says to be a fundamentalist Christian. I define fundamentalist Christians as to be blind of anything that is not written in the Bible and I have shown you that the Bible is self admittedly with lost text.

This is the problem with bringing non-believers to Christ. People as yourself proclaim to have all the answers and you don't know SHIT. It is your way or the Highway. The Bible is full of interpretation of the Truth. You have elected to lock on to one way and not listen to any other. It is just like the Old lady/Young Lady picture. Until someone points out to you that there is an

547

alternative, you will fight to the death to prove your own beliefs. This is what creates wars.

I truly pray for you my brother in Christ, that you will somehow be delivered from your own microscopic frame of reference and realize that there is a Big world out there and not everyone has your frame of reference.

The Prophet Nathan

P.S.

I still haven't heard your rebuttal to the seven sealed two-sided scroll. I don't get my check from God and you do. So lets have your interpretation.

Nathan Isbell

Judge lest ye be Judged 'O Sinless one.

Pastor Facebook Friend

Nathan, stop your BS right here. Let me clue you in, sir.

First of all there is only one True and Living God - and His name is Jehovah. None of the other names you have uttered even come close. Stop your blaspheming mouth.

Secondly, sir - I am not judging you in any way - if you feel convicted - then the Holy Spirit is trying to drive some sense into you.

I can assure you, when I stand before God I will have PLENTY to account for - but judging you will NOT be on the list. You see, you have a very prideful issue - in your words "judging" you are saying "you do not agree with me so you are judging me". It is a theme I have watched with you on many occasions on Facebook, Nathan. And for some time now.

If you choose not to follow God's word, then you sir condemn yourself - it is not I who condemns you - your actions do this all on their own. You have turned against the very Word of God and chosen a path of your own making - and one that will lead to your own destruction.

And lastly, Nathan - I am in no way sinless. I miss that mark every day. However, I am smart enough to know I do not not know it all, and I surrender to God completely. I do not have my own agenda within my heart. I am quite sure you cannot say the same thing.

One thing about the verse where loveless knowledge is likened to a clanging gong and a resounding cymbal. The physical law of those items is simple - if you activate them, they make noise - if you leave them alone - they grow silent.

Consider this my leaving you alone - and unlike where you said it - I mean it.

I pray God blesses you, Nathan, and removes the smoke from your eyes.
9 hours ago

Nathan Isbell
I do have an agenda. To deliver God's Gift. The Vessel and the Lamb. The secret to the Seven Sealed, Two-Sided Scroll. I will Endeavor to Persevere.
Take Care Pastor Facebook Friend and God Bless.

COOOOOOOOOOOOOL................ I was de-friended by Pastor Facebook Friend. I can not be accepted by the Fundamentalist Christians. I was not accepted by the Atheist. I should have kept that dialogue, it was freaking cool. Arguing with those goofy bastards is just like arguing with these goofy bastards. Every one seems to have their head shoved so far up their own ass, that the senses are shut down. They have given up their ability to make rational decisions based on the now. They make decisions based on the then and their own frame of reference. Wow, I can see why this has caused such an uproar. Lord, you know me. I love to stir me some shit. LOL Screw you all, you Goofy Bastards. I ask you this my Goofy Brother, how has it been working out for you thus far? I tell you right now, you goofy, arrogant, self righteous brother of mine. Our Father will have His pyramid built with the bricks of Mankind and after you wash the egg from your face. You will line up to be at His service. You are my brother. You are blind. You will see the light of our Father in Heaven. His Will will be done, if I have an ounce of spirit left in my self beaten body.

Lord,
I so want to tell them to freak off. They tell me that I am not witnessing for you, but for myself. Lord, tell me. Am I doing all of this for me, all that I have been through, all of my losses. Please Lord, I'm crying, I'm sad, I'm dying. Tell me.

**ENDEAVOR
TO
PERSEVERE
MY SON**

**FOR ALL
THAT THY DO
THY DO FOR
ME**

LAST ACT OF
NATHAN
THE PROPHET

BELIEVE IN
ME

This is the World's Greatest Sin. If you can not believe in our Creator, SCREW YOU. BURN IN HELL. Dude, I'm not getting paid extra to tell you this. It is the Truth.

**WHAT IS
TRUTH
TRUTH
IS WHAT**

**TRUTH
IS HEART**

**HEART IS
TRUTH**

You're so WAY cool Jesus. We're going to make a fortune on Greeting Cards. LOL

**GIVE UNTO
ME
WHAT IS
MINE**

**MINE IS
WHAT I
GIVE UNTO
YOU**

**FOR AN
ETERNITY**

What if your people do not heed your word, your Gift Lord.

Frankly my dear, I don't give a damn
- Gone With the Wind

I AM
THY GOD
I LOVE YOU
UNCONDITIONALLY
I WILL
LIVE AMONG YOU
I WILL...

Lord, I want nothing from my brother. Why does my brother want from me and not you?

ALL
WANT
ALL
NEED
ALL
DESIRE
ALL
CONSPIRE
ALL
MANIPULATE
ALL
HUNGER
ALL
THIRST
ALL
THRIVE
ALL
CREATE
ALL
DREAM

I'm sorry Lord, I still got that bad ear thing going on. Please Lord, a little more so that I may understand.

YOUR BROTHER
IS YOU
YOU ARE
YOUR BROTHER
YOUR BROTHERS
KEEPER IS YOU
YOUR KEEPER IS
YOUR BROTHER
JUDGE THY BROTHER
LEST THY BE JUDGED
LOVE THY BROTHER
THY BROTHER
LOVES YOU

FOR THOSE YET...
LET ME INTRODUCE
MYSELF TO YOU
I AM
YOUR BROTHER
I WILL
SAVE YOU

Thank you Lord. Thank You. Will your people manipulate your words given to them through me?

MAN WILL MANIPULATE WORDS
GOD'S WORDS WILL MANIPULATE MAN
LET THOSE THAT WOULD
STAND FOR... ON THIS SIDE
LET THOSE THAT WOULD
STAND FOR... ON THAT SIDE
TOO EASY

Lord, doesn't that put us at odds with one another over our Faith in you?

I
I AM
FAITH
THEIR FAITH
IS IN ME
MY FAITH
IS IN THEM
MANKIND WILL HAVE
FAITH
OR MANKIND WILL HAVE
DEATH
ONE WITHOUT FAITH AND PURPOSE
IS NO ONE AT ALL
THEY ARE THE WALKING DEAD
THEY ARE THE CRABS
PULLING AT YOU TO
SUPPRESS YOUR
DREAMS
I AM
ALIVE
I AM
WELL
FIND YOUR PURPOSE FOR ME
AND FIND YOUR PURPOSE FOR YOURSELF
OUR PURPOSES ARE ONE IN THE SAME CHILD

Lord, some will say that I manipulate your words as my own, even with all of my disclaimers. What say you?

SCREW 'EM
NO WORRIES

But Lord, they are my brothers and sisters in Christ. I love them and I don't understand. You say Screw Them and Love Them., what do you mean?

**YOU ARE
CHRIST LIKE
OR
ANTI-CHRIST LIKE**

**WORDS CAN BE
MANIPULATED**

**WHO YOU ARE
CAN NOT**

**SERVE THY GOD
THEN SERVE THY BROTHER**

**THY BROTHER
SERVES ANOTHER
GOD**

JUST AS YOU ALL HAVE

**YOU ARE NOT YOUR BROTHER'S
JUDGE AND JURY**

I AM

GOOD FRIDAY
2010
HIS KINGDOM
WILL ARISE
THANK YOU
JESUS

Okay Lord,

I got to tell you, I'm laughing my ass off right now. It is not that your words are funny, it is that they are full of wisdom and I can't believe I am being blessed to hear them.

I beg of you Lord. Give me a final statement that you want me to make sure that they hear. Lord, we need your guidance. We need a Shepard.

I AM
THY GOD

I WILL

Dude, I get it. I was just hoping for a little more inspirational words. You know like AHHHHHHH....

DANCE FOR
THY GOD

THY GOD
DANCES FOR
YOU

Mr. Martini,
How about some music...

Lord,
How can we fix our mess?

ME
FAITH
HOPE
LOVE
CHARITY

Lord, I wanted to give you the last word but I can't. I have so much more to talk to you about. There is so much more that your people want to know. I am fixing to ask you how they can find their answers and you have already answered me. PRAY You are such a cool God. Let's burn one and really connect.

MY GIFTS
ARE TO
ENJOY

OR
DESTROY

OF YOUR
OWN
FREE WILL

Good Friday, I'm drunk and fixing to go to bed. I'm having difficulty conveying what was once on my heart. Wow, what can I say. Our Creator procreated a Son and sent Him to save us from our sins. This Man died on the cross so that we may live. Because He is a Man God, He was risen from the grave to sit at the right hand of God. I just don't understand what is so hard to believe about that. Rocks banging into one another sounds more far fetched to me. I must tell you the truth, there is a Heaven. If you don't believe that there is something greater than yourself and a better place, why do you continue to exist? I'm so sick of you hypocritical bastards. I am not here to judge you, you may judge yourselves before meeting Jesus. Bring all the rocks you want, they will only save you if you proclaim them to be the rock of Jesus that you molded your life around. Jesus came as a Lamb, I my brother am a Lion and I don't put up with your shit. Been there, done that. I will not buy that T-Shirt that brings you entitlement. Get off your freaking ass and buy your own damn T-Shirt. You Assholes.

Oh speaking of assholes, I have another joke. C'mon, just one more. Pleaseeeeeeeeeeeeeee.............

You know that every racist joke begins with looking over your shoulder, but this one is not racist. This one applies to everyone that has an asshole and is capable of being one.

Heyyyyyyy.... What did you expect? Did you think I'd be beating a tambourine and passing out flowers at the airport. Screw You.

Okay, here goes. One day the brain was feeling quite full of himself and proclaimed that no one could function without him. The arms chimed in and said, you could not lift anything if it were not for us. The legs said, you could not go anywhere if it were not for us. The heart said, please understand that we are all part of the body and we need each other. The asshole said, screw the lot of you. I am the most important one that you will ever have to report to. They all laughed at the asshole and he puckered up. He did not allow anything to pass. Soon all began to cry for relief. The moral to the story is that we all work for assholes. Just figure out how to lubricate the asshole that is in charge of you.

Lord, give of me to proclaim your words.

LIVE BY MY WORDS
OR DIE BY YOUR OWN

It's Good Friday, what's so good about it. Jesus got the Hell beat out of Him. A bloody freaking mess. I Will tell you about it. I Am a bloody freaking mess. My heart lays open with blood as I witness for our God. Please crucify me my Lord, so that I may be of benefit to you and your people. It is not a hard decision to make when your heart is with God. Love thy neighbor as thy love thy self. When you can truly believe in this, you are ready to meet your savior. There is no scoreboard. There is only your heart with

Christ. I implore you to break away from your peers and realize that you are judged by just one God. He is all forgiving and always there for you to call upon.

Brothers and Sister in Christ, do not allow the trials to defeat you. You are being tested and will continue to be tested. Do not test our God and do not allow Satan to determine your decisions. Remember Pinocchio, it is very attractive. We are so easily persuaded to pursue rabbits. It is called dreaming. Never give up dreaming, it is what continues to create comfort for God's people. I can not analyze your dreams without hearing them from you. I am not a bullshit voodoo psychic telling you what you want to hear. I can't see shit in your hand or a ball. I can tell you that you will find what you seek. I can tell you that you can emulate any personality that you admire. I can tell you that you are not given what you do not seek for yourself.

Damn, I thought I was out of jokes. Would you pacify me with one more?

Shit, I forgot it before I could type it. How about a riddle instead?

There are thirty steps in a well and you step up two and back one each day. How many days will it take for you to emerge from the well?

If you were to reach your hands from the well only to be smacked by a boat oar, you would retract your hands. How many times would you reach out your hands to be smited before you would give up? That is life my brother, keep reaching because the one that smites you will get tired and that is when you will come out of the well that holds you hostage.

Oh, the answer to the riddle is 29. Once your out, your dumb ass don't have to go back. It is your decision. Of your own free will.

LAST DANCE WITH
(2ND WIFE)
ONE MORE TIME
TO FEEL THE PAIN

I had hoped to find out if there was anything to my second marriage or not. I had booked the cruise for the summer and invited (2nd Wife) and her boys to come along.

(2nd Wife)
So can you put me and the boys together, cause the way this looks, we are staying together.

Nathan
If you don't feel comfortable staying with me, I can take (Step son 1) or (Step son 2) in my room. I just didn't want to bunk up three to a room. I would like to stay in a cabin with you, but I don't want you to feel like there is something expected. (2nd Wife), can we be adults and just be friends on this trip? I have told you that I have an ulterior motive and it is to see you for who you are. You are the keeper of my heart, I hope to be able to either leave it with you or ask for it back. It is something that I must do to be able to move past you. That is why I have invited you and the boys. Yes, it's all about me. LOL Please understand that I have been in complete turmoil and have a need to move past you. Every time we communicate helps for me to move to that point. I'm sorry for being in love with you, I hope you will humor me in falling out of love with you. I know this is weird, but I have a vision of a man I met in Orlando and I don't want to be him. If this does not sound like the type vacation you are looking for, please tell me. I bought insurance and can cancel.

(2nd Wife)
I'm sorry, we will not be able to go with you and Austin. I am an adult, I just don't feel like Being put in this position. Sorry, the boys and I will not do a vacation this year. I specifically asked to be by myself, and you said ok, now you want me to room with you So you can fall out of love with me, that is just a tad too much pressure for me. I should have known this wouldn't work. I'm not gonna be naive this time. Take care and thank you for financially

helping Me, I have put every penny to bills and good Use. It's much appreciated

Nathan
My Dearest (2nd Wife),
Christ has my body, mind and soul. You are the keeper of my heart. I will take this as the final sign that you want to give it back. I accept it back and appreciate your honesty. It's quite bloody, but it will heal this time because I have it back, I can guard it carefully and I can give it to God. I have made every attempt for you to see my heart, but something is blinding you and I can not penetrate this shield. I will live with no regrets for my actions and I pray that you can do the same. I must accept the fact that you never loved me and never will. I will resolve myself to finishing this second book and websites because that is what I am compelled by the Holy Spirit to do to fulfill prophecy. It is my purpose for God. Then I will move on with my life. As I have said before, if creating God an Everlasting, Earthly Entity so that He may dwell among us and Heal us is wrong, then I don't want to be right. I am not sure what your definition of a "Godly Man" is, but I pray you can find Him someday. Thanks again for being the catalyst in my life to complete my purpose I don't think that I could have done it without you. I will be praying for you.
Take Care (2nd Wife),
Nathan the Prophet - A humble servant of the Lord

(2nd Wife)

Take care, My definition of a Godly man is to wait to have sex and not badger to get his way, who attends church and wants to serve the people in the here and now, Who is kind to people and NOT EXTREMELY judgmental and cynical. I'm sorry Nathan, but your manic ideas of creating an earthly entity for Jesus is not real. He doesn't want you to do that, he wants you to live for today and to help the many hurting people all around you, I'm sorry.

Nathan

We can always agree to disagree. I pray that you are wrong, we will see soon enough because I am almost done. I have nothing to lose and everything to gain. The ones that are closest to us, are the ones that are the last to see. Thank God for the people that are willing to step outside the box and look inside to find ways to better our lives. They met with enormous obstacles and endeavored to persevere and so shall I. I have God on my side, so who can be against me? All I do is for Him and He has shown me what to do. Interesting definition of a "Godly Man". Were King David and Solomon "Godly Men"? I wonder if Bathsheba would say they are. I guess it would depend on her own frame of reference. Duck, there is a judgmental arrow headed your way. Take Care.

(2nd Wife)

I don't want to argue with you! I'm not judging You, you asked me a question and I answered You, king David paid the consequences of those choices he made, just because He did those things doesn't give you a free ticket to live that way. If the spirit were leading you, He would be leading you into truth and conviction over your sin, not constantly defending it!!!Take care of yourself, Nathan You never made it easy for me to love you, You badgered me and hassled me about everything. I just couldn't take it any more

Nathan

My intent is not to argue with you at all. I was merely pointing out that as men, we have flaws. If you think otherwise, then you are the naive woman you portray yourself to be. Flawed men can be great Godly Men. Wouldn't you agree?

(2nd Wife)

I know we are all flawed Nathan, I'm done. We can go on and on

Nathan

Yes, we can always go back to our unchallenged beliefs. Fundamentalist Christians find refuge in a very funneled belief system. If it is not in the Bible, it is not real. Unfortunately for them, I am in the Bible as a lost book and I will speak my mind about what I have seen, heard, read and experienced, it is prophecy. (2nd Wife), please don't take our chat as confrontational, I want to pick your brain so I know who you are. I am so over you now, but I want to know the minds of someone that has blinders on so I can reach them. I learn so much from you, so that I may witness for our Father. It will take a lot of convincing to get all the folks on your path over to God's path. Please don't shut me off, I will even pay you for the opportunity to see what it is that you believe and what others believe to be able to bring you all back to Christ. If that is possible. Some people still believe that Jesus will come back on a surfboard shooting fire balls from His ass. I believe He is coming back through me, just as it was prophesied in literature. It is not in your frame of reference so you only see crazy 'ole me. Worldwide they will see a Man of God that is trying to make a difference. Good luck with the celibate, check writing, front row sitting hypocrite. He is Lukewarm.

(2nd Wife)

What is unchallenged about doing what the bible says, do not eat with fornicators, drunkards, do not get drunk on wine, but be filled with the spirit.

You are the one with your situational ethics, you think because you think it is right, it is right. You don't get fed from the word, because you don't go to church, you are lying to yourself.

Nathan

Let me tell you about church. It is filled with hypocritical, lying, cheating, stealing, fornicating, drinking bastards and it's leader could possibly be the worst. It is still full of money changers. They will look down upon you and secretly do the same thing as you. If that is your thing and it makes you feel good about yourself, then do it. Do no judge me because I elect to hold worship in my own way. I can not go to a place where I feel like they are raising their arms in praise for their neighbors sake and their own Glory, not Gods. If you think that by going to church you are saved and it is good, then you are destined to be deceived once again. You say you don't want to be argumentative, yet you want to get your jabs in. It has become quite apparent that we can not ever be together. You're beliefs are way too sheltered for me. You are very narrow minded, but why should I have expected more. You've lived in La. your whole life, your frame of reference is so limited. How could you be able to comprehend any more than what you have been taught. When have you ever stepped out of your shell to do something for God and His people that required more than pulling your checkbook out? You personify exactly what turns people away from the Church. I have allowed you to get your verbal harpoons in without retribution. If you wish to continue this discussion, I will let you know what I honestly think of you and your Christian Fundamentalist friends. You have freed my heart and now I can live without regret. I guess I never really knew you and only now am I able to see into you.

I didn't want to accept the fact you are cold. I wanted to find the good in you. I saw a (2nd Wife) that was foot loose and fancy free. I fell in love with her. This (2nd Wife) only emerges when a need is to be met. Her own self fulfilling prophecy. I am not bashing on you, because I understand what it is that you have been through. How can you ever trust a man again? What you have gone through with your dad is something that I can only articulate and I am blessed to have never experienced. It is controlling your life whether you realize it or not. You truly can not in your heart relinquish control to another ever again. I will confess, as I thought there was a chance for you and I, I envisioned buying you a quaint little older home in downtown Foley. You could see your dreams fulfilled with your own health food store. No worry, no stress. It's all paid for. I don't know when that (2nd Wife) will wake up and realize that her life has past her by. How many other men will you disregard about this situation? He is your son and all sons need direction. Honestly, how much direction are you giving him? What are your hours by the way? Don't damn yourself, you are a victim of an economic environment. But he is a result of your direction and you will support him forever because you have not taken the time to inspire him.

(2nd Wife)
You mean sort of like your parents are paying For you? Go to hell!

Nathan
My parents have facilitated for me. I have made great money due to their compassion for their son. I pray that I can be that compassionate. I love the fact that you continue to throw darts of judgment and don't even realize it. Your financial situation is all due to your own decisions. You may want to pass the blame to me, but you must know by now that they are all on you. I will not tell you to go to hell. I wish for all believers in Christ to go to Heaven. What kind of believer would I be if I wished someone to Hell anyway?

(2nd Wife)
You can, but I can't!!!!!whatever

Nathan

Thank you for responding. I need to hear your ignorant Louisiana heart to the point that I don't care for you anymore. I am there now, thanks. Wow, what everyone said about you is true. I just didn't want to believe it because I was in love with you. You need to come with a disclaimer. Break glass only when desperate.

(2nd Wife)

Oh ok messenger of God!!! Ugly mean hateful Man, crazy manic fuck.

You started with your meanness because you didn't get what you wanted.

You call yourself a prophet and a godly man, but look, the minute you didn't get what you want and look at the venom that spews out of you, you attack me, where I'm from, my sons, my economic problems, you have some nerve to call me cold, it poured out of you in a flash. Then to say what everyone said about me is true!!!!!! What did everyone say Nathan??? You are by far, the most hate filled person I know. Go live your lie and think you are doing something for God.

Do they know you were in an institution and you have bi polar with a hint of schizophrenia? Do they know you should be on meds but you refuse?

Hi (2nd Wife),

Let me start off by apologizing for my hurtful words and forgiving you of yours. I had a glimmer of hope that one day we could reconcile and obviously that is never going to happen. I have finally resolved to the fact that you will never be a part of my life ever again. With that said, I understand that you are making a transition in your career and financially things are tough. As I have told you, I never want to hear that you have no food and have to go to charity. I will send you gift cards for the next two months to help you make it through your transition. I expect nothing in return but an email or text that you are receiving them, it is just like cash. I do not wish to correspond with you because

I am trying to heal and it seemingly continues to cause pain for both you and I. I can only speak for myself when I say that our emotions are still very raw. I truly do pray for your success and I realize that I am the last person you would go to for help. When I heard from you, I guess I got elated that somehow we could work things out. The truth is, we can't even be friends. However, that will never kill my spirit for caring for you. You were the catalyst to fulfilling my purpose for God whether you giggle about it or not. I believe it and I am not alone. I will not stop until I am heard.

Take Care (2nd Wife),

The "Crazy Manic Fuck" Nathan

ALL MEN

Lord,
Is Christ in me speaking for You?
- Your Forgiven Servant Nathan

**DON'T BE
ARROGANT**

**I AM
IN ALL
THAT WOULD
PRAISE OF
ME**

**ALL ARE
MY (2ND WIVES)**

**I AM
YOUR BRIDEGROOM**

NOW COME

**LET US
REJOICE**

**FOR OUR FATHER
HAS HIS
EARTHLY ENTITY
AND HIS
KINGDOM
WILL RULE
ON EARTH
AS IT IS IN
HEAVEN
FOR AN**

ETERNITY

Lord, have I asked all the questions? Have I given all the answers? Have I not served you well? Have I not given you my heart? What more can I do Lord, that I haven't already done? I am still in unrest and my friends laugh at me that I am not done. I want to be done Lord, but I can not, until our Father's Devine Plan is heard. Why do you choose to punish me in this way? Don't get me wrong, I would rather take a verbal lashing over what my brother Jesus Christ got any day of the week and twice on Sunday. Man, did you have to be so brutal on my brother Jesus?

EVERY LASH
WAS A LASH FOR YOU

THE PAIN WAS IMMENSE
BUT COMFORTING

MY SOUL WAS WITH
THE FATHER

MY BODY
DESTROYED BY MAN

I HAVE NO PAIN
MY FATHER
WEPT

I AM
HIS SON

You have this way of capturing my heart Lord, I just go to tears. I am your slave Lord, please use me in anyway you see fit.

Am I done? Lord, please tell me. Am I done?

Nathaniel, my brother. You will remain in unrest until our Father's Divine Plan is fulfilled. You are in good company. I

am with you, so are all that have proclaimed their love for God. We live in unrest as we watch our Father's direction. No one knows the hour of our deliverance, only the Father. Even now I can not share with you what I do not possess. Just know, He keeps His promises and you are merely a facilitator.

Why did you choose me Lord? I am not worthy. I am the lowest of the low. I am a sinner.

THE MEEK SHALL
INHERIT THE EARTH

THE HUMBLE
SHALL WITNESS

THE PRIDEFUL
WILL PERISH

ALL THAT ASK
SHALL BE FORGIVEN

What about the really bad stuff, do you forgive them as well? You know where I want to place my vote on these bastards. How can you have mercy on them Lord?

CONFESS THY SIN

SHOW THY HEART

JUDGE THYSELF

THEN BE
JUDGED

JUDUS ISCARIOT
NOW ACCOMPANIES

THOSE IN UNREST
AND EXITS THOSE IN
TORMENT

YOU HAVE PAID
THE SILVER OF JUDAS
THE BETRAYER OF MANKIND
FORGIVEN
BY MY
GRACE
FORGIVEN
BY YOUR HEART

Wow, that is just too deep. I'm listening Lord. I may not get it now, but I know that it will come to me. I wish I could call in a lifeline to know what else to ask you. I can think of nothing else, can you just elaborate?

LOVE THY GOD
AS THY LOVE
THY SELF

LOVE THY MOTHER AND FATHER
LOVE THY PARTNER
LOVE THY BROTHER AND SISTER
LOVE THY CHILD
LOVE THY NEIGHBOR
LOVE THY COUNTRY
LOVE THY WORLD

LOVE MY SON
AS HE LOVES YOU

LOVE THY GOD
AS I LOVE YOU

ALL MEN

A SINGLE SHOE
CAN CHANGE
A LIFE
-CINDERELLA

A SINGLE BOOK
CAN CHANGE
THE WORLD
-THE HOLY BIBLE

BUSH ADMINISTRATION REPLY "ON AND ON MY FRIEND"

November 1, 2004

Ms. Nathan J. Isbell
Post Office Box 592254
Orlando, Florida 32859-2254

Dear Ms. Isbell:

On behalf of President Bush, thank you for your letter. The President appreciates learning your views and welcomes your suggestions.

President Bush is dedicated to pursuing policies and programs that serve the American people, secure our homeland, fight terrorism around the world, strengthen our economy, and ensure that all our citizens can realize the promise of America. Best wishes.

Sincerely,

Heidi Marquez
Special Assistant to the President
and Director of Presidential Correspondence